THE WEB NAVIGATOR™

THE WEB NAVIGATOR™

Paul Gilster

WILEY COMPUTER PUBLISHING

John Wiley & Sons, Inc.

NEW YORK • CHICHESTER • WEINHEIM • BRISBANE • SINGAPORE • TORONTO

Executive Publisher: Katherine Schowalter
Editor: Philip Sutherland
Assistant Editor: Kathryn A. Malm
Managing Editor: Carl Germann
Text Design & Composition: North Market Street Graphics, Lancaster, PA

Designations used by companies to distinguish their products are often claimed as trademarks. In all instances where John Wiley & Sons, Inc., is aware of a claim, the product names appear in initial capital or ALL CAPITAL LETTERS. Readers, however, should contact the appropriate companies for more complete information regarding trademarks and registration.

This text is printed on acid-free paper.

This publication is designed to provide accurate and authoritative information in regard to the subject matter covered. It is sold with the understanding that the publisher is not engaged in rendering legal, accounting, or other professional service. If legal advice or other expert assistance is required, the services of a competent professional person should be sought.

Library of Congress Cataloging-in-Publication Data:

Gilster, Paul, 1949–
    The Web navigator / Paul Gilster.
      p.   cm.
    Includes index.
    ISBN 0-471-16495-X (alk. paper)
    1. World Wide Web (Information retrieval system)   I. Title.
  TK5105.888.G55   1997
  004.67'8—dc21   97-3517
                                          CIP

Printed in the United States of America
10 9 8 7 6 5 4 3 2 1

For my children Miles, Alec and Caroline.

Contents

Acknowledgments   xiii
Introduction   xv

Chapter 1 The World through the Web   1

The Power of the Networked Machine   2
The Browser as Revolution   3
A Sampling of Internet Sites   4
    The On-line Newspaper   4
    A Networked Encyclopedia   6
    A Cornucopia of Programs   6
    Real Time in Antarctica   9
    The Sound (and Sight) of Music   11
    The Interactive News Channel   11
    The Fruit of the Vine On-Line   14
    Digital Learning   14
    Community Building on the Web   17
    The Specialized Discussion   19
    Hunting for What You Need   20
    Finding Friends and Family   22
The Long Result   22
Internet Addressing in This Book   24

Chapter 2 The Web Defined: History, Terminology, and Potential   27

The Visionaries of Cyberspace   27
Connecting the Machine   30
Birth of the Internet   33
The Nature of a Network   37
How TCP/IP Manages Traffic   38
Client/Server Computing   42
The World Wide Web Emerges   43
    How Modern Physics Changed the Internet   45
    HyperText Transport Protocol   47
    Hypertext Markup Language at Work   49
    URLs: The Location of Information   54
    The Rise of the Browser   56

Gateways to External Programs through the
    Common Gateway Interface   59
Search Engines Index the Web   61

Chapter 3   Logging On to the Web   **63**

The Evolution of Internet Access   64
The Modem Connection   68
    Making the Call   69
    Routing Computer Data   70
    From Computer to Telephone: SLIP and PPP   71
    The Winsock Link   71
    Types of Internet Access   72
    New Technologies for Dial-up Users   73
Major Internet Providers   80
    AT&T WorldNet   80
    internetMCI   83
    Sprint Internet Passport   85
    UUnet AlterDial   85
    NETCOM   88
    Mindspring   89
    America Online   92
    CompuServe/SpryNet   94
    Using a Local or Regional ISP   97
Choosing the Right Provider   99
    Service   99
    Access   99
    Modems   99
    Price   100
    Documentation   100
    Web Page Hosting   100
    References   100
    Software   101
    Related Services   101
    Domain Name Aliasing   101
    Mail Forwarding Options   102
    Set-up Fees   102
    Multiple Use   102
    800 Access   103

Chapter 4   Inside the Browser   **105**

The Browser Interface   106
    Using Hyperlinks   107
    Exploring the Screen   109
    The Netscape Toolbar   110
    Directory Buttons   111

The Major Browser Functions   112
     Downloading Files   113
     Saving Pages or Images onto Your Hard Disk   118
     Printing a Web Page   118
     Finding Text on the Current Page   119
     Creating a New Browser   119
     Copy and Paste   120
     Using Bookmarks   121
     Using the History List   130
The Fine-Tuning the Browser   131
     Rethinking the Toolbar   131
     Choosing a New Home Page   132
     Changing Your Link Expiration Time   135
     Experimenting with Fonts   135
     Adjusting Your Screen Colors   137
     Image Options   137
     Setting Language Preferences   139
     Enlarging the Content Area   140
     Using Keyboard Shortcuts to Major Commands   141
     Turning Off Inline Images When Necessary   142
     Reducing the Size of Your Cache   143
The Ongoing Customization   143

Chapter 5   Plug-Ins, Add-Ons, and Helper Programs   145

Plug-in Programs Extend the Browser   146
     What Plug-ins Do   148
     MIME Formats and Browser Configuration   150
Macromedia Shockwave: A Must-Have Plug-In   153
     Downloading Shockwave   154
     Installing the Software   157
     Viewing the Shocked Site   157
Streaming Audio: The Sounds of the Internet   159
     RealAudio: An Upscale Audio Player   160
     Listening to Files with RealAudio   162
Video (Live and Otherwise) on the Web   166
     The InterVU MPEG Player: Downloading a Video File Viewer   167
     StreamWorks and VDOLive: Real-Time Video Players   168
     CU-SeeMe: Teleconferencing and Live Events   173
The Printed Page On-Line: Adobe Acrobat   176
Assorted Additional Plug-Ins   180

Chapter 6   The Uses of Electronic Mail   181

Configuring the Browser for Mail   182
     Simple Mail Transfer Protocol (SMTP)   183

Post Office Protocol   184
Completing the Configuration   184
Using Electronic Mail   188
Reading Your Mail   188
Replying to a Message   192
Deleting Messages   195
Creating a New Message   196
Using Folders for Mail Organization   197
Saving Messages   199
Working with the Address Book   199
Endora: An Electronic Mail Alternative   199
Electronic Mail Manners   202
The Internet Mailing List   205
Finding and Subscribing to a LISTSERV   206
Running a Sample Search on a LISTSERV Archive   214
Using the LISTSERV Database Function   217
A LISTSERV Search Methodology   219
ListProc, Majordomo, Mailbase, and More   221
Sources of Mailing List Information   227
Read before You Post   228

Chapter 7   Interpreting the Net: Newsgroups, Telnet, and Gopher
            through the Browser   231

Reading USENET Newsgroups   232
How the Newsgroups Work   233
Newsgroup Hierarchies   233
Configuring Netscape to Read the News   239
Reading the Newsgroups   240
Marking Groups Read   244
Setting Up Newsgroup Subscriptions   244
Searching for Messages in a Newsgroup   247
Responding to Articles   247
Posting a New Message   249
Saving Interesting Newsgroup Postings   249
Decoding Graphics and Photographs   249
Newsgroup Do's and Don'ts   252
The Newsgroups through Forte Agent   255
Telnet: Logging In to Remote Computers   256
Downloading a Telnet Client   256
Configuring Netscape for Telnet Use   257
Telnet and Terminal Emulation   257
HYTELNET: A Directory of Telnet-Accessible Resources   263
tn3270: Terminal Emulation for IBM Connections   267
Gopher: A Trusty Tool Soldiers On   268

Chapter 8   Breakthrough Web Technologies   275

Modes of Interactivity   276
     Java: Toward an Interactive Web   278
     Using the Java-Enabled Page   282
     Java and the Network Computer   284
     The ActiveX Alternative   285
The Internet Telephone   288
     Net Telephony and the Search for Standards   290
     Making Phone Calls from Your Browser   291
The Virtual Web   295
     The Language of VR   297
     Enabling the Browser for Virtual Reality   300
     Exploring the Virtual World   304
     Browser Tips for the Virtual Reality Experience   305
Agent Technology   307
     PointCast: The World of User-Defined News   311
     Smart Bookmarks: A Clientside Agent   315
     Agents to Watch   316

Chapter 9   Searching the Internet   319

A Sample Search through AltaVista   320
     The Anatomy of a Search Engine   324
     Methods of Indexing a Site   324
     The Art of Relevancy Ranking   325
     Tuning Up the Burroughs Search   326
HotBot: Adjusting the Search with Menus   329
Typical Search Issues   336
     Search for Phrases Where Possible   336
     Use Capitalization to Restrict Searches   336
     Make Certain Keywords Mandatory   337
     Use Wildcards When Necessary   337
Targeted Searching within the Document   338
Major Web Search Engines   338
     Lycos: Hunting for the Right Image   339
     Excite: Using a Concept Search   340
     Infoseek: Text and Precision   344
     Open Text: Full Text, Full Power   344
     WebCrawler: The America Online Solution   347
     DejaNews: Looking for Newsgroup Messages   347
Search Engines versus Directories: A Meeting of the Ways   349
     Yahoo!: A Classic Directory Revisited   352
     Magellan Internet Guide: Web Sites Rated   352

Four11: Finding People   355
Switchboard: Locating Physical Addresses   355
Other Web Directories   355
Metasearching: Combining Your Tools   357
Intelligent Software and Off-Line Browsers   358
Autonomy: An Intelligent Search Tool Using Agents   358
A Sample Search Using Web Compass   360
Other Web Search Tools   363
Off-Line Browsers: Search Filters and Automated Downloads   364

Chapter 10   Publishing on the Web   **367**

Who Publishes on the Web?   368
The On-Line Print Magazine   368
Independent On-Line Magazines   374
The Cyberspace Newspaper   378
The Digital Book   382
The Personal Web Page   389
Creating Web Pages   394
HTML Editing Tools   395
Using Claris Home Page to Publish on the Web   397
Critical Jobs for the HTML Editor   402
HTML Reference Sites   404
Tips on Page Design   405
Where to Publish Your Web Pages   407
Posting Pages on a Commercial Information Service   409
Using an Internet Service Provider   411
Uploading Your Pages to the Server   413
Publicizing Your Site   413

Chapter 11   Commerce, Security, and Privacy   **417**

Business Takes to the Net   418
Business and Security   426
The Assumptions of a Purchase   427
Browser-Level Security   428
How Encryption Works   432
Digital Signatures and Authentication   433
The Digital Certificate: Verifying the Transaction   435
SET: Toward a Secure Credit Card   437
Payment Methods: Varieties of Digital Money   439
Is There Privacy On-Line?   444
Tracking Your Mail and Newsgroup Habits   444
Monitoring Web Use   445
Recording Your Personal Information on Disk   447
Storing Information in Cookies   449

Making Yourself Anonymous   450
Pretty Good Privacy for Secure E-Mail   452
The Rise of the Junk Mailers   459
The Clipper Chip: Federal Law and Privacy   459
Privacy and Security-Related Sites   461
Implications for the Web's Future   462

Appendix   **465**
Index   **477**

Acknowledgments

The Web Navigator owes much to the labors of Kathryn Malm, this book's editor, whose insights helped me see what most needed explanation of today's complicated Net. Janice Borzendowski, whose close reading of all my books has flagged the trouble spots and made the rough places smooth, provided the needed check against verbal extravagance. I would also like to thank the many people responsible for this book's production, including Phil Sutherland, under whose guidance the book was conceived, and Carl Germann, whose unenviable chore was to decipher my marginal notes as we edited the manuscript. Working with the Wiley team on this book proved to be unusually smooth sailing. Special thanks to Frank Taylor, Web guru extraordinaire, for last minute course corrections. And I'd like to thank my wife Eloise for her patience, a debt so long-standing that I almost forgot to mention it.

Introduction

The Web Navigator is a broad survey of the Internet's fastest growing technology, with abundant references to the related tools that, although not based on the Web itself, nonetheless provide key Internet capabilities. I've emphasized not just the Web experience here, but also your ability to customize it through manipulating the browser itself as well as downloading plug-in and helper applications that extend the browser's range. Netscape is my tool of choice, although the same principles apply to Microsoft's Internet Explorer. Tweaking the software to reflect your own needs is not only enjoyable but necessary, for many Web sites today link to content that can only be viewed through third-party software. This book shows you where to get that software and how to install it.

Readers of my book *The New Internet Navigator* should understand that *The Web Navigator* is an entirely new book, written from the ground up to reflect the fact that the Net has changed dramatically in the past two years. The Web has become the standard medium for Internet publishing. Most new users first go on-line through a Web interface, using software supplied by their service provider. Whereas the issue used to be, how do I get on-line and which programs do I use, the issue today is, how can I customize my browser to do everything I need, and add to its capabilities? Thus *The Web Navigator* looks long and hard at how browsers work and suggests practical tips for using them more efficiently.

Because it covers everything from Internet definitions and access options to newer technologies like Java and ActiveX, this book is intended for a wide range of readers. While total novices can use it by working their way sequentially through its chapters, I've shaped it toward the more experienced user, who should find the methods suggested here for personalizing the browser helpful, while the material on plug-ins and developing technologies like Internet telephony, audio, and video will help those who haven't yet explored these options. We're all learning as we go in this facile medium, and it's my hope that this book will ground readers in the key issues of the Web today while offering a model for tracking its exciting new developments.

1

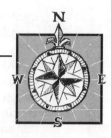

The World through the Web

No one can say how large the Internet has become. Unlike a city, this global network of linked computers doesn't respond to the niceties of demography, and if there were such a thing as an Internet census bureau, it would find its work almost impossibly complex. A network is a libertarian's dream. It connects to the broader Internet with nothing more than a few thousand dollars of hardware and a unique address so that computers around the world know how to reach it. Behind that address lie perhaps 10 people, perhaps 100, perhaps 5,000, depending on the organization behind the network and its own internal divisions. Not to mention the millions of individuals, people whose access to the Internet is through a service provider. They use modems to connect to a network that, in turn, connects to the Internet. Counting them means contacting all the service providers, large and small, and reaching a definitive figure which, in any case, is in a state of constant change as new customers sign on and established ones change services in the restless process known as "churn."

But think big. Does it matter whether the Internet's ranks have swollen to 40 and not 35 million? Perhaps 40 million is a reasonable estimate, and certainly we've pushed global networking into over 150 countries in one shape or another. But what counts just as much are rates of growth that make the Internet the fastest growing medium in history. No technology—not television, not radio, not fax—has grown so fast, and the remarkable thing about Internet penetration is that it continues its pace with seeming inexorability. Surely the Net will slow down one day, if for no other reason than the limits imposed by the numbers of people who own computers, or telephones, but for now, its robust dynamism is a cause for wonder. It's a community, this Internet, a place where you can talk to people without regard to distance, listen to digital radio archives, watch moving video, download programs, text files and images, conduct research in large databases and, perhaps most significantly, search worldwide for information by means of ever more powerful software search engines.

Most of all, the Internet is a global phenomenon, which means that the computer around the corner from us with news about local school closings is as accessible as the one in France that helps us plan our trip to Giverny. Because we can access publicly available information with ease, the barriers of distance drop dramatically; we find ourselves going to the source for information about customs, cultures, cuisines. And because the Net can also be a personal place, we learn to join in discussion groups that talk about the things that interest us, from coin collecting to nuclear physics. A sense of community develops with odd resonances; it's a place where we make friends we never meet face to face, and forget about time and space because we're in the malleable world of cyberspace, which is a conflation and enlargement of both. Local news can quickly become world news, and a store that sells handcrafted walking sticks suddenly becomes an international presence through the use of a consumer-oriented World Wide Web page with accompanying catalog.

The Power of the Networked Machine

Hollywood pundits told us it would happen, but never in the way it actually did. Computers in the movies of the 1950s and 1960s were always mechanical devices the size of railway cars; their huge panels were stuffed with flashing lights and reel-to-reel input devices that looked like tape recorders. When they spoke, which they often did, it was with a low, jerky, mechanical voice that mimicked what that era saw as the machine's great limitation—its inflexibility. Yet these were machines with sinister power. Used improperly, they brought merciless logic to bear upon the problems of existence and sometimes solved them by attacking the people who made them. When they talked to each other, it was to unite against humanity before being ultimately defeated.

But real computers do talk to each other, and not with sinister intent. What Hollywood never anticipated—what few but the most visionary could have anticipated—was the advent of the desktop computer and the fabulous expansion of processor power. The box on our desktop quickly became as powerful as the old mainframe style computers, and it didn't need a refrigerated room or a whole cadre of operators to make it work. And while its software seemed needlessly complex to people unused to operating computers, that very complexity was the result of the machine's ability to perform lightning-fast calculations and offer options we rarely knew we needed. Linking machines like this gave us the ability to communicate by moving information digitally, a fertile ground for innovation and ideas. The language of binary arithmetic pumped data through telephone wires and back out again; the desktop became a way station, a place where we tapped the worldwide muttering of thought.

And the old machine, the centralized behemoth running its programs in majestic isolation before handing off the results to its programmers, faded before the power of the network. Link two computers together and you don't just double their power, you quadruple it; link three computers together and you boost functionality by the square of three. Office workers first saw these advantages take hold as business moved away from the centrist model of computing to embrace local area networks, but today it's the individual—the home user and the small businessperson—who is finding out how to access the unique resources available on-line. These people are entering the world of cyberspace by the millions. Who knows where the Internet they will encounter —consisting of computers talking not only to business, government, and research labs, but also to individual users riding in on ever-faster modem connections—can lead us?

The Browser as Revolution

But if it took processor power and a revolution on the desktop to make the Internet of today possible, it was software that brought the point home to the consumer. Blasting digital data around the globe isn't something most people grew up thinking they would do, and even today, the intimidation factor associated with these technologies is high. But the Internet is rapidly being enmeshed in the phenomenon we've learned to call the World Wide Web, and it is the Web that has made all the difference. The Web links data in intuitively obvious ways; it sets up connections that tie computers together with a simplicity that even a classics buff like me, head filled with stories of ancient Athens and Rome, trained for everything but technology, can understand. Using the right software, we can simply point and click our way to download files, call up images, listen to sound, display video, and send electronic mail. With a Web browser on our computer, we're in touch with a graphical Internet that is linked through hypertext—we jump back and forth between documents and fuse the various forms of media.

They come in several varieties, these browsers, but they all harken back to the same model of moving data, and they all tend to work in pretty much the same way. The original browser was called Mosaic, and it was born out of research and experiment at a government-supported organization. But Mosaic would spawn many offspring, including the two in widest use today: Netscape Navigator and Microsoft Explorer. Both are descendants of the original model; Netscape, in fact, was built by many of the same people who conceived the idea for the original Mosaic. Today, they're locked in a fierce war for market dominance. New versions appear every few months, each laden with additional features, and either can be downloaded from the Net. But whichever browser you choose, the basics of Web navigation remain the same. And so does the goal—to customize your browser so that you can get the maximum benefit out of it, and hence maximize your presence on the Internet.

A Sampling of Internet Sites

Without the Web, the Internet would have remained the domain of programmers, computer scientists, and researchers. With the Web, it has become home to anyone with an idea to publish, a product to sell, or a subject to research. For a look at how diverse its holdings have become, let's walk through some interesting sites, or Web pages, the places where you can find information. And bear in mind that the examples that follow were chosen from literally tens of millions of World Wide Web pages.

Before we set out, though, a note about what you'll see here. I believe in customizing everything. After all, the default settings in most software are established to provide you with someone else's idea of what you need. But programmers build in the necessary functions to enable you to change the way the program operates. The figures that follow show a Netscape display that has been customized to reflect my own needs; it's one with a larger content area so I can get as much text and graphics on the screen as possible. In Chapter 4, I'll show you how to duplicate this screen in your own browser; I'll also point out the changes this kind of display makes in the way you issue basic commands. You won't see a toolbar here, for example, but Netscape's designers have built in the ability to issue commands by pull-down menu, pop-up menu (via right mouse button click) and keyboard shortcuts. My method may or may not work for you, but I hope it suggests the power you have to alter the browser environment in search of your own best model.

The On-line Newspaper

Newspapers weren't early adopters of the Internet's technology, but the publishing capabilities offered by the Web were so spectacular that more and more of them have begun to come on-line. What the Web provides for newspapers is what the Internet had previously lacked: formatting. In the formative days of the Net and lasting until the late 1980s, using networked computers meant working with straight text. It was possible to generate an image, but only if that image was sent as a coded text file, downloaded on your machine, and then decoded to make it work. And the text in question couldn't be manipulated by changing font and point size. It had to be monospaced ASCII text, meaning that about the only variation you could bring to it was the distinction between lowercase and capital letters.

But the Web made it possible to view information with the pleasing visual variations of the physical newspaper. Take a look at Figure 1.1, which shows you how this magic looks on your screen. We're examining *The Washington Post* in its on-line edition, complete with photographs, headlines, and capsule summaries of the news. The address is http://www.washingtonpost.com/.

But if you study the figure, you'll see that while this version of *The Washington Post* bears similarities to the printed paper, it also shows significant dif-

Figure 1.1 *The Washington Post* on-line shows how newspapers can readily adapt to the multimedia format of the World Wide Web.

ferences. You can see that certain parts of the text are underlined, and if it were possible to show you this page in color, these parts would also appear in blue. The presence of the underlining and color highlight indicates a *hyperlink;* click on this item and you are taken to the underlying story. You'll find hyperlinks scattered throughout the on-line edition, which enables the newspaper to create a flexible and powerful on-line presence. You can't page through a digital newspaper in the same way you scan a physical one, with its sheets spread out on your breakfast table, but you can use hyperlinks to jump immediately to the story of your choice, avoiding all those pesky pointers to pages inside the print edition. And when you're through, you can quickly click on the Back command in your browser software to return to the front page of the newspaper. For that matter, if you run into an article you'd like to save, you can print it out for future reference, or save it to disk for later redisplay.

Notice, too, that the on-line version of *The Washington Post* contains a search box at the top of the screen. Using it, you can navigate quickly to the section of your choice—sports, international news, classified ads. A major part of Web page design is the creation of such features; they allow you to use the site productively, without wasting time going back and forth between pages of related information until you find the precise story you need. Another feature of the on-screen page is the button that lets you click to update the image. Web pages work like this: Each time you download one, you have completed the process, but if the page subsequently changes through a news update, you must download it again. Many of the more interesting new Web technologies are finding ways to solve this problem.

A Networked Encyclopedia

When one of my sons was planning to come in from California for a summer visit, he wrote me (via e-mail) to ask if we could visit any North Carolina historical sites associated with the Civil War. In a noncomputer world, I would have headed for the local AAA office, asking for maps and guides to local tourism, or else I would have checked with a public library. But I was able to run a quick search on the topic using the *Encyclopaedia Britannica*, which has gone on-line in full-text format coupled with a handy search engine. You can see the *Encyclopaedia Britannica* search page in Figure 1.2. The encyclopedia's address is http://www.eb.com/.

By entering a few keywords, I was able to target the encyclopedia's articles on the subject, homing in not only on the entry for North Carolina itself, but also on a variety of other entries in which my search terms were mentioned. The beauty of searching an encyclopedia this way is that you can pull up mentions of your topic in articles you might never have found otherwise. I found links to numerous articles that dealt with or at least mentioned some aspect of the Civil War in my state, and was able to construct a list of places my son and I could visit. Durham Station was certainly in reach from Raleigh; it was the place (now Durham) where Joe Johnston surrendered the last major confederate army to General Sherman in April 1865.

A Cornucopia of Programs

One of the great achievements of the early days of computer networking as the ability to make software programs available on-line. The advantages quickly became obvious. If you could call into a remote computer and simply download a program, you could have that program up and running on your own machine within minutes. And whereas local bulletin board systems were designed to enable people in the same area to share ideas and programs, the

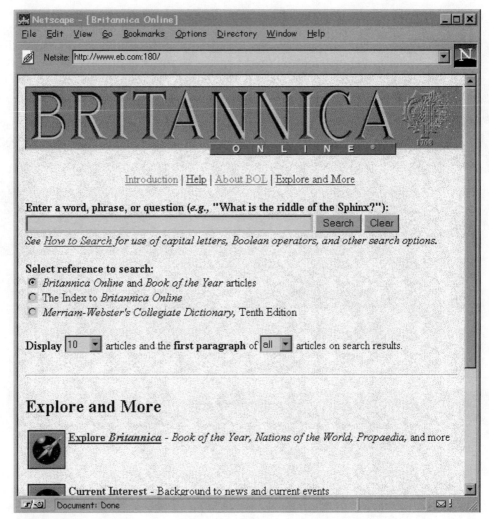

Figure 1.2 An on-line encyclopedia allows you to retrieve information with scalpel-like precision.

Internet upped the ante by giving them access to hundreds of thousands of computers where some kind of downloadable software is posted for public use.

But distributing software this way poses an obvious challenge to companies that are in the business of selling products. After all, computers let people duplicate digital information, and a program is nothing but a collection of coded data that, when understood by the computer's microprocessor, can handle a particular task. Thus the concept of shareware was born: People would write programs that could be downloaded for free, but if the user decided the program was worth keeping, he or she was expected to pay a fee. Other software, called freeware, was simply given away, with no fee implied. The success of early shareware products such as PC-WRITE (a word processor) and PRO-COMM (a communications program) kept shareware authors in the hunt, but it was probably the mammoth success of the game called DOOM that put this method of distribution on the map, because the people who wrote this popular game, distributed free but with commercial upgrades, became wealthy. In Figure 1.3, you can see a site that specializes in shareware products. Its address is http://www.shareware.com/.

The World Wide Web format allows SHAREWARE.COM to use the same kind of formatting that we saw with *The Washington Post;* that is, we see a mix-

Figure 1.3 SHAREWARE.COM is a site that specializes in making software programs available, frequently updating its holdings as new entries come in.

ture of various screen fonts and illustrations. And just as the newspaper also folded in a search engine to help you find your way around the site, so SHARE-WARE.COM sets up a search box you can use to track a particular program. You can click on the window to search for Windows 95 software, or Macintosh, or UNIX, or else you can choose to search through the entire database. New programs that the Web page administrators find particularly interesting are highlighted with their own hyperlinks; if you click on one of these, you wind up with a full description of the program and another link that, when clicked upon, lets you download the software.

As the Internet grows, we're moving to a model of software distribution in which you routinely upgrade your existing programs, whether commercial or shareware, by using Web sites; you can check demonstrations of popular software *before* you buy. This extension of services from the shareware domain into the commercial world is all but inevitable, for the Internet is becoming so widely distributed that sending physical disks through the mail or buying them from a local dealership is no longer the optimum way to ship binary data. That day hasn't yet arrived, but when you see a site like SHAREWARE.COM housing 200,000 programs, you realize that the method has teeth.

Real Time in Antarctica

Among its other virtues, the Internet can be a window. Mount a camera that can feed a digitized image onto the Net and leave that camera running 24 hours a day; pretty soon you will acquire an audience of curiosity seekers who, tempted by the live nature of the event, want to see what's on the other side of the lens. In Figure 1.4, you can see one such experiment, a scene from Mawson Station, in the Australian research zone of Antarctica.

The bleak landscape shown here is not quite live; the image is actually updated every hour, but that's probably close enough for those of us who aren't likely to see Antarctica any other way. That the image is real can be verified by following it through the year; the Antarctic winter is a long one, during which, the picture is mostly black. In this shot, we see Mawson Station coming into summer. To track Mawson's fortunes yourself, use the following address:

http://www.antdiv.gov.au/aad/exop/sfo/mawson/video.html

The process by which this image is generated is as follows: The video camera that shoots the scene feeds it into a Macintosh computer at the site. The computer processes the image and sends it by satellite to the Australian Antarctic Division's headquarters in Kingston, Tasmania. Mawson is six hours ahead of Universal Coordinated Time (also known as Greenwich Mean Time), which puts it in the same time zone as Novosibirsk, Russia, and Hyderabad, India. Details of its weather and a convenient map are also available through hyperlinks on this home page.

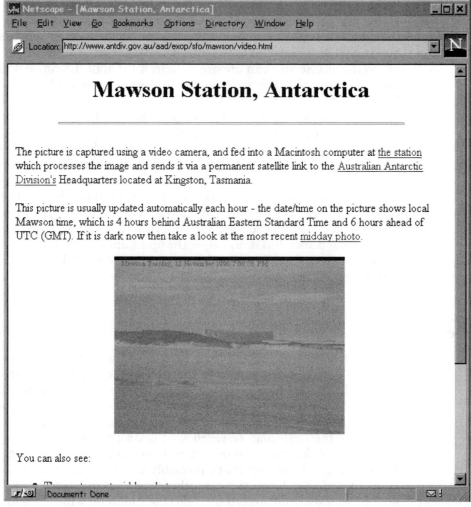

Figure 1.4   The Internet as remote viewer—a glimpse of Antarctica, updated hourly.

Not all Internet cameras factor in a one-hour delay. Some shoot their scene every 10 minutes; some every one. And their subjects vary widely. You can take a look at what's happening near the Arc de Triomphe in Paris or view events in Rockefeller Center Plaza in New York, both courtesy of France Telecom. And because the Net is as much the domain of hobbyists as it is of telecommunications companies, you can also look inside a college student's dorm room, see what's going on in a nightclub, check out live images from a control room at NASA's Goddard Space Flight Center, or view Sydney, Australia, through the window of a resident. There's even a live camera trained on an ant farm! A good place to find these and many more sites is:

http://www.dsu.edu/anderbea/machines.html

The Sound (and Sight) of Music

The great notion behind the World Wide Web is that content of any kind can be digitized. It's just as easy to turn a photograph into binary data and send it through the Net as it is to send a simple electronic mail message. But a curious thing happens when you digitize sound or video files. They become quite large, by orders of magnitude larger than straight text. Until recently, that meant that when we wanted to listen to a sound file, we had to download that file to our computers and then use playback software to hear it. The process was lengthy because the files were big; it made sound and video on the Internet little more than a curiosity, fun to try but not a contender for serious work.

That situation has begun to change with the advent of so-called streaming technologies that let us play the content as it is being received. Through sophisticated compression techniques, companies like Progressive Networks and Xing Technology Corp. are bringing full multimedia capabilities to the Internet. Using Progressive Networks' RealAudio software, for example, I can listen to radio shows that have been stored at the RealAudio site in archival format (http://www.realaudio.com/). Or I can play music—not FM quality, it's true, but eminently listenable—from an on-line jukebox. Hundreds of radio stations around the world have begun to put their programming on-line live.

Xing's Streamworks software can perform comparable feats with video. In Figure 1.5, you can see streaming video presented in an on-screen window. Early live video has been devoted to experimental transmissions, including live coverage of the Democratic and Republican conventions (via White Pine Software's CU-SeeMe video product), concerts from a variety of performers, and business news. But as we increase the size of the data channel to homes and businesses, we will make it possible to use live video on a more frequent basis as the vehicle for videoteleconferencing and other specialized applications.

The Interactive News Channel

The World Wide Web has attracted the attention of traditional content providers like television stations. And that only makes sense, considering its ability to carry audio and video and to marry them with live, hyperlinked text, jumping between sites to provide background information on news stories. A case in point is CNN Interactive, the Internet presence of Cable News Network. This is a site that makes full use of digital multimedia by providing a constantly updated base for news, sports, weather, and feature stories, each of which can be explored at the user's leisure through links to such resources as video and audio files, text documents and databases, both in-house and located elsewhere on the Internet.

In Figure 1.6, you can see CNN Interactive at work. Notice that, on the left of the screen, a bar of options is presented; click on any one of these to visit the named section, which could be anything from stories on show business to health or international news. Unlike the traditional news broadcast, the Inter-

Figure 1.5 Live video is a major growth area for Internet content. Here, Xing's Streamworks software is displaying an interview with *X-Files* star Gillian Anderson via C|Net.

net's paths are user-determined; when you want to learn more, you point and click. The content is rich and diverse; a story on President Clinton's response to provocative moves by Saddam Hussein is shown in full-text with photographs of the president, along with U.S. military maneuvers. It is backed by a sound file of Clinton's statements about the issue, detailed maps of Iraq that can be expanded for closer inspection, a streaming audio speech by Saddam Hussein, and several videos showing various aspects of the story; the latter are downloaded and played through Apple Computer's QuickTime software, linked to World Wide Web browsers as a so-called plug-in program.

And when CNN forges links to other sites on the Internet, it allows the user to go to the Department of Defense's computers, providing backgrounders on weaponry, and to sites devoted to the coverage of Arab affairs. In this way, a

Figure 1.6 Hyperlinks allow a news organization like CNN to provide extended coverage through a variety of media types.

news organization like CNN becomes an enabler as well as a broadcaster; it makes content available both in its own internally edited materials and through its choice of remote sites that provide useful materials for the news seeker. And because computer storage is relatively cheap, CNN can provide a complete archive of its stories on a particular issue, so that reading through the background of events in order to understand them becomes easier than ever before. The site thus takes on elements of an archive as well as a news dispenser; it is part library, part wire service. You can view it yourself at http://cnn.com/.

The Fruit of the Vine On-Line

The World Wide Web has also transformed the Internet commercially. As barriers to the use of networking for business purposes were lifted, what remained were the very real barriers caused by the Net's unyielding interface. The Web, with its drop-down menus and mouse-driven commands, made navigation easy; coupling its helpful front end with features like on-line forms, frames, and enhanced security has meant that consumers can now use the Web for their shopping. On-line commerce is still in its infancy, but there is little doubt that it will occupy a significant part of the consumer market within a few years. The advantages of shopping from one's desktop are all too obvious; they're many of the same factors that have created a boom in catalog sales—simplicity, speed of delivery, lack of hassle.

In Figure 1.7, you can see Virtual Vineyards, a site devoted to selling wine. Like many sites that have grown up around the idea of on-line commerce, Virtual Vineyards has learned that business must offer both a buying opportunity as well as free information. At this site, you can enroll in a monthly wine program that delivers bottles to your door according to a set of preferences you itemize by filling out an on-line form. But you can also do background research on wine through an interactive question-and-answer section, or study food and wine pairings via linked pages stuffed with recipes.

The Virtual Vineyards site (http://www.virtualvin.com/) is thus an interactive and user-determined journey through the wine purchase. When you are ready to sign up for delivery, you can choose to use a secure server, a computer that has been enhanced with security features so that your credit card or other information will not be compromised. Your browser software knows how to work with this server to provide you with the privacy you expect in a commercial transaction. Creating an account is a matter of entering the necessary information and choosing a user password, so that you can identify yourself to the server. Buying items involves reading descriptions and clicking on the appropriate icon, which adds the item to your shopping list. You have the chance later to submit the list or change your mind about particular items. And the convenience of wine delivered to your door has a way of convincing even the skeptical that on-line commerce offers something unique.

Digital Learning

The Web's communications links provide powerful reasons for considering the Internet a learning tool. Education was, in fact, an early driver of Internet growth, as scholars used electronic mail to contact their colleagues and discuss ongoing projects. Today, the enhanced media capabilities of the Web are adding new dimensions to the educational process. Take, for example, the idea of a virtual museum, an on-line version of a physical museum that gathers resources and connects them in ways otherwise impossible.

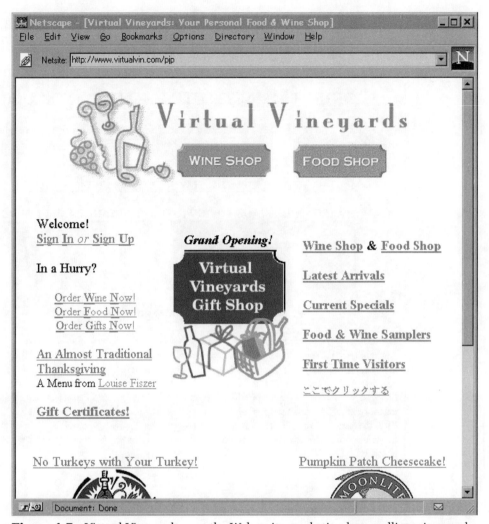

Figure 1.7   Virtual Vineyards uses the Web as its marketing base, selling wines and a variety of food products.

In Figure 1.8 you can see an example of such a museum, the Oriental Institute Virtual Museum. A part of the University of Chicago's Oriental Institute, the physical museum is a collection of antiquities from Egypt, Mesopotamia, Iran, Syria, Palestine, and Anatolia; over 5,000 artifacts are on display here. Its virtual analogue   (http://www-oi.uchicago.edu/OI/MUS/QTVR96/QTVR96_Tours.html) draws on Web-based video to move the user alcove by alcove through the museum, providing links to background materials, photographs, archaeological sites and more. The downloaded movies are panoramic, meaning that you can move your mouse to see different parts of the display while the video is playing.

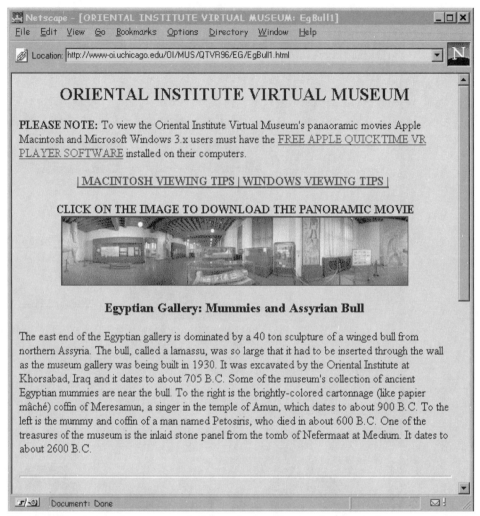

Figure 1.8 A virtual museum provides enhancement to the physical museum by linking to related sites and offering multimedia background materials.

Step by step, for example, you can move through the Egyptian Gallery, starting with the Predynastic Pottery exhibit, where various views of the gallery are presented. Each is clickable; choose one and the download process begins. When the file has been transferred to your computer, your browser will work with the associated playback software to display the image. When a browser uses an external program to display content like this, it is using a plug-in program, one that functions in conjunction with the browser itself. Many plug-ins are now being built right into the browser, making the task of configuration for the end user that much easier.

From objects from everyday life in the ancient Middle East to writing samples, pottery, religious materials, and funerary customs, the Oriental Institute Virtual Museum offers a unique take on some of the world's oldest civilizations. Its work is a precursor of the ongoing development of so-called virtual reality, which will allow us to create simulations and exhibits of even greater complexity as the software continues to develop. In a virtual world like the museum tour, the user controls movement through the scene by moving the mouse. This makes the world of sight and movement as controllable as the world of text when manipulated through its set of hyperlinks, and provides for a learning experience that can be both customized and readily repeatable.

Community Building on the Web

Communities are elastic things on the Internet, where geography is transcended by the global topology of linked computers. Ideas become transcendent; people with common interests find compatriots in a host of countries, meeting to discuss their views in the on-line discussion areas called newsgroups. Well over 20,000 such groups exist, on topics as diverse as classical music, old movies, coin collecting, hypnotism, and almost anything that captures the attention of professionals or amateurs. What happens is that each group builds up a core of regulars, who meet to share their thoughts in a generally unmoderated forum. The isolated individual gives way to the connected user, and diverse people can profit from the experiences of others.

The Web wasn't the original home of the newsgroups, which grew out of early networking experiments at the University of North Carolina and Duke University, and matured into a global cluster of discussions called USENET. But as the Web model becomes ubiquitous, helped along by the easy-to-use interface built into browser software, more Internet functions are becoming folded into the browser. Thus you can access any newsgroup your system provider makes available by calling it up through Internet Explorer or Netscape, reading the postings on-line, collecting them into "threads" and contributing your own messages.

In Figure 1.9, you can see an example of a newsgroup displayed through the Netscape browser. The list of newsgroups, on the left of the screen, is complemented by the list of postings to each; the highlighted group on the left is the one currently viewed on the right. And when I click on a particular posting, it appears in the bottom window on the screen. The browser interface brings more than simplicity to the task of reading newsgroups; it also provides such useful features as hyperlinks, so that if someone posts a message on a newsgroup that mentions a particular World Wide Web site, that site's address will be active; you click on it to go there. In this way, the newsgroups take on some of the multimedia aspects of the Web itself, and the dividing line between the two becomes blurred, which is why many new users assume that the newsgroups have been part of the Web all along.

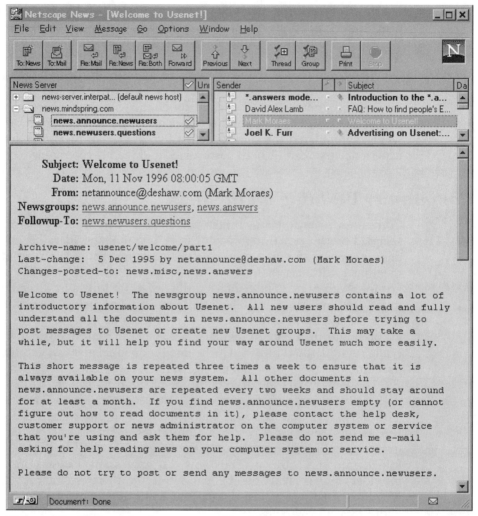

Figure 1.9   Thousands of newsgroups like this one, news.announce.newusers, break topics into tight areas of discussion, all viewable through a good browser.

The newsgroup shown here, called news.announce.newusers, is a good one to sign up for. Getting a subscription is simply a matter of telling your browser software to subscribe to the particular group, after which its postings are made available to you every time you access the newsgroups. Many useful background documents can be found here, on such topics as copyright on the Internet, how to find Frequently Asked Questions (FAQs) documents to answer common concerns, basic rules for posting to the newsgroups, and discussions of on-line etiquette. It's a good idea to read through this newsgroup for such information before becoming an active participant in any group, as doing so can help you make your on-line debut a graceful one.

The Specialized Discussion

While newsgroups are popular, easy to subscribe to, and often filled with chatter, a more serious tone prevails in the discussion groups known as mailing lists. A mailing list is distributed directly to the electronic mailboxes of its subscribers. When you check your mail, which you can do through your browser or by launching a specialized mail program like Eudora, you find the messages that have accumulated during the time since your last check. Any messages posted on the list will appear there, making it easy to follow a discussion as it forms and to trace the flow of ideas. Other mailing lists are set up to disseminate information, such as updates on Internet news. You can see an example of such a mailing list message, as shown through a Web browser, in Figure 1.10.

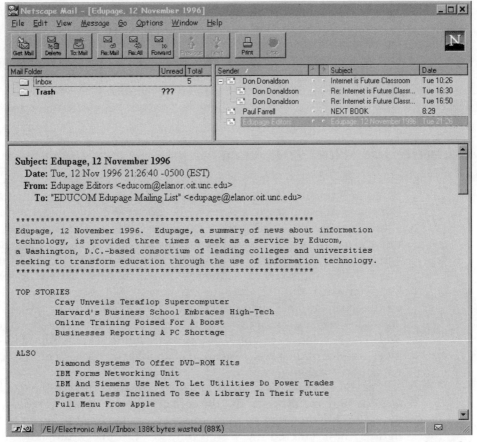

Figure 1.10 While the Web abounds in graphics, low-bandwidth text, as shown by this mailing list message from Edupage, is still a major reason why people sign onto the Internet.

The distribution of mailing list messages is frequently automated. To subscribe, you send a message to a computer that manages the list. Any messages you want to contribute are sent to a different address, which has been established specifically to handle the routing of the list's traffic. And as far as subjects go, mailing lists are as diverse as newsgroups, although, as noted, generally somewhat more serious. They originated in the early days of ARPANET, the precursor to today's Internet, and spread rapidly in the academic community. It's possible to sit in on serious discussions about esoteric issues on such a list. One list I frequently use, for example, is ANCIEN.L. This list is populated by classics scholars and other enthusiasts interested in the cultures of ancient Greece and Rome.

The first browser, Mosaic, was unable to handle mail functions, but later versions of both it and other browsers can do so with ease. Both Internet Explorer and Netscape Navigator can be used to send and receive electronic messages, both to mailing lists and individuals, and each allows you to manage your mail through specialized functions, such as the creation of mailboxes by person, subject, or list to which you subscribe. Mail has always been text-based, but browsers simplify the process of incorporating multimedia materials like graphics or sound in your messages, not to mention the fact that using a single browser program for the bulk of your Internet work keeps your computer screen uncluttered with external programs.

Hunting for What You Need

Since the explosion in its growth began several years ago, the Web has always posed an information challenge; specifically, how do we find what we need? Hypertext allowed us to connect one document to another, and thence to another, ad infinitum. But the experience of using the early Web was something like rummaging through a vast curio shop, bumping into endless numbers of interesting things as we worked our way into the back of the store, but finally becoming so overwhelmed with possibilities that we forget where we had seen which thing. Fortunately, ingenious Net programmers went to work on this problem, producing the tools we now call search engines. Using such an engine, we can specify what we're looking for and home in on it. In Figure 1.11, you can see an example of a search engine. This is AltaVista, one of the most popular of the numerous engines that have appeared on the scene (http://www.altavista.digital.com/).

As you can see, AltaVista is accessed like any other Web page, by entering an address in the browser. But the core of this page is a search field, into which we enter keywords that tell the remote computer what we want to find. In the figure, I have entered the search phrase "st. louis cardinals", setting off the name in quotes because I want the search engine to look for those three terms only when they appear next to each other. AltaVista will generate a list of Web pages on which my search phrase appears. Better still, the software will also

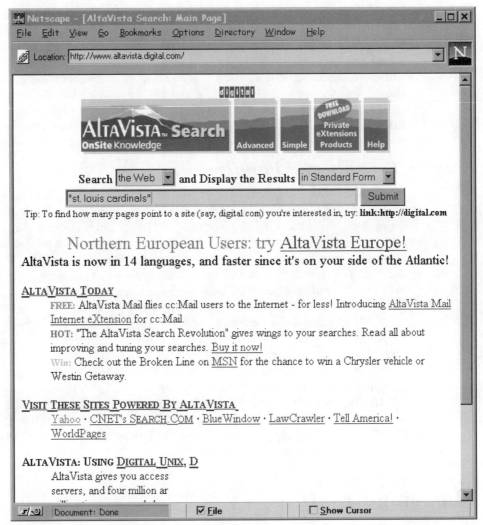

Figure 1.11 The AltaVista search engine includes information from almost 300,000 servers around the Web.

provide that list in the form of hyperlinks, so that I can click on any one of them to see it. This makes finding particular information fast, but it also places a burden upon the user to specify exact terms, and to learn how to narrow down searches. I found, for example, over 3,000 Web pages on which my key phrase appeared, but on many of them, it made only a brief appearance. Usefully, AltaVista attempts to cluster the sites it calculates as most relevant to my search at the top of the list, but there are other techniques you can use to focus your search, as we'll see later in this book.

The number of dedicated search engines is growing constantly. The importance of the genre is seen in the fact that some of these companies have gone public; Yahoo! is an example, as is AltaVista. Just as spreadsheets were the software tool that made the desktop computer a necessity in business, so search engines are the network tool that make the Internet into a fully functional and necessary vehicle for research. And you'll find numerous sites that, while not set up to be dedicated search engines, nonetheless use some kind of search technology to help you find material at their site. We've already seen such sites at work, at the *Encyclopaedia Britannica*, *The Washington Post*, and SHAREWARE.COM. And they're equally helpful at locating people.

Finding Friends and Family

Perhaps the most frequently asked question I get as an Internet author is, how do I find someone on the Internet? There are a variety of answers, and they depend on the nature of the question. For example, do you want an e-mail address for this person, or are you looking for a street number? Do you have an idea of the person's present location? Do you know who he or she works for? In the past, Internet directories were largely confined to people with some kind of previous Internet connection, such as those who worked at major universities; but today, that story has begun to change with the advent of new tools. In Figure 1.12, you can see an example of an Internet directory that extends the old model considerably. Switchboard is a nationwide residential and business directory that allows you to search by first or last name, street address, and city (http://www.switchboard.com/). When Switchboard finds the person you're looking for, it will produce a street address and telephone number.

Nor do these directory services labor in isolation. If you find the address of a person but still don't know how to get there, you can use a mapping service like Yahoo! Maps (http://www.vicinity.com/yahoo/), a service that lets you enter the address and generate a map on the fly.

The Long Result

Maps that draw themselves while you wait. Search tools that let you sift through millions of pages of material in seconds. Customized news presented with text, audio, and video. Cameras peering into the Antarctic twilight. No one who worked on the original projects that led to the Internet could have imagined it would come to this. Nor would any of those engineers and scientists have foreseen the huge influx of ordinary citizens, many of them coming to computers for the first time, who would wind up considering the Internet an adjunct to their standard work day or their recreation. But it has happened, and it happened largely as a result of the World Wide Web. It's true that we have to distinguish between the Web and the broader Internet (numerous network resources exist that are not carried by the Web's technology, even if many of them are accessible through a browser). But for newcomers, usually armed with software supplied by their service providers, the Web and the Internet are

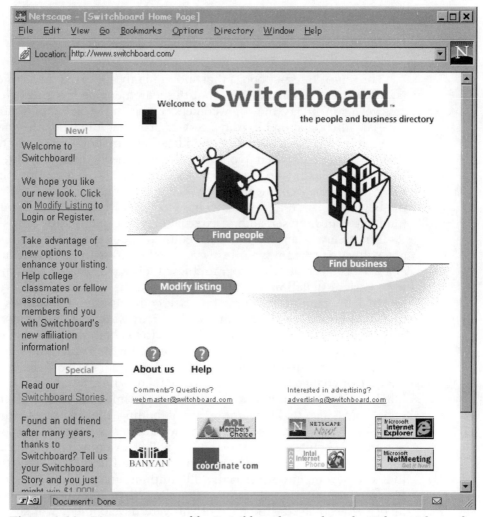

Figure 1.12 Directory services like Switchboard are making the Web a quick stop for locating friends and relatives.

virtually synonymous. The first thing they see when they launch their connection is a browser, and it is the program that navigates through cyberspace to find and display information. And it's clear that the Web will continue to grow apace, far outstripping other forms of Internet content as business and consumers alike learn to find and create new banks of information on-line.

The advent of the search engine has turned the Web into a research device of remarkable power, and this is a factor you should bear in mind as you master the Internet. For when questions arise, they're often to be found on the Net itself. In earlier books, I always called this phenomenon "the Internet Catch," and it could be framed in the form of two questions:

Q: What do you need to get on the Internet?
A: Information about the Net and its service providers.
Q: How do you get that information?
A: On the Internet.

The raft of Internet books that subsequently appeared made finding information easier than ever before, but the search engine has simplified the process yet again. Today, most newcomers can be on the Net within minutes after receiving their sign-on kit from a service provider. And when they need to supplement information from that provider, they can look first to printed sources for background and then to on-line sources to flesh out and update what they have found. Making the Net easy to search, which is a huge accomplishment of the World Wide Web, means that you can be doing productive research from the beginning, even as you learn how to refine your Web work through customizing your browser, adding external plug-ins, and finding new sites.

But it's my belief that the Web requires fine-tuning for optimum use. Like any software program, your browser is delivered with certain default settings enabled. The people who program these tools have decided what makes sense for a basic installation, but after you've used the Web for a while, you'll want to tweak the parameters of the browser, going through the various settings to find the ones that work best for you. You may want to make your screen fonts easier to read, or reduce the time it takes to load graphics, or change the Web page that appears when you first sign on in the morning. You may decide to create a complicated bookmark list, nesting folders of bookmarks one inside another, or change the way your browser shows links you have already visited. Maybe you'd rather not have those links underlined in the first place. And perhaps you'd like to know more about adding the latest software to your browser's bag of tricks, so you can view data in new ways. All these things are possible, and quite a few more, and all will be examined in these pages.

If we can make any assumption about the Internet, it's that the changes that will accompany its growth will continue unabated; indeed, considering how fast computer power grows—doubling in intensity every 18 months, even as prices are halved—the pace of software development will soon go supersonic, if not transluminal. So we'll talk in this book not only about customizing the browser you have, but keeping up with the browsers that are forthcoming, equipped with everything from enhanced virtual reality to built-in Internet telephone capability and videoconferencing. In the long run, your use of the Internet will revolve around your ability to customize every aspect of its interface.

Internet Addressing in This Book

All addresses provided in this book will use the Uniform Resource Locator (URL) format. URLs needn't be intimidating; they're just like the street addresses we use to send postal mail. Any such address must include not only specific information, such as the name of the person to whom the mail is addressed, but also more general data, such as the name of the street and, of course, the name of city and state. We wrap up an address with a zip code that ensures (we hope) that the mail will find its target.

A URL is constructed in much the same way. In the sampling of Internet sites given in this chapter, I used URLs to tell you how to find each site. What I called the "address" for *The Washington Post,* for example, was actually a URL, and it looked like this:

http://www.washingtonpost.com/

The address part of this statement is www.washingtonpost.com. The letters http in front of it tell the network that you are requesting information that is in the World Wide Web's format, called HyperText Transport Protocol. For you the user, the fact that HTTP is at play hardly matters; your browser performs the necessary work of negotiating the contact with the remote computer. But which one? The rest of the URL tell us by giving us a specific address.

The www generally appears at the front of Web addresses, although it doesn't have to; when it's there, it stands, as you might surmise, for World Wide Web. But a Web address might leave those letters off, as we saw above at the CNN Interactive site, whose address was simply cnn.com (and whose URL, then, would be http://cnn.com/). The rest of the statement names the domain in question (thus washingtonpost at the newspaper site) and tells us that this is a commercial operation (thus the com at the end).

URLs can get relatively complicated when they home in on a particular page. The preceding URL, for example, points to the home page at *The Washington Post,* but if I move around at that site, I can generate a URL like this one:

http://www.washingtonpost.com/wp-srv/digest/ent2.htm

This URL begins the same way, but as we move from left to right, it gets progressively more specific, until it has named a particular story at *The Washington Post* site. What we are actually doing is working deeper and deeper into the file structure on a particular remote computer, in order to track down the final page we're after, which is ent2.htm.

We can specify any kind of Internet-based information this way. Here's a brief rundown of how non-Web related URLs are presented, using real-world examples:

gopher://world.std.com/: A Gopher site, in which information is presented in textual form, albeit with the help of menus. You can access a Gopher site as easily with a Web browser as any Web page.

ftp://ftp.isoc.org/: A File Transfer Protocol, or FTP, site. FTP is the original method used to transmit and receive computer files over the Internet. Like Gophers, FTP sites can be accessed with any Web browser, with the benefit that instead of having to enter textual commands to perform file downloads, you only need to use mouse clicks.

telnet://locis.loc.gov/: A Telnet site. Telnet is a method for using the tools available on a remote computer. You could, for example, Telnet to a site to connect your computer to it and run searches on a database you found there, or cause the remote computer to provide a report on local conditions. Telnet sites are giving way almost entirely to the World Wide Web, but you still run across them occasionally.

news:news.announce.newuser: A newsgroup. You can use a Web browser, as mentioned, to access any newsgroup made available by your service provider. While thousands of newsgroups exist, you are only able to use those your provider specifically offers. Notice that newsgroup URLs do not contain the double slash marks found in the previous URL formats.

mailto:gparker@tamerlane.ejd.com: An electronic mail address. Again, the URL uses not slashes but a colon, as opposed to the URLs for Web sites, Gophers, Telnet, and FTP. This URL, incidentally, is fictional.

In practice, most of the URLs you see in this book will refer to Web sites, but we'll occasionally look at Gophers and FTP possibilities as well. Before the Web took hold, Gophers were growing at a fast clip; they allowed system administrators to post information in a format that people without a computer background could readily use. But the Web has all but halted Gopher development in the United States and western Europe, as sites migrate to graphical front ends built using Web tools. It should be noted, however, that text-based software like Gopher still has a place, particularly in those parts of the world where bandwidth is expensive and users are working with older equipment. If it's true that some 100 million personal computers are in active use around the world, we shouldn't forget that many of them lack advanced graphical capabilities.

2

The Web Defined: History, Terminology, and Potential

Intellectual breakthroughs can be subtle, growing by the accretion of insight and experiment. Like the lightbulb and the telephone, the Internet started out in the laboratory. But unlike the drama accompanying the first filament flicker, or Bell calling to Watson, the Net's beginnings went largely unnoticed by the public. For all its technological brilliance, the Internet of today is far removed from the concepts that propelled initial research. And the Internet's story—which has become the World Wide Web's story—has not been so much one of planned development as of individual genius, at least until recently.

You need to understand that story because while the Net of today is outpacing its original 1960s-era definition, it has yet to catch up with the vision of several people who came into the process early and realized that it could change the world. In a similar way, the breakthroughs that will change tomorrow's Web are likely visible only to the few. If there is one thing the Internet has taught us, it is that technology often extends its own definition. Its reach is elastic and its implications can be profound.

The Visionaries of Cyberspace

The visionaries who developed the key network concepts put them together out of brainstorming and intuition. Visionaries like Vannevar Bush, a mathematician who directed the Office of Research and Development for the U.S.

government during World War II. Bush's groundbreaking article "As We May Think" appeared in *The Atlantic Monthly* in 1945, not long before the stunning news of the atomic blasts at Hiroshima and Nagasaki. You can access this document, which originally appeared in *The Atlantic Monthly* in July 1945, at a Web site: http://www.isg.sfu.ca/~duchier/misc/vbush/, as seen in Figure 2.1. In fact, the benefits of using the Web as a publishing tool are graphically illustrated here, allowing you to jump about in the article as required and link to related information.

Bush described a device called the *memex* that could access information and thus amplify the powers of human memory. His ideas would resonate with

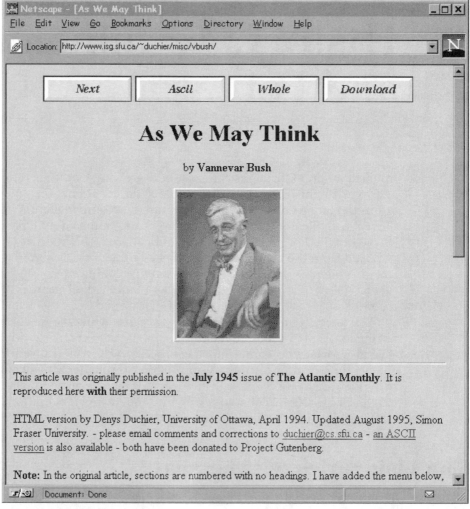

Figure 2.1 Vannevar Bush's seminal article forecast many of the properties of today's Net-connected computers.

fellow engineer and dreamer Doug Engelbart, who realized that computers could be facilitators of communication, used to teach as well as to perform feats of numerical calculation. The vision of both men was of the computer as mind-amplifier, as idea-enhancer. Significantly, the machines were envisioned as tools for a broad audience, devices whose social consequences would be as significant as their impact upon subsequent technology.

Engelbart's pioneering work at the Stanford Research Institute (SRI) in Menlo Park, California, explored questions like how best to organize and display networked information and use it to think better, both individually and collectively. It was in 1957, the year of Sputnik, that Engelbart went to work at Menlo Park, where SRI's Augmentation Research Center would become a nexus of early research on using computers to share knowledge; SRI would also become one of the original nodes on the Internet. Many of the premier intellects at the Augmentation Research Center would later drive research at Xerox's Palo Alto Research Center (PARC), a seedbed for the use of individual microcomputers on the desktop. Here, concepts such as the mouse Engelbart had created would be fine-tuned, and key designs such as graphical interfaces and pull-down menus would arise, much to the interest of Apple Computer's Steven Jobs, who used them on the Macintosh.

J.C.R. Licklider, who worked for the U.S. government's Advanced Research Projects Agency (ARPA) after distinguished tenure at MIT, was another such visionary. In the mid-1960s, when Licklider coined the term "Intergalactic Computer Network" to describe, if whimsically, a paradigm that would use computers to allow people to communicate, the hot concept was *time-sharing*, the ability for many programmers to communicate with a machine simultaneously. It was the era of Vietnam and the Beatles, and the idea of linking computers on a global level, much less an intergalactic one, was pure science fiction, but Licklider's early work demonstrated the promise of the concept. Its motif would later be echoed in Vernor Vinge's science fiction novel *A Fire Upon the Deep* (New York: Tor Books, 1992), which presupposes a galaxy-spanning network amusingly modeled on the USENET newsgroups. That Licklider came up with this concept when he did is testimony to his foresight, for the idea that the isolated computers of his day could link communities of users was by no means obvious. It would take a revolution in computer technology that put machines on the average desktop to bring his words back into focus. Licklider was also something of a polymath, who found inspiration in the past as well as future. Describing the spirit of the network enterprise, he was fond of quoting Shakespeare: "What's past is prologue; what's to come, in yours and my discharge"; these words could be considered a battle cry for the rising generation of network builders.

Yet it was an odd enterprise they foresaw, one that blended a sense of possibilities with the hard-headed realism of the engineer. Robert Heinlein once said, "Never worry about theory as long as the machinery keeps working," and in many ways, it was this pragmatic attitude that made the network happen, even as its proponents began to see the potential results of their endeavors.

What they were trying to do was to fundamentally alter the relationship between human and computer, and in the process, extract more benefit from the growing processor power in their machines.

Connecting the Machine

For the businessperson in the 1960s, mainframe computers were huge data factories that were virtually inaccessible save to the specialists who maintained them. To run a program on such a machine, you sent a reel of magnetic tape with your program on it to the computer's operators, who would execute the code and send you the results, unless you were one of those fortunate enough to be able to use the machine in person. Those not fluent in programming were compelled to bring their needs to the same operators, hoping one of them would find the time to reduce their project into code.

Needless to say, such a relationship between individual and machine was intimidating for average users. The likelihood of the average worker understanding how mainframe computers worked was about the same as their knowing how to fly a jetliner or to conduct brain surgery. And this highly centralized model was also self-contained; it all but eliminated the possibility of collaboration between people at different sites, for in that era, no means of connecting geographically separated computers and using the connection existed. The Cuban missile crisis in 1962, among other events, made it clear that making such connections would become a priority, for government if no one else. Better computer connections would allow the military to extract maximum benefit from its own machines. But how could it be done?

To get around the problem, it was necessary that information find its own way across the network. The insight, which would later become known as *packet switching*, was developed at the Rand Corporation, under the guidance of Paul Baran. Simply put, the new mechanism set up each network communication as a series of data parcels, each with its own routing information. The parcels would be forwarded from one computer to the next; if a particular site were unavailable, the routing data would provide the other computers on the network with all they needed to ensure that the content reached its destination successfully. The data itself was thus self-contained, while the network was intelligent enough to route it through changing pathways depending upon the situation. This elastic data packaging and transmission technology is the definition of packet switching.

Tip: You can read Paul Baran's original work on packet switching at http://www.rand.org/publications/RM/baran.list.html.

As numerous writers have pointed out, packet switching follows a model not terribly dissimilar from what happens with the delivery of postal mail. When you write a letter, you place it in an envelope that contains complete addressing information. You then commit it to a physical network of post offices and delivery systems. The letter does not leap directly to its destination, even though it will likely travel by air if the distance is long enough. Instead, it makes its way from post office to post office until being committed to the long-haul part of its route, during which it travels at higher speed to a post office near its destination. There, it again enters the local system, finally finding its way to the post office that will deliver it to the recipient. Packet switching works in much the same way, except the data moves through routers rather than post offices. These machines examine the header information and pass the data packet along, always routing it in such a way that it will reach its destination.

By 1967, Larry Roberts had proven that computers could connect and operate successfully even at transcontinental distances by linking machines in Massachusetts and Santa Monica. The Department of Defense had proceeded to fund research at a number of universities and research laboratories, which would eventually be hooked together in a network called ARPANET (after the Advanced Research Projects Agency that created it). The ARPANET contract was awarded in 1969 to Bolt, Beranek, and Newman in Cambridge, Massachusetts, whose job was to build the switches that would become the computer nodes for the fledgling network. With the nation's attention diverted by Cambodia and Kent State, few in the mainstream press took notice when initial sites were set up at UCLA, the Stanford Research Institute, the University of California at Santa Barbara, and the University of Utah. This testbed project established the need for a common set of commands that would allow the different computers on the network to communicate.

Computer scientists Vinton Cerf and Robert Kahn made this vision into reality. The two developed TCP/IP (Transmission Control Protocol/Internet Protocol), the standard that enabled the data sent on the network to be placed into packets and reassembled at the other end. A single electronic mail message could be broken into several of these packets, each of which could wind up traveling by a different route to its destination. When you received this message, it appeared as unified text, but behind the scenes, it had been reassembled by the remarkably engineered TCP/IP after its passage through a complex system of router computers, forwarded from site to site. Unlike conventional software, TCP/IP worked on any kind of connected computer, a major plus in a world where differing computer standards challenged anyone trying to connect a variety of machines. You can find a great deal of information about TCP/IP and the Internet's early history at The Internet Society's site on the Web; its home page is shown in Figure 2.2.

The early ARPANET days were marked by three kinds of networked computer activity. File transfer was the ability to move a program or text file from

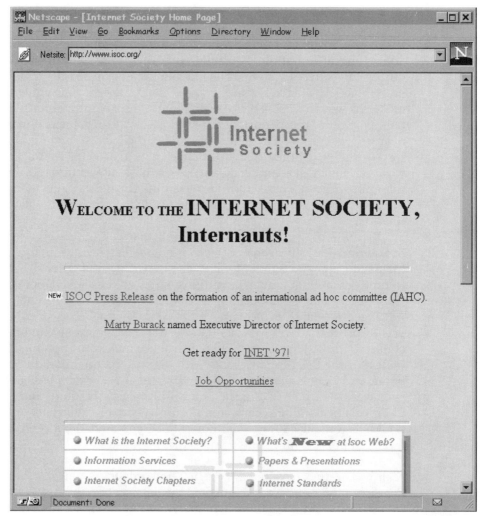

Figure 2.2   The Internet Society, which has supported and developed standards for the Internet, offers useful background materials on the Net and its history.

Tip: If you're looking for materials on Internet history as well as current developments, check The Internet Society's home page at http://www.isoc.org/. The Society exists to promote internetworking technologies and their coordinated development. Its membership consists of corporations, government agencies, nonprofit organizations, and individuals. Perhaps its most significant role is in the development and maintenance of network standards for the Net, to ensure that new technologies are usable throughout the range of standard computers and operating systems. A major thrust continues to be the promotion of network technologies around the globe, particularly in developing countries. But The Internet Society is also active in maintaining archives of information related to the Internet's history and use. Its regular print magazine *On the Internet* is an excellent source of current news.

one site to another over the network; today, its known as File Transfer Protocol, or FTP. Telnet was the ability to log on to a remote computer and use the software and information available on it. Finally, the network made it possible to use devices like printers that existed at other computer sites. These three capabilities foreshadowed a day when the average business office would be linked by local area networks (LANs) and users would take for granted their ability to access files on different computers as easily as those on their own.

ARPANET grew at a relatively rapid pace. Fifteen sites were on-line by 1971, 35 by 1973, including a satellite connection between California and Hawaii. Connections in Europe were added to provide greater connectivity and to test the system for reliability. By the early days of the Carter administration, over 100 computers were established as network sites, or "nodes"; by Ronald Reagan's third year in office, over 4,000 were available. As a testbed, ARPANET took advantage of the immense skills of people like Licklider and Vinton Cerf, who became the first president of The Internet Society (and who, it is said, once sketched the basic network architecture on the back of an envelope in a San Francisco hotel lobby in 1973). As participants in the heady infancy of ARPANET recall, theirs was a time of intellectual excitement driven by a creative team that was given free rein to investigate the issues. Those who remember the period still consider it a golden age of research. If you'd like a unique perspective on this period, the reminiscences of Eugene Miya, a student at one of the ARPA sites, were posted on a USENET and can now be read in excerpts at Michael and Ronda Hauben's Web site: http://www.columbia.edu/~hauben/netbook/. I know of no more lucid account of this period than the Hauben's work, a sample of which is shown in Figure 2.3.

Birth of the Internet

It's hardly unusual when a primary driver for technological growth is military; radar and air traffic control systems, for example, grew out of our experience in World War II. The Cold War era highlighted the fact that early military computers were linked in ways that seemed fragile. A nuclear strike on one would destroy not only the computer at that site, but the communications moving along the entire network. In 1975, the Defense Communications Agency (DCA) took control of ARPANET, whose packet-switching technology fit well with the military's need to maintain its networks under the worst possible conditions. The model was alluring: While a central command site would be the first to be attacked in the event of war, a packet-switched network has no central site; all

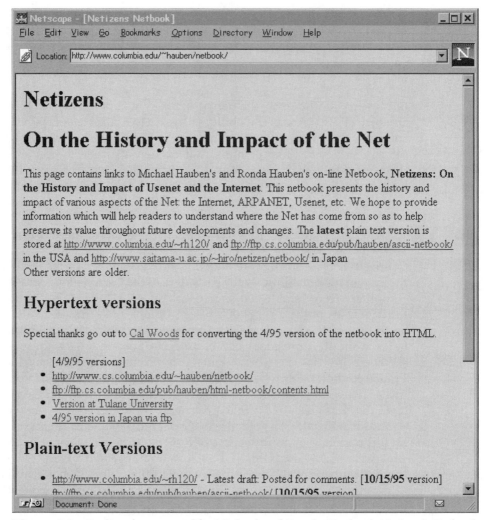

Figure 2.3   On-line documents like Michael and Ronda Hauben's Netizen's Netbook provide a useful view of the Net's history.

nodes are equal to all other nodes, and can route information with similar ease, rerouting if necessary.

The beauty of the packet-switching technology, as shown by ARPANET's example, was that new networks could be added; the use of common protocols placed no real limitations on the ability of remote computers to communicate through gateways. The advantages of networking had become apparent to numerous user communities, especially those in the sciences, but not all of them fit under the ARPANET research mandate. By the late 1970s, numerous networks were using TCP/IP to connect. The concept of the network as an "internet"—a network composed of other networks—took hold as the number of connections increased. And the greater the Net's reach, the greater its value to users. By 1983, ARPANET had split into MILNET, the unclassified portion of the military network, and the remaining network, ARPANET, whose growth would be the catalyst for the appearance of today's Internet. ARPANET would later be taken out of service, but its mark on technological history was profound.

The Reagan years were the time of the Internet's adolescence, during which it grew out of its origins in research and began to spread into a broader community of users, with all the growth pains that entailed. In 1984, the National Science Foundation created NSFNET, a network that began the process of connecting the nation's universities to the supercomputer sites where the world's fastest and most powerful computers were located. Similar networks took hold at NASA, the National Institutes of Health, and the Department of Energy, but it was NSFNET that set the tone for technological advance in this period, driving research and deploying faster and faster long-haul connections. NSF also provided funding for the creation of regional networks that would support the delivery of computer data from NSFNET's backbone to the universities. At this point, the Internet remained a government-funded operation subsidized by taxpayer dollars, giving rise to the unfortunate assumption that the Net's resources were free. They were free, of course, to the university faculty and students who used them, but the taxpayer still footed the bill.

The NSFNET era was crucial for the development of today's Internet. For most of its life, it served as the Net's "backbone," the carrier for long-distance data that routed messages to regional networks for delivery. Access to that information changed the way many academics did their job. Most of them were not computer specialists but researchers in a wide range of academic disciplines. It had been one of the great surprises of the early ARPANET days that electronic mail was a key application; no one realized how useful it would become for exchanging ideas until mail systems at early sites were linked together and researchers could compare notes. Mailing lists, in which people could send a message to a central location and receive the messages sent by fellow members of the list in their own mailbox, quickly became popular as well, some of them serious, some lighthearted (one of the earliest mailing lists in the ARPANET days, in fact, focused on science fiction, a passion among the early network pioneers). These same communications tools took root in the academic community and, through exposure to students, gradually began to fan out into the rest of society. The idea of electronic mail became established in the public mind, as did the notion of "virtual communities," clusters of users connected by ideas rather than geography. Meanwhile, commercial information services like CompuServe, The Source, and DELPHI continued a parallel but separate development, offering access by modem to their own proprietary networks. For most people in the 1980s, the commercial services and local community-based bulletin board systems were the entirety of the on-line experience. Where the Internet was known at all, it was as a government-sponsored research enterprise.

By 1989, as communism was collapsing throughout Eastern Europe, ARPANET was decommissioned. It was one of the most successful research projects in the nation's history. Universities had grown accustomed to communicating through electronic mail and mailing lists, while the communications protocols that supported the Internet had become established on a global basis. NSFNET itself would be decommissioned in 1995, an equally successful project whose successor is a high-speed network dedicated to boosting the Internet's speeds to accommodate the huge number of users and the demands of advanced multimedia applications. The home page for the NSF's Very High Speed Backbone (http://www.vbns.net/) is shown in Figure 2.4.

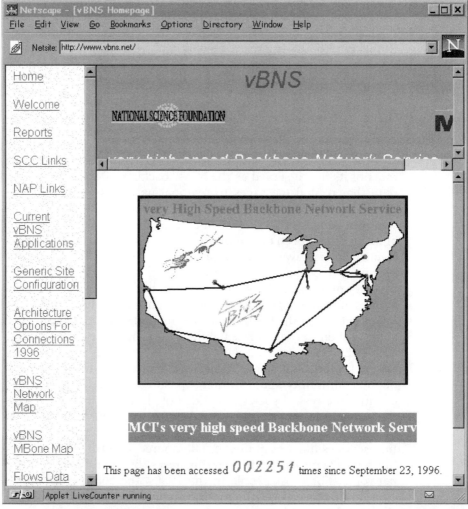

Figure 2.4 You can track cutting-edge research in data delivery at the NSF's Very High Speed Backbone site.

Today the Internet has no single backbone. In place of NSFNET are a series of networks, some run by the long-distance telephone companies, some by full-time network providers like UUnet and PSI. The changing landscape of government regulation means that the Internet has become self-sustaining and subject to the play of market forces. No one today believes that Internet access is free; the key question now becomes, at what price level is the Net sustainable, and how will the industry find the pricing model that supports the continued expansion of bandwidth?

The Nature of a Network

A network isn't just made up of computers. We have to include the software that makes the connections on the network interoperate, the media that make up the connections themselves, and the devices other than computers that the network uses to perform its functions. Such devices might include printers, for example, or routers—the specialized machines that direct the flow of Internet traffic. And, of course, the computers on the network are not limited by size, power, or operating system. We can create networks linking Macintoshes to supercomputers to IBM ThinkPads, neatly sidestepping the issue of incompatibility.

So think of a network as a group of computers and related machines that are connected by some kind of communications software. The Internet, as we've already seen, is not one but many networks, all of them communicating using the TCP/IP protocols. The Internet includes each computer and connected device on those member networks and all the information available to them (or, at least, all the information they want to make available to the public at large). You can see why we need a set of rules to manage all these transactions between different technologies. TCP/IP is what does this for the Internet.

If you work in a business office, you're probably familiar with another kind of network, the one you use to access files from an office computer and to send e-mail to colleagues in the same building. This is a local area network, or LAN, which uses its own technologies to link computers that are close to each other, usually in the same building or in adjacent buildings at a commercial site. A wide area network, or WAN, is a network that connects computers over a wide geographic area, joining local area networks together through special hardware. TCP/IP can run over both LANs and WANs; connect any two such networks and you create an internetwork, or internet (note the small i). Connect them to the international network of networks using TCP/IP and they have become members of the Internet.

Tip: The concept of an internet (with a small i) is undergoing a change in terminology. Today the word is *intranet*, referring to a network established using the TCP/IP protocols that operates independently of the worldwide Internet. Such a network might be

> established, for example, at a corporate site to connect employees and provide services like e-mail and file transfer. This network could be connected to the broader Internet, but it does not have to be; indeed, for security reasons, many companies have decided to mine the flexibility of TCP/IP while keeping their operations in-house. We'll be seeing more and more intranets established by business as the benefits of TCP/IP connectivity are recognized.

What kind of media can we use to connect computers on this globe-spanning network? The choices are actually quite wide. Most individual users make their connection with modems, which means that their computers are only on the network part-time, when they are connected to their service providers' machines using the copper wires and fiber-optic cables of the telephone system. Fiber-optic cable itself uses light instead of electricity to transmit its signals; a chief advantage of fiber is that the signal degrades only slightly with distance, which is why this medium is used for both transcontinental and international telephone connections. Fiber is also used extensively in local area networks and in long-haul data transmission over the Internet.

But we're not through yet. Internet data destined to cross oceans may equally well pass through satellites, an interesting application of wireless networking. Microwave transmission is a possibility, as is line-of-sight laser communication and even so-called packet radio, in which Internet traffic is moved through an amateur radio connection. The deregulation of the telecommunications industry invariably means that we'll soon be seeing yet another form of Internet media, the cable television connection. As you can see, the idea that the Internet is a set of specific wired connections rapidly begins to break down; in fact, the supple TCP/IP protocols can be routed over a wide variety of media, leading us to expect intriguing changes in the way we send and receive information, particularly on the wireless front. Setting up an Internet connection over a cellular telephone, for example, is doable but expensive today. Tomorrow, it may well be a common way to connect. The deregulation of the telecommunications industry will invariably have profound consequences for how telephone, cable television, satellite, and other industries scramble for Internet market share.

How TCP/IP Manages Traffic

The crucial thing to understand about how Internet traffic moves is that TCP/IP arranges it into packets for sending. Each packet contains data along with the routing information to get the data through to its destination. Hardware devices called routers examine the packet and move it along to the next site that would logically follow the route to the receiver. If a particular site stops working, the data can be routed to a different site. Routers have sufficient intelligence to examine the status of the network and determine which path will be most efficient for a given packet at a particular time. All of this will be determined by such factors as the flow of network traffic and changes to the hardware available on the network itself.

But let's look more closely at TCP/IP. The IP part of the equation stands for Internet Protocol, which is the crucial tool for creating an Internet address. Every computer on a TCP/IP network uses a numerical address; it is IP that determines how your computer will deal with those addresses. And just as each computer boasts its own IP address, it also must have a unique name that identifies it. On the Internet, the Domain Name System (DNS) is what translates computer names into IP addresses computers can understand.

Here's an IP address: 140.147.254.3. And here is the name that corresponds to the numeric address: locis.loc.gov. If I use a Telnet client program, I can enter locis.loc.gov as my destination, and the Domain Name System will translate that into a numerical, or IP, address. The DNS matches the name to the number; it's the latter that the Internet's routers work with as they move data across the network. In this case, my connection would result in my moving into the catalog at the Library of Congress; I would be using the library catalog, a service offered by the server at the site, through a client program running on my own computer.

Why go through the confusion of using both names and numbers? Because names are much easier to work with than numbers. It's hard enough to remember a series of seven-digit local telephone numbers, much less 10-digit long-distance ones. Internet addresses, as you can see from the preceding example, can be quite lengthy. Using names allows us to identify each computer on the Internet uniquely. In this case, locis.loc.gov, the first part of the address, locis, is the actual name of the computer. The second part is an organizational name at the site; the final part of the name is a so-called domain name. In this case, it's gov, which tells us that this is a government institution.

Tip: The Domain Name System that underlies the Internet is the crucial element in network activity, whether it be moving a file from one computer to another or calling up a World Wide Web page on your screen. Your computer needs to know which computer to contact to obtain information, and the contact data is found in the IP address. So-called nameservers are specialized computers that deal in translating between numerical addresses and their word-based counterparts, all of which happens behind the scenes for you the user. The packetized information that carries its routing instructions can only be delivered when your typed address can be turned into an IP address.

A number of these top-level domains exist; we can find them at the end of most Internet addresses:

com	A commercial operation
edu	A 4-year, degree granting educational institution
gov	A U.S. federal government agency
org	A miscellaneous, usually non-profit organization
mil	A military site
net	A network organization

Normally, we call the periods that separate the various parts of an address like locis.loc.gov "dots"; if you wanted to read the entire address aloud, you might say "locis dot loc dot gov." This is getting more important these days as World Wide Web sites are getting more play in the media. Thus you'll hear a Web site like www.mindspring.com referred to as "www dot mindspring dot com." Don't be put off by the complexity of the address; in fact, Internet names and addresses are logical and the format remains the same throughout. With a little practice, you'll master the address scheme, and you'll realize that your browser software lets you save addresses that you want to return to with a single click, sparing you the need to enter the whole complicated thing again.

Here's another example. An electronic mail address is what you use to send e-mail to a particular person. It takes on the following format: david_johnson @wallaby.aussie.com. If we take this address apart, starting from the left and proceeding to the right, we move from greater to less specificity. The user name is david_johnson (note the underscore, which connects the first and last name into a single user name). The @ sign is the Internet symbol, pronounced "at," that signals us that what follows will be the computer on which this person maintains his or her account. The next term, wallaby, is the name of the computer at the site on which this person's account resides. The following term, aussie, is an organization name; in this case, it's the name of a (hypothetical) company that uses the com suffix to indicate its commercial status. The com part of the address is the top-level domain name, as shown in the list. And the connected statement aussie.com is likewise a domain name, uniquely identifying the network at the site. The entire statement wallaby.aussie.com is known as a Fully Qualified Domain Name, or FQDN.

Once you've been on the Internet for any length of time, you'll run across some addresses that don't seem to fit this model. Outside the United States, top-level domains, the statements to the far right of the address, are given in two-letter format and used to identify the country of origin. You might, for example, encounter an address like this one: amelini@mbox.giovanni.it. Here, while the format of the address seems familiar, the final two letters, it, tells us that this is a site in Italy. You will run into numerous examples of country codes as the Internet continues to grow. Some that are widely seen are these:

ca	Canada
uk	United Kingdom
de	Germany
it	Italy
jp	Japan
nl	Netherlands
sg	Singapore

And so on.

If Internet Protocol, or IP, handles the network addressing chores, making sure that messages sent to a particular address are properly sent, the TCP part of TCP/IP is what makes sure the data actually arrives. Transmission Control Protocol ensures that any data that is lost on the network is resent; it's critical for network reliability. Bear in mind, too, that TCP/IP is actually a protocol suite, meaning it's a complete set of network applications and services. Thus the term FTP, which we've already discussed, stands for File Transfer Protocol, which lets you move files between computers. Another you may have heard of is Network News Transfer Protocol, or NNTP, which handles the movement of newsgroup postings between server and client. TCP/IP is multifaceted, and flexible enough to allow for the continual evolution of new services.

TCP/IP mandates that there's no single route for getting it to destination. The protocols always assume a worse-case scenario; they'll send data packets no matter what it takes, bumping them from one router to another, jumping oceans by satellite or transoceanic cable, crossing plains by fiber or microwave, rerouting around network outages the long way. But what does "long" mean? Here in Raleigh, if I want to send a message to Chapel Hill, about 35 miles away, I can use a UNIX program called traceroute to see how that message moves. The result is a study in complexity.

My message first goes, as you would expect, to my service provider, where it jumps from one computer to another before being routed to the huge switching center called MAE-East outside of Washington, D.C. From there, it's switched between three computers before being sent to Greensboro, North Carolina, about 80 miles from here. It winds up shuffling between routers in that city before feeding into the North Carolina Research and Education Network machines in Research Triangle Park, which is perhaps 15 miles from where I sit. It then flows to my destination.

Round trip? Hmmm. I just drove to D.C., and I made it in 4½ hours. Figure 310 miles one way; add 20 to get to MAE-East, which makes roughly 680 to get from here to Greensboro, another 70 or so to return to Research Triangle Park, and then 15 to Chapel Hill. So 765 miles as the packet flies to go 35 miles in a straight line. This is TCP/IP for you; it isn't always efficient, but it sure does carry the mail. You can imagine the kind of routes it dreams up when hauling traffic across entire continents.

Client/Server Computing

The necessary element of any Internet connection is to set up the TCP/IP protocols, which manage the connection. Most service providers include the necessary software in their start-up kits, including the Serial Line Internet Protocol (SLIP) or Point-to-Point Protocol (PPP) software that manages the connection over a telephone line, but also a number of programs that you will use while on the Internet. If you will think of the network itself as a kind of computer, this concept may become clearer. What we do on the Internet is to run programs that take advantage of its riches. That means sending commands out on the network and working with responses the Internet delivers. The software programs we use for this purpose are called *clients*.

Don't be misled: a client is just a computer program, like your word processor or appointment scheduler. But in this case, it's a program that was designed to function in a network environment. Rather than running only on your system's microprocessor and taking advantage of your hard disk, the client is developed to send a communication out over the Internet, to reach a remote computer and tell it what it wants to do. The remote computer, wherever it happens to be located, processes the request from the client and acts on it, returning the specified data.

Netscape, for example, is a client program; its job is to sit on your computer and mediate your presence on the World Wide Web. In doing so, it processes your requests; every time you click on a hyperlink, for example, it goes out on the network and retrieves the information found at that hyperlink's address. When it returns that information, it might show you a photograph or a map; it might play you an audio file of a radio show or display a multipage textual document with full formatting.

Client programs can do all kinds of things. They can request a specific program from a remote computer and download it. They can set up a connection with a computer that lets you query a database or search an archive. They can create a virtual reality chat room where you can talk to people around the world by typing in your responses to their questions and watching their on-screen presence move about in the form of a so-called avatar, an image they have chosen to represent themselves. Client programs can put on presentations that teach and display unread messages in newsgroups to which you have subscribed. They can play live video or let you edit network images. In general, clients are the tools we use to make the Internet work for us.

The model I am describing is called *client/server* computing. This dry term refers to the two parts of the network data-handling process. The client is the computer program that requests some kind of service from another computer. The server is the computer that offers that service. The service in question could be anything from disk space on the remote machine to a database program that can be run on it or a set of files for downloading. When you use Netscape to look at pages on the World Wide Web, your client, a Web browser like Netscape, has requested data from a remote computer, which has returned the desired information in a format Netscape can display. This back-and-forth transaction is at the heart of the sea change in computing whose most striking element is the Internet itself.

The World Wide Web Emerges

And what of the Web? We can trace its origins best if we examine how search tools developed on the Internet. The Net's great problem has always been its size and its diversity. As more and more individual networks joined, the content available on their machines was invariably unknown to current Internet users; how could they track down particular information, given the sheer number of sites? Yet the rapidly accumulating data was a priceless resource if it could be harnessed for productive use. A basic way to do that, built into the earliest Internet protocols, was by copying files from one computer to another. This activity was managed by File Transfer Protocol, FTP.

Moving files from one computer to another meant that the network could be accessed as a giant software library. System administrators at various sites could make information available to users at the same site or throughout the world. Through so-called anonymous FTP, files could be made accessible to the public at large; when users logged on with the word anonymous, the computer holding the files would allow them access to anything put in the public areas. Large collections of software and data were built, there for the taking but largely unused by modem users because they didn't know where to find them.

The search problem was tackled ingeniously in 1990 by Peter Deutsch, Alan Emtage, and William Wheelan at McGill University in Quebec. Their program, called archie, was designed to let users search through the holdings of a large number of Internet computers by entering a keyword (the lowercase "a" on archie is a convention of the early Internet days, when most software was developed on the UNIX operating system, and uppercase filenames were rare). Rather than randomly examining the directories at remote computer sites, users could enter a filename and let archie search for files that corresponded to it. If a file existed that matched the term, a list of "hits" was produced that showed where to go to download it. Other sites soon began running archie, which became the first widespread Internet search tool, if a cumbersome one to use. You can see a current take on archie at the Bunyip Information Systems home page (http://archie.bunyip.com/archie.html), as shown in Figure 2.5. As with so many Internet tools, the Web has become the easiest mode of access to archie.

Gopher was another take on the search problem, although its method was to simplify the way we use on-line information by making it easier to view. Developed at the University of Minnesota in 1991 by Mark McCahill and a team of programmers, Gopher allowed system administrators to put content on-line within a menu structure. Users who were unfamiliar with the complicated commands required to use networked computers needed a way to point at what they wanted and retrieve it quickly. Making this possible would allow

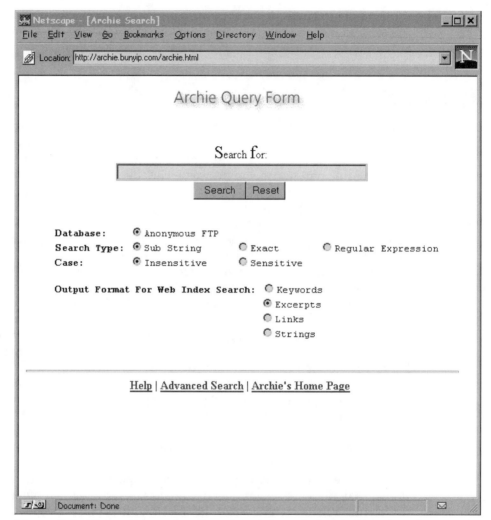

Figure 2.5 The archie search tool as viewed through the World Wide Web at Bunyip Information Systems.

faculty members at the university to take advantage of network resources without having to go through intermediaries. In that sense, Gopher was the first step toward populist networking, the goal of making Internet access available to all and usable by anyone.

Word of the original Gopher at Minnesota spread quickly; before long, thousands of sites were running the software with pointers to local content. Gopher could point to text files, or directories, or libraries of software; it could also point to information stored on other Gophers. By 1993, the Gopher model was firmly established, and a search tool called Veronica had sprung up to allow users to search Gopher menus for items of interest. Other search engines appeared to tackle specialized tasks, from a database search program called

Wide Area Information Servers (WAIS) to several systems designed to display and retrieve directory information on university campuses. Yet it remained for a mind-bending concept we would learn to call the World Wide Web to make the Internet mainstream, and to provide the search tools that would democratize the data hunt.

How Modern Physics Changed the Internet

The World Wide Web was born at a physics center called CERN, for Conseil Européen pour la Recherche Nucléaire (in English, the European Laboratory for Particle Physics), near Geneva. CERN's specialty is the study of the smallest building blocks of matter; you can't open a book about breakthroughs in physics without running into its name. Here, the scientists who study bosons, leptons, and quarks—the exotic inhabitants of the quantum world—perform research that is watched by colleagues at universities and research centers around the globe. But physics, like any science, is a collaborative enterprise; it builds upon the findings of its entire community. That means that scientists need to communicate, and computers provide a unique way for that communication to take place.

Enter Tim Berners-Lee, a British-born physicist at the laboratory, and Robert Cailliau of CERN's Electronics and Computing for Physics (ECP) Division. Their insight was to apply hypertext—embedding links in documents to point to related materials—to perform information exchange between researchers. Berners-Lee proposed the project in March 1989, and the first Web software made its appearance in 1990, running on a NeXT computer at CERN. While Cailliau focused on the needs of the physics community itself, Berners-Lee performed broader work on Web development that would take the project far beyond its original constituency. Now at the Massachusetts Institute of Technology, Berners-Lee continues this work through the World Wide Web Consortium, whose home page is shown in Figure 2.6.

Hypertext is a provocative model. It provides for links within documents that lead directly to other documents. Today's hypermedia is an extension of the original idea; a document can likewise point to video or audio files, or graphic images. What Berners-Lee had done was to connect network resources in a powerful new way. Beginning with a simple file server and then a hypertextual phone directory at CERN, his work established a system in which finding your way to a particular item on a remote computer was a matter of simply following the right hyperlink, which concealed the computer address behind the link. Ideas became central; physicists were freed from the need to master intricate computer skills while sharing their work. Berners-Lee put it this way in an interview in the *World Wide Web Journal* (Issue 3, "The Web after Five Years." Summer 1996): "When you turn on your computer, what you should see is information; what you should deal with is information. You should be able to create it, to absorb it; you should be able to exchange it freely in the informational space. The computer should just be your portal into the space, in my view."

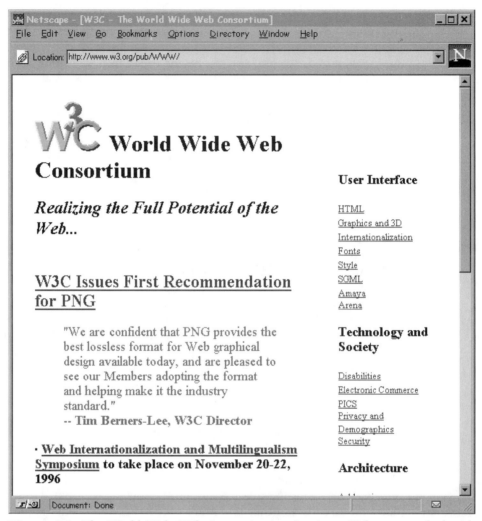

Figure 2.6 The World Wide Web Consortium maintains a Web page packed with information about technical specifications and standards for technically-minded users.

Tip: On technical issues concerning the Web, The World Wide Web Consortium (http://www.w3.org/pub/WWW/) is a priceless asset. Hosted both by the Massachusetts Institute of Technology and the French National Institute for Research in Computing and Automation (INRIA), the Consortium (W3C) promotes the standards-making process that ensures that Web-based software will be able to operate seamlessly. While individual memberships are not available, the W3C does provide the *World Wide Web Jour-*

nal, offering articles on Web protocols, security issues, and the broader concerns raised by the Web in society. You can read sample articles from the current issue of this journal, published by O'Reilly & Associates, at http://www.w3.org/pub/WWW/Journal/. Archives of past issues are also available here.

HyperText Transport Protocol

HyperText Transport Protocol (HTTP) is the breakthrough that makes the World Wide Web function. In networking parlance, a protocol is simply a set of agreed upon rules that allow disparate computers to work together, using a set of commands that both can understand to perform network functions. We can refer to it as part of the Web's architecture, in the sense that it is a building block without which the essential transactions of the Web could not take place. And it is the http prefix that you see on a Web URL, alerting you to the fact that the site address that follows is using the Web's protocols to display information.

Shorn of its technical complexity, HTTP functions rather simply. The client/server model we've already examined is used to handle the transaction. A document is requested when the user clicks on a hyperlink on a particular World Wide Web page. That click sends out an HTTP information request from the browser (the client), causing it to contact the computer named in the hyperlink (the server) to call up the file in question. The file is returned to the client in the Web's Hypertext Markup Language (HTML) format, which allows it to be displayed with a full range of graphical and formatting features. You can see the basic HTTP transaction in Figure 2.7.

Tip: We say that an HTTP transaction is *stateless,* meaning that once the server has returned the requested information, the connection ends. This has interesting ramifications for how we use the Web. A television signal, for example, is broadcast to your set; any new content appears immediately, so that you receive news of breaking stories as they occur. The Web page you download now, however, because of the stateless nature of its connection, is a completed transaction. To update it, you would need to reload the page. This is why new technologies like Sun Microsystems Java language and Macromedia's Shockwave plug-in have emerged, to provide updatable information by allowing you to download and run small programs on your computer. We're moving, if slowly, toward a Web with more animation and immediacy, one in which content can be delivered in a fashion more similar to that of the broadcast media.

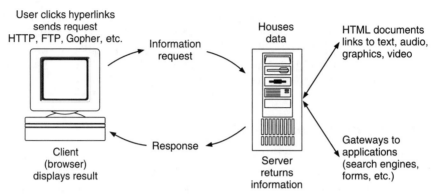

Figure 2.7 A basic HTTP transaction between Web client and HTTP server.

A Web client normally works with HTTP to deliver Web pages, but it can also send an information request using any of the other protocols available for TCP/IP work, which is how we can access Gopher servers, FTP sites, and WAIS databases through the same browser with which we access the Web itself. The Universal Resource Locator system described in the last chapter (and more fully explained later in this chapter) can point to any of these resources no matter where they're located. This creates a system that is not only indexable through search engines and their databases, but also one in which a consistent set of standards allows anyone to create a Web page or, if he or she chooses, a Web server itself.

Tip: In order to operate, all Web servers and clients have to use HTTP to exchange hypertextual and hypermedia information. A Web server is thus often referred to as an HTTP server, but you will also see the term HTTPD, which stands for HTTP Daemon. The word daemon stems from the UNIX programming language, where it refers to a program that executes in the background to provide a particular service. In this case, the HTTPD reference means "a server computer running the HTTP protocol on the Web."

The beauty of this system is that the entire range of networked information is made accessible via nothing more than mouse clicks or, in the case of search-enabled sites, by typing in keywords and then clicking a button to launch the search.

When we view a Web-based document, we normally talk in terms of "pages" of information, although as we've seen, a page in this sense is enlivened with links to multimedia resources and can connect documents on one computer with those on numerous others. Home pages are those that represent our entryway to a particular organization's Web site, which can contain numerous pages of its own in the form of hyperlinks. We don't have to access a home page to see other pages at the site in most cases, but it's the home page that provides the overview of what's available there. With servers now managing home pages in the hundreds of thousands around the world, we have access to millions of linked pages of information of all degrees of quality.

Tip: The W3 Servers page at the World Wide Web Consortium is a great way to get a global view of World Wide Web servers. You can access it at http://www.w3.org/pub/DataSources/WWW/Servers. html. If you're interested in a particular region, it's helpful to see the list of servers broken down by country and continent. This site allows you to do just that, with quick links to the servers you find. Clickable maps make it easy to find servers in the country of your choice and access them; you can see one of these in Figure 2.8. You will also find pointers here to lists of other types of information servers, from Gopher to FTP to phone book systems like WHOIS, or search tools like Wide Area Information Servers (WAIS).

Hypertext Markup Language at Work

Let's see how the HTML language works in a practical example. Figure 2.9 shows the home page at CERN itself, with a splendid photograph of the facility and the surrounding terrain. Immediately beneath the photograph is a short block of text that welcomes readers to the site. The photograph is from a file in GIF format called CERN.GIF, a fact that can be determined by using a Web browser to view the underlying computer code that has assembled the page in question. You can see that code in Figure 2.10.

The CERN.GIF reference tells the browser which image to display on which part of the page and where to find that image. What we are looking at here is Hypertext Markup Language which, for all its apparent complexity, consists of nothing more than a series of pointers to computer files and references to the proper formatting of their information. Notice that HTML documents appear as plain text; while a host of HTML editing tools are available, you can create an HTML file with a simple text editor if you choose. HTML tags key items of a document—headers, tables, paragraphs, illustrations—in particular ways using brackets. You can see that the CERN photograph, for example, is tagged. The section reads as follows:

```
<BODY>
<H2>
<IMG SRC="/CERN/CERN.GIF" ALT="CERN"> European Laboratory for Particle
Physics </H2>
<HR>
```

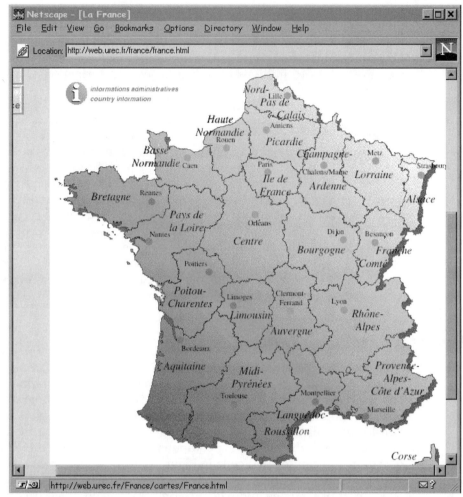

Figure 2.8 A clickable map at the World Wide Web Consortium is available for all countries offering Web sites; this map of France makes targeting a resource a matter of point and click.

Untangling this text, we find the following: BODY refers to the content of the Web document displayed in the browser window. H2 is a second-level heading; HTML allows you to display heading text in larger fonts than normal body text. IMG SRC refers to the photograph, which is found on the server through the path shown. It is listed as part of the second-level header H2, so that the image appears first, followed by the text: "European Laboratory for Particle Physics." The /H2 statement ends the heading. The HR tag produces a horizontal line along the browser window.

As you can see, looking behind the scenes at HTML reveals that it is a relentlessly logical way of creating Web-based information, and one that read-

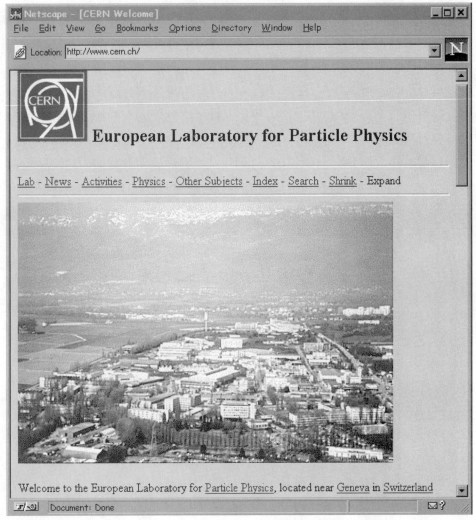

Figure 2.9   The home page at CERN, where the World Wide Web was created.

ily yields to automation through various software tools. An HTML editor is a program that does for HTML and the Web what a word processor does for the creation of textual documents: it simplifies the process and removes from the user the need to know the complexities of the coding behind the program. Conversion software is likewise available to translate documents from numerous formats into proper HTML coding.

While the specifics of Web page creation are beyond the scope of this book, be advised that you can learn a great deal about how HTML produces its effects by studying source code like that just shown. To do so, look for the View

```
Netscape - [Source of: http://www.cern.ch/]                    _ □ x

<HEAD>
<TITLE>CERN Welcome</TITLE>
</HEAD>

<BODY>
<H2>
<IMG SRC="/CERN/CERN.gif" ALT="CERN"> European Laboratory for
Particle Physics </H2>
<HR>


<A HREF="#z01">Lab</A> - <A HREF="#z02">News</A> -
<A HREF="#z03">Activities</A> - <A HREF="#z04">Physics</A> -
<A HREF="#z05">Other Subjects</A> -
<a href="/CERN/AlphabeticalIndex.html">Index</a> -
<A HREF="/CERN/Search.html">Search</A> -
<A HREF="/NormalWelcome.html">Shrink</A> -
Expand
<HR>


<IMG SRC="/CERN/CERNview.gif" ALT="">
<P>
Welcome to the European Laboratory for
<A HREF="http://www.w3.org/hypertext/DataSources/bySubject/Physics/Overvie
Particle Physics</A>, located near
<A HREF="http://www.isoft.ch/GenevaGuide/">Geneva</A> in
<A HREF="http://heiwww.unige.ch/switzerland">Switzerland</A> and
<A HREF="http://web.urec.fr/france/france.html"> France</A>.
CERN is the birthplace of the
<A HREF="/CERN/WorldWideWeb/WWWandCERN.html">World-Wide Web</A>.
<P>
The <A HREF="/WebOffice/Contacts.html">WWW support team</A>
provides a set of <A HREF="/WebOffice/">Services</A>
to the physics experiments and the lab.
<HR>

<H2>About the <A NAME="z01">Laboratory</A></H2>
```

Figure 2.10   A browser can show you the computer code underlying a Web page; note the reference here to the file CERN.GIF.

menu in your browser and click on the Document Source header to see how a particular page was created. This is particularly useful when you're looking at unusual effects and want to learn how they were achieved.

Tip: Numerous books have appeared detailing the tags now available through HTML, and HTML itself continues its development with the release of version 3.2. The latest version supports such features as tables, text flow around images, superscripts and subscripts. But you should be aware that the ongoing evolution of HTML is controversial. Driving development of their browser products, Netscape Corporation and Microsoft have both pushed at times past the standards process supported by the World Wide Web Consortium, which has caused difficulty for developers at other companies. HTML 3.2 is an attempt to consolidate the situation; it represents the Consortium's work in coordination with major vendors like IBM, Microsoft, Netscape Communications Corporation, Novell, SoftQuad, Spyglass, and Sun Microsystems. Nonetheless, version 3.2 has yet to reach final form; version 2.0 continues to be the choice of many Web page designers, despite its inability to work with some of the extensions developed by Microsoft and Netscape. In a field as fluid as this, you should continue to monitor developments through the World Wide Web Consortium to track the fortunes of HTML.

The text beneath the photograph reads as follows: "Welcome to the European Laboratory for Particle Physics, located near Geneva in Switzerland and France. CERN is the birthplace of the World Wide Web." In hypertext form, this statement is notated as follows: Welcome to the European Laboratory for <u>Particle Physics</u>, located near <u>Geneva</u> in <u>Switzerland</u> and <u>France</u>. CERN is the birthplace of the <u>World Wide Web</u>." Each of the underlined terms is a hyperlink, all but one referencing a file on a computer different from the CERN server. The particle physics hyperlink, for example, resides on a computer at the site http://www.w3.org/, at the World Wide Web Consortium. As we've seen, this is a valuable site for background material about the Web and documents about its future direction.

In a similar way, the hyperlink for Geneva references a site, http://www.eunet.ch/, which is actually a rather charming guide to the city, whereas the comparable links for Switzerland and France lead, respectively, to a guide to Switzerland created by the Graduate Institute of International Studies (http://www.heiwww.unige.ch/) and a directory of France containing a clickable map that makes it easy to point to an area you want to learn more about and go straight to the information (http://web.urec.fr/). The final hyperlink, on the term World Wide Web itself, points to a file on the CERN server that explains how the institution uses the Web to handle its own information. You can check these links in your Web browser; in Netscape, for example, moving the cursor over any hyperlink causes the URL of the link to be displayed at the bottom left side of the browser window. In each case, a click on the appropriate hyperlink causes the HTTP protocols to create the necessary communication between client and server to ensure that the right page is displayed.

Tip: We used to speak of system administrators as the people who run servers, but the growth of the Web has spawned a new term: the *Webmaster*. Anyone in the business of creating and fine-tuning a Web server can be considered to be a Webmaster, a term that will surely enter the job description dictionary for thousands of companies over the next few years.

URLs: The Location of Information

Using HTTP, a page of information referencing any form of multimedia can be sent across the Internet to a distant computer and displayed. Critical to the process is the Universal Resource Locator, or URL, a format we examined briefly at the end of the last chapter. A URL is like an address—it points to a particular resource no matter where it's located on the Internet. Take a look at the URL for the Internet Society site we looked at earlier. The statement http://www.isoc.org/ starts out by telling us what kind of resource we're about to examine. The http statement is a reference to HyperText Transport Protocol, the mechanism by which HTML Web pages are moved through the Internet. Only Web pages will be referred to with http designations, so we know to expect, in most cases, the www that follows, which is a relatively standard method for indicating Web sites.

Tip: Confusingly, many Web sites are listed using their URL, while others are shown with the address only. This is particularly the case now that advertising Web sites has spread so widely in commercial venues. In earlier versions of Web browsers, it was necessary to enter the complete URL in your browser; this included the http statement at the beginning and its accompanying colon and two slashes, as in http://www.quarterdeck.com/. Some browsers have now shortened the process; Netscape, for example, lets you enter a simple company name in its Location box, and the browser itself will supply the surrounding URL information. You could, in other words, access the Quarterdeck site just referred to by typing, simply, "quarterdeck" in the Location box, but this method wouldn't work for noncommercial sites like http://www.isoc.org/. Similarly, you can type in an address, not the full URL, in Netscape, and the browser will supply the http header. But this method will not function if you are hoping to access something other than a Web page—a Gopher site, for example, requires a full URL statement. Thus, if you type the address world.std.com into the Location field in Netscape, the browser will take you to a Web page; to reach the site's Gopher at gopher://world.std.com/, the complete URL is required.

If we keep reading from left to right, we encounter the address: www.isoc.org. It uses the domain names we're already familiar with, and tells us that we're dealing with an entity called isoc (we know now that it stands for

Internet Society), and that it is a nonprofit organization, as revealed by the org domain statement at the end.

The final slash in the URL is resonant. It tells us that we're not really through, that there is underlying content to be found if we explore the site. For a URL can be quite specific; it can point to something as small as an individual file. Suppose I wanted to tell you where an interesting document about classical music could be found. I might say, "I know about an FTP site where they keep a directory of composers' biographies. Check into the classics directory there and you'll find a subdirectory called schumann. In that directory is a file called clara.doc. The address is ashkenazy.piano.com." If you understood FTP procedures, you'd know to log on to the site ashkenazy.piano.com using anonymous FTP; you could do this through your Web browser by entering the site address in URL form: ftp://ashkenazy.piano.com/. Then you'd have to find the classics directory, which might be located just about anywhere in the directory structure at the site, based on what I said. From there you'd go to the schumann directory. And then you'd have to locate the individual file in that directory to download it. All in all, my statement has pointed you in the right direction, but with cumbersome methodology that adds to your work.

But suppose I gave you an address like this one:

ftp://ashkenazy.piano.com/classics/schumann/clara.doc

That's a URL as well, but it's a lot more specific than the preceding. The ftp designation tells you it's an FTP site that contains files made available through anonymous FTP. The address follows, but after the com we find a slash, and after that, a complete directory path to our destination. In other words, the URL has been constructed to tell us how to find this file. By looking at it, we know that the right path to the file is to log on to the site, go first to the classics directory, then to the schumann directory, then to the individual file: clara.doc. Note that the file itself has no final slash in the URL. Once we get to it, we've taken the URL to as fine-grained a specificity as we can. Having done so, we can shorten the actual process of finding the file; by entering the complete URL in our browser, we can access the file directly, without making the changes of directory that work our way down into the layered site. In pre-Web days, we'd have had to follow through this process one step at a time, entering commands the whole way.

URLs, in other words, compress address information into as small a space as possible, and transfer the workload from ourselves to our software. The URL thus tells us everything we need to know to find a particular thing on the Internet. URLs always tell us what we're going to see at the other end of the connection. If http statements tell us we're referring to World Wide Web pages, Gopher statements (as in gopher://gopher.mountolive.edu/) tell us we're looking at a Gopher site, which makes information available in menu format. Newsgroups and e-mail addresses can be designated by URLs, too, as in news:rec.music.classical, or mailto:jones@samarkand.org. Note that the news and URLs don't contain slashes like the others.

URLs are pointers, so they make it possible to set up an Internet that is indexed, no mean feat on a network encompassing millions of pages of Web-based information and terabytes of files and programs. They also make it possible to combine Internet material, files of all kinds, into single pages of information. Take a file from this computer and another from that one; both can be displayed on the same World Wide Web page, for the HTML language can point to each; to the user, moving between them is transparent. Between HTTP, HTML, and the URL concept, we lacked only one thing to make the Internet take off: a simpler user interface.

Tip: Security remains an issue on the World Wide Web, as it does on the broader Internet. The Net was never designed as a secure medium for handling electronic transactions, for example, and electronic mail is just one type of communication that can, theoretically, be intercepted, or read by an unscrupulous person at a service provider's site. To get around many security issues, corporations often set their networks up behind so-called firewalls. These security devices—a combination of hardware and software—make it difficult for anyone from the outside to access the company's server; people working at the firm can easily use the Internet, but those trying to get in from the Internet can't do it unless they have been given accurate password information. Firewalls are what make it possible for companies to create intranets; without them, the corporate network would simply be too insecure.

The Rise of the Browser

With all the technical brilliance of the Web, the challenge that remained was to create a program that would display it on our screens and let us use it with ease. The program that met the challenge was called Mosaic. Developed by Marc Andreessen, Eric Bina, and a team of programmers at the National Center for Supercomputing Applications in Urbana-Champaign, Illinois (on the campus of the University of Illinois), Mosaic could take information available over the infant World Wide Web and display it with full graphical capabilities, enabling users to point and click their way around the Internet without having to enter complicated commands. The Mosaic model took off in much the same way Gopher did, although with considerably more momentum. Copies of the program were made available for free from the NCSA site, and users downloaded them by the hundreds of thousands. The change in interface was driven by the obvious strength of the software, with the clear implication that the Web browser in some form would become the standard means of Internet access. In Figure 2.11, you can see the current home page for the NCSA, a good place to check for cutting edge developments in computer science.

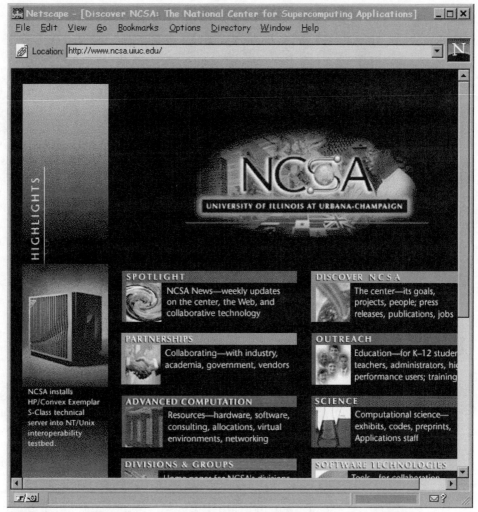

Figure 2.11 The home page at the NCSA, where Mosaic was developed, remains a lively site for the technically oriented.

By making network navigation simple, Mosaic pointed to an Internet with broad popular appeal. The once exotic concept of the hyperlink entered the public vocabulary; people realized that when they encountered blue or underlined text, they could click on it to jump to the underlying link, which could be on the same computer or on a machine across the ocean. From a text-oriented Internet, we entered a world of graphical formatting, photographs, and multimedia, in which information could be displayed with magazine-style clarity and approachability. Suddenly the Internet took on the shape of a publishing enterprise, a place where screens of information were like the pages of a book, turbocharged with connecting links between documents.

Tip: What was life like before Mosaic changed the Internet interface? While scientists and researchers had access to a variety of programs, some of them graphical, for tapping the Net's resources, most dial-up users were confined to a text-based interface that was not only nongraphical, but also required the user to enter commands to perform basic operations. One mistake in entering a command meant that the action would fail. A key virtue of the browser interface is the presence of pull-down menus; these not only suggest the next step in the command sequence, but perform the action itself when the user clicks on the item in question. Take the example of the classical music file mentioned. In the text-based days, I would have had to enter multiple commands to change directories at the site until I had worked my way down to the appropriate file, at which time I would enter a command such as "get clara.doc" to download it. With a browser, I can enter the file's URL and begin the download process with a few mouse clicks, or else simply read (or print out) the resultant file on my screen.

By 1995, the browser model had become ubiquitous. Andreessen and many of the original Mosaic team had gone on to develop a second-generation browser called Netscape, while the start-up company he helped to create made a spectacular initial public offering on Wall Street that saw its price soar. Mosaic itself, now commercialized and licensed by a company called Spyglass, appeared in improved versions and was incorporated in CompuServe's full-access Internet offering. By then, Internet stocks of all kinds, from network provider UUnet to hardware manufacturer Cisco Systems, were setting records on Wall Street as public interest in networking technology grew. Microsoft's Explorer browser began to cut into Netscape's market share, while a host of browsers from smaller companies continued to offer their own takes on Web page download and display. And the changing nature of the Internet's user base meant that individual users in homes and small businesses were signing on in the millions; for most new users, a browser was part of the start-up software provided by the service provider.

Tip: The growth of the Web, propelled by improvements to our browsers and a tsunami of new content, is a fascinating thing to track. Various Web sites specialize in statistics.
They include:

> http://etrg.findsvp.com/index.html: This is the FIND/SVP site, from a
>   research firm that has conducted numerous studies on Internet
>   growth and use.
> http://www.cc.gatech.edu/gvu/user_surveys/User_Survey_Home.html:
>   Here you'll find the GVU User Surveys (from the Graphics, Visual-

ization, and Usability Center at the Georgia Institute of Technology); these provide, better than any other source, a look at who is using the Web today.

http://www.jpmorgan.com/MarketDataInd/Research/: The J.P. Morgan Research Reports site.

http://www.netcraft.co.uk/survey/: The Netcraft Web Server Survey.

http://future.sri.com/vals/vals-survey.results.html: SRI International's look at the growth of the Web.

http://www.ora.com/research/: O'Reilly & Associates has been a major player in tracking the Net's development since pre-Web days.

http://www.nua.ie/Choice/Surveys/SurveyMaster.html: Nua's Internet Surveys, a set of varying takes on the state of the Web today.

http://www.mit.edu:8001/people/mkgray/net/: Matthew Gray's Internet Statistics site, from a long-time observer of the Web's growth.

Gateways to External Programs through the Common Gateway Interface

In a basic Web transaction, your browser sends a request to a server, which processes the request and returns the desired information in the form of an HTML document and associated graphics or multimedia files. A Web document, after all, frequently contains multiple items; a typical page is usually a mixture of file types, containing, at the very least, textual and graphical files. Each of these objects will be returned individually by the server to the client requesting the information, and built on your screen. And as we've seen, a Web page can refer to objects that exist not only on a single server, but also on computers all over the Net. Thus a page can be a composite of data stored in widely dispersed locations. For that matter, a page can also use elements found on your own computer, such as objects it has placed in its cache. Caching such objects allows them to be called up quickly, because they do not have to transit the Net again to reach the client.

But a request can be more complicated than this. In some instances, we might want to use a search tool to find information. At a Web site that makes this possible, a search box appears in which we can enter keywords and then click a Search or Enter button to start the process. In this case, the server has to process the information request, forward it to another software program, wait for the reply, and then return these results to the client. When such transactions occur, we use the Common Gateway Interface, or CGI, as the link between HTTP server and external program. Although both server software and external program probably exist on the same machine, CGI is the element that allows them to work together. The CGI program simply takes Web server data and manipulates it; in the case of a search request, it uses the data to run a database search, using your keyword as input.

But CGI can handle more than search requests; it can work with any external program to increase the functionality of a Web server. A Web page can be used, for example, to create forms, such as the one you see in Figure 2.12 at amazon.com, an on-line bookseller in Seattle.

Many on-line newspapers and magazines set up forms that users must fill out to get access to the site. Although the content may be free, it is useful to the system administrators to build a database of information about their audience; obviously, this same strategy is valuable in Net-based advertising, in which a company can quickly determine a user profile of interested people and pitch its products accordingly. CGI can track usage at a Web site as well, which is how counters can appear that show the number of people who have accessed a particular page. In general, a Webmaster will use CGI whenever it

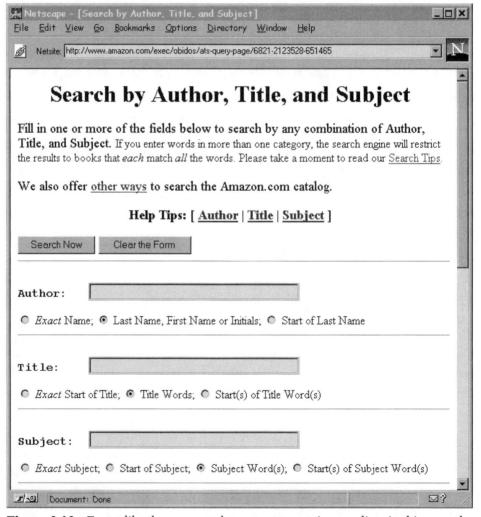

Figure 2.12   Forms like these are used to enter transactions on-line; in this case, the completed form can be submitted to begin the process of order handling at the Amazon site.

is necessary to gather input from the user, or whenever the information he or she wishes to send is fluid, as would be the case, for example, in a site that returned an accurate time of day or day of the month to any user who accessed the home page.

In a broader sense, think of CGI as an enhancement to the Web's information model. Whereas a standard Web transaction is cut-and-dried—you make the request, your client delivers it, the server responds, the client displays—a CGI-enabled site can perform a wide variety of actions based upon the kind of CGI script to which the server has been linked. As we will see in subsequent chapters, the move toward a more dynamic, interactive Web is one of the key themes of network development. It shows up not only in CGI but also in such diverse applications as streaming audio and video—in which we view or listen to information without download delays—as well as computer languages like Java, which bring animation and screen updates to the information presented by the browser. In one form or another, the Web is becoming a livelier, more interactive place to be.

Tip: You will often encounter the term *cgi-bin* in the URL information for sites that use CGI. It is typical for Webmasters to create a cgi-bin directory on the server, so that when a client requests the CGI gateway, the information request is sent to the cgi-bin directory for processing. The server then runs the program and returns the results to the client. The term bin comes from the word binary, which has long been used to designate programs; today, the average files found in a cgi-bin directory are text files that contain scripts used by gateway programs.

Search Engines Index the Web

As the Web seized the public imagination, the problem of information retrieval gradually moved to the forefront of Internet research. The Web was particularly troublesome to information seekers because it was all too easy to lose your place when you followed hyperlinks from one page to another. Locating information on the Web would be a hit-or-miss affair, until the next generation of search engines arose. These tools, with names like Yahoo!, Lycos, AltaVista and InfoSeek, were designed to search through the universe of Web pages looking for references to specific keywords. They did this by creating a database of keywords found on Web pages and allowing users to search that database. Soon the standard model was to search the entire text of such pages, allowing the user to enter a single query that would examine millions of hypertext pages for the term in question.

The development of Web-based search engines is an ongoing story; each engine boasts its own search parameters, and each consults a proprietary database. But despite these limitations, the search tools now available on the Internet provide us with the enabling software the network has long needed to make its content accessible by anyone. Keyword searching is a simple matter of entering a term and starting the search; the results are shown in hyperlink fashion, so that all we need do to retrieve the information is to click on the item of your choice and let your browser take you to it. In many respects, search engines are the final piece of the puzzle; they tell us that the Internet is taking on the shape of a library, with indexed resources and retrievable content. What remains is to settle the issue of how that content is provided and how its publishers are compensated.

The vision of a Vannevar Bush or a J.C.R. Licklider remains alive in today's Internet. Its mesh of connections open the individual computer screen to the possibilities of communication, boosting not only one-to-one discourse through electronic mail, but also changing the nature of research through links to libraries and publications. If we think of the Internet as a huge publishing enterprise, we can see that its content remains its greatest conundrum. On-line books, magazines, and newspapers vie with personally produced and often slick home pages from voices outside the normal channels of production. The Web thus becomes in the digital era what the printing press was for the late fifteenth century, an unprecedented technique for disseminating ideas, bringing the power of the printed word to people who had hitherto remained voiceless. Publish a Web page and your thoughts can be found by search engines and read by anyone with an interest in your idea. It remains the province of the reader—the information consumer—to make the necessary judgments about the reliability and verifiability of Web-based materials.

3

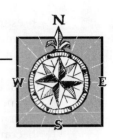

Logging On
to the Web

Internet access has changed so much in the past few years that newcomers will have no idea how difficult the process used to be. Just five years ago, logging on by modem involved first tracking down a service provider, of which there were few who serviced the individual user. Documentation was sparse if it existed at all. Getting on-line meant calling the provider's telephone number, then once connected, you needed to type in commands to activate network functions like electronic mail or file transfer. The interface was text-based; no graphics were possible. Using the World Wide Web in its infancy involved typing in the number of the hyperlink you wanted to see, and the result was displayed in monospaced text. Help was all but nonexistent, because most dial-up providers offered the service only as an adjunct to other activities; the full-service provider of today had not yet entered the picture.

Today's graphical world makes signing up for the Internet a far simpler process. Among the great advances for individual users is that providers now offer set-up software that is supported by relatively straightforward documentation. Armed with one or two disks, you have to enter only a few commands in a graphical environment by clicking on the appropriate item; you then fill in information supplied by your provider to set the TCP/IP parameters. At this point, you are able to load the necessary client programs, for most providers today offer a World Wide Web browser like Microsoft's Internet Explorer or Netscape as part of the sign-up package that includes other tools. Logging on may not be problem free, but it is far easier than before; a good service provider can make the process straightforward enough that you can be navigating the World Wide Web within minutes of loading your software. And the presence of easy-to-use directories like Yahoo! point you in the right direction, no matter what topic you'd like to explore.

And the provider picture itself has changed. In keeping with the Internet's scientific and educational background, early dial-up providers tended to be associated with research laboratories or similar organizations. My first dial-up connection came through a research consortium that offered accounts largely as a convenience to the local technical community. Today, providers have become numerous; any large city is bound to be served by numerous companies offering Internet access. The type of company varies from tiny start-ups with a handful of computers and a local user base to national firms like MCI and AT&T, offering access through a global network. The oddity of Internet access, then, is that the route onto a global network began as a local phenomenon and has only recently moved to a regional and national level. Local providers are still out there, many of them excellent, but your options now include the major telecommunications companies, other nationwide providers, and commercial on-line services, with new entries expected from the world of satellite and cable television.

The Evolution of Internet Access

The Internet didn't grow up as a modem-accessible service. Instead, it was conceived as a means of connecting large computers and providing access to them through terminals. In a research laboratory or a government agency, a terminal would allow users to take advantage of the processing power of the computer they were connected to, and the connection would be maintained on a full-time basis without using dial-up telephone lines. Later, networked computers—not terminals—within offices and agencies would offer the same kind of connectivity. Fed by a full-time, or "dedicated" high-speed link, they wedded desktop computers whose Internet connection remained available 24 hours a day.

It was only in the early 1990s that practical modem access became available for an ever-widening group of individual users. This happened because companies began to sense a market building for Internet connectivity. Starting with a company called The World in Massachusetts and spreading to other early providers like Panix, PSINet, The WELL, and others, modem access made it possible to set up an Internet connection to the home or small business without the expense of a full-time connection. These early forays into modem connectivity were almost experimental, in that the size of the Internet market had yet to be established. But their success made it clear that if the individual user was to get connected, it would be through the modem model.

It's ironic that it took the Internet, today the industry's hottest technology platform, so long to move to widely available modem capability, because modems are hardly new. The 1980s was the decade of the bulletin board system, or BBS. These local and sometimes regional services, usually run by volunteers but later increasingly commercial, were places where users could call to leave messages and participate in discussions about various topics; they also provided file libraries with the latest free- and shareware (you pay if you like it) software. BBSes are still healthy; one recent survey found over 60,000 of them.

From a structural point of view, a bulletin board is a relatively simple system. A person with a minimum of computer knowledge could set up a BBS with a single computer and one incoming telephone line. Software to manage the bulletin board's activities was available either for free or for a nominal fee, depending on the system operator's choice of programs, and once installed, the BBS would largely run itself, accepting incoming calls and managing the flow of discussion group and electronic mail traffic.

Because of their local nature, bulletin boards were readily accessible via a local telephone call. They became places where communities could form to discuss issues affecting neighbors; companies sometimes started boards as a way of staying in touch with employees on the road. A popular system called FidoNet sprang up that let system operators automatically move electronic mail and discussion group traffic between sites late at night; a message could go coast to coast from one computer to another through a series of local telephone calls, each one moving the traffic closer to its destination. Later, improvements in the bulletin board technology would establish nationwide and even international conferencing capabilities.

Commercial on-line services like CompuServe and Prodigy sprang out of this environment, along with competitors like The Source (now defunct), DELPHI, GEnie, BIX and others. The model in those days was a variation on the bulletin board theme: You still called a central computer to connect to the various services it made available; but in this case, the central computer(s) was located at some distance; to handle telephone charges, networks like CompuServe set up their own local access numbers, so that the only charge you paid was the one that took care of your use of the system. Billing usually took place on a by-the-minute basis.

Because the Internet is decentralized, there was no decree from above that a particular model of service should be made available. But as individual users began to express an interest, companies offering Internet access by modem began to spring up on the local level. We call such companies Internet service providers, or ISPs. The World, for example, gained most of its clients from the Boston and Cambridge, Massachusetts areas, while The WELL began as a San Francisco–based organization that quickly grew into surrounding cities. In my area, the research organization known as the Microelectronics Center of North Carolina (MCNC) was the first to offer dial-up access by modem; it was joined within a short time by a host of other companies. Some providers went regional, while others concentrated on serving a limited geographical area. A few became national players—NETCOM is an early example, and both the long-distance telephone carriers and the regional Bell companies are more recent entrants into this market. But whatever their range, service providers were responsible for taking a modem signal and putting it to work over the Internet.

The Internet, then, offers not one but numerous entryways into its resources. Computers on the system operate on a so-called peer-to-peer basis. This means that no computer is assumed to have priority over another until a particular action is performed. When you use your computer to download a file, for example, your machine is entering into a relationship with a remote computer in which the other machine provides the data. But your computer is also capable of providing data to a different machine. The old model of central computer dishing out services to computers that acted like terminals is replaced by an interactive network in which computers participate on an equal basis.

Tip: The term *bandwidth* is used to refer to the amount of data that can be sent over a given connection. This amount is normally measured in bits per second (bps) so that when we talk about a 28.8Kbps modem, we're referring to a device that can move 28,800 bits per second. Bandwidth also defines the kind of connections we can use on the Internet:

56K   Many businesses use leased telephone line connections that operate at this speed, which translates to 56,000 bits per second. The line is digital and roughly twice as fast as a 28.8Kbps modem.

T-1   A leased line connection that operates at 1.544Mbps per second, or 1,544,000 bits per second. Bandwidth of this nature is what is normally used to connect office networks to the Internet.

T-3   A connection capable of moving data at close to 45Mbps per second (45,000,000 bits). Bandwidth of this calibre is what is used to handle much of the long-haul backbone traffic on the Internet today.

By comparison, a typical Ethernet connection in an office network operates at 10Mbps (10,000,000 bits per second).

As modem users, the bandwidth feeding our computers is determined by the speed of our modem as well as the rate that data is flowing on the Internet itself, which varies depending on use and routing. In general, though, a faster modem means faster data transfer, an important factor when considering how long it takes to download some Web pages.

Today, connecting to the Internet with a modem is the most practical alternative for the individual, while medium to large businesses connect using dedicated telephone lines. T-1 lines may be out of reach on grounds of price for the individual user, but the rapid transformation of Internet bandwidth means that within a relatively short time, we will enjoy data rates far higher than T-1's 1.544Mbps access in our homes through satellite, cable television modems, or fiber-optic lines from the telephone companies. Even now, 56Kbps modems are in the works, effectively doubling the rate of today's fastest modems.

And the range of access choices has become enormous. Full-service providers like NETCOM, Performance Systems International, and UUnet have moved into the direct connection business, having previously marketed exclusively to business. AT&T, MCI, and Sprint also offer individual Net access, with the regional Bell companies moving to unveil their own services at a rapid pace. The commercial on-line services—CompuServe, America Online, Prodigy—have expanded their connectivity to the Net, even as regional providers like Atlanta's Mindspring continue to grow into nationwide suppliers. And as we'll see, local providers remain an option, with compelling advantages for several categories of user. Making sense out of it all can be daunting, but information is available to help you find providers in all categories no matter where you live. You can see one useful Web page specializing in ISPs in Figure 3.1. The List arranges information about more than 3,000 ISPs worldwide in a hypertext format. You can examine this source at http://thelist.iworld.com/. Another good ISP list is The Directory (http://www.vni.net/thedirectory).

Tip: The entrance of the telephone companies, both long-distance and regional Bells, into the Internet service provider business will have profound consequences. With their economies of scale and regional to nationwide networks already in place, the telcos operate according to models that local Internet providers cannot match. Standard pricing models have unlimited Internet access in the range of $20 per month, but price isn't the only attractive feature. The telcos can also offer support packages that combine Internet access charges with your regular telephone bills, and they benefit from their high visibility. They can aggressively target large customers and can afford to go after content providers that would be out of reach to the smaller operators. Expect the number of independent ISPs to drop dramatically over the next few years; unable to compete on price, they will increasingly turn to local service options, including Web page hosting and highly specialized content, to try to stay alive. The survivors will learn the value of market niches.

Figure 3.1   The List tracks Internet providers globally.

The Modem Connection

A modem is the computer component that lets you connect your machine to the telephone system. Modems can be either external, in the form of a flat box with lights on the front that connects to the back of the computer, or internal, in the form of a card that fits into a slot inside the machine. The modem takes the information inside the computer, which is digital in nature, and turns that information into analog format. Put more simply, a modem turns data into music.

Music? If you were to listen to what was happening as your modem sent and received information, you would hear a series of tones that were being sent through the telephone system. The modem takes the data, which is stored on your computer in binary form, and translates it into the analog form—sound—the telephone system can handle. Let's assume you want to download a file to your computer. When you call the remote computer with your modem, the modem dials the number and makes the connection to a modem connected to the other computer. The two modems send signals back and forth to ensure that the connection is viable and then, when you have given the appropriate command, the remote modem begins to send you the data you need. It does so by converting the bits of binary information into sound that it pumps through the telephone connection to your modem. At your end, the modem converts the sound back into digital data. The sequence, then, is digital to analog to digital.

A number of things are involved in handling this transaction, which explains in capsule form why so many industries are now converging to explore the possibilities of the technology. Your computer has to work properly with your modem; to do so, it uses software that manages the dataflow back and forth between computer and modem. The telephone line, built as part of a system that was designed to handle voice traffic, must now accept the data and deliver it with as few errors as possible. The computer and modem at the other end of the connection must be running and able to receive the incoming call and act upon it. And throughout the process, the modems are checking for errors, which invariably creep into telephone line communications.

As the telephone system moves away from twisted-pair copper wire to the home and gradually supplants it with fiber-optics, we will see the nature of modems change. The word modem is short for modulator-demodulator, a description of what the device does. And in a fiber-optic world, as mediated by telephone companies or cable television firms or, indeed, new forms of wireless communication, the connection will already be digital. Your computer will be connecting directly to the kind of network that can understand digital data without translation. In the interim, as we'll see, hybrid technologies are springing up to provide broad bandwidth over today's copper wiring. They too establish a digital connection between computer and telephone line that feeds into the now all-digital long-distance network to provide Internet access.

Making the Call

Let's walk through what happens when you use your provider to get onto the Internet. In most cases, the number you call will be a local one. The huge growth in Internet connections means that companies are trying their best to expand the number of local numbers they make available. We call these numbers *points of presence*, or POPs. A provider who puts a POP in your town saves you the expense of making a long-distance call to get access. This model may be familiar if you've used CompuServe or America Online, both of which offer local telephone numbers that get you into their network and let you use their services. The method has become well nigh universal as Internet providers, including the commercial information services like CompuServe and America Online, compete for market share.

When you install your service provider's software, you'll be putting onto your computer the necessary TCP/IP tools to make a full-fledged Internet connection. The bulk of your provider's software packet is made up of these TCP/IP protocols in a form designed for your computer, whether it be a Macintosh or an Intel-based PC running Microsoft Windows. Installing the software is relatively simple, as you'll see in a moment. The catch is entering all the right parameters, which means telling the software the specifics of your network address. One wrong entry there and the connection will refuse to initiate. A good provider will offer you documentation that tells you precisely what to put where, and will back up these directions with a 24-hours-a-day help staff. One cheerful note: Once your connection is working, you shouldn't need to tweak its parameters again unless you change providers.

Routing Computer Data

But let's back up a moment. The first thing to understand is how your telephone call routes your data onto the Internet. During its normal life, your computer is not on the network at all. When you call the telephone number your service provider has given you, you're dialing into a computer at your provider's site. The modem at the provider's end accepts your data and establishes the connection. At this point, with the TCP/IP software kicking in, your computer becomes a functioning Internet machine. It uses your provider's computer as its way into the Net.

Protocols are just rules for computers to use as they communicate. Think of TCP/IP as a set of procedures that make it possible for all the different kinds of computers on the Internet to work together. This independence is what has made TCP/IP the worldwide standard it has become. It's immaterial to the protocols what kind of network they flow over, and they're immune to changes in transmission systems, which means your data can move along telephone lines or through satellite dishes with equal dexterity. TCP/IP can work with any computer operating system on any kind of computer. And because it was developed by the federal government, it's in the public domain. Numerous vendors have incorporated it into their own software because it's not vendor-specific.

Tip: Windows 95 comes with TCP/IP built in (we call this software a TCP/IP *stack*), while earlier versions of Windows, like Windows 3.1 and Windows for Workgroups 3.11, do not include the software. Most service providers will offer you software that can be installed on any of the versions of Windows, but if you want to use the Windows 95 integrated TCP/IP, you should tell your provider, who should be able to provide specific instructions for using the built-in tools of the operating system. I find working with the Windows 95 stack to be advisable, as it seems more stable than any other TCP/IP stack I've used on a PC. But Microsoft's instructions for enabling TCP/IP within Windows 95 are inadequate, which is why help from your provider is essential. If you're still having trouble, the appendix provides a checklist for installing the Windows 95 stack.

From Computer to Telephone: SLIP and PPP

With TCP/IP now workable on your machine, you still need a way to handle the transactions between your computer and the telephone system. On this score, two acronyms will become familiar. SLIP stands for Serial Line Internet Protocol; it's a way to set up the basic Internet protocols on a computer using a telephone line and modem. PPP, or Point-to-Point Protocol, does the same thing, only in a different and much improved way. As a modem user, you'll need either SLIP or PPP software to get you onto the Internet. These days, PPP is considered preferable because it is an actively supported standard; that means new options for fine-tuning it are constantly being investigated and improvements are being made, whereas SLIP is static, and does not support advanced telephony features like ISDN, a digital way of connecting over a telephone line. SLIP will eventually die, which is why most service providers have now embraced PPP (this is what Microsoft builds into Windows 95). The necessary software will be delivered to you as part of your sign-up package; if you are offered the choice between SLIP and PPP, don't hesitate to choose PPP.

The Winsock Link

You will doubtless run across the term Winsock in your network travels. The word stands for Windows Sockets, and it is the interface that allows a particular program to work with the TCP/IP protocols. Think of Winsock as existing between the program itself and TCP/IP; this means that TCP/IP software from any developer can work with any client program written to conform with the Winsock standard. Winsock compliance means that it is possible to run any standard client software in this environment.

One of the most popular versions of Winsock is Trumpet Winsock, which is often provided as part of a service provider's start-up package. But beware: a critical file called winsock.dll is created when you install many Internet programs. If you attempt to install more than one version of TCP/IP, you may set up a conflict. When an application tries to load its winsock.dll file and can't find it in its own directory, it will next look in the Windows system directory and will load the winsock.dll file it finds there. Windows 95's own Winsock won't work with an external winsock.dll file, but if you overwrite it with a different winsock.dll, the operating system will overwrite it again with its own version of the file.

The solution: If you need to use two winsock.dll files because you're using multiple communications programs, keep any versions of Winsock that didn't come with Windows itself out of the c:\windows and the c:\windows\system\ directories. Check to see that you have saved their winsock.dll files in the same directory in which the programs themselves are located. Trumpet Winsock users, for example, should make sure that winsock.dll is placed in the working directory for each application containing its tcpman.exe program. And if you use Windows 3.1, be sure to keep that directory out of your PATH statement to avoid further conflicts. In general, one stack at a time is good advice.

Tip: Finding background information about Winsock software and how it operates is easy. Martin Hall, now at Stardust Technologies, performed early development work on the standard. You can check out the Stardust Web site at:

http://www.stardust.com/

for background Winsock information. Or you can go to a site maintained by the developer of Trumpet Winsock, Peter Tattam, at the following site in Australia:

ftp://ftp.utas.edu.au/PC/trumpet/

Here you will find the Trumpet Winsock software.

Types of Internet Access

SLIP and PPP have become so standardized (PPP in particular) that we almost don't see them anymore—they're built into our set-up software and operate behind the scenes to manage our dial-up call to our service provider's computers. But they perform a service that was uncommon just a few years ago. Using either, our computer becomes a functioning part of the Internet while it is connected. When we download a file, it comes directly to our machine. When we receive electronic mail, it appears on our own hard disk. The modem connection may be a temporary one, activated only when needed, but it operates while we're on-line in the same way that a full-time connection does.

The older model of dial-up access was called a *shell account*. Using it, you dialed into your service provider's computer, but once connected, your machine could only operate like a terminal, which is another way of saying that the remote computer treated your machine as if it had no processing power of its own. This had important ramifications, for it meant that you were dependent on your service provider's computer to run all your client software. If you wanted to read electronic mail, you had to run a mail program on the remote computer and read the results; to actually get your mail onto your hard disk, you had to download it a message at a time. Transferring a file was similarly complicated; you first downloaded it from an Internet site onto your provider's computer, and only then would be able to download it onto your own.

In that text-based world, your range of movement on the Internet was limited; you depended upon your service provider to supply any client software you wanted to run. Today, using Point-to-Point Protocol to connect directly to another network computer, your own machine becomes as much a part of the Internet as any other. That means that if you see a new network tool you'd like to try, you can simply download it and go. You'll be seeing an explosion of network software as more and more individual users create a market for it. Each new browser version is downloaded directly to your computer and run there, while clients to handle specialized tasks like newsgroup reading or electronic mail can also be test-driven. The Web makes the old shell account method seem too limited for serious use; when viewed as pure text, the Web loses its graphical punch.

Tip: If you scout the local software stores, you'll doubtless run across products designed to help you access the Net. These "suites" of Internet tools generally include the basic TCP/IP software plus assorted client programs, from Web browsers to newsgroup readers and e-mail programs. Examples include Quarterdeck's Internet-Suite, NetManage's Internet Chameleon, The Wollongong Group's Emissary for Windows 95, and FTP Software's Explore. Products like these vary in quality and ease of installation, but any can be used to connect you to the Internet.

That said, I recommend that new users avoid Internet suites. The reason: Your first step in dealing with the Web is to get connected, and your service provider, whoever that may be, will provide you with the necessary software to make the connection, as well as enough client programs to at least get you started. Your first navigation on the Web should be within the context of your browser, so you don't need to worry at this point about additional client software. In short, the Internet suites may prove their worth by offering features you'll one day want to explore, but at the beginner level, they're an unnecessary purchase.

New Technologies for Dial-up Users

The technology driving Internet access continues to change. For dial-up users, the biggest roadblock is the wiring that feeds the home telephone system. Most homes are connected with twisted-pair copper wiring, a less than ideal medium for moving data at high speeds. Fortunately, a variety of methods are available to extract unexpected bandwidth from balky copper lines. And not a moment too soon, for today's Web is a place enlivened with audio and video links, enhancing straight text with graphics, animation, and sound. But these features are demanding; a slow connection will leave you staring at the monitor while you wait for the data to download. And the situation will only be exacerbated as we move to teleconferencing, interactive virtual reality, and real-time videos and music.

No wonder communications companies, from Northern Telecom to Ericsson to Lucent Technologies, are working so hard on upgrading transmission methods. If the Internet is to grow into a true consumer-oriented communications tool, capable of carrying live telephony and switched broadband video on a massive scale, then pumping up the dataflow emerges as priority number one. The telephone companies have a huge stake in this, if they can be persuaded to follow through on the technology they themselves have implemented. So do the cable television companies, although technical issues have them, at least for now, at a disadvantage.

ISDN: The Switch to Digital Telephony

ISDN—Integrated Services Digital Network—offers simultaneous transmission of data, voice, and video over the same telephone line, and at peak speeds roughly four times as fast as a 28.8Kbps modem (although data rates vary depending on a host of factors). You'll pay more for ISDN than a standard telephone line, and the service requires a pricy terminal adapter (a so-called digital modem) to manage the connection. Installation fees can also be high. But ISDN offers one key ingredient that competing technologies find hard to equal: it not only upgrades the speed of your connection, but it's also available today.

Standard modems are analog devices—they translate digital data into the kind of analog "music" the telephone system can ship across copper wire. ISDN is digital, which is why it requires a different kind of modem. Its speed can go as high as 128Kbps; it can be used for voice or data or, indeed, simultaneous transmission of both. Bringing digital connectivity to the home is a significant last step in modernizing the telecommunications process, for once a call leaves the local switch, it moves primarily through a digital network. It is the last stretch of connection between the central office and the home that makes the difference; it is here that the roadblocks are worst.

Tip: When is faster not really fast? When a fast modem runs into a slow network connection. It's important to realize that the speed of your download, whether it be a file transfer or a Web page displaying itself on your screen, depends as much on the network connections between you and the desired data as it does on the speed of your modem. Run into a balky link and you will wait, no matter whether you're using a 14.4Kbps analog modem or the latest generation of digital equipment. Suffice it to say that over a good connection, an ISDN line can make your Web experience snappy and enjoyable, but there will be times when you find yourself drumming your fingers while a remote server gets around to handling your request. If the information you need is on a popular server that operates at the end of a narrow-bandwidth connection, you won't see a noticeable difference in speed even with a T-1 connection.

All of which should remind us that the Internet's bandwidth problems continue, despite massive injections to the infrastructure like MCI's 155Mbps backbone network. We're still years away from the kind of reliable, fast connectivity in the megabits-per-second range that will make Web audio and video genuinely ubiquitous. Until then, practiced users will master the various tricks of the trade, such as turning off the graphics option in their browser when they need to move quickly between sites, or clicking on the Stop button to halt the download of cumbersome images when what they really want on a particular page is the text.

ISDN has been slow to be implemented, but today, a variety of manufacturers offer digital modems in the $500 range, while telephone companies have begun to provide it throughout their service areas. Although many have yet to fully come to terms with ISDN installation and customer support issues, the chances of setting up an account are improving. The process involves requesting the service from your telephone company, which will configure your line to handle two 64Kbps channels; these can act together as a single 128Kbps connection. No special line is required, for ISDN works over the same copper wires that exist in the home today. With the line properly configured, the next step is to connect and configure the digital modem, after which perhaps the greatest challenge is to get your software to recognize it. Expect to ask questions of technical support people as you tweak these parameters.

Pricing remains problematic. The basic service can cost anywhere from $20 to close to $100 per month, depending on local tariff structures. You should investigate monthly fees as well as installation charges carefully before making the ISDN leap; installations can vary from $50 to $500. The service is spreading rapidly despite such variations; almost all metropolitan areas in the United States are now serviceable, as are a majority of suburban areas, although connectivity in rural regions remains spotty at best.

But an ISDN connection does you little good if it's not recognized by your Internet provider. Fortunately, more of them, and many commercial on-line services as well, have made a move toward ISDN (both CompuServe and The Microsoft Network support it). Always compare charges between ISDN and analog connections; ISDN normally costs more, and this can become a factor in your choice of service provider. And be aware that numerous on-line services have yet to upgrade to ISDN, which means that analog modems still have their place on the desktop, at least as a backup system when all else fails.

Tip: The ISDN world is as encumbered by acronyms as any other part of the computer scene, but one you will run into early is BRI, for Basic Rate Interface. This is the standard ISDN service for the home user, and it comprises two 64Kbps channels for voice and data, as well as a 16Kbps channel for signaling purposes. The division of channels makes BRI a good choice for home business, since you can set up one channel for voice calls and the other for data.

ADSL: Adding Muscle to the Infrastructure

The idea behind ADSL—Asymmetric Digital Subscriber Line—technology is to split a standard telephone line into three separate channels, one of which is used for voice traffic, another for data transmission upstream from your home to the Internet, and a third for a high-speed downstream hookup. ADSL surmounts the problems of noisy copper wiring by using digital signal processor chips to send data only over clear frequencies, increasing capacity by hundreds of times. A variant of ADSL called VDSL (the V stands for very high bit rate) can up even that rate by a factor of six. A video clip that took 45 minutes to download over a 28.8Kbps modem and 10 minutes with ISDN would take just 30 seconds with ADSL.

Standard ADSL technology (insofar as there is a pure standard for a technology so new) uses bandwidth asymmetrically. In other words, data flows into your computer at speeds as high as 9Mbps, while the command you type goes back out onto the Net at 640Kbps. While it sounds lopsided, the asymmetry makes profound sense. Most of what we do on the Net is wait for pages to load; the actual data request is a matter of a few keystrokes, or a mouse click. ADSL allows us to submit that request at one speed and receive the inflow of data at rates that dwarf those we use on our desktops today.

The ADSL technology requires a modem at each end of the connection, and is effective only at ranges of about two miles, which means connecting to an ADSL modem at your phone company's local central office, from which point your data can be routed to its destination. The future of the access provider business may be bound up far more tightly with the local telcos than we imagine. With data speeds running as high as four times a conventional T-1 line over copper wire, ADSL could allow the telcos to attract a huge audience if the price is right. As you'll see shortly, telco involvement with the Internet is increasing and will become a major factor in Net access.

But there are many imponderables. Like so many technologies, ADSL's promise is belied by a scarcity of real-world applications. In Virginia, Bell Atlantic has launched a 1,000-home test. In Dallas, GTE is linking 30 sites using ADSL products developed by Aware and Westell Technologies. Speeds vary depending on the manufacturer: Swedish telecommunications company Ericsson's new system works at 512Kbps, Westell modems can receive data at 1.5Mbps, while Aware technology can receive at speeds of 4Mbps. With a variety of competing systems, few products in the pipeline, and field trials in their early stages, it's too early to declare ADSL the next breakthrough in home-based Internet access. But it seems safe to say that ADSL's potential is great, and that if it succeeds, it could relegate ISDN to the status of useful but interim step.

Tip: One of ADSL's bright attractions for the telephone companies is that it points to a future for copper wiring, allowing the telcos to offer high-speed access without huge upgrades throughout their infrastructure, and keeping them competitive with the emerging competition from cable companies. Another is the fact that ADSL connections are permanent. An analog modem connection ties up a telephone switch, while ADSL bypasses the switch with its direct connection, lowering the cost of service for the telcos. This is why the cost may not be out of line. US West, for example, estimates that ADSL prices will soon establish themselves in the $35–$40 per month range.

Cable Modems

Cable television companies are holding out bandwidth prospects of their own, touting access speeds as high as 10Mbps with next-generation technology. The move makes sense; after all, cable companies possess advantages even the telcos can only envy. Two-thirds of American homes are already wired for cable, and the connection they receive arrives not over twisted-pair copper wiring but coaxial cable, a high-bandwidth medium that can be adapted for data.

In California, the @Home service, owned jointly by several cable companies, offers Internet access and intranetworking features through cable to a test audience; the launch of its full consumer service will be watched with great anticipation by Internet users, even as the first cable modems are deployed. Among cable's problems: Most cable networks are analog, requiring a new kind of modem that can convert their signal to digital data for passage across the pipe. So-called cable modems are now being bought up by the big cable television suppliers, but they face the additional challenge that the networks they service were never designed as two-way information carriers. Putting them to this use will require upgrading the infrastructure with fiber-optic cable, a movement already underway as the cable firms seek to expand their offerings, both in the number of television stations they provide as well as possible Internet connectivity. New routing and switching equipment will likewise be a necessity, as will filters to eliminate noise. And the service component is another factor. The telephone companies are used to managing a communications system that can be repaired quickly; is cable television as an industry really ready to support a two-way communications infrastructure?

As for cable modems, speed projections for them may have to be proven in the field. A figure widely touted in the media, 10Mbps, may be a pipe dream. The problem is that, at least in their earlier iterations, cable modems will be dependent upon the user base being fed by the company. A 10Mbps connection will degrade quickly if it's being divided up among several hundred neighbors. Add to this the cable companies' lack of expertise with Internet connections and their lack of customer support personnel. Clearly, the cable companies have their work cut out for them if they are to emerge as reliable network carriers. But given their presence in the home, you should watch them carefully to see whether competitive service offerings emerge.

The Net by Satellite

With all the question marks about rival technologies, what should the Internet user with a yen to be on the cutting edge do? One possibility is to look at satellite-based network delivery. DirecPC is an Internet access service that receives data via satellite dish at an average of 200 to 300Kbps, while routing user commands back through the telephone system at conventional speeds. As with ADSL, this asymmetrical access doesn't appear to be a problem, since download time is what counts. But DirecPC, an offshoot of fast-growing DirecTV (the satellite television people), still charges a healthy tariff for the receiver, PC adapter card, and necessary software, not to mention a per-month user fee, which must be factored in on top of the charges you pay your Internet access provider. Being on the cutting edge may be fun, but it's also expensive.

Another take on satellite technology comes from the estimable Bill Gates and McCaw Cellular founder Craig McCaw. Their plan is to envelop the Earth with a cloud of 840 satellites, providing direct links to computers on the planet below. The project, named Teledesic, plans to orbit its satellites far lower than the geostationary orbit used by the average communication satellite (22,500 miles above the surface). The result is that satellites will be able to deal with smaller numbers of users, offering higher bandwidth levels, and avoiding delay times caused by the higher orbits of their competitor's satellites. Perhaps the most intriguing part of this project is that it seems to open up the possibility of extending Internet access to areas that will not be immediately served by wired options, especially in rural areas and the developing world. The plan—improbably optimistic—is to have Teledesic operational by 2002.

The Wireless Option

Today it's possible to link a laptop computer through a cellular modem into the Internet, though for reasons of price and speed, the option is seldom exercised by individual users. Another possibility is packet radio, long the domain of ham radio operators, and now available from various companies for local access through specialized modems. A third offering is so-called wireless cable, the broadcasting of Internet data from local transmitters, just as some companies now offer television access without wires.

The advantages of wireless access should be obvious. Without the need to plug into a wall socket, your computer goes with you and takes the Internet along for the ride. Imagine taking a laptop to the library and connecting from the reading room to supplement your book and magazine research, or popping into the Web site at your employer's office to double-check on project status while you're on the road. Ultimately, wireless will prove hard to resist if the price of access can be brought in line with other service options. We're years away from that outcome, but it's not beyond possibility that wireless will emerge as the method of choice in the first part of the next century.

Tip: Should you take the digital route to high-speed connectivity? One of these technologies—or something very similar—will eventually make its way into your home as the need for bandwidth expands. But my view is that the Internet is complex and rich enough to keep you occupied using a now conventional 28.8Kbps modem (or its slightly faster 33.6Kbps successor). The advantage of sticking with analog modems in a time of transition is that, after all the teething pains of the last decade, we know now how to configure modems and make their installation relatively simple for the first-time user. It is ease of use that has expanded the Internet's base, and a mass move to ISDN or, in a few years, ADSL, would probably slow that advance until these technologies became equally transparent.

Of all the new technologies, ISDN is the one most available today. Had it been widely used five years ago, I would recommend it unhesitatingly, for the difference between a slow modem and ISDN is huge. But today, ISDN can offer you, at best, an advantage of roughly four times that of a 28.8Kbps modem, not enough, in my opinion, to justify the additional expense, particularly since so many of the Net's delays are now attributable to problems upstream. Both ADSL and cable modems will provide huge speed increases, with the likely winner being ADSL. Unless you have a need for squeezing the last data bit out of your connection, I recommend holding off on ISDN.

But monitor ADSL, cable modems, and wireless; they will shape the way we log on to the Internet in the next century. For your own use, unless you're a determined pusher of boundaries, stick with a fast analog modem as the new technologies define themselves. You will have several years to evaluate the successors to the analog modem; by then, you'll be able to make a choice based not only on what looks attractive on paper, but on reports from those users who went ahead and worked out the worst of the bugs.

Major Internet Providers

Let's take a look at the companies that have brought Internet access to a national level. They break into three distinct categories, each with a claim to your business, and each with key advantages and, in some cases, disadvantages. These are: the telephone companies like AT&T and MCI; the national Internet providers like Performance Systems International and UUnet; and the commercial service providers, like CompuServe, Prodigy, and America Online. While price structures have undergone, and will continue to undergo, dramatic change, quality of service remains the biggest variable, with factors we will consider next.

AT&T WorldNet

Telephone companies possess key advantages in entering the Internet market, not the least of which is their familiarity. Internet users often speak of "Internet dial tone," meaning access to the network; it's often said, for example, that an Internet jack will be standard equipment in any new home or office built in the twenty-first century. That being the case, the convergence between telephones and the Internet in the public imagination seems to be growing. A company that can offer a one-stop solution for voice telephony as well as Internet access is bound to be attractive, as is the notion of unified billing for both services, particularly in the realm of on-line transactions. Telephone companies possess obvious expertise at dealing with directory information, one of the Internet's weak points. How this will continue to play out as the telephone companies begin to experiment with delivery of content like movies and interactive games to the home remains to be seen.

Nationwide providers of all stripes likewise offer something local and regional providers cannot—a wealth of access numbers. Obviously, making a local call to gain Internet access is far preferable to having to pay toll charges while on-line. But a network with numerous POPs (points of presence) in other areas gives you great flexibility if you travel. Internet service providers charge higher rates for using their 800 service; if you can log on through a local number no matter where you are, your business trip or holiday will feature Internet connectivity at the same price as your on-line work at home. And you'll be able to use the same software and connectivity parameters that you've been using all along. A wealth of POPs also means that a busy number can be bypassed in favor of an alternate. These used to be key advantages of commercial on-line services like CompuServe or America Online; today, they have been preempted by the nationwide ISPs, who will market them aggressively.

AT&T has been a major player in the Internet market since the announcement of its WorldNet service on February 27, 1996. With 80 million long-distance customers, the telecommunications giant dwarfs almost all other access providers save the other long-distance carriers, and it remains the largest of these. In many ways, the AT&T announcement legitimized the Internet for a generation of computer users who remained skeptical or concerned about the network's complexity. By tying network use in the minds of these people with standardized telephone service, AT&T put other providers on notice that brand name has clout, and a secure user base is any company's greatest asset.

But smaller Internet providers haven't necessarily run for cover. Among the problems facing both AT&T and its brethren in the telephony business is the fact that their businesses come from a different environment than the one that spawned the Internet. And one of AT&T's first moves was to limit access to its Internet service to ensure that its network could handle the anticipated traffic, causing unexpected waiting periods for Internet accounts (the company activated 150,000 customers in its first nine weeks out of some 600,000 requests). Another issue: Can the telephone giants deliver high-quality technical support to Internet neophytes? Certainly the local providers will make the case that they remain closer to the individual customer and his or her problems. Another strategy for the smaller players will be to target business-to-business networking and Web hosting services, niches that may remain open as the telephone companies build a consumer-oriented user base.

Tip: Don't expect the RBOCs—the Regional Bell Operating Companies—to take the long-distance companies lightly as competitors. Due to the rules that govern their relationship with the long-distance carriers, they are forced to exempt AT&T, MCI, and Sprint from the local access charges that normally would apply to their calls. That makes attractive offers like AT&T WorldNet's five free hours a real problem, because it increases usage without accompanying benefits to the local companies. And the RBOCs, of course, plan to offer Internet access themselves.

BellSouth, for example, recently announced its BellSouth.net service, offering flat-rate prices of $19.95 for unlimited usage. With a customized version of Netscape Navigator, electronic mail, and a Web site devoted to local information, BellSouth.net provides the same benefits of unified billing offered by the long-distance companies. Local or regional content provided with high-quality technical support could make the difference for the Bell companies, but the transition between telephone company and Internet provider is a tricky one to navigate.

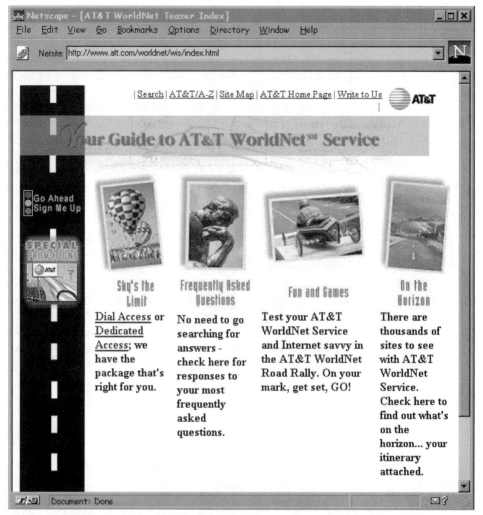

Figure 3.2   The home page for AT&T WorldNet services, which is rapidly becoming the most visible of the service providers.

In Figure 3.2, you can see AT&T WorldNet's Web site. By offering an initial price for unlimited dial-up access of $20 per month, AT&T forced the hand of other providers, who had to either match that price or make the case for enhanced services that would cost more. The company also offered an alternate plan of five free hours per month to residential AT&T customers, with a $2.50 per hour tariff after that. This pricing model is unlike that of voice telephony, which is both time- and distance-sensitive, and it remains to be seen whether burgeoning Net traffic will make the price sustainable.

AT&T WorldNet offers points of presence nationwide and an 800 access number. The service uses a customized version of the Netscape Navigator browser, although Microsoft's Internet Explorer is also compatible with the system. Launched as a U.S. service in early 1996, WorldNet has now moved into overseas markets with a variety of business-based offerings.

Minimum system requirements for Windows users: an IBM compatible PC 80386sx processor with Microsoft Windows 3.1 or higher, 8MB of RAM, and 11MB of free hard disk space; the service demands at least a 14.4Kbps modem. At present, only Microsoft Windows-based systems are supported, but the system is to become Macintosh-compatible in the near future. Minimum equipment requirements for Macintosh users: Macintosh or Power Macintosh running System 7.1 and above; Apple Open Transport 1.1+ (if machine uses Open Transport); 8 megabytes of RAM, and 8 megabytes of hard disk space; 14.4Kbps (or faster) modem.

Price: For AT&T residential customers: Five free hours per month for one year; $2.50 per hour for anything over five hours (minimum use of one hour per month); or unlimited access for $19.95 per month. For non-AT&T residential customers: Three hours for $4.95 per month; $2.50 for additional hours; or unlimited on-line time for $24.95 per month.

For more information or to sign up for AT&T WorldNet, take one of the following options:

- Access the AT&T WorldNet Service home page on the Internet at http://www.att.com/worldnet/wis/.
- Send e-mail to worldnet@attmail.com.
- Call 1-800-WORLDNET.

internetMCI

MCI has been an aggressive soldier in the Internet wars as well, and was the first of the long-distance carriers to set up an Internet access service for individual users, which it calls internetMCI. Long-time Net users were intrigued when Vinton Cerf, whose work in the development of the Internet was seminal, joined the company to implement its Internet strategy. But MCI's involvement with the Net has been long-standing. In 1987, it signed a cooperative agreement with the National Science Foundation that saw it join IBM and Merit, Inc. (a nonprofit consortium of Michigan schools) to provide high-speed fiber-optic lines to NSFNET, the network that served as the Internet's U.S.-based backbone until its decommissioning in 1995. The backbone connected the six supercomputer sites in the United States with seven regional networks. In a recent move, MCI has upgraded its backbone speeds from T-3 levels (45Mbps) to 155Mbps, and there are predictions of backbone speeds as high as 622Mbps within a year.

The MCI service includes a customized version of Netscape Navigator and access to the Internet via over 300 local points of presence. Its TCP/IP connections use Point-to-Point Protocol and offer speeds of up to 28.8Kbps for analog

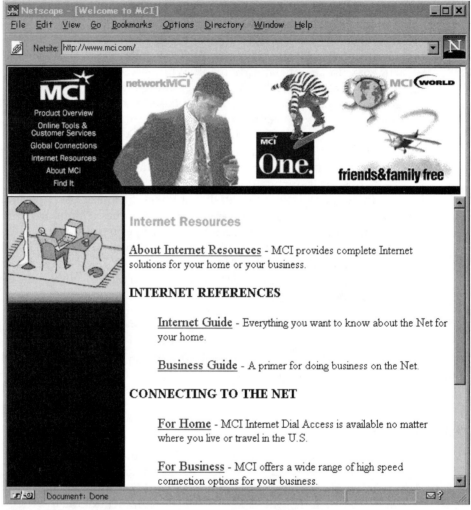

Figure 3.3 The home page for internetMCI provides links to a variety of Internet resources, including subscription information.

modems and ISDN connections up to 64Kbps. You can see the internetMCI Internet resources page in Figure 3.3.

Minimum System Requirements: Windows version 3.1 or 3.11; 386 PC or higher; 3.5″ disk drive, 4MB of RAM, 10MB of available hard disk space; 9600bps modem or greater modem (at least 14,400bps recommended). Price for MCI long-distance customers: five hours per month free for one year; $2.50 per hour for additional hours, and $5.95 per hour for 800-number access; or $19.95 per month for unlimited access; $5.95 per month for 800-number calls. For noncustomers: three hours for $5.95 each or $24.95 for 20 hours per month; extra hours at $2.50 each.

For more information or to sign up for internetMCI:

- Call 800-550-0927.
- Check the company's Web site at http://www.mci.com/, which provides links to its Internet services.

Sprint Internet Passport

Unknown to most Internet users, Sprint is now the largest carrier of Internet traffic in the United States, selling unused capacity on its network to Internet service providers. The Sprint Internet Passport service, debuting later than the offerings of both AT&T and MCI, competes directly on price, with the same $19.95 per month charges as its competitors. Sprint offers points of presence nationwide and uses the Netscape Navigator browser as its primary client program. You can see Sprint's Internet Passport home page in Figure 3.4.

The Internet Passport service provides PPP-based connectivity accessible by 14.4Kbps modems or higher. As of now, the service is available only to Sprint long-distance customers. Its software is limited to Windows 3.11 and Windows 95, although a Macintosh version is planned. Price: $1.50 per hour or $19.95 per month for unlimited use.

For more information or to sign up:

- Call 800-359-3900.
- Check the company's Web site at http://www.sprint.com/

Tip: All seven Regional Bell Operating Companies are planning Internet connectivity packages in the immediate future. The effect will be to continue the price war, with benefits for end users as the RBOCs jockey for position against both the long-distance carriers and the other national ISPs. The RBOCs can offer many of the same advantages found in using a long-distance carrier as your provider, including integration of billing with your standard telephone bill. You'll want to weigh their price and features, and in particular, their customer service, against that offered by their larger competitors.

UUnet AlterDial

When MFS Communications, an independent telephone company, acquired UUnet Technologies in 1996, the latter became the first of the national Internet providers to be taken over by a telecommunications company. The event was interesting on several levels, not the least of which was the point it made about the instability of the service provider market. For UUnet has been a major

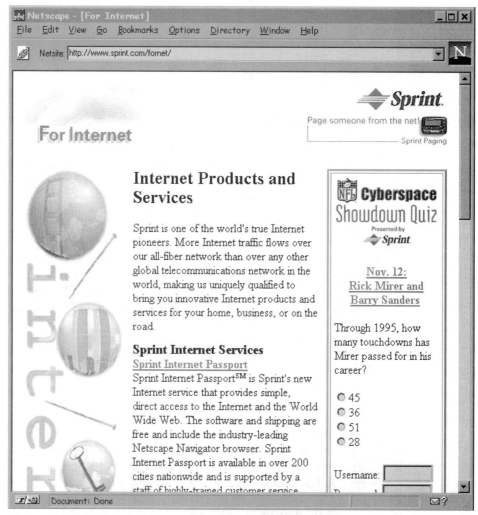

Figure 3.4 Sprint's late entry into the residential Internet market challenges the other long-distance carriers as well as the Regional Bell Operating Companies.

provider for some time now, joining NETCOM Online Communications Services and PSINet as nationwide ISPs. AT&T's aggressive pricing upon release of its WorldNet service clearly made waves; ever since, prices have fallen and mergers have become more likely as companies have looked over each others' shoulders. And mergers between telcos and ISPs make sense for the telcos; they provide needed expertise in an area where the focus of business is considerably different from voice telephony. With its purchase, MFS acquired an established Internet backbone with almost 300 points of presence. And some people saw the merger as the beginning of the end of the era of separate voice and data networks.

Nationwide Internet providers like UUnet, PSINet, and NETCOM represent a second type of Net access. Whereas the long-distance carriers own their own high-speed lines and equipment, these companies must lease their lines from the telephone companies and manage their own points of presence in local communities. Most offer high-speed connectivity for business, resell bandwidth to other Internet service providers, and make individual accounts available as well.

UUnet's AlterDial service is that part of the company's offerings designed for the individual user. Connections are available in standard analog form for modems up to 28.8Kbps in speed, as well as ISDN connections using a terminal adapter. PPP is the standard protocol. AlterDial supports both Windows-based PCs and Macintoshes. You can see the UUnet home page in Figure 3.5.

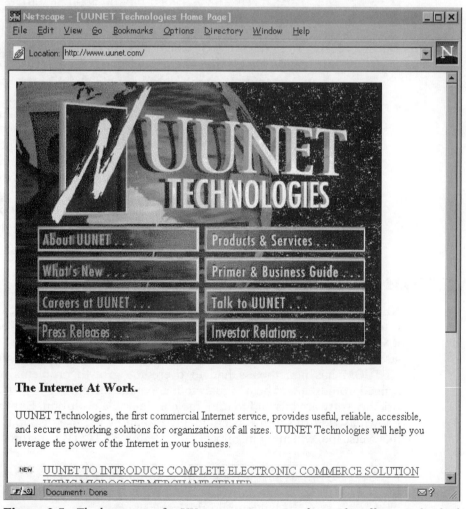

Figure 3.5   The home page for UUnet, a major national provider offering individual access through its AlterDial service.

Price: $30 per month, including 25 hours of local usage, Internet mail, and USENET news for one user; $2.00 per hour after first 25 hours; $6 an hour surcharge for 800-number calls; $10 per month optional charge for each additional POP e-mail account; $25 one-time start-up fee.

For further information or to sign up:

- Check the firm's Web site at http://www.uunet.com/.
- Call 800-488-6383.

 Tip: Is there any reason to consider setting up accounts with more than one Internet provider? Curiously, the answer may be yes, particularly if you work out of a home office. The large national companies offer many advantages, but they also leave you vulnerable to sudden outages, as users of America Online discovered to their dismay when the network went down for 19 hours in August 1996. Suddenly left without connectivity, users found themselves cut off from electronic mail and access to the Web. If you're using your Internet account in ways that make electronic mail or the Web crucial to your business, then a backup account with a different provider may make sense. It can keep you on-line when your primary network goes down for maintenance or unexpected repairs. And with capacity on the Internet already challenged by the influx of new users, we can expect more outages as the infrastructure is stressed. Ultimately, bandwidth upgrades will leave us with a far more reliable network than the one we have today, but that outcome is at least several years away, and it always pays to be prudent.

NETCOM

NETCOM is an example of what happens when a company switches to a flat-rate pricing model. The firm says its subscriber list grew some 300 percent after it switched to a $20 flat-rate fee, the price that is rapidly becoming an industry standard due to pressure from the long-distance companies. Consumer-driven, NETCOM has nonetheless had to overcome growth problems, which have ranged from frequent busy signals to inadequate technical support; and its proprietary software has had to undergo considerable evolution. But the software, known as NetCruiser, has been adapted to allow the use of popular browsers like Netscape, widening its appeal and firming NETCOM's customer base.

 Tip: What's wrong with a proprietary interface? Almost everything, if the software doesn't conform to the Winsock standard. From its beginnings, the Internet was never conceived as a proprietary place, where one vendor's standards would work in isolation from the rest. Indeed, the ability to interoperate, so that a program would function seamlessly over a TCP/IP connection no matter what kind of computer was in use, is at the heart of the Internet experience. Today's Internet clients are being developed, with certain significant exceptions that we'll examine later, with this premise in mind. That means that a user wants to be able to run and evaluate a Netscape, an Internet Explorer, a Eudora (an electronic mail program) or an Agent (a newsreader program). If a service provider's software limits the user to a single way of looking at the Net, it has removed one of the great attractions of cyberspace—the ongoing traffic in new and improved software. Like NETCOM, other providers with proprietary front-end software are being forced to reevaluate their policies, making it possible to run other programs using their systems.

NETCOM provides over 330 points of presence worldwide and offers a variety of additional features, including a personalized news page delivered daily to subscribers and personal Web page service. ISDN speeds up to 128Kbps are now becoming available in addition to standard SLIP connections. The NETCOM Web site is shown in Figure 3.6.

Price: $19.95 per month for unlimited use. New subscribers receive their first month of service for $5.00.

For more information or to sign up:

- Sign up on-line at http://www.netcom/com/.
- Call 1-800-638-2661.

Mindspring

In an intriguing move (given the ongoing reshuffling of the Internet service provider business), one of the oldest nationwide ISPs recently sold its base of individual customers to Atlanta-based Mindspring, Inc. The ISP, PSINet, had provided two access routes for individual users: Pipeline (for PC users) and InterRamp (for the Macintosh). Under its new arrangement, PSI acts as a wholesaler of bandwidth to Mindspring, which itself moves from a position as a fast-growing regional provider to a nationwide presence. The move triples Mindspring's customer base.

Minimum equipment requirements: For Microsoft Windows 3.1, 3.11, or Win95 users, a 486 processor or better and 8MB or more of RAM. Also needed: a serial port with a 16550 UART chip, and a 14.4Kbps modem or higher. For Macintosh users: System 7.0 or higher, and 8MB RAM, as well as a hardware handshaking cable for the modem.

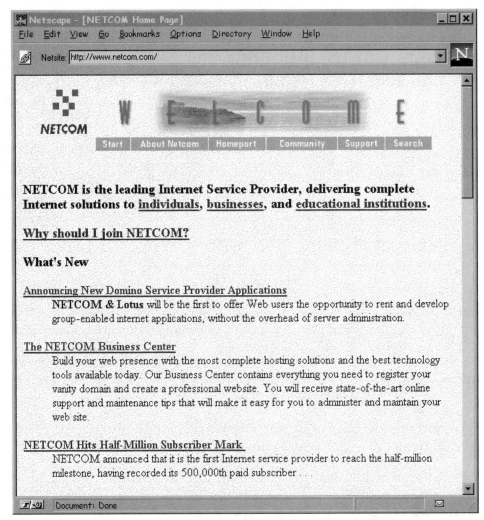

Figure 3.6 NETCOM has become the largest of the nationwide service providers other than America Online, with an estimated customer base of 500,000.

Price: Unlimited access for $19.95 per month, with a $35 start-up fee. Light access plan $6.95 per month for five hours of use; additional hours at $2 per hour. Standard plan $14.95 for 20 hours of use; additional hours at $1 per hour. Several other pricing options are available.

For information or to sign up:

- Check the company's Web site at http://www.mindspring.com/.
- Call 800-719-4664.

You can see the Mindspring home page in Figure 3.7.

Figure 3.7   Mindspring has moved from a regional to a national Internet provide with a rapidly expanding customer base.

Tip: Don't feel limited by the Internet software package offered by service providers. Your primary goal in setting up your account is to get your Web browser functioning. After that, two considerations come into play: First, most major Internet tasks, like electronic mail, file transfer, and newsgroup reading, can be handled through the browser itself, so putting it on-line creates a fully functioning Net presence for yourself. Second, most good Internet software for specialized tasks exists in shareware and often freeware form, meaning you can download the program to try it out before deciding to buy, or in the case of freeware, download it and use it without charge. Thus, if you don't care for the e-mail program supplied by your service provider, it's a simple matter to go out on the Web and download a different program. Far more important than what your provider offers by way of software options (other than the browser itself) is the stability of the connection supplied, and whether you can get on-line as necessary or will encounter frequent busy signals.

America Online

America Online is perhaps the best known of all Internet providers, but like CompuServe and Prodigy, it remains one of the most misunderstood. The reasons for this are found in its very visibility. For AOL first made a name for itself as a commercial information service, a proprietary network offering a wide range of databases, forums, and chat capabilities that worked under a pay-by-the-minute model. It was only later that AOL, and the other commercial service providers, began to connect to the Internet, first through electronic mail and, gradually, through other Internet options like Gopher, FTP and, finally, the World Wide Web. This method seems to have succeeded particularly well for America Online, which now connects more households to the Internet than all other Internet service providers combined, according to a 1996 report by market research firm Odyssey. Contrast this with NETCOM's 8 percent and you can see how large AOL has become in this market, towering over the other 3,000-plus ISPs.

The commercial services have thus begun to merge with the Internet model by reason of necessity, as it has become obvious even to the most devoted America Online or CompuServe user that the Internet is where the growth will be for the foreseeable future. This has meant a host of problems for the commercial services, not the least of which is how they model their connections. Both America Online and CompuServe have adopted a proprietary interface that makes using their services more graphical and user-friendly, but it has proven difficult to meld to the Winsock standard. It has only been in the last year that the commercial services have made the transition, allowing their users to work with Netscape or Microsoft's Internet Explorer as well as their own software, and many rough edges remain. In particular, the ability to set up a true Winsock connection to use standard Internet clients is still cumbersome.

Pricing issues likewise come to the fore when considering one of these services as a primary Internet provider. The by-the-minute model is fine if you are evaluating the Internet to see whether a full-service account makes sense for you. But once you have made that decision, using the Internet heavily while paying a by-the-minute charge can quickly result in astronomical bills, and the comparison between this method and the flat-rate billing of the full-time ISPs obviously favors the latter. For this reason, all the commercial information services have had to dramatically revise their price structures to compete; AOL, for example, has had no choice but to offer unlimited use for $19.95 per month. Whether it can build a successful bridge between itself and the Internet remains to be seen, for despite its large number of subscribers, its "churn" rates—the rate at which customers sign up and then leave—are high.

You can see the America Online take on the World Wide Web in Figure 3.8. Here, we are looking at AOL's proprietary browser. As you can see, one way in which the commercial information services have always distinguished themselves is by offering edited content. In this case, the AOL Web page offers a list

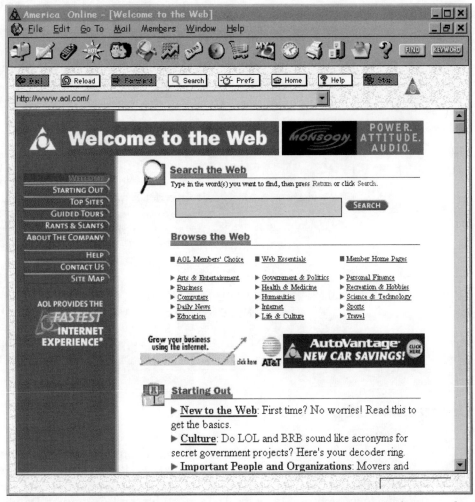

Figure 3.8 America Online offers a fast way to begin your Internet explorations, but its interface options quickly pale when compared to using third-party software.

of popular Web sites and provides links to the WebCrawler search service that America Online now owns. The Web page is full-featured, but interestingly enough, AOL insists that its proprietary front-end software remains viable for most Internet tasks, although it does make connection to popular browsers possible, enhancing that access with its new Windows 95 software. Its competition, CompuServe and Prodigy, have both announced that they will migrate their entire services into the Web format; The Microsoft Network has moved in the same direction. The magnitude of this transition is such that users will continue to see proprietary front ends, at least for CompuServe for the foreseeable future, as programmers work on the adaptation. Further complicating the picture is the fact that both CompuServe and America Online software will be offered as an integrated part of Microsoft's Windows 95 operating system.

Price: $9.95 per month for five hours; additional hours at $2.95 each; or unlimited use for $19.95 per month.

For more information or to sign up:

- Use one of the diskettes America Online distributes in computer magazines; these contain the complete start-up package.
- Visit the company's Web site at http://www.aol.com/.
- Call 800-827-6364.

Tip: Don't forget, your choice of browser is entirely up to you. Whether or not your service provider sets you up with Netscape Navigator or Microsoft Internet Explorer or possibly a third alternative from a smaller software house, you can always switch at a later date. The TCP/IP connection makes this possible; good Internet software must run over TCP/IP, not a proprietary system devised by your service provider. And because you can download Netscape for evaluation or Internet Explorer for continual use (it's free), you can easily move between different browsers as new versions come out, deciding for yourself what features you like and which you'd just as soon discard. The end user is the beneficiary as Microsoft and Netscape slug it out by offering frequent and powerful upgrades to their core browser products.

CompuServe/SpryNet

While the fortunes of the market tend to favor America Online, at least in terms of user numbers, CompuServe has continued to make a bid to reengineer its operation. The well-established service has made a name for itself through the quality of its on-line forums and databases, including full-text offerings such as Magazine Database Plus and Computer Database Plus. A major attraction has continued to be the service's wide range of businesses on-line, many offering technical support for their products in specialized forums. But access has continued to be provided through the CompuServe Information Service software (the Windows version used to be known as WinCIM; it's now called CompuServe 3.0), a proprietary front end inferior to America Online's, but like it in the sense that it offers a nonstandard route to the Internet. A deal cut with Microsoft, however, means that future users will receive the Internet Explorer browser as part of the package. You can see the CompuServe home page in Figure 3.9.

In addition to replacing its interface with a browser based on Microsoft's Internet Explorer, CompuServe will also offer support for Netscape Navigator;

Figure 3.9   CompuServe's home page as seen through Netscape.

both represent a significant upgrade from the Spry Mosaic browser that CompuServe had been providing. An interesting variant on using CompuServe as an on-line service is SpryNet, which allows you to use the CompuServe infrastructure to access the Web directly. SpryNet is accessible from any place that CompuServe has a POP, which covers most of the United States and almost 150 other countries. SpryNet, in sharp distinction to CompuServe itself, offers pricing competitive with other ISPs. SpryNet members can post up to 5MB worth of personal Web pages.

Minimum System Requirements for CompuServe 3.0: 486/33 Processor (or higher); 8MB RAM (16MB recommended); VGA monitor running 640 x 480; 15MB available on hard drive; 9600 baud modem (or higher); CD-ROM drive.

Price for CompuServe: $9.95 for five hours of use with additional fees based on the type of content accessed; some specialized databases can add significantly to your bill. Additional hours at $2.95 each.

Price for SpryNet: $19.95 per month for unlimited access, or $9.95 per month for seven hours with $1.95 for each additional hour, or $4.95 for three hours with $1.95 for each additional hour.

For more information or to sign up:

- For CompuServe, call 800-769-6747 or try the Web site at http://www.compuserve.com/.

- For SpryNet, call 800-777-9638 or send e-mail to info@sprynet.com. The Web site is http://spry.com/.

Tip: Two other commercial information services deserve mention here, although both are in such a state of transition that I cannot recommend them until it is clear where they will settle. The Microsoft Network, launched to great fanfare as Microsoft's answer to CompuServe and America Online, has moved from on-line service to Web-based content provider. Certainly, the money behind this project will make MSN a force to be reckoned with, and its user numbers put it in the same category, at least for the time being, as AT&T WorldNet. Time will tell how the difficult transition to the Web pans out. You can keep an eye on The Microsoft Network at http://www.msn.com/, or call 206-882-8080. Its premier pricing plan offers five hours of access to the Internet, e-mail, and all MSN services and original programming for $6.95 per month, with additional hours at $2.50 each. Its unlimited plan offers access at $19.95 per month. There are also several plans for customers who already have Internet access, including one with unlimited usage of all MSN content for $6.95 per month.

Much the same situation holds true at Prodigy, late of Sears and IBM joint ownership, and now in the hands of International Wireless Inc., a communications company with Internet as well as cellular telephone properties. A move to the Web would eliminate the Prodigy interface and pose the same questions for this struggling service that it does for any commercial information company—how do you adapt proprietary forums, download areas, and databases to the wide-open Internet format? The new Prodigy Web-based service, called Access Net Direct, will offer Internet access at $1 per hour. You can track Prodigy's fortunes at its Web site: http://www.prodigy.com/, or check out the Access Net Direct site at http://www.and.net/; or call 800-776-3449 for more information.

Using a Local or Regional ISP

Many factors come into play when choosing a service provider, and geography is certainly one of them. The national providers—telephone companies, ISPs like UUnet and NETCOM, and commercial service providers—offer a certain permanence due to their size. When you sign up for an account with them, you can be reasonably sure that your e-mail address will remain fixed (or at least as sure as you can be with any provider, given the flux in which the industry finds itself), whereas with a smaller regional or local provider, the possibility of a change of ownership always exists, as does the possibility that the business will fail, leaving you needing a new provider and, perhaps, stuck with a set of business cards with a now defunct address on them.

Yet it is difficult to rule out using local and regional providers. Some regional services have moved rapidly to the top, as witness the growth of Atlanta's Mindspring, once a regional serving only the southeast, now a nationwide provider through its agreement with PSINet. And local providers likewise have their place. I have been using a statewide provider here in North Carolina called Interpath since its inception, and have found the service stable and well managed. One benefit local services can offer is their access to the local community. Interpath, for example, maintains a Web site with tie-ins to community-based news and directories of events in my area. It is probably by fostering such content—aimed at a specific community in its user area—that a smaller provider can combat the industry consolidation that so threatens it.

Whether you opt for national, regional, or local, you will find the set-up procedure relatively fixed. Your provider will always offer you the necessary TCP/IP software and accompanying browser, probably with other Internet client programs as well. The actual installation should be handled by a set-up program that makes your biggest chore nothing more than pointing and clicking to launch the operation and filling in form-based information with the help of your provider. Having done this, calling the local telephone number provided in your documentation should get you on-line. These are minimum expectations for any service provider, and you should avoid any provider who cannot meet them. From that point on, you will need to evaluate whether there exists any compelling reason for using a provider in your immediate area, or whether the benefits of nationwide access, particularly in terms of widely available points of presence, make a national provider more attractive.

Points of presence, though, should be evaluated carefully. If you live outside a major metropolitan area, check to see just where the provider's POPs are located. It will do you little good to sign up to a nationwide provider if the nearest POP is a toll call away, leaving you with much higher bills than you had anticipated. In that case, a local provider may be your only choice. Several of my friends live in Henderson, a small town just north of Raleigh. The only provider available without a toll charge is Vance.Net, a local ISP that has become the only game in town. AT&T WorldNet, internetMCI, and even CompuServe and America Online have yet to make a POP available there.

But beware the small provider whose apparently unbeatable price conceals some very big catches. For one thing, many smaller providers are run on a shoestring, often by people whose technical expertise leads them to believe that details like configuring a TCP/IP connection are relatively simple. Pressed for time, they're unlikely to offer good technical support, which is just what you need when you realize that in place of a solid setup program, they're offering a demanding, bare-bones program with few pointers. TCP/IP isn't brain surgery, but it is difficult enough for the first-time user that you don't want to have to install it without explicit instructions and a helpful voice at the other end of the telephone if needed.

Another catch is access. Many smaller providers offer too few modems for the number of clients they have signed up. The result is that when you try to log on to your Internet account, you're likely to run into a busy signal. The best rate in the world won't make up for the aggravation of needing to get work done and not being able to get on-line. It is usually a good idea to check with other customers of any provider you are evaluating to see if they have any complaints. An ISP who is operating forthrightly should be willing to provide you with such contacts. You can then use the suggestions given in the next section to help you complete the ISP search.

Tip: If you already have some form of Internet access and are looking for another, one good way to check for customer reaction to a given ISP is to read the newsgroups. Both alt.internet.services and alt.internet.access.wanted include postings from users and potential customers of ISPs. You should be able to ask there about how good the service is and find out about any common complaints. And if it's a larger service you're looking at, check for specialized newsgroups devoted to it. America Online, for example, can be discussed in alt.online-service.america-online, while CompuServe can be checked out in alt.online-service.compuserve.

Choosing the Right Provider

As we've seen, price is only one of the considerations involved in choosing an ISP. If you're unsure whether a national provider is your best choice, you may want to extend your search by checking any local computer-related publications. Here in North Carolina, for example, we have a monthly newspaper called *Carolina Computer News* that contains ads from providers as well as articles about how to use computers and the Internet. If you're coming up short on the names of local ISPs, make your way to a nearby computer store and see if anyone there has any ideas.

Having found the names and numbers of any companies that provide Internet access in your area, make a call to each and ask for brochures or any other sales materials they may have available. Read these with care. Consider the following issues and be prepared to ask questions if you're not satisfied with what you see in the printed materials. These issues are equally applicable to nationwide providers, and you should weigh them with your particular needs in mind. Obviously, a traveling executive is going to have different provider preferences than a work-at-home writer.

Service

How easy will it be to get help when you need it? Does the provider offer a 24-hour help desk? And if so, does it connect you at all times to a person, or does it more often lead to an answering machine, with callback uncertain?

Access

Can you get a call through when you need to, or are you going to run into busy signals a good proportion of the time? The answer depends on the kind of modem-to-customer ratio your provider offers. A ratio of 1 modem to every 10 customers is excellent; it means you'll almost always get through. Any service provider should be willing to tell you what ratio he or she can provide.

Modems

Speed is essential for accessing the Web, and it only makes sense to ensure that your provider offers 28.8Kbps access at the various points of presence. If you are fortunate enough to be considering ISDN, check to see whether your provider can support that option. And be sure to check the fee structure for ISDN versus standard analog access.

Price

Although flat rate is getting to be the accepted model of Internet access, you should weigh commercial on-line services with their various pricing strategies against your own needs. If you truly believe you will be on-line rarely, perhaps only to send the occasional electronic mail, then an America Online or a CompuServe might make sense for you. But be aware that limited usage may come back to haunt you; as you explore the wealth of information on the World Wide Web, you'll find yourself increasingly drawn to it, with a corresponding increase in your on-line time. If your usage begins to run over five hours per month, it's time to switch to a full-service ISP and a standard flat rate.

Tip: Be very cautious when evaluating price! Flat rate should mean unlimited access day or night throughout the week and weekend. Beware providers whose flat rate extends only to particular hours, such as nighttime or weekends.

Documentation

In a computer world, some providers offer you nothing more than a disk, with any documentation available for you to print out. You should look for providers offering hard-copy documentation for their systems; this will especially be useful in the set-up process if you run into difficulty.

Web Page Hosting

If you're thinking about producing your own Web pages, you should look for a provider that offers Web page hosting options. Usually, you will be charged by the megabyte for storage space, and in general, local ISPs charge less than nationwide providers. Web services like this can be an inducement to stick with a local ISP.

References

Who else uses this provider's services? Asking for selected references can be helpful, although companies are usually careful to choose people they know are satisfied with their service. A better idea is to track down customers on the newsgroups; they may have a different tale to tell. Another option: Check your potential provider's Web site to look for customers with their own Web sites (you can do this through a friend's account or at one of the burgeoning number of Internet cafés now popping up). Having found the addresses for people who do business with this provider, you can send them e-mail to ask about their opinion of the service. If you're setting up a business account, a sales representative from the ISP should be willing to let you call customer names at random, and you should feel free to demand it.

Software

Does the potential provider offer all the software you need to get on-line? It has become standard practice to do so, and you should expect to receive as part of your account a packet of diskettes and a user manual. What you want to avoid is the company that tells you to go out and download what you need from the Internet itself. As a newcomer, you're in no position to do that; you want enough good software to get on-line quickly and efficiently.

The programs your provider offers should include a standard Web browser like Netscape Navigator or Internet Explorer, an FTP client for file transfers, a mail program like Eudora, and a newsgroup reader like Forte's Agent. Remember that you can always use the Net to download freeware and shareware versions of other programs, so the client programs you receive aren't crucial. But you'll doubtless want to use them to learn the ropes on the Net, so they should include all the functionality just itemized.

Another key issue: Is the provider's software proprietary? This is no time to be stuck inside a proprietary interface when the Internet is undergoing the most exciting period of software development in its history. You want to be sure you can run the new client software using your ISP's service, and that includes not just Netscape Navigator or Internet Explorer, but also all the sophisticated mail and newsreaders now entering the market. Bear in mind, too, that the Web is undergoing change as companies like Netscape push standards into new territory; you want to be able to view Web sites using these new technologies without difficulty. Be prepared to ask pointed questions about software compatibility to Net standards.

Related Services

As the provider wars intensify, ISPs in all sizes are looking for ways to catch your attention. Depending on your needs, you will want to evaluate additional services they may offer you or your business. These may include: consulting services; security arrangements; Web site development; network design and management services.

Domain Name Aliasing

A major advantage of an ISP over a commercial information service is that ISPs can offer *domain name aliasing*. This means that you can possess an on-line address based on your company name, such as the (fictional) gilster@ navigator.com. Choosing ISPs that offer such aliasing means you can, if needed, switch providers and maintain the same address. You also provide your company with an impressive-looking address. A one-person office suddenly looks like an office with its own server. The ISP can set up this "virtual domain" for you with the InterNIC, the body governing the use of domain names on the Internet. The application fee for a domain name is $100, and an annual maintenance fee of $50 is also due to the InterNIC.

Mail Forwarding Options

Does your provider guarantee your mail will be forwarded if you change addresses? This is an extremely useful service, as I found out when I moved from a previous account to my present address. After several months, my old provider stopped forwarding my mail, despite the fact that I was receiving numerous messages from readers. I determined at that time to work only with providers who would guarantee mail forwarding in the event of such changes.

Tip: A mail forwarding service can help you avoid address changing. One of the best of these is Pobox, which offers forwarding for a small yearly fee. With an address at Pobox, your underlying address is shielded from users; if you change providers, you simply notify Pobox while retaining your Pobox address. For more information, contact Pobox at new@pobox.com or http://www .pobox.com/.

Set-up Fees

Charging you for installation is an idea whose time has come and gone. In today's competitive market, there is no excuse for a set-up fee. The only reason to pay one is if the service you want to use offers such powerful incentives for your business that you find the fee acceptable. Also look for a free trial period, which most providers should be willing to offer. Such tactics will ensure that you can try different services at minimal charge to find the one you need.

Multiple Use

Families may want to investigate where a given ISP will allow several different e-mail addresses to be used through the same account. Many do provide this feature, usually for a small fee. In this way, you can get several people on-line without having to open separate accounts.

800 Access

Be careful about this one. A provider who promises 800-number access while you're on the road may have forgotten to mention that the access comes at a higher price. It's not unusual to pay from $5 to $10 per hour for 800 access on top of your normal account fees. In such cases, it makes more sense to look for a provider with a larger number of POPs in the areas you're likely to travel.

Internet users have never had such a wide choice in service providers, which means you can afford to shop around. The company you choose should be able to explain itself to network novices and should be able to provide all the tools you need to make your network connection. If you know any Internet users among your circle of friends and colleagues, be sure to solicit their opinion as well about which provider is best. The process is a lot like choosing a long-distance telephone company, but it's packed with more variables because the technology is so unfamiliar. Don't let anyone cow you with jargon you don't understand. You should expect a good provider to be able to deal with you in plain English and explain his or her services clearly.

And be willing to switch. If you have chosen carefully, you'll have found a provider who offers a free or low-priced introductory period and who demands no long-term commitment from you. If you find service to be questionable, you can always try a different provider until you've isolated the one you want. Tying yourself up with a long-term relationship to a provider you don't know is asking for trouble, and isn't necessary in today's market.

4

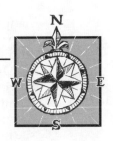

Inside the Browser

The browser you use, whether it be Netscape Navigator, Microsoft's Internet Explorer, or a third-party program, is the most critical tool you will bring to the Internet. The battle over browsers is now in full fury, as Microsoft seeks to cut into Netscape's enormous lead in marketshare, and both companies provide improvements and frequent upgrades to their products. Your job in all this is to ensure that the browser you use has the horsepower to do everything the Net offers, and that means customizing it for your own use.

An uncustomized browser is still a functional tool, but after you've used it to examine a variety of sites on the Internet, you'll discover that it can be made better. This chapter looks at how the browser can be tweaked internally to improve its performance or to accomplish particular tasks. Many of these changes are not difficult, but most people fail to take advantage of them because they're reluctant to meddle with a program that seems to work just fine as is. So we'll walk through the options and discuss how changing a few settings can simplify your Internet life. I will scatter tips on improving your browser use throughout these pages. The next chapter shows you how so-called plug-in and add-on programs can extend the power of the browser to handle a wider variety of data types. I'll be using Netscape Navigator to describe these issues, but the same principles are at play in Internet Explorer. They are the same because the job of any browser is to represent Web pages to maximum advantage using the same Net protocols.

I choose Netscape because I find it superior to the Microsoft product in terms of interface, elegance of design, and especially installation. Because it can be downloaded and tried out for free, I recommend that people who have used only Explorer download Netscape and make the comparison themselves. Both browsers enable you to do almost everything you need to do on the Internet, so the question isn't one of functionality as much as it is one of preference. Since Explorer is free, Internet users can keep up with both browser versions if they choose, benefiting from the intense pace of development as the two companies try to outdo each other. My view, though, is that mastering a single browser backward and forward is the best way to turn the Internet to your advantage, and the best browser for accomplishing that task is Netscape.

One thing this chapter assumes is that you already have a browser in place. Service providers, after all, routinely provide browsers to all new customers. But if you are using a different browser and want to evaluate or switch to Netscape Navigator, you can easily download the program from the Netscape site on the Web:

http://home.netscape.com/

or call 800-426-9400.

Browsers are getting to be like America Online software—you can find them almost anywhere. But whereas America Online has packaged its interface program on floppy disks and included them with magazines and postal mailings, both browser companies have made their products visible by striking deals. Microsoft has contracted with numerous providers to put Explorer in the hands of first-time users, while both Netscape and Explorer can be used with commercial on-line services, and hence are readily downloadable from them as well. Netscape is not free software, although you are able to download an evaluation copy from the site without charge; the product costs $49.

Tip: Hardcore Internet mavens will doubtless want to evaluate both Internet Explorer and Netscape Navigator, particularly since the browser wars promise fast technical innovation as one browser leapfrogs past another, only to be surpassed by the next iteration of the competition. But you'll probably want to maintain your favorite as the default browser. This is the browser that comes up when you click on an HTML file or an Internet Shortcut. The problem with this is that both Internet Explorer and Netscape install themselves as the default browser. If you're working with the wrong default, it may be necessary to reinstall the browser you want to see as the default; simply, whichever one has been installed last is it.

The Browser Interface

Because the World Wide Web was created to simplify communications, we should expect that it will be easy to use, and on many levels, it is. The browser interface is designed to place difficult to remember commands within a friendly graphical environment, one supported by pull-down menus, mouse-driven commands and hyperlinks. The latter are shown by underlining and color changes; click on a hyperlink and you're taken to the appropriate file or site. This flexibility and intuitive approach has been the key factor in expanding the Internet's population into the millions.

Let's walk through the basic browser operations by examining its screen. As with most windowed, graphical software, there are two levels of commands: The first are the most often used actions. These are shown by buttons and icons on the main screen. They are also found on the pull-down menus, but their presence as easily clickable buttons makes them more readily available. The second type of commands are those actions that are invoked less frequently; most of these are found on the menus themselves. We'll examine these as we look at customization options, for in many cases, changing the browser means exploring its menus.

Using Hyperlinks

The main screen of Netscape Navigator is shown in Figure 4.1, along with pointers to its relevant parts. You'll notice that this screen includes the toolbar along the top of the screen, with buttons for quick access to common commands. This is the default screen, which we'll change later in the chapter to maximize the display area.

The model for using browsers is simplicity itself. Clicking on an underlined hyperlink (the color of the text should be blue—but read the next paragraph for more on this) causes you to go to that page. Clicking on the Back button moves you to the previous page. Once you've clicked on several pages, you can move back and forth between them using the Back and Forward buttons. As you can see, having these functions available as buttons keeps you from having to pull down menus each time you want to move.

If you are using a black-and-white monitor, you'll see hyperlinks only as underlined words; on a color monitor, they are shown in blue, but this color can be modified according to your preference. When you click on a hyperlink and are taken to the linked material, the hyperlink will change color the next time you see it; from blue, it will turn purple. In other words, if you move back to the page from which you jumped to the linked material, you'll find that the hyperlink is now magenta (or purple, depending on your monitor and your eyesight). This tells you that you've already explored that hyperlink, a useful feature when you're moving quickly between large numbers of Web pages.

But other things happen as well when you click on a hyperlink:

The status indicator goes into motion. This indicator is the company logo found in the upper right portion of the screen. In keeping with a high-tech software tool, the indicator's motion will appear to be a field of meteors streaking across the blue field.

The progress bar at the bottom right of the screen will show the percentage of the page that has completed loading, in the form of a bar moving across the rectangular box.

When the page is being loaded, you will notice two things happening on-screen: The text is displayed first, which means that you can start using a given page almost immediately, without having to wait for possibly extensive graph-

Title bar

Location field

Menu bar

Tool bar

Link icon

Status indicator

Directory buttons

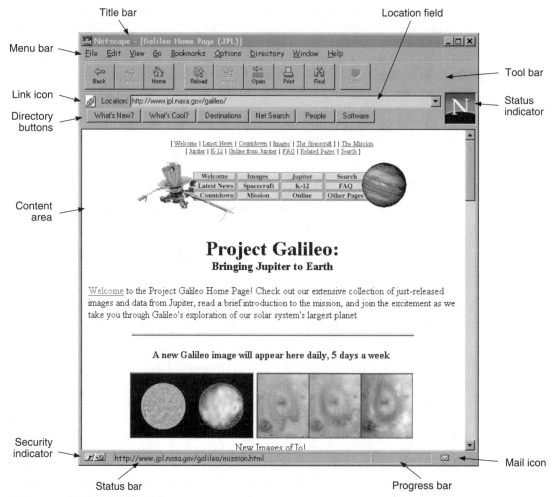

Content area

Security indicator

Mail icon

Status bar

Progress bar

Figure 4.1   The primary screen of Netscape Navigator. Note the buttons along the top.

ics to load. Second, the download of images seems to proceed in waves. This is called *progressive rendering;* it allows the browser to hasten the download by displaying the image in several passes, each with increased screen resolution. The image thus seems to fade in, gradually increasing in sharpness. If you decide it's not something you need to wait for, you can move to another site or simply halt the download using the Stop button on the toolbar.

Tip: Internet Shortcuts are a way to return quickly to the page of your choice, launching the browser as you do so. Available through Windows 95, they are created in several ways. You can drag the URL link icon to the desktop or click on the right mouse button and choose Internet Shortcut from the ensuing menu. Either will create the shortcut on your Windows 95 desktop. When you double-click on the shortcut, your default browser will be launched and the link specified by the URL will be displayed.

Exploring the Screen

The Netscape Navigator screen provides a great deal of useful information about your Internet activities.

Title Bar
: Located at the top of the screen, the title bar shows you the name of the page you are currently accessing. This title is established by the author of the HTML page.

Menu Bar
: Immediately below the title bar, this contains the names of the various menus, which can be activated by clicking on the text of each.

Toolbar
: Contains the large buttons that allow you to perform major Netscape tasks with a mouse click.

URL Link Icon
: Immediately to the left of the Netsite or Location field, this icon can be dragged to the Windows 95 desktop to establish an Internet shortcut there. It can also be dragged to the Book-marks window as one of several ways to create a bookmark that takes you quickly back to the site.

Netsite Field
: This is the location field. It gives you the URL of the page currently being displayed. It will be labeled Netsite when you're connected to a Netscape server; otherwise, it will appear as the Location field. You can enter a new URL here by highlighting the current one with a mouse click and typing over it. Notice, too, that you can pull down a menu of recently accessed URLs by clicking on the pull-down icon at the right of this field. A click on any of these items returns you to that page.

Tip: Netscape makes it easy to enter a new URL directly. If you are moving to a commercial site (one with a .com extension), all you need do is type the name of the company in the Netsite or Location field and press a Return. Going to the Netscape site, for example, I could simply type netscape in the Netsite or Location field and go; the browser supplies the necessary surrounding information. This means you can always leave out the http://www prefix and the .com suffix. Sites with other types of URL will not work this way, however; you'll have to type in the complete URL.

Directory Buttons
: These buttons take you to information available at the Netscape site that can help newcomers find their way around the Internet.

Status Indicator	This animated icon, a Netscape company logo, comes alive when you are loading a page.
Content Area	This is the largest part of the display. It is where the content of a particular page is shown. Text from the content area can be selected and copied.
Status Bar	Beneath the content area, the status bar provides information about the connection to a particular page. If you move the cursor over a hyperlink in the content area, the status message will become the URL of the hyperlink in question.
Progress Bar	To the right of the status bar, the progress bar tells you what portion of a download has been completed.
Security Indicator	At the bottom left of the screen (below the content area), the security indicator provides information about the security of a particular document (i.e., whether or not it is safe from prying eyes). If the document is secure, the icon appears as a door key on a blue field. If the document is insecure, the icon appears as a broken key on a gray field. The status of security is indicated by the number of teeth on the key—two teeth indicate high-grade encryption, while one tooth indicates medium-grade encryption. You can click on this icon to produce a screen of information about the document's security.
Mail Icon	Located directly opposite from the security indicator, the mail icon can be used to display the mail window. If a question mark appears next to the mail icon, this means that Netscape cannot check the server automatically for new messages. If an exclamation mark appears there, this means that new messages are available.

The Netscape Toolbar

Using just these basic actions, you can move around the Internet with ease. But understanding the other options available to you will give you much greater flexibility. Let's run through the available screen buttons and their uses. We begin with the large buttons shown on the toolbar.

Back	Moves to the previously viewed document.
Forward	Moves to the next document. This option will be grayed out until you have moved the Back button to return to a previously viewed page. At that point, using Forward will take you to the page you were viewing before activating the Back button.
Home	Takes you to your home page. By default, the home page in Netscape Navigator is the Netscape site (http://home.netscape.com/), but you will be able to choose any home page by adjusting the program's options.
Reload	Causes the currently displayed page to be reloaded. This can be useful if you are dealing with a page that is frequently changed; various news services, for example, update on a regular basis, and the Reload button will cause the software to check such pages for changes. If none are found, Netscape will

reload the page from your computer's cache; if changes are
found, it will download the revised page.

Tip: A *cache* is a place where information can be stored on your
computer. By storing various pages in the cache as you view them,
Netscape is able to keep them available. Returning to such a page
is therefore much quicker than retrieving the page from the network itself, because the page is now local. When you access a page
for the first time, the software must retrieve the page from the network. Using the Back button will take you to pages in the cache
from your current session. Using the Reload button will cause
Netscape to check the cache and, if the page has changed in the
interval, reload it from the network. If the page remains the same,
Netscape will always use the cache. You can force Netscape to
reload a page regardless of the status of the cache by pressing the
Reload button at the same time that you hold down the Shift key.

Images	Loads images on the page you are viewing. You would use this button if you have set Netscape to download icons instead of images, thus causing faster downloads. In such a case, you would be able to override this setting for the page in question by using the Images button.
Open	Lets you type in a URL to move directly to a new site.
Print	Prints the current page, after offering you a dialog box in which to set printing parameters. When you print such a page, Netscape will send only the content of the page to the printer; you will not, in other words, see a screen display but only the HTML page you are printing.
Find	Allows you to move directly to a particular word or phrase on the Netscape page. A dialog box will let you choose the direction in which to search—up or down within the document, and you can decide whether to set up a case-sensitive search. The Find command is crucial when you are dealing with long documents and are hoping to isolate particular information without reading the entire text.
Stop	Another crucial button, this one stops the download of infor-mation from the remote server. It is useful when it becomes obvious that a given page is not what you are looking for.

Directory Buttons

Netscape also includes a set of directory buttons that point to specific content.
These are useful primarily to Netscape itself as a promotional device, since
they all point to internal content at the site, and the materials available here
can be duplicated elsewhere around the Internet using search engines and

other tools. But if you're a newcomer, you'll find it easy to start your network explorations by clicking on these buttons and following their hyperlinks.

What's New	A variety of recent Web pages, with a Go button that can take you to assorted types of content.
What's Cool	Netscape's links to what its marketers think are the hottest sites and trends on the Net.
Destinations	A handy page if you want to view the latest Netscape technology; a showcase for the company's products, but handy for seeing how developers are using them.
Net Search	A page devoted to various search engines.
People	A page devoted to directories of people on the Net. Helps you locate electronic mail addresses.
Software	Information on Netscape Navigator upgrades.

Tip: One innovation of Netscape Navigator 3.0 was the introduction of tables and frames, which have become standard tools for Web page designers. A frame is a part of the content area of a page that has been segmented into its own window. Each frame can contain its own page of information, making it possible for designers to create easily navigable Web sites; point to a table of contents in one frame, for example, and you can see the results in another, while the original contents remain in the first frame. The page that contains the frames is known as the *frameset;* toolbars and icons affect it, whereas navigation between frames is handled by whichever frame is active at the time. Frames are selected by clicking inside them. You can see a page using frames in Figure 4.2.

Welcomed by many designers because they offer additional options for directory and content display, frames are nonetheless confusing and often off-putting. A 15-inch screen showing a page divided into three frames will make you feel claustrophobic; it divides the text you're reading into such a small area that, in the absence of sharper screen displays, it becomes a chore to work through. Frames can, however, be resized by positioning the cursor between them and dragging the frame to a new position. Whether you will find this an acceptable solution or will tend to avoid pages with frames altogether depends on your disposition.

The Major Browser Functions

The Netscape toolbar buttons refer to many of the major browser actions, and these are also available within the pull-down menus, as are a range of other, more specialized functions. Rather than going through the entire menu structure, then, let's simply target the major activities that you are likely to be doing

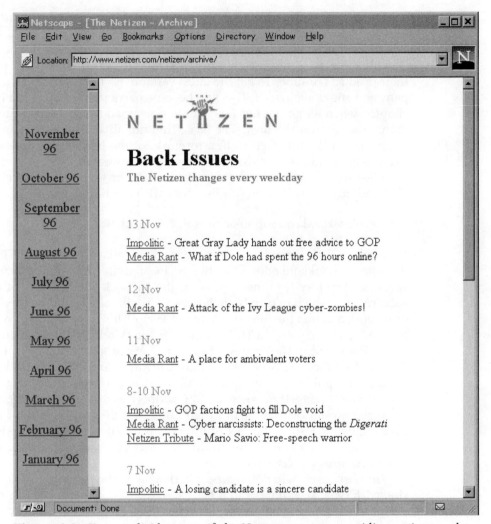

Figure 4.2 Frames divide areas of the Netscape screen, providing options such as tables of contents and other navigational aids.

on-line, with reference to the ways to implement them. Once these are familiar, it will be a logical step to customizing the browser by altering its key parameters. I will leave electronic mail and newsgroup options for later chapters. As with any Internet activity, the way to master it is to acquire basic skills in the browser and then add on to these through selective Net explorations and downloads.

Downloading Files

To download a file is to transfer a copy of it from a remote computer to your own hard disk. The file could be textual in nature, a photograph, an animation, a video clip, an audio file, or a program. Its exact nature doesn't matter to your browser, because HTTP allows for the transfer of any kind of digital information as long as it can be tagged by HTML and thus recognized by your browser. Downloading is significant because more and more companies are putting their products on-line. To get the latest version, it's necessary to go to the company site and download it. This will become particularly important in the next chapter, when we go out onto the Net to download Netscape plug-ins, the programs that extend the browser's basic functionality. You will find all of these programs on the Internet itself, a foretaste of the Net's future role as the primary distribution mechanism for the programs we run.

File downloads used to be managed solely through File Transfer Protocol, FTP. Indeed, you will often run into files with the FTP prefix, as in this URL:

ftp://oak.oakland.edu/pub/simtelnet/win95/winsock/twsk30c.zip

In standard URL format, this statement tells us that we can use FTP to access the site oak.oakland.edu. Our file is located in the /pub/simtelnet/win95/ winsock/ directory (in other words, in the winsock subdirectory of the win95 subdirectory, which in turn branches from the simtelnet subdirectory of the pub directory), and that the filename is twsk30c.zip. This is the Trumpet Winsock file referred to in Chapter 2, a TCP/IP stack for the Windows environment.

FTP was one of the earliest of the Internet's protocols. It took advantage of the fact that thousands of system administrators around the world had made various files publicly accessible. By allowing users to sign on with the login of anonymous (using their own e-mail address as their password), these site managers would restrict part of their computer disk space to their own organization, while letting the rest of it be open for file downloads. In Figure 4.3, you can see a typical FTP site, in this case the one known as oak.oakland.edu, as shown through Netscape.

In most cases, what Netscape will display is the directory structure at the site, with type, size, date, and a brief description of each available file. If you examine the figure, you can see that text files are shown with text icons, the image of a typed page with a turned-down corner. Folder icons indicate subdirectories; clicking on one of these calls up a list of the files and folders available within that subdirectory.

Let's assume for a moment that we want to download the SIMW95-L.ZIP file shown in this URL. To do so, we can simply click on the filename on-screen. The dialog box shown in Figure 4.4 will appear. The dialog box gives you the option of saving the file to disk. To download it, click on the Save File button. This will call up the Save As dialog box, allowing you to specify into which directory you want to put the file. You can take the default by clicking on Save or specify a different directory by clicking on the downward-pointing triangle in the box at the top of the Save As dialog box itself. This will cause a directory tree of your hard disk to appear, in which you can move about until you've located the place you want to put the file. Click on Save to begin the download process.

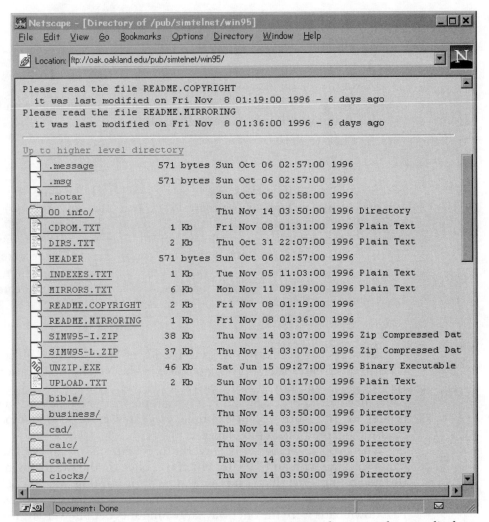

Figure 4.3 An FTP site viewed through Netscape. Note the minimal screen display.

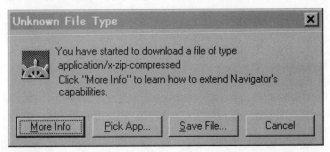

Figure 4.4 This dialog box indicates that Netscape does not know what you want to do with the file in question. Click on Save File to save the file to disk.

To summarize, file downloading proceeds like this:

1. Find the file you want to download.
2. Click on it.
3. In the dialog box, click on Save File.
4. In the Save As dialog box, check the location for the file and change it if you want to put it somewhere else.
5. Click on Save.

 Tip: When Netscape is working with a binary file, the download proceeds as just defined. When you click on a text or a graphics file, Netscape will attempt to display that file. This is handy for working your way through FTP sites, because it allows you to check the content of files that you may not want to take the trouble to download. If you do choose to download them, you can save them to disk by using the Save As command from the File menu.

Browsers can access FTP sites as readily as World Wide Web sites; all you need to do is enter the appropriate URL in the Netsite or Location box that specifies location. But in many cases, a file will be retrievable through a Web page, in which case, downloading it is a simple matter of clicking on the appropriate link. In Figure 4.5, for example, you can see the download page for the RealAudio streaming audio player.

When you download this way, the procedure is much the same as it is when working with an FTP site. When you click on the file to download it, the Unknown File Type dialog box will appear, prompting you to click the Save button after confirming the location of the file. Previously, command-driven FTP downloads were the only way large amounts of data were transferred over the Internet; now, the Web has largely replaced them for average Internet users, for whom downloads are a matter of following prompts and pointing and clicking with the mouse.

 Tip: After you've downloaded a few files, working through two dialog boxes each time seems unnecessary—and it is. You can avoid one of the boxes by pressing Shift as you click on the link to download the file. Rather than looking first for a file viewer and presenting you with options, Netscape will simply show the Save As dialog box, allowing you to choose the location for the file and begin the download process.

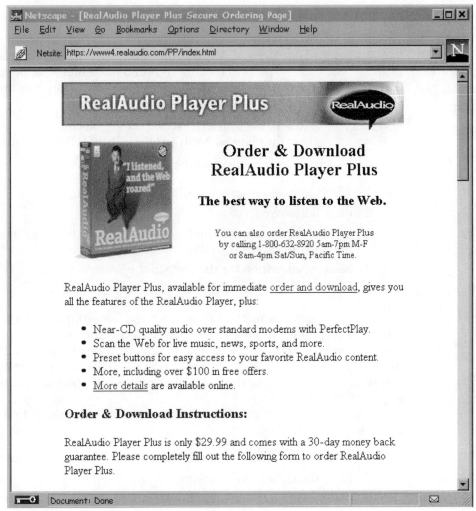

Figure 4.5 A Web page can contain links that allow you to download a file.

The Web-based delivery of files also makes sense for business. A software company can, for example, set up a download that can be accomplished only after the user fills out a form, thus building a useful database of customers for the company. Features of the program can be discussed in screens leading to the download area, while links to information about the company's other products can also be provided. In general, making downloads more graphical and wrapping them in the context of other information benefits both consumer and developer. While shareware and freeware continue to be found on FTP-enabled sites, Web-based downloads are the way most users will acquire commercial software on the Web.

Saving Pages or Images onto Your Hard Disk

There will be occasions when you run across something on the Web that you'd like to keep for later perusal. Various options are available: You can print out the page; you can clip parts of it using copy and paste methods; or you can save the entire page onto your hard disk. In the case of the latter option, you can save files in either of two formats:

HTML File   Saves the file with all its HTML coding intact.
Text   Saves the file as an ASCII text file without HTML formatting.

To save a page to your disk, do the following:

1. With the page on-screen, call up the File menu.
2. Click on Save As.
3. Choose the format in which you want to save the page by clicking on the Save As Type box in the Save As dialog box.
4. Select the location for the page in the Save As box.
5. Click on Save.

When you use this method to save a page, you go through a manual procedure using pull-down menus as opposed to clicking on a filename. But in all other respects, saving a page to disk is similar to downloading a file through the FTP method. In both cases, you initiate a procedure that results in your choosing a destination for the file. A click on the Save button results in its subsequent download.

Pages and files can also be saved directly to disk without first displaying them on-screen. To do so:

1. Position the mouse over the link or image you want to save.
2. Click the right mouse button.
3. In the ensuing dialog box, choose either Save Link As or Save Image As.

To view files you have saved in HTML format or to view graphic images, simply choose the Open File command from the File menu. A page's inline images may be replaced with icons, but the text of the HTML page should remain viewable.

Printing a Web Page

The current page in Netscape's contents window can be printed out easily. To do so:

1. Pull down the File menu.
2. Click on Print.

3. In the Print dialog box, choose any options, such as number of copies, pages to print, or type of printer.
4. Click on OK to print the document.

Note that you also have the option of previewing any print function by choosing Print Preview from the File menu. This will create a screen display showing an image of the page as it will appear when printed.

Tip: Printing Web pages takes on a slightly different slant when you're dealing with frames. Instead of a Print option, you'll discover that the File menu contains a Print Frame item. Using it, you can print the page of the currently selected frame, using the same dialog options as are available for any printed page. The same sort of change occurs with other menu options. Thus the Mail Document and Save As commands become Mail Frame and Save Frame As commands.

Finding Text on the Current Page

Netscape can provide you with information only one screen at a time, but it's frequently the case that a Web document may consist of numerous pages of information. Rather than paging through such a document scanning for the particular item you need, you can use the Find function. To do so:

1. Pull down the Edit menu.
2. Click on Find.
3. Fill in the Find what field with the keyword of your choice.
4. Click on the Match case box if case is important in your search.
5. Choose the Up or Down button depending on whether you want the search to proceed down into the document or back up through material you have already paged through.
6. Click on Find Next to launch the search.

Netscape will take you to the first occurrence of your keyword, which will now appear highlighted on the screen. You can click on Find Next once again to find the next occurrence of the word.

Creating a New Browser

The day will come when you are working with a particular home page and need to simultaneously view a second one. You could accomplish this by moving back and forth between the two pages, but Netscape makes it simple to launch a second version of the program to display the second page.

To accomplish this:

1. Pull down the File menu.
2. Click on New Web Browser.

Alternatively, you can launch the process directly by typing a Ctrl-N command (hold down the Ctrl key while pressing the letter N). A second copy of Netscape will be launched; you can move about the Internet with it independent of what is being displayed in the first copy. I find this function particularly useful when I'm doing something that depends upon an incoming data stream, such as listening to a streaming audio file while I work on something else. The second browser lets me move about the Net as needed, while I can keep the first locked onto the incoming audio materials.

Another, more targeted way of launching a second copy of the browser is to use the right mouse button. You might do this if you were reading a particular page but decided to examine a link mentioned there, while maintaining the page you were reading. Here's how:

1. Move the mouse cursor over the link you want to open in the new window.
2. Right click.
3. Choose Open in New Window command.
4. A second version of Netscape will appear and will load the URL in the chosen link.

Copy and Paste

You can quickly move material found on the Internet into a local program, such as a word processor, by using basic copy and paste techniques. To do so:

1. Highlight the textual material in question.
2. On the Edit menu, click the Copy command.
3. Move to the program in which you want to insert the information.
4. Use its Paste command (on its Edit menu) to paste the material directly into the new document.

This function is something you will do often in your work, because the connection between the Internet and your desktop is becoming more seamless. While compiling information about a particular subject, you'll want to be able to paste segments of it into your own notes. I often work this way when assembling background materials for a story I'm writing, thus building a reference document that supplies statistics, provocative quotes, or explanations.

Using Bookmarks

Bookmarks are a key feature of any browser. They allow you to set up a direct link to a page that has particularly caught your attention. The next time you want to view that page, you don't need to enter a complicated URL, but can move directly to the site by clicking on it in the Bookmark menu. Bookmarks have been vastly improved since the early days of browsers; today, you can drag them into position, categorize them with subfolders, and separate them with dividers to mark off different kinds of subject matter.

Tip: Customization of any browser begins with its bookmarks; indeed, a browser without a full set of bookmarks, built up over time from your network travels, is one that fails to take advantage of the medium. The Internet is a vast and largely uncataloged terrain, a landscape so preposterously random that without appropriate search tools and markers, we would be left to wander aimlessly until we stumbled across data that might, or might not, reflect what we need. If there is one area where putting your personal stamp on a browser is critical, it is in building your bookmarks.

To add a bookmark to the Bookmark menu:

1. Call up the page you want to be used as a bookmark.
2. On the Bookmarks menu, click on Add Bookmark.

When you add a Web page to your Bookmark menu, the title of that page will henceforth appear as a menu item. The next time you want to travel to that page, you simply click on the item and go, without entering a complicated URL.

The Bookmarks Window

Note that we have not one but two choices on the Bookmarks menu. In addition to the Add Bookmark command, we can also choose Go to Bookmarks, which will produce the Bookmarks window shown in Figure 4.6.

Notice that the Bookmarks window contains a hierarchically arranged set of folder icons. Each folder represents a group I have set up under a particular category of information. Thus I have created a folder called Science in which to place sites like James Gleick's home page; the author of *Chaos* and a fine biography of Richard Feynman offers a site that archives his recent writings. Project Galileo is here as well; this NASA site tracks the ongoing fortunes of the Galileo orbiter around Jupiter, with frequent updates and photographs from the probe. In Figure 4.7, you can see the Science folder and its contents. I expanded it by double-clicking on the Science folder icon.

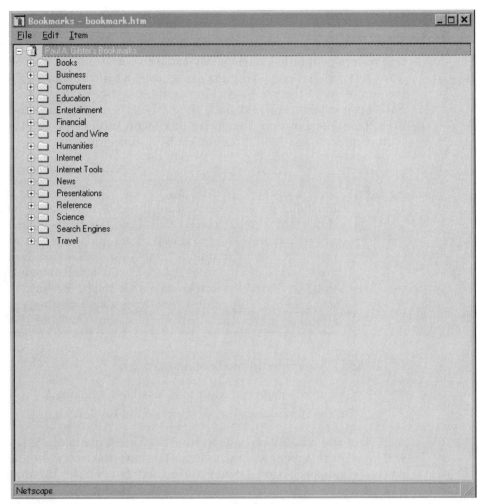

Figure 4.6 The Bookmarks window is the place where we can categorize and arrange bookmarks from our Net travels.

The model is provocative because it allows us to arrange information as necessary, a necessary first step in customizing a browser for personal use. It is possible to include folders within folders; I could, for example, create a sub-folder within the Science folder that would house all Web sites devoted to astronomy, or all sites dealing with chemistry, or whatever category I needed.

Tip: The Bookmarks window also provides an alternative way of adding bookmarks to your list. You can pull down the Item menu and click on Insert Bookmark to do so. After you have filled out the title and URL information and any optional comments, the new

> bookmark will appear below the current selection in the bookmark list. If this is an open folder, the bookmark will appear as the first item in the folder's sublist. If the folder is closed at the time, the new item will be inserted after but at the same level as the folder.

Creating New Folders

You can use the Bookmarks window to create new folders with ease. To do so:

1. Pull down the Item menu.
2. Click on Insert Folder to call up the Bookmark Properties window.

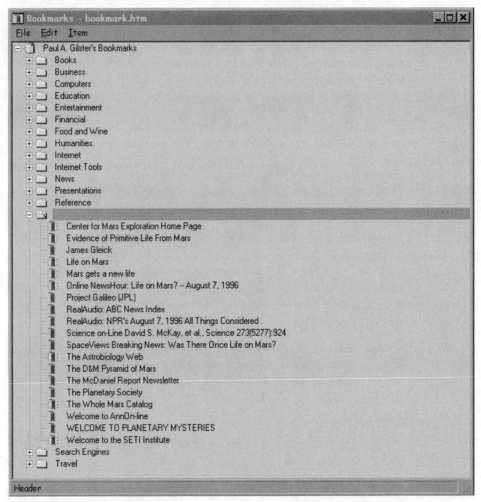

Figure 4.7   A double-click opens a folder for inspection; each site within it is reachable through another click.

3. Fill in the title of the new folder in the space provided.

4. Click on OK.

You can see the Bookmark Properties window in Figure 4.8.

The folder you add will appear beneath the item currently highlighted in the Bookmarks window. This allows you to create a top-level folder or to nest a folder within another to reflect a hierarchy of subject matter.

Sorting Bookmarks

Bookmarks work through a drag-and-drop model. When I want to move a bookmark into a particular folder, I simply highlight it, hold down the left mouse button, and drag it to the place I want it to go. This will drop the bookmark into the folder of my choice; but note that it inserts the bookmark without regard to alphabetical order. This can make finding the page in the future a tricky proposition, unless there is some way to sort the Bookmarks page itself. Fortunately, there is: by using the menus at the top of the Bookmarks window. To sort your bookmarks:

1. Pull down the Item menu.

2. Click on Sort Bookmarks.

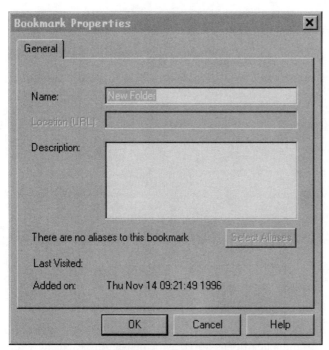

Figure 4.8 The Bookmark Properties window is where you create folders and edit their names.

Tip: Don't forget that Netscape provides a drag-and-drop model for its bookmarks. You can, for example, highlight a Netscape bookmark and drag it to your Windows 95 desktop to create a shortcut. If you work with a page frequently, you can create this shortcut and then activate it by double-clicking or by dragging it to the Netscape icon. Either action will launch Netscape and cause the browser to access the page indicated by the bookmark. Another possibility is to drag the URL link icon from the main screen to the desktop; this likewise creates a shortcut to the site.

Changing Bookmark Properties

When you sort your bookmarks, you may still be unsatisfied with the results. What Netscape does is to insert the title of the home page in the folder of your choice or on the Bookmarks menu itself, depending on your preference. The title itself is dependent on the home page designer who created the page. Thus a page titled "The Planetary Society" will file itself not under the Ps but the Ts, since the first word in the title is "The." Trying to remember a title rather than a subject can be confusing, so you'll want to edit that title to reflect its content.

To do so, do the following:

1. Highlight the bookmark in question.
2. From the Item menu, click on Properties.

The window in Figure 4.9 will appear. Notice that the title of the page shows up in the Title field here, which is highlighted. By overwriting the title, you can insert whatever information you choose. The best course is to change the title to reflect the subject of the home page in the first word. In this example, "The Planetary Society," I might choose to change it to, simply, Planetary Society, if I were content to look under the Ps to find it; or else Astronomy—Planets, if I wanted to subcategorize it. Your decision will probably depend on your folder structure, and how careful you have been to make it a precise one. Here, if I already have an Astronomy folder, for example, I might just use Planets to reflect a reasonable subdivision within my collected URLs.

Notice that there is also a Description field in the Bookmark Properties window. This can be used to fill in any background information you might find useful. This is particularly handy if you are exchanging bookmark lists with another user. The Description field can clue in that person to particular reasons why a given page should be examined, or how it fits into a broader scheme of research, and so on. Additional information on when you last looked at this home page and when it was added to your Bookmarks list is also provided.

Finding Bookmarks Quickly

After you've accumulated 10 bookmarks, pulling down the Bookmarks menu will make it easy to find what you're looking for, particularly if you've remem-

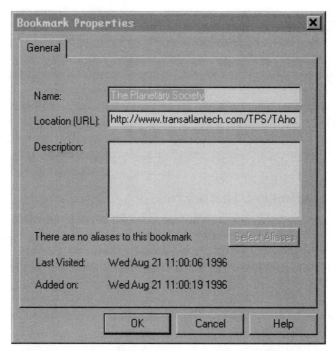

Figure 4.9 The Bookmark Properties window allows you to modify the title of a particular page to reflect its content.

bered to sort the bookmarks and have used intuitive titles to replace misleading ones. But once you've added several hundred bookmarks, there may be times when you still can't find what you need; the bookmark in question may be buried deep within a set of nested subfolders, for example. To get around this, you can use Netscape's Find function. To do so:

1. From the Bookmarks window, pull down the Edit menu.
2. Choose Find.
3. In the resulting dialog box, enter the word you're looking for. Note that you can choose whether case is significant in this search.
4. Click on OK to start the search.

Note that you can also use the Find Again item from the Edit menu to repeat the search; conveniently, this function is also accessible through the F3 key.

Creating Multiple Bookmarks Lists

Each bookmark list is a separate entity. Netscape allows you to create as many of these lists as you choose, which can come in handy depending on the kind of work you do. I often give presentations based on Internet content, for example, and it's easier for me to set up separate bookmark lists for such presenta-tions rather than to load down my main list with numerous addresses that I'll probably not use again. Thus I create a bookmark list for presentations to gov-ernmental groups, another for presentations to the library community, and so on. A second advantage of this is that it keeps the bookmark list I use in the presentation simple and easy to read, a benefit for the audience I'm addressing as well as for me as I work.

To create a new bookmark list:

1. From the Bookmark Properties window, choose the File menu.
2. Choose Save As to save the active bookmark list in HTML format.
3. Enter a filename for the bookmark list.
4. Click on OK to save it.

To move between bookmark lists:

1. In the Bookmarks Window, pull down the File menu.
2. Click on Open.
3. Choose the list you want to use.

To add the contents of a bookmark list to the currently active list:

1. From the Bookmark Properties window, choose File.
2. Click on Import.
3. Choose the file you would like to append.
4. Click on OK to append the file.

Using Separators to Format Your List

A separator is simply a line that can be drawn between two items on a book-mark list. Separators can be useful when you are trying to show logical divi-sions between your bookmark materials; this is especially helpful if you are working with several ongoing projects. To create a separator:

1. From the Bookmarks window, choose the Item menu.
2. Click on Insert Separator to insert the line.

The separator will appear below the current selection in the bookmark list.

Bringing Your Bookmarks Up to Date

A fact of Web life is that many Web pages change frequently. This can be bless-ing or curse depending on what you're looking for. Updating content means you can follow breaking news stories or do regular follow-ups on trends in the industry. But on non-news pages, keeping up with changes is tricky; it involves going back into the site and looking for new content, which is always readily apparent. I'd like to know, for example, if the Tech Classics page at MIT has added any new editions of Greek or Roman authors, but I don't always want to take the time to go through its contents, especially not when there are other pages out there I'd also like to follow.

Netscape's solution is to provide an update feature that is accessible through the Bookmarks window. To access it:

1. From the Bookmarks window, pull down the File menu.
2. Choose What's New.
3. In the resulting dialog box, choose either All bookmarks or Selected bookmarks to determine the parameters of the search. Multiple bookmarks can be selected by holding down the Ctrl key and clicking on the bookmarks in question.
4. Click on Start Checking.

Netscape will now go out onto the Net to check for changes to the bookmarks you've specified. If it finds them, several things will happen. First, a dialog box will appear that tells you how many pages were accessed and how many of these have changed since the last time you checked. Pages that have been changed will be shown with accentuated lines in the bookmark icon, as shown in Figure 4.10. A bookmark that cannot be reached for the check is displayed with a question mark next to it; you'll want to run the check again at a later time to check its status. In Chapter 8, we'll download a more advanced version of the software that makes this possible; it's called Smart Bookmarks.

Tip: It's not infrequent that a given URL will change as people move their home pages either on their own server or from a commercial provider's server to their own. When this occurs, you may receive either a changed page icon or else a question mark, indicating that the site cannot be reached. It's worth investigating all pages with either icon to verify that you are not dealing with a different URL, in which case, it will be necessary to change your bookmark.

When you run a check for changed bookmarks, you may be surprised. The last one I ran covered 244 bookmark entries in a particular list I maintain. Of these, 109 were changed; 16 were unreachable at the time of the check. I find this Netscape feature extremely useful because it saves me time; I don't have to look back at sites I've already viewed if I know for a fact that nothing has been altered there. Keeping track of changing content is going to be an ever more important issue as the Internet continues to grow.

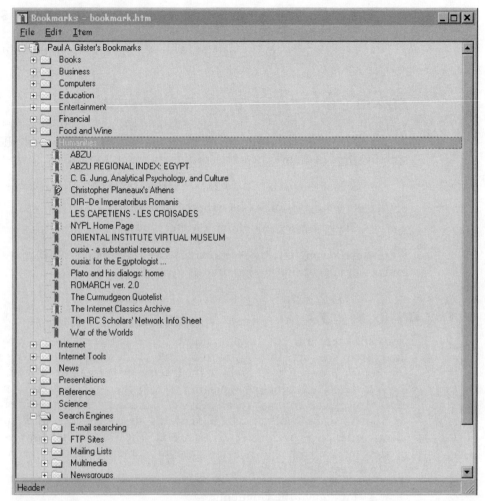

Figure 4.10   A sweep for altered Web pages pulls up several changed sites, shown by the modified folder icon here. Note the question mark alongside the bookmark icon at one site, which indicates it could not be reached for checking purposes.

Selective Bookmark Insertion

When you work with Netscape bookmarks, by default, the topmost folder in the bookmark list is the one in which the added bookmark goes. Netscape isn't terribly demanding, so it's easy to move a bookmark from that folder to the one you want it to appear in. But if you'd rather not go through that process, it's easy enough to specify that added bookmarks should go into a different folder. To do so:

1. Select the folder into which you want the bookmark to go.

2. From the Item menu in the Bookmarks window, click on Set to New Bookmarks Folder.

3. From this point on, new bookmarks will appear in the folder of your choice.

Limiting the Display of Menued Bookmarks

You can also choose to display only the contents of a particular folder as your Bookmarks menu from the main Netscape screen. This would allow you to simplify the bookmark menu for presentations, for example. To do this:

1. Select the folder you want to appear on the Bookmarks menu.

2. From the Bookmarks window, choose Item.

3. Click on Set to Bookmark Menu Folder.

From now on, only those bookmarks and subfolders starting at the chosen folder will appear on the Bookmarks menu.

Using the History List

Netscape keeps track of a certain number of Web pages that you have visited in the current session. If you want to see one of these pages again, it's not necessary for the browser to go out onto the Internet to retrieve it. Instead, it will look in its cache to recall the page, placing the most recently viewed item at the top of its History list. You may recall that we do the same thing by using the buttons on the Netscape toolbar, which allow us to move backward and forward through the pages we've already accessed. The History list simply makes the process more obvious, by providing us with a menued list of sites we've seen.

To access the History list:

1. Pull down the Go menu.

2. At the bottom of the menu are the pages viewed in the current session.

3. Choose the page you want to revisit and click.

You can also view the current list using a different menu:

1. Pull down the Window menu.

2. Click on History.

The History list isn't a permanent record; it will vanish when you exit the browser. It will also reflect only a particular chain of home page visits; if you back up through pages already viewed at a site and then move forward onto a new set of pages, the new links will replace the old. For quick movement between related pages at a particular site, the History list will supplement your use of the toolbar buttons to get you back to the page you need. If Bookmarks are a permanent record of your Web visits, the History list is a temporary navigation tool.

Fine-Tuning the Browser

Browsers offer a range of customization options that will allow you to fine-tune them for your particular needs. We can consider these options in two ways. First are the internal options that allow us to set specific parameters for our browser use. Second are the external options—programs that provide additional functionality beyond that offered by the browser itself. In this chapter, we'll look at the options Netscape provides to change the way it operates through controls on a wide range of features. Later, we'll look specifically at the plug-in programs that provide other, more complex customization possibilities. Mail, newsgroup, and security options will be discussed in subsequent chapters, so that as you read deeper into this book, your browser will become increasingly customized.

In Figure 4.11, you can see the window that appears when you click on Netscape's Options menu and move to the General Preferences item. As you can see, the metaphor is of a file folder with multiple tabs. You can click on any of these tabs to move to screens that allow you to adjust such features as fonts, colors, images, and helper applications. The initial screen is the one affecting the appearance of Web pages. What follow are my recommendations for a customized setting.

Rethinking the Toolbar

I'm not a believer in toolbars—the strips across the top of a program's screen that contain icons for performing common commands. Icons are usually representative of the actions they represent, but it's easy to forget which icon does what without a textual jog. The Netscape toolbar is a prominent feature of its interface, so it's not surprising that the toolbar can be adjusted in various ways to affect its appearance. The default is set to Pictures and Text, but you can choose to see only icons or buttons with text inside them, or you can turn the toolbar off altogether.

It's best to use the default initially, since you're still learning how the program works, but once you've adjusted to the Netscape buttons, I recommend eliminating the toolbar entirely and using alternative command entries, as explained later in the chapter. But you can improve your display area and still maintain easy pointers to commands by turning off the icons and going with text buttons only. Consider the home page in Figure 4.12, viewed with Netscape's default settings, and compare it to the same page shown with toolbar icons eliminated, as shown in Figure 4.13. Then compare both these pages to Figure 4.14 showing the Netscape screen with the toolbar as well as the

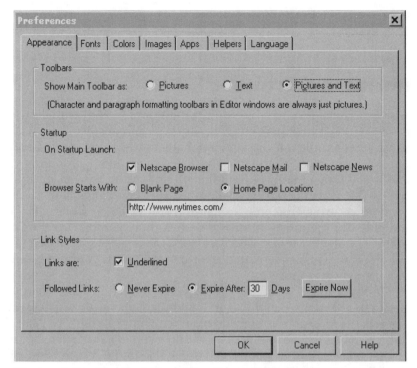

Figure 4.11   The Preferences panel contains tabs that let you move between screens controlling key Netscape features.

directory buttons completely eliminated. For now, remove the icons by clicking on Text in the Appearance tab.

Later in this chapter, I'll show you how to make the transition to an alternative command strategy, and do away with the toolbar altogether.

Choosing a New Home Page

The Startup section of the Appearance dialog box also allows you to launch Netscape either as a pure Web browser or with its mail or news functions running. A more significant choice, depending on your preferences, is the next one, which allows you to set the home page location. Netscape's default is the Netscape server, but given the huge demand on Netscape's machines, it makes sense to choose a home page that is more specifically focused on your Web use. I use *The New York Times* Web site as my home page, so that every time I launch Netscape, I wind up with a synopsis of the news and a clickable interface to more information. Your own choice should reflect the kind of content you want to see every day, and it should also be based upon a server that doesn't take too long to load an average page. Nothing is more frustrating than launching your browser only to have to wait while extensive graphics cross a balky network connection.

Figure 4.12 Netscape's default display settings provide point-and-click functionality but use up too much screen space.

Figure 4.13 With icons eliminated, the textual buttons take up less space, giving the Web page greater area to work with.

Figure 4.14   The fully customized screen eliminates toolbar and directory buttons for maximum exposure to the Web page.

It's also possible to download a home page and use it from your own hard disk as your default. Having downloaded it using the methods given, you simply enter the file location in the Startup section of the Appearance tab, using a URL in this format:

    file:///E:/htmlfile/homepage.htm

inserting whatever name you have given the page. Note that this URL uses a third slash as opposed to the normal two slashes, because it must also provide any necessary path information for the browser to find your file. In this case, my home page is located on my E drive in the htmlfile directory, and is called homepage.htm.

Why would you want to operate with a home page based on your own disk, if the information on it was external to your site? Mostly for reasons of speed. If you find a home page that provides numerous useful links but you don't like waiting while your browser loads it each day, pulling it up off your disk will greatly speed the process. The only problem is that you'll have to keep checking when changes to the home page are made so that none of your disk-based links become obsolete.

Tip: If you save HTML pages to disk and work with them frequently, you may want to consider another home page option. In the Appearance box, you also have an option for starting the browser with a blank page. Clicking on this will cause the browser to load faster because it is not connecting across the network as it does so. The URL for your home page will still appear in the Location box, but the browser will not contact the site. Now you have the option of using the File menu and the Open File command to work locally, or you can go out onto the Net with a Return, which will cause Netscape to make the home page connection.

Changing Your Link Expiration Time

Netscape defaults to a link expiration time of 30 days. This means that when you click on a particular hyperlink, that link will maintain its purple color, indicating it has been visited by you, for 30 days before reverting to the original blue. In my own work, I find that moving back and forth between sites is frustrating when I have no clear idea of where I've been recently. The 30-day time limit is too short for me, since I find myself looping back to sites unintentionally and thus wasting time. I recommend setting the expiration option to Never Expire to provide a continually present statement of where you have journeyed on the Web. You can always reset this length of time later if you choose; you can even choose to make all links expire simultaneously by clicking on the Expire Now button. But having a record of your travels is a useful reminder that helps you avoid redundancy as you search.

Experimenting with Fonts

Fonts have a lot to say about how your eyes fare during an Internet session. For the casual user, the Netscape defaults are doubtless fine, but for heavy Net readers, it becomes necessary to adjust the fonts to reflect the screen you are using and your own eyesight. In my case, I move back and forth between a desktop computer and a laptop; each machine demands its own set of parameters, complicated by the fact that I use the laptop with a docking station and an external screen when I'm not on the road. Figure 4.15 shows the Fonts and Encodings panel, a simple one to adjust.

A font is a collection of letters, numbers, punctuation marks, and other characters in a consistent typeface and size. Notice that on the Netscape menu we are dealing with two types of fonts. Proportional fonts are those that are adjusted in relation to the shape of the character itself, so that, for example, a narrow character, like an i, takes up less space than a wide character, like a w. Most Web-based text is found in proportional format, whereas fixed fonts are those in which the width of all the characters is the same; fixed fonts give the appearance of typed text.

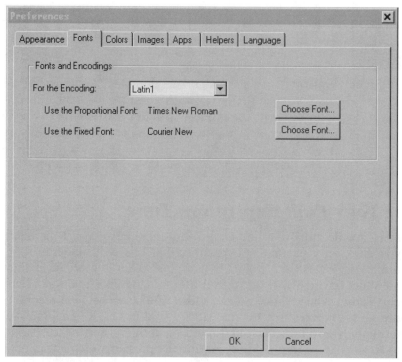

Figure 4.15 The Fonts and Encodings panel is seldom used, but altering options there can prevent headaches when you do a lot of close reading on-screen.

In each case, you have an option for setting the font by clicking on the Choose Font button, which opens the dialog box shown in Figure 4.16. Note that you can adjust both the base font (the default is Times New Roman for proportional text, and Courier for fixed text) as well as the point size. I recommend experimenting broadly with these settings. The key will be the font size, which will determine such things as how much text you can fit on a screen, and trade this off against readability. If you're finding yourself with a headache after a long session on the Web, an adjustment to a larger font size will probably pay off, assuming you can still work with enough text on the screen. You can adjust the Fixed Font as necessary as well, although it will be less significant; your use of the fixed font will largely be in filling out on-screen forms and other editable text.

The Encoding menu is set with Latin1 as the default, a setting that you will want to leave as is. The pull-down menu selects the character set that is used with the two types of fonts; a change of encoding can accommodate languages other than English. If you want to view the fonts involved with any particular encoding scheme, you can pull down the Encoding menu, choose an item, and then examine the fixed and proportional font options available through that encoding by clicking on the Choose Font buttons.

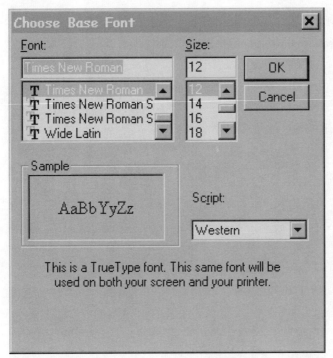

Figure 4.16 The dialog box for changing fonts in Netscape.

Adjusting Your Screen Colors

Browsers give you enormous flexibility in your choice of screen colors, but I generally find that the default settings work best. We are well past the days when the average Web page was constrained by limited HTML coding to appear in one of a small range of formats. Today, Web page designers are using all the special effects used in traditional presentations, including a large palette of color options, to highlight the pages they produce. In most cases, we should let them do their work and gauge its effectiveness, even if Netscape gives us the option of overriding their colors with our own.

You can see the Colors panel in Figure 4.17. Using the options available here, you can change the color of links or followed links to suit your preference, create a different color for standard text, and adjust background colors by clicking on Custom and Choose Color. The option for using your own colors exclusively is set by clicking the small box at the bottom of the window.

Image Options

The Images dialog box lets you make changes to the way Netscape displays graphics, by adjusting image loading to fit your own computer. Figure 4.18 shows the Images panel.

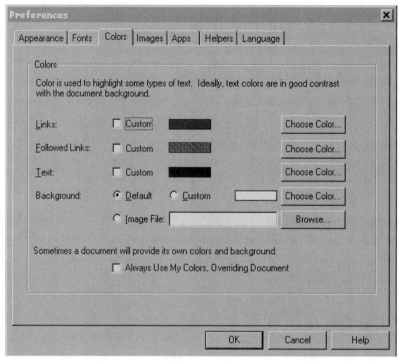

Figure 4.17   The Colors panel allows you to adjust screen backgrounds and hyperlink colors.

Images can be loaded in three ways:

Automatic	The default setting; this allows Netscape to determine the best type of screen display.
Dither	This setting adjusts the available colors in the computer to match the image's colors as closely as possible.
Substitute Colors	Substitution allows Netscape to use an available color that comes as close as possible to the image's colors. This setting takes slightly less time than the dither setting.

The issue at work here is that the colors available within a particular image may not precisely fit the color capabilities of your computer. Unless you are having significant problems with image display, the default setting is preferable. The same is true of the While Loading default, which displays images as they are being received. No significant advantage is available for modem users by choosing the After Loading option, which displays the image only after the transmission is complete. Using the While Loading option allows you to stop a download before it is complete if you realize that the image forming on your screen is not one you particularly want to see.

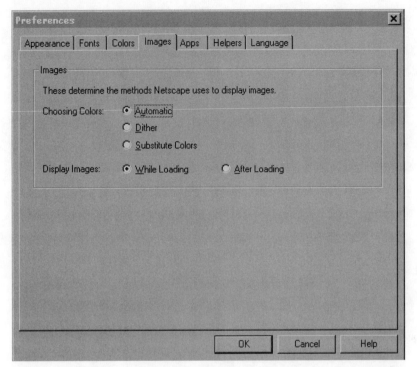

Figure 4.18   The Images panel adjusts the display of Web images for your screen.

Setting Language Preferences

A global network is one that increasingly uses languages other than English to present information. Netscape allows you to tell remote computers which language you would like a given page presented in, assuming the remote server has the capability of fielding multilingual requests. Such servers will interpret the HTTP information sent by Netscape and return a page in the appropriate language where possible. This option is controlled from the Language panel, accessible through the Preferences screen, shown in Figure 4.19.

If you examine the Language/Region box on the left of the Language panel, you'll see that each language has its own code. Dutch, for example, is [nl], while Italian is [it], and so on. Some languages also add a region suffix, as in the case of Portuguese, which is the primary language not only of Portugal, but also of Brazil, and which is shown as [pt-BR]. Similarly, the code for French is [fr], but the code for French Canada is [fr-CA]. The language identifiers are all based upon standard tags developed by the International Standards Organization, an international group concerned with standardization in numerous technical fields.

To adjust your language list, do the following:

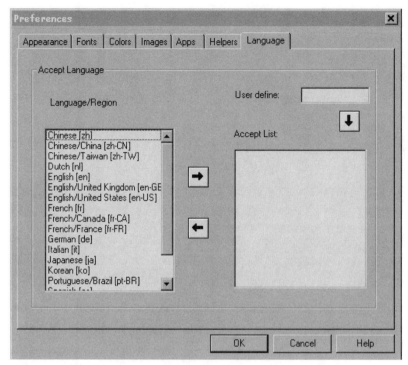

Figure 4.19 The Language panel offers a wide range of language options in an increasingly multilingual network.

1. Select the appropriate language from the Language/Region list and highlight it.
2. Use the Right arrow button to place the language/region in the Accept box.

Alternatively, you can enter a language/region manually in the User Define box and click on the down arrow to put your entry into the Accept box. Languages you have decided not to use can be removed from the Accept box by using the left arrow.

Enlarging the Content Area

One of the frustrations of reading lengthy documents on-screen is that it requires you to continuously scroll through the text by clicking on the scroll bar. The Netscape Options menu provides several toggle switches—click once to turn off the option, click again to turn it back on. Using these, you can enlarge the content area of the browser, thus packing more text onto the screen. This will also have the effect of removing some key screen elements, so you should consider which of these you may be willing to do without. The options are as follows:

Show Toolbar	Clicking on this item will turn off the toolbar.
Show Location	Clicking here will remove the Location or Netsite box.
Show Directory	Buttons Clicking here will remove the Netscape buttons that provide directories of various sites.

My recommendation: Turn off the toolbar as well as the directory buttons. Yes, the Back, Forward, Print and Find buttons represent some of the most common commands you'll use on the Net. But these options can be handled by a Netscape trick that's just as fast: the pop-up menu. To access the pop-up menu for common commands, click on the right mouse button.

What you see next will depend upon the contents of the window you are looking at. We just saw that if you right-click with the cursor positioned over an image, you produce a menu with commands that apply to that image, allowing you to save the image to disk or to use it as a background image in your work. If you are viewing text, however, clicking on the right mouse button produces a short menu with Back, Forward, Add Bookmark, and Internet Shortcut commands. You can quickly move back and forth at a given Web site or through your History list using these commands, and you won't need the toolbar to do it. Working without the toolbar enlarges your content area significantly.

Similarly, I recommend turning off the Netscape directory buttons. After your initial network explorations, you'll find many of these sites on your own, and will, in any case, be able to return to them easily through the menus. They are the least used buttons on the Netscape screen, and as such, they simply take up space that could be used for textual display. Turn them off.

The Location box is a different story. It gives you a quick reminder of the site you're logged in to and the URL of the file you're examining; without it, you're driving blind. Besides, a quick way to move to a new URL is to highlight the existing one and simply type another in over it. I find this much quicker than using the File menu and its Open Location command. However, for those who don't mind remembering key combinations, there is another method.

Using Keyboard Shortcuts to Major Commands

Now that we've all grown used to window-based graphical environments, we forget the keyboard shortcuts that let us accomplish many tasks without using a mouse. If you are comfortable using the keyboard alone, you can turn off the toolbar as well as the directory buttons, thus adding to the amount of space available for text. Here are the major keyboard options for common tasks:

New Web Browser	Ctrl-N
Open Location	Ctrl-L
Open File	Ctrl-O
Copy Text	Ctrl-C
Find Text	Ctrl-F
Reload Page	Ctrl-R

Back   Alt-Right Arrow
Forward   Alt-Left Arrow
Stop loading   Esc

You can see that between keyboard commands and pop-up menus, there is no reason for you to take up valuable screen space with the toolbar or the directory buttons. Optimize your viewing space and you'll get more out of a Web page.

Turning Off Inline Images When Necessary

An inline image is one that is loaded automatically as a page is displayed on your screen. One of the great breakthroughs of the Web was, of course, its ability to provide graphics and images in conjunction with text, and numerous designers have taken advantage of this fact to produce carefully crafted and appealing Web sites. Unfortunately, however, too many images on a page can slow down loading, because images are larger than text files and take longer to download through the network. A good page designer tries to minimize the amount of time a viewer must spend waiting for images to load, but even a well-designed page sometimes falls victim to a crowded network, slowing your work considerably. When you're pressed for time and need to do research, turning off the automatic loading of images is a good idea.

To turn off automatic loading of images:

1. Pull down the Options menu.
2. Click on the Auto Load Images toggle.

When you turn off automatic loading of images, any inline images Netscape finds will be replaced by small icons, sometimes accompanied by text. Now you can proceed with your work and move between sites with minimal loading time. But if you do choose to see images, you have two options:

- To see an individual image, click on the image's icon (alternatively, you could right-click on the icon and select the Load Image command).
- To load all images on a given page, click on the Images button in the toolbar, or pull down the View menu and click on Load Images. The keyboard shortcut to this is Ctrl-I.

Tip: If you have turned off automatic image loading, then change your mind, resetting the toggle will affect subsequent pages only. If you want to display all the images on the current page, you can click on the Reload button (or choose the Reload command on the View menu) to cause it to be displayed with all images available.

Tip: Two types of images are available within Netscape. An inline image is one that loads automatically. But the browser can also display external images, which are shown in their own screen windows. You view such an image by clicking on a link to it; external images have their own URLs, and are not automatically loaded, unlike inline images. Netscape can display images in GIF (Graphics Interchange Format), JPEG (Joint Photographic Experts Group), and XBM (X Bit Map) formats, but other types of image require an external viewing program, a helper application of the kind we'll discuss in the next chapter.

Reducing the Size of Your Cache

A cache is a useful tool, because it allows Netscape to quickly call up pages you've already seen. The downside of a cache, however, is that it takes up disk space. Depending on the amount of free disk space you have, this could be a problem, but it's one that can be addressed simply:

1. Pull down the Options menu.
2. Choose Network Preferences.
3. In the Cache tab, change the number in the Disk Cache field. The default, 5000K, can be cut in half if necessary.

The Ongoing Customization

You'll find as you work with your browser that customization isn't something you finish. For one thing, new browser generations keep changing what's included in each version; for another, people's work habits vary depending upon their assignment. So don't be surprised if you find yourself returning again and again to the various customization options offered by Netscape and adjusting them as necessary. In my own work, I turn inline images on and off frequently depending upon the type of sites I need to access, and I'm always looking at new programs that can work with Netscape to extend its basic functions. These programs form the subject of the next chapter, which focuses on plug-in and add-on products. But we won't be through with customization even then, for issues such as electronic mail, newsgroup reading, and security will be addressed in subsequent chapters, with tips on adjusting the browser to optimize these functions as well. With the Internet evolving as rapidly as it has, frequent customization is the only sensible way to keep pace with technology.

5

Plug-ins, Add-Ons, and Helper Programs

The original Mosaic program was a proof-of-concept product, at least in its early versions. It demonstrated that a browser that incorporated graphical elements and wrapped the Internet in a sensible menu-based structure could succeed at moving information through the World Wide Web's protocols. But many of its functions depended upon external programs. If you wanted to view a graphics file, a click on its hyperlink would download it and send the result to a separate file viewer program, which would open and display the results. If you wanted to watch a QuickTime video, you needed QuickTime, which would run as a separate program after the file you were after had been acquired. The model worked because the browsers could be configured to send data to these programs, provided you knew which switches to throw.

Today, the situation has become more flexible. Both Microsoft and Netscape have continued to improve their products by incorporating more add-on programs into the browser itself. This means that when you click on the appropriate hyperlink, the file is displayed within the browser; no separate window appears. This works for many things, including basic graphics file viewing, moving videos in various formats, and audio files. But a host of data types and formats remain unsupported within the browser. To use them, you must get the software and install it; in most cases, the install program automatically configures your browser to recognize the new program.

The combination of easy-to-use install programs and hooks within the browser that let external programs work closely with it will change the face of the Internet. Rather than working with a huge program that tries to be all things to all people, we have the opportunity to pick and choose which applications are specifically of use to us. This extends our customization of the browser; in the last chapter, we customized its internal options, and in this one, we will add one or more extended capabilities that pick up on the activities we find interesting on the Web. Third-party developers are thus encouraged to push the boundaries of network computing, and because their programs are usually made available either for free or through demonstration copies that let you evaluate them, you'll have the chance to participate in some of the Web's most exciting developments.

This chapter is designed to walk you through the process and help you discover the tools you need to make your browser fully functional. When you're through, you should be able to view everything from on-screen animations to live video; you'll be able to explore archives of radio shows, read magazines on-screen that are formatted exactly as their printed counterparts, and view compelling presentations wrapped in video effects and sound. Finding and installing these programs keeps you one step ahead of the game as third-party programmers change the Internet. My recommendations are only starting points, of course, but they're designed to show you what I consider to be a minimally equipped browser for today's Web.

Most of the plug-ins I talk about here work only with the 32-bit version of Netscape Navigator, which means that you have to be running your Internet connection through Windows 95 or Windows NT's TCP/IP stack to make them work. If you're able to run only a 16-bit version of Navigator under Windows 3.1 or Windows for Workgroups 3.11, be advised that some (though not all) of these plug-ins will function, you should check download pages carefully to make sure you are requesting the version designed for the correct operating system. And note: In most cases, I have given you the home page for the plug-in developer in question, rather than a URL that takes you directly to the file. This is to prevent a change in the file structure at the site causing the address to fail. You may need to browse the home page to find the necessary link to the plug-in, but in all cases, the links are obvious.

Plug-in and helper applications are a way of making the Internet more interactive. Both Microsoft and Netscape have also built two other innovative technologies that download from the Web page and run on your own machine into their browsers. One is the Java programming language; it uses small programs called *applets* to create lively effects on a Web page. These applets are downloaded without user intervention and they bring life to an otherwise static screen. Both Netscape and Internet Explorer now support Java, and Microsoft is actively developing its own ActiveX technology, a different take on making content come alive (and one that can be viewed in Netscape through another plug-in). We'll examine Java, ActiveX, and the fascinating world of virtual reality in Chapter 8 when we look at the Web's breakthrough technologies. In that area, too, we'll see that third-party applications are significantly extending the range of our browsers.

Plug-in Programs Extend the Browser

But first, a word about terminology. A *plug-in* is a Windows program that allows you to add viewers for sound, video, animation, and other kinds of Web page effects. A plug-in can turn Internet content into an interactive event, sending a continuously updating ticker of news events across your screen, or showing you a live concert complete with audio and video. It can put you in touch with radio stations around the world, many of them broadcasting live. It can produce screen effects with punch, a novelty to those used to a static and unmoving Web interface. These programs, also known as add-ons and helper applications, are critical weapons in your Internet arsenal, so we'll walk through basic installation requirements and discuss how you can find plug-ins and keep up with new versions. The list of plug-ins has grown large enough that what I show you here can reflect only my own views as to the most important ones.

Tip: A good source for information about browsers in general and plug-ins in particular is the BrowswerWatch page:

http://browserwatch.iworld.com/

Here you'll find breaking news about the latest plug-ins, a useful gathering point given how fast events are occurring in this sector. The site includes a complete list of plug-ins and a month-by-month breakdown of new applications.

Each new browser generation will incorporate more plug-ins, much as word processors evolved by folding in tools from desktop publishing and other forms of high-end editing. An early word processor used a third-party dictionary or thesaurus program, and had to be linked to external programs to edit graphical images or manipulate pages for proper layout. Today, word processors are all-purpose packages, design tools that have effectively subsumed most of the products originally built to support them. In the same way, browsers have become more self-sufficient, so that a newly downloaded copy of Netscape Navigator provides you with everything you need to perform many multimedia tasks. But the browser also provides a plug-in architecture that allows you to add third-party solutions. This is important because it encourages the industry to continue its innovation, finding new ways to display Web content.

Netscape today includes former plug-in tools, including support for streaming audio, streaming video in two different formats, and three-dimensional virtual reality. Think of *streaming* as meaning *real time* or *continuous delivery*—you listen or view content without having to download a file first. The program also supports Sun Microsystems Java language and JavaScript, a language based on Java, which promotes interactive Web pages with dynamically updating pages. Finally, Netscape is now available with built-in support for Internet telephony in the form of the CoolTalk program. It was Netscape 2.0 that added Java as well as the crucial plug-in technology to the basic browser package; version 3.0 refined that model.

Tip: In programmer talk, we refer to Netscape's *plug-in API*, a term you'll doubtless encounter if you read a few computer magazines or check into sites that discuss browsers on the Web. API stands for Application Program Interface. An API is the set of software resources that enable programmers to create basic interface features, so a plug-in API is the set of tools that programmers use to connect external programs to the browser, thus making it possible for those programs to run from within the browser when activated. The CGI standard we discussed in Chapter 2 is one way to make Web pages more interactive, but APIs are more desirable. They need less memory; moreover, server programs can remain connected to client software after each information request, a function CGI cannot perform. Because of this, a server can store information passed along by the client and recover it when a new connection is initiated by that client. Moreover, APIs are easier to customize, which is why Webmasters like them; they can more easily integrate their own programs into the operations of the server.

What Plug-ins Do

What is the purpose of all these tools? Whether included in the base program or available as plug-ins, applications like these are designed to bring full multimedia capabilities to Web sites designed to exploit them. Some plug-ins are designed to let you play back or display content built with desktop applications. You can, for example, download a plug-in to view a presentation developed in Microsoft's popular PowerPoint program, while similar plug-ins from other developers handle file formats based on other software. Asymetrix, for example, offers a plug-in that lets you work interactively with files created with its multimedia authoring software.

But you can see the dilemma already. Many of these plug-ins operate with only one particular file type. Web Player, a plug-in from Gold Disk Astound, will not display a PowerPoint presentation, while Macromedia Director, a plug-in for multimedia applications, can't display files created by Asymetrix software. We run the risk of needing plug-ins from each software house, an ultimately untenable situation given the constraints of disk space and user patience.

Plug-ins take time to download, and each requires installation if it's not built into the browser. And while plug-ins are relatively easy to link to the browser, tools have yet to be developed for plug-in management, making it difficult to tell which plug-ins you have and which you need. A final problem: A plug-in might disable other plug-ins previously installed to work with the same file types, creating confusion and perhaps a system crash. All in all, plug-ins are fertile ground for growth but still present difficulties that will be remedied only as install and uninstall routines are improved and browsers provide better controls for their management.

With today's Netscape, however, you can call up a screen of information about your existing plug-ins. To do so:

1. Pull down the Help menu.
2. Click on About Plug-ins.

The screen shown in Figure 5.1 will appear. While the screen provides only limited information and no install or uninstall functions, it does give you a quick overview of the plug-ins now operating in your system.

Figure 5.1 This screen provides Netscape information about the plug-ins that are currently installed and where they're located on your hard disk.

Tip: Another way to check your plug-in situation is to look in the Plugins folder. In Netscape 3.0, this folder appears in the Program folder within the Netscape folder. A double-click on this folder will reveal a series of .dll files. These are dynamic link library (DLL) files, all of them needed by the various Netscape plug-ins. The first two letters of each of these files will always be np. Thus Npaudio.dll is obviously a .dll file of significance to audio functions. The point, though, should be obvious: You shouldn't have to be trolling deep into the Netscape folders looking for .dll files when all you want to do is to manage your plug-ins. Future iterations of the browser should incorporate a plug-in manager that allows you to try the plug-ins of your choice, evaluate them, and easily discard the programs if you decide they don't measure up to your expectations.

MIME Formats and Browser Configuration

Netscape can use a plug-in as though it were built into the program from the beginning, while maintaining its own interface and command structure. Operations like the History list, basic page navigation, and other Netscape features aren't affected by the work of the plug-in. Remember, we need plug-ins because they handle types of data that Netscape can't normally handle. When the browser encounters a Web page offering data of an unknown type, it looks to see whether it has a link to a plug-in that can handle it; if so, it loads the plug-in and displays the result.

Data types are determined through so-called MIME, or Multipurpose Internet Mail Extensions. MIME was developed as a standard for sending nontextual information as part of an Internet mail message. Such information could include everything from video files to spreadsheets, sound files, graphics, photographs, or word processor documents. In broader terms, MIME file types have become a standard way of identifying the kind of file we are talking about and how that file can be sent over the Internet before being converted back into its original form for display or playback. Servers on the World Wide Web use MIME to identify the kind of data they are sending to their clients.

Tip: It's easy to confuse plug-ins and helper applications, but there is a difference in how the browser treats them. Helpers are actually external programs; Netscape can send data to such a program to display that data as needed, but when you've viewed the data, it will remain in its separate window until you close it. Plug-ins work more closely with the browser, using programming hooks built into the software, and are displayed from within it. When you finish with a plug-in and move on, Netscape is able to exit the plug-in as though it were a part of the browser itself; there is no need to close down a separate program. In both cases, you are able to see the data, but the helper application, being external, is not, strictly speaking, a plug-in.

In real-world terms, however, the distinction between helper applications and plug-ins is quickly becoming obscured. Is RealAudio a plug-in or a helper application? It's actually a plug-in, but when we download it in the next section, we'll see that to listen to a RealAudio file, the click on the linked audio will usually launch a separate program that appears on your screen (Netscape does this automatically). Yet RealAudio can also play within the Web page itself (you don't see the separate program box), and in other respects functions as a plug-in. In popular usage, the term plug-in has taken on the meaning of "any application that enhances the browser's functions by adding the ability to read a new data type." The distinction is obviously more significant to developers than to end users.

Netscape offers a screen for specifying its helper applications and associating them with specific MIME types so they can operate within the browser. In Figure 5.2, you can see the Helpers tab, which is accessible in the following way:

1. Pull down the Options menu.
2. Choose General Preferences.
3. Click on Helpers.

Here you can see the file types listed in the window at the top of the screen, which is presented in a scrollable field. The particular MIME type highlighted is then displayed within the Helpers box, along with its subtype, file extensions, actions associated with it, and the name and location of the helper application to which it applies. Highlighting a different type results in a change to the information within the rest of the tab. Note: Only the UNIX and Macintosh versions of Netscape currently show plug-ins in the Helpers tab; the Windows 95 version (as well as the Windows 3.1 version) shows only helper applications. To examine plug-ins, check the Installed plug-ins screen.

In the Helpers tab, you can see that the highlighted file type is application/x-cu-seeme, which is the format used by the CU-SeeMe videoconferencing tool. The Action column refers to the player used to display the data referred to by the particular MIME type; the CU-SeeMe player is listed as Cuseem32, as you can confirm by looking at the bottom of the screen next to the Browse button, where the filename, Cuseem32.exe, and the path to the file are displayed.

Now look back at the top right of the Helpers tab. The Extensions column shows the particular file extensions associated with each MIME type. Files

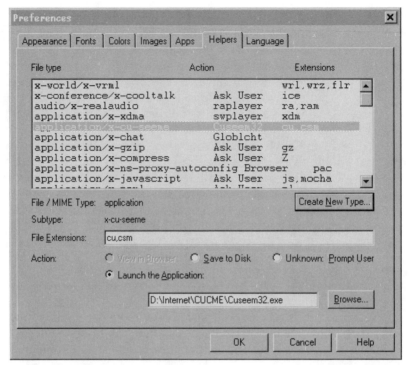

Figure 5.2   The Netscape Helpers menu, which identifies plug-ins and the MIME file types associated with them.

made available in CU-SeeMe format can be found with two different extensions, .cu or .csm. This is important, because it tells Netscape that when it encounters a file with this extension, it should launch the CU-SeeMe program. The file extension is also displayed in the File Extensions field toward the bottom of the Helpers tab. Note, too, that we are given a choice of actions:

View in Browser	Causes the information to be displayed within the browser, provided that this particular file type is supported.
Save to Disk	Causes the file to be saved to your hard disk.
Unknown: Prompt User	Causes a dialog box to appear, giving you options for disposing of the file.
Launch the Application	Launches an external application.

As you can see, the CU-SeeMe player requires that it be launched as a separate application. But if we were to click to highlight a different helper application, we might find that the View in Browser button was used. To view a file in the JPEG format, for example, I click on the file on any Web page where I find it, and Netscape displays the image without having to launch a separate application to handle the task.

In addition to providing background information about helper applications, the Helpers tab can be used to configure a particular program. Today, more helpers and plug-ins are ready to go once installed; the installation program itself establishes the correct settings within Netscape. But some applications will install themselves on your computer without creating the necessary connection to Netscape. For these, it's necessary to read their documentation, which includes instructions on how to edit the Helpers tab to include the file type they manage. I'll demonstrate how to handle this process later with another key helper program called StreamWorks.

Macromedia Shockwave: A Must-Have Plug-In

Let's examine how a plug-in can be downloaded and installed by carrying the process through with Macromedia's Shockwave plug-in. This set of tools is designed to bring enhanced interactivity to Web pages, including animation and various types of audio and visual effects. Adding animation, sound clips, video, and other forms of high-resolution screen effects to a Web site makes the page fun to view, but it requires the right software. What Macromedia has done is produce a plug-in that incorporates a complete range of interactivity in a single product. A site that uses Shockwave is said to be "shocked," and the powerful capabilities of the software have enabled numerous businesses to create vivid advertising, virtual tours of catalogs, animated company logos, and a variety of other eye-catching effects. Prominent firms using the technology include Disney, General Motors, Sony, MCI, CNN, and Paramount. But you can't view any of these special effects without the right software, which for now, involves installing the files, although Microsoft and Macromedia are making arrangements to include Shockwave eventually in the Windows 95 operating system itself.

Tip: Shockwave is actually a bundle of several software components, including Shockwave for Director, Shockwave for Freehand, and Shockwave for Authorware. Director is a multimedia authoring tool—a program that helps designers create multimedia applications, first created for the Macintosh but now available across the major computing platforms, including Windows. Using Director, they can create so-called movies, which are actually combinations of animation and sound. Shockwave for Freehand allows them to use Freehand graphics on the Internet, just as Shockwave for Authorware allows the use of that format on the Web.

The Shockwave toolset provides multimedia functionality for the Internet, by making it possible to enclose Director-style movies in an HTML page. You should view Shockwave, then, as a file viewer for particular types of content, movies that have been created on the Web using the Director product along with other Macromedia tools. The uses of the "shocked" page are broad, but they clearly extend to entertainment, where games can be enhanced by a variety of visual effects, and to advertising and marketing, making a company's Web site a colorful and lively place to be. Even those pages that don't employ multimedia for major effects will still benefit from offering animated logos and unusual display features.

Downloading Shockwave

The Shockwave plug-ins are available from the Macromedia Web site:

http://www.macromedia.com/

and you can see the Shockwave download screen in Figure 5.3. Notice that it includes a form asking for user information, and provides various pull-down menus to help you choose the correct version of the software for your computer.

Having filled out the on-line form (and notice that in this instance, most of the fields are optional, and can thus be left blank if you choose), you are now ready to click on the Get Shockwave button to initiate the download. A click produces a Security Information box, advising you that the information you are transmitting is not secure and could theoretically be intercepted by someone else on the Internet. This is a standard warning, but as we'll see in a later chapter, a common-sense approach to Net security encourages us to send non-vital information without worry. Click on the Continue button to send your information. The site will now produce a list of FTP sites from which you can download the product; you can see this screen in Figure 5.4. In general, choosing a site close to you is the best approach; it minimizes network congestion.

Note that installation instructions are provided via a link on this page. Your next step should be to follow this link and print out the ensuing instructions. This can be done easily within Netscape by:

1. Pulling down the File menu.
2. Clicking on Print.
3. Clicking on OK in the Print box.

Printing out installation instructions is always a good idea; it allows you to check any particular tips that the developers of the plug-ins may pass along regarding their product. This is not a matter of trifling detail, either. Because the plug-in process isn't standardized, you can expect some to be better than others, especially with regard to their installation. A little time spent printing out any relevant information can result in fewer headaches when you try to install a product only to find that its installation routine is tricky and you need help.

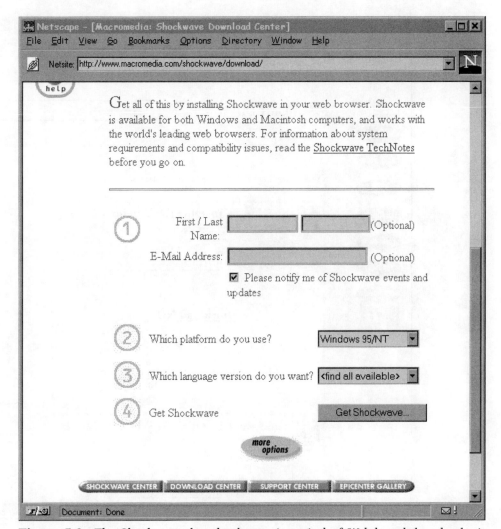

Figure 5.3 The Shockwave download page is typical of Web-based downloads; it includes a form and information about the product.

Having printed out the instructions for installation, you can now return to the previous screen and click on the Download Now link. Now you are in familiar terrain. As explained in the previous chapter, downloads follow certain conventions. The Save As box will appear over part of the Netscape window, allowing you to select the place to which you'd like to download your program. You can choose any destination you wish depending upon the organization of your hard disk. In my case, organization is important; I like to know exactly what program is sitting where, so I set up separate folders for each plug-in, thus making it easier to locate and remove them if I decide they're not for me. As a part of this, I've created a Software Unpack folder

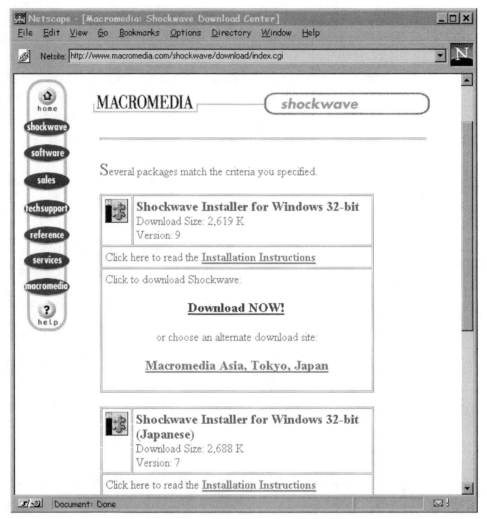

Figure 5.4 The site selection screen for Macromedia's Shockwave software allows you to pick the FTP site closest to you, thus minimizing network congestion.

where all downloaded files go; after they're installed, I can remove their install program or save it to their own folder if I choose. This method keeps my hard disk from becoming too cluttered with unneeded installation programs.

A click on the Save button begins the file download.

Tip: Plug-ins vary in length, and your download time will depend upon not only the speed of your modem, but also network conditions and the load upon the server you're accessing. Don't be surprised if things seem noticeably faster one day than another; this is just normal network variation. The beauty of multitasking, of course, is that you can proceed with other work while waiting for a long file to download. But the broader question is, given the number of plug-ins and the download times required, how much time are you willing to put into collecting them? A judicious attitude is to use those that have proven themselves in the user arena, acquiring others only as reliable reviews validate them for your browser. Collecting each and every plug-in may be an absorbing hobby, but it's a guaranteed way to reduce productivity.

Installing the Software

Having downloaded the software, you should now exit your browser to run the installation, as advised in the Macromedia installation instructions. I would also recommend closing all other Windows programs at this time, to prevent conflicts that may disrupt the installation.

The actual installation is surprisingly simple:

1. Locate the Shockwave installation program by clicking on the Windows 95 My Computer icon.
2. Double-click on the file to launch the program.
3. Follow the instructions that appear on your screen.
4. Restart your browser.

The installation proceeds through a software *wizard,* a program that makes the difficult decisions for you and allows you to get the program up and running with a few mouse clicks. You will be prompted for your choice of browser (choosing between Netscape Navigator and Internet Explorer); a progress bar will then display the course of the installation. After this point, the installation program will offer you the chance to read a file that lists program updates and other news. The installation is now complete. From this point, you will be able to access Shockwave-enabled sites by entering their URLs in your browser.

Viewing the Shocked Site

The best way to get a look at Shockwave is to visit some of the sites that are now using it. Bear in mind that some of these sites may take some time to load, given that the files they are accessing can be relatively large; while they're loading, you'll be looking at nothing more exciting than a Macromedia icon. Nonetheless, Shockwave does a remarkable job of compressing information so that developers can achieve interesting effects even over a 28.8Kbps modem connection. An example is a page created by DC Comics, accessible from the directory of Shocked sites at Macromedia itself (http://www.macromedia.com/).

Here the effect is very much that of watching an animated slide show. In one presentation, for example, for a comic book called *Sovereign 7*, you are shown an animation of a house with a view that changes as you watch, even as various audio effects play over your speakers. An illustration showing both the writers and artists working on the comic book as well as its major characters now appears, along with two arrows; using these, you can move the field of view to the left or the right, while along the bottom of the screen, animated logos provide additional information. Moving the cursor over any of the people in the illustration causes that person's name to pop up at the bottom of the screen. Clicking on one of the people's images creates a pop-up screen with a drawing of that person and a scrollable, personal message concerning his or her work at DC Comics or his or her role in the Sovereign 7 universe. All mouse clicks are followed by lively, comic-style sound effects.

The DC Comics project is mirrored by rival Marvel Comics, both companies obviously realizing that the potential uses of Shockwave-style animation ideally suite their own type of content. The Marvel site (http://www.onslaught.com/shock/main.htm) is even livelier, with thunder-and-lightning screen and sound effects and the howl of wind coming through the speakers as the page loads. The story line is based on the popular Marvel comic book *The X-Men,* and deals with a new threat to their existence, which can be explored by following links. On-screen tickers feed information while characters' eyes flash, and eerie sounds add atmosphere to the experience.

But Shockwave effects aren't confined to animators. A company called @dver@ctive, based in Chapel Hill, North Carolina, uses Shockwave to highlight its home page in intriguing ways. Menu items are surrounded by icons that pulse, while messages flash and change color as various Shockwave items are loaded. This company (http://207.69.132.225/) specializes in creating Shockwave effects for advertisers, so it's no surprise that its own work should be loaded with interactivity, color video, and supporting sound. Icons display textual information when you move the cursor over them; text assembles itself out of a blank background; images create themselves on-screen and swing into motion. An interactive radio icon swells to full-screen size, lets you click on a choice of stations, and feeds jazz into your speakers, with a clickable volume control. A library of Shockwave effects is available for developers to download.

The important thing is that the user doesn't have to take any special pains to view Shockwave-enabled sites. When properly installed, a good plug-in takes over the transaction: After you've clicked on the icon to travel to the Shocked Web site, Netscape will launch a second copy of itself, in which the Shockwave site will appear. This can be confusing, because the Back and Forward commands within that window will affect only your experience within the Shocked sites you visit, just as the Go menu will include a history of only those sites. You need to remember that when you want to return to your previous on-line work, you must click on the other copy of Netscape, which will take you back where you started. The second window can then be closed.

Shockwave's popularity seems destined to increase rapidly, given its recent deal-making activity with Microsoft, so we'll see the number of such sites rise dramatically in the coming year. Beyond animating icons on home pages and providing effects for advertising, we'll see much more development in the area of interactive games, and perhaps experimental use in education and training. As to the latter, check what Tufts University has done with an animation called *Synapse—The Movie*, which is used in undergraduate neuroscience courses, graduate and medical neuroscience courses, and postgraduate neurology and psychiatry curricula throughout North America. The on-screen version provides a snippet of the film, but points to the ability to house educational modules on the Web in Shockwave format. Or consider the Bayeux Tapestry site at http://orion.it.luc.edu/~mfoys/bayweb.html, which provides a movable view of parts of this famous tapestry. I recommend checking the Macromedia home page (http://www.macromedia.com/) frequently to look for new sites like this and other innovative uses of Shockwave.

Other companies, of course, are working on Web-based animation and multimedia presentation. In particular, you will want to check out the following:

http://www.narrative.com/: Narrative Communication's Enliven, a plug-in for viewing multimedia presentations.

http://www.futurewave.com/: FutureWave Software's FutureSplash, a plug-in for animations created with the company's software.

http://www.golddisk.com/: Gold Disk's Astound Web Player, for viewing presentations created in the Astound and Studio M formats within the browser.

http://www.totallyhip.com/: Totally Hip Software's Sizzler, a streaming player for real-time animation and multimedia for files in Sizzler format.

http://www.excite.sfu.ca/NCompass/: Ncompass Labs' NCompass OLE Control, a program that lets OLE (Object Linking and Embedding) controls operate inside HTML pages, executing them when pages are retrieved.

http://www.spco.com/asap/asapwebs.htm: Software Publishing's ASAP WebShow, a viewer for on-line presentations in the WebShow format.

http://www.mbed.com/: mBED Software's mBED, a plug-in for the display of animation and presentation-oriented materials.

http://www.micrografx.com/: Micrografx's QuickSilver, a plug-in handling interactive graphics.

Streaming Audio: The Sounds of the Internet

Progressive Networks' RealAudio program has more or less taken the Internet by storm by offering audio content in a new format. So-called streaming audio plays audio content as soon as you click on the appropriate icon. Streaming audio is a sharp contrast to previous methods for providing sound on the Web. In the early days of Mosaic, for example, to hear audio, it was necessary to download an audio file. When you clicked on the file icon, the browser would download it and, if you had configured Mosaic to send the download to a helper application, you could then hear the file. The problem: The download process took time, and audio files, unlike text, were relatively large. That inevitably consigned audio to a minor network role; after you had downloaded a few audio clips and listened to them, the relatively short playback time coupled with the lengthy download process made it seem easier to stick with text. In fact, most audio files worked on a 1-to-5 transfer ratio, meaning that it took five times as long to download the file as it did to play it back. An hour-long radio show, in other words, would take five hours to download.

Streaming media changed all that. When you clicked on a RealAudio file, the sound began to play almost as soon as the RealAudio plug-in was launched. And rather than being consigned to a short playback time, RealAudio content could be continuous. It was possible, for example, to access archives of radio shows—National Public Radio was an early entrant in this arena with a library of its *All Things Considered, Talk of the Nation,* and *Science Friday* shows. Even live audio became possible, with radio stations offering their broadcasts over the Net in real time. Click on the icon and suddenly you were receiving audio from a station that might be located virtually anywhere in the world. And though the sound wasn't as good as real FM radio, later versions of RealAudio and other streaming media players upped the quality surprisingly.

Tip: How fast is fast? In modem terms, a 28.8Kbps modem is close to the maximum, although 33.6Kbps modems have begun to appear. But in broader terms, 28.8 kilobits per second isn't much— it works out to a throughput of roughly 3.6 kilobytes per second (8 bits make up a byte). Consider that even a single-speed **CD-ROM** player can transfer up to 150 kilobytes of data each second, making it 40 times faster than your new modem. This is the data bottleneck, and why developers have to resort to compression technologies to pump streaming audio and video into your machine.

Streaming audio provides other useful capabilities. In the days of huge file downloads to listen to audio, you didn't have the option of sampling a file to see if it interested you. To listen to even a few minutes of audio required that you download the entire file. Streaming audio lets you begin to play the file, then change your mind and close it, moving on to the next possibility. Another key difference is disk space. A 30-minute radio show in digital form takes up a lot of storage, whereas streaming audio does not store the file on your hard drive, meaning you can listen to as many radio shows or concerts as you want without overloading your hard disk. Finally, most streaming audio players let you move quickly to a different part of the file. If you're stuck in a tedious description of a band's travel arrangements, for instance, you can fast-forward to the point where they begin to play.

RealAudio: An Upscale Audio Player

Beginning with Netscape 3.0, streaming audio capability has been built into the browser through its LiveAudio plug-in. But you'll need to acquire the latest version of the RealAudio program as well, because it operates on files that work with different formats from those supported by LiveAudio. File formats are pesky things because there are so many of them, but once you've got the browser running, Netscape's LiveAudio plug-in can handle the following formats:

AU	The most common of all audio formats.
AIFF	An audio format originally developed by Apple Computer and now in common use. Designed for high-quality audio for speech and musical instruments.
WAV	Microsoft's audio file format, used by Windows 95.
MIDI	Musical Instrument Digital Interface. The format for the exchange of information between musical instruments and computers.

And when you add the RealAudio plug-in, you'll be able to deal with files in the RealAudio native format. Considering the diversity of content now appearing for the RealAudio player, this is a format you won't want to miss.

The current version of RealAudio offers sound that is perfectly understandable and enjoyable, and the number of sites offering content in this format is growing rapidly. Clearly, RealAudio is a tool you need for your browser. Its VCR-style features are easy to use, with volume control, pause, fast-forward and rewind functions that let you navigate through a sound file, replay parts of interest, and move easily between files. And while a 28.8Kbps modem is optimal for this kind of work, a 14.4Kbps unit will suffice for pleasurable listening.

Tip: Just how does streaming audio work? By compressing incoming data so that it more closely matches what your modem can provide. A streaming audio program includes a *codec*, or compression/decompression unit. Built in to it is the compression function itself and a player that unpacks and plays the audio stream. Because of the amount of data provided by an audio transmission, the audio file can't be reproduced exactly. Using so-called lossy compression, the codec represents the original data in its own format, with some loss of sound quality. In general, the higher the compression, the more the likelihood of distortion. The playback function of a well-designed codec will reassemble the compressed data and present it in a form so close to the original that for all intents and purposes, what you are hearing on the computer is what you would have heard on the radio. Where the difference will be the most noticeable is in the realm of music (although this is improving); for most talk shows, it hardly matters. And if everything works the way it should, the codec will buffer incoming data, storing it so that the player always has audio data to work with and no delays from the server result. At least, that's the theory. In reality, packet loss of various kinds occasionally occurs, resulting in choppy sound and sometimes arcane sound effects.

Compression uses mathematical formulae to reduce the amount of redundant data available in a given file. In video programs, if a certain screen background remains static while the person in front of it talks, that background can be represented by a formula produced by the compression software, thus reducing the total amount of data that must be continuously sent over the network. Some scenes are more susceptible to radical compression than others, but the important thing to realize is that the image you see is not the original but a cleverly constructed simulacrum of it. The difference between Internet video and standard television is painfully obvious.

To get the RealAudio program, visit the Progressive Networks site at http://www.realaudio.com/. You can see its home page in Figure 5.5. System requirements for the program, assuming a 28.8Kbps modem, are these: at least a 486/66 CPU with 8MB of RAM, a Windows-compatible sound card, and 2MB of free disk space.

To download RealAudio, follow the links to the download page. As with Shockwave, the download requires that you fill out a form, selecting operating system, processor speed, type of connection; and supplying your name and e-mail address. Note that you will be able to download (and pay for) the commercial version of the product, which includes a number of enhancements, or the basic player, which is free for individual use. The program will install itself on disk and configure itself to work with Netscape Navigator; it will also configure itself automatically for Internet Explorer and most other browsers.

Listening to Files with RealAudio

To launch a RealAudio file, simply access a page with a link to one and click. For example, Figure 5.6 shows the archive at National Public Radio for its *Science Friday* program, available off a link at the RealAudio site. (http://www.realaudio.com/contentp/npr/scifri_index.html).

A mouse click on any of these programs causes the RealAudio program to launch the player. An illustration of the RealAudio player is shown in Figure 5.7. To listen to the program, you need do nothing; the software will add content to the buffer for a few moments and the audio will begin. The program can be stopped by a click on the Pause button, or closed entirely by clicking the close box in the top right corner. Note, too, that you can slide the indicator with your mouse to move back and forth within the program; RealAudio will hesitate as it locates the new portion of the streaming content; it will then play back the show from the point you have chosen with your mouse.

Numerous sites are bringing RealAudio content to the Internet, so the best thing to do is to look for directories; these give you a listing of pages you'll want to visit for the various kinds of audio content now available. Some of the better choices are these:

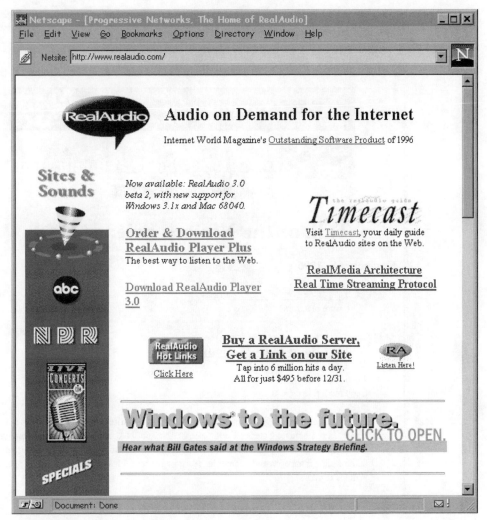

Figure 5.5 The RealAudio site offers one of the Internet's major attractions, a player for live audio content.

The RealAudio home page (http://www.realaudio.com/), with links not only to National Public Radio, but also to ABC, and collected sites covering everything from movie reviews to old-time radio shows.

Timecast (http://www.timecast.com), a guide to daily programming in the RealAudio format. This one is particularly useful at locating new sites.

The DJ (http://www.thedj.com/, a wonderful site for music lovers, with a wide selection of styles.

NetRadio (http://www.netradio.com/), for Netwide radio.

Audionet (http://www.audionet.com/), a comprehensive directory of live radio, archived talk shows, music, sporting events, speeches, and other audio content.

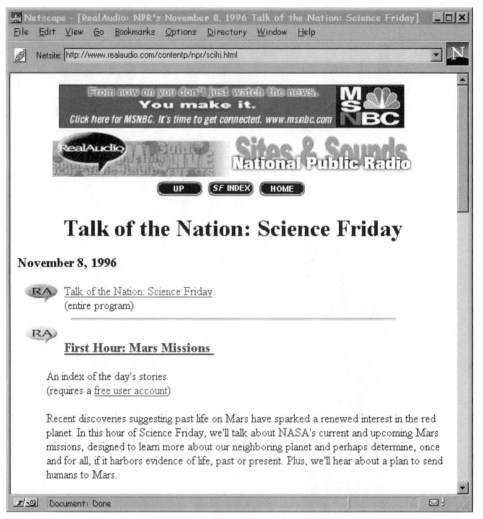

Figure 5.6   National Public Radio maintains an extensive archive of radio shows on the Internet.

Tip: Don't minimize the importance of streaming audio technology. Today it's being used to enliven advertiser's pages and to provide links to stored music and live radio. But archival sites like the one provided by National Public Radio indicate where this is all heading. We have a whole battery of tools, for example, in the battle to organize textual libraries of printed books, magazines, and newspapers. But multimedia libraries are more challenging—along what principles should they be organized, and how cataloged, and how made accessible so that finding what we need is as easy as using a library's card catalog or on-line search engine?

With RealAudio and similar technologies, we can foresee the day when vast collections of audio materials will be fully switchable; that is, they will be usable when and where we need them by clicking on the appropriate icon.

I use NPR like this all the time. While I enjoy shows like *All Things Considered*, I rarely have time to listen to them in their entirety, and even when I do, I often miss crucial parts of a given story because someone is talking near me, or I become busy doing something else (I usually listen while I'm cooking dinner). A tape recorder would make it possible to play back the show later, but then I would be reduced to listening to it in its entirety, just as with the live broadcast, to find out what was in it. With an audio archive, I can find links to each NPR story within a given day's *All Things Considered* broadcast. I can then decide to listen on one, or two, and no more than these, and can decide whether I'll listen the week after they're broadcast, or next month, or next year, because the archive, once on-line, remains available. This is how I've uncovered some extremely useful interviews locked in the NPR archives that have helped me not only in my computer work, but in my studies of classical languages and physics and astronomy.

Numerous other firms are experimenting with audio technologies from the standpoint of plug-in players as well as various kinds of editing tools. Their sites are always worth visiting for updates and links to Web pages with audio. They include the following:

http://www.syntrillium.com/: Syntrillium Software's Cool Edit 95, a sound editor that works with a variety of audio formats.

http://www.vocaltec.com/: VocalTec's Internet Wave, an audio player that works with the streaming Internet Wave format.

http://www.liveupdate.com: LiveUpdate's Crescendo Plus, an audio player for MIDI files.

Figure 5.7 The RealAudio player, showing its VCR-like controls for manipulating audio content.

http://www.prs.net/midigate.html: PRS Corp.'s MidiGate, a helper program for playing MIDI files accessible from Web pages.

http://www.voxware.com/: Voxware's ToolVox Web Player, an audio player with unique playback capabilities; you can adjust the speed of the audio on the fly.

http://www.yamaha.co.jp:80/english/xg/html/libhm.html: Yamaha's MIDPlug, a player for MIDI music files.

http://www.dpsg.com/: DSP Group's TrueSpeech Player, an audio player that works with the Windows 95 Sound Recorder.

It's not likely you'll work with all of these, but it's not a bad idea to keep an eye on these companies if you're interested in audio developments, and in streaming technologies in general. Companies like them are pushing the boundaries of multimedia on the Net and developing the products that will become standard issue in the future.

Video (Live and Otherwise) on the Web

Audio isn't the only thing that can stream on the Internet, as these last technologically turbocharged years have proven. It was in 1993 that the first rock music concert was broadcast, or "cybercast," on the Internet, showcasing a band made up of members of the Xerox PARC research team. The broadcast made use of the MBONE, or Multimedia Backbone, technology then being developed, which allowed for the transmission of audio and video simultaneously over the Net. The Rolling Stones put cybercasting onto the map with a 1994 concert, while The Grateful Dead's late-1995 concert at San Francisco's Fillmore theater was backed with a Web site and included digital photographs and a live chat with band members after the concert. Clips of the band could be accessed from around the world along with real-time views of the action at the Fillmore.

Since then, the movement of live multimedia content over the Web has grown apace. Whereas early uses of the MBONE included such technically focused events as meetings of the Internet Engineering Task Force (the group that helps to establish standards for Internet technologies), more recent uses of live multimedia have focused on social issues. The Future of Hope teleconference took place in late 1995, linking former president Jimmy Carter with South Africa's Nelson Mandela and Israeli prime minister Shimon Peres; and popular music continues to widen the audience: Jimmy Buffet's 1996 Net concert was a smash. All signs point to a multimedia future encompassing talk shows, museum tours, sporting events, and any other type of cybercast in which video and audio combine to deliver unique content. In fact, the ability to back the cybercast with the tools of the Web trade—electronic mail, linked newsgroups, graphics, chat—means that the Web takes video and audio into an interactivity far beyond the range of standard television.

But video is also a challenge. Fast-moving technology invariably means differing standards for everything from file formats to compression techniques. Differing standards can mean different plug-ins, and as you'll see, you have your choice of two interesting formats for the plug-ins I'll show you. And live video is only one of your choices. Video can also appear on a Web page in the form of playable files. CNN Interactive, for example, includes links to short videos that support its news stories, all playable through the QuickTime plug-in that was built into Netscape starting with version 3.0. The well-equipped browser is one that can handle all these formats, which calls for several new plug-in acquisitions as we proceed. It also calls for a computer with enough muscle to handle the demands of streaming media. To buffer and extract incoming material requires a minimum of a 486-based PC running at 66MHz or better, and 8MB of RAM.

The InterVU MPEG Player: Downloading a Video File Viewer

To understand the video challenge, you should know that there are two ways of proceeding. In the first, you download a file and play it back on your own machine. Some players require that you download the file before you can see it, but others use streaming techniques that let you view the file as it is being downloaded, while also preserving it on disk for future viewing. Streaming video downloads are imperfect at best; it's far better to wait for the entire download than to expect to see anything but jerky and uneven video over a modem connection. As you'll see, other forms of streaming video offer a superior alternative.

Tip: If streaming video downloads aren't that attractive to watch, why offer them at all? One reason is that downloading video takes time, since video files are large. With streaming techniques, you can get a glimpse of the video as it's arriving and make a decision about whether you want to download the whole file. If the video doesn't seem interesting, you can simply stop the download by clicking on the Stop button or pressing the Esc key.

Video files are made available in several major formats:

QuickTime	This is Apple Computer's video format for the Macintosh. Netscape included streaming QuickTime capability beginning with version 3.0. QuickTime movie files use an extension of .mov.
Video for Windows	This is Microsoft's Video for Windows format. AVI stands for Audio Video Interleaved files; these are recognizable by the file extension of .avi. Netscape built in the LiveVideo plug-in to its browser starting with version 3.0, again with

MPEG

streaming video capability. While widely distributed, AVI files are at a disadvantage compared to the MPEG standard, next. In comparison to MPEG files, they are generally much larger.

MPEG is named after the Moving Pictures Experts Group, a committee of the International Standards Organization that creates video compression standards. MPEG is a form of compressed video that can provide full-screen 30-frame-per-second video images on the desktop, either from hard disk or from a CD-ROM. MPEG-1 refers to computer-based video on the Internet, while MPEG-2 is designed for broadcast applications. This is a demanding format, as you might expect; optimum MPEG use requires either a Pentium processor with at least a 100Mhz clock speed and 16MB of RAM or a video card that can decompress MPEG files. Before MPEG, video on a PC screen tended to be small-scale; the image would open in a tiny window on the screen, and video quality wasn't high. MPEG offers a dramatic upgrade to that situation, which is why it has been so widely embraced by software developers, particularly in the games industry. The file format for MPEG is shown by the .mpg extension.

With viewing capabilities for .mov and .avi files, Netscape provides two-thirds of the necessary file viewers, although you'll still need to acquire a viewer for MPEG files. I recommend you consider InterVU's MPEG Player plug-in. The program will play MPEG-1 video from any Web server, including videos that are embedded within Web pages. You can view them during the download or play them later from your Netscape cache or hard disk. Best of all, it's free. You can find the InterVU MPEG Player at http://www.intervu.com/. You can see the InterVU home page in Figure 5.8.

The player will run on a 486-based PC as well as a Pentium, but a clock speed of at least 66MHz is needed for reasonable video performance. To install the program, click on its icon and the set-up routine will run. The InterVU home page contains links to numerous sites that make video in MPEG format available.

StreamWorks and VDOLive: Real-Time Video Players

When you use the InterVU MPEG Player, the program downloads a video file to your disk and saves it for later viewing. Other players work through tight coordination between client and server, using compression on the server end and a client-based player for viewing content. The latter do for video what RealAudio does for sound, playing the content as it arrives in real time, and like RealAudio, they do not save files for later viewing. And each of them works in its own format, meaning that player and server must understand each other.

Figure 5.8   The InterVU site is where you'll find the player you need to handle MPEG files.

And as with audio, transmission challenges center around the bandwidth bottleneck. In both audio and video, the answer is compression. As the technology has evolved, several companies have emerged as major players in this arena. Xing Technologies offers a product called StreamWorks, a downloadable helper application for Netscape that can be configured for a variety of transmission speeds depending on your connection. VDOLive from VDOnet offers similar capabilities, but as is the case in many areas of Internet development, the two offer formats that are incompatible—you can't use the VDOLive player to view content in the StreamWorks format, or vice versa. To get started in real-time streaming video, I recommend StreamWorks, after which you can download the VDOLive player for comparison. Keeping up with video developments will demand you keep an eye on both these companies.

To download StreamWorks, access the Xing Technology Web site at http://www.xingtech.com/. You can see the Xing home page in Figure 5.9. The download requires that you fill out a simple form, and installation follows a standard set-up routine after you click on the icon for the downloaded file. The Xing Technology home page contains a contents guide from which you can select video in StreamWorks format. Options include television from KSL in Salt Lake City, pop music from Capitol Records, as well as numerous radio and Web-based sites, live concerts, music videos, talk shows, Telecom Finland's

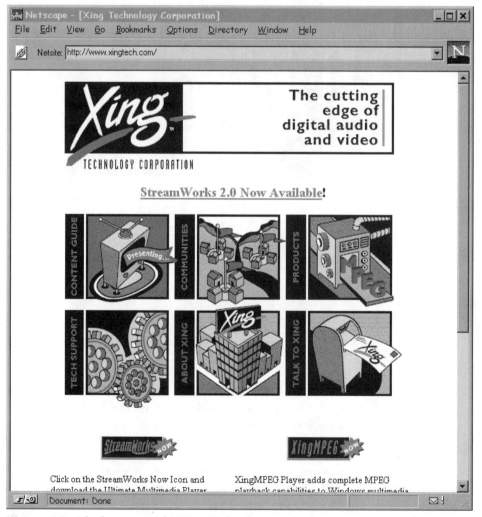

Figure 5.9 The home page for Xing Technologies, where you can retrieve the StreamWorks audio and video player.

MediaLab site, and an audio book club with readings from novels and plays (I'm actually listening to classical music via WKSU radio at Kent State University as I write this).

Tip: After traveling the Internet for a time, the term TCP/IP gets to be second nature. But you should also know about another protocol, UDP. User Datagram Protocol is a way to deliver a data stream across the Internet that can be faster than TCP methods because the client program is not required to acknowledge the receipt of data packets. TCP is a reliable protocol because of its receipt of each data packet; when packets are lost, they can be retransmitted. When speed is at a premium, as it certainly is in the realm of streaming video, UDP makes a great deal of sense; both Xing Technology and VDOnet use UDP. But UDP also has a downside. Because packets are not acknowledged upon arrival, the server doesn't know if one has been lost. This can result in missing video frames, so developers have had to factor into their software ways of working around missing data while still producing an acceptable image. The image degrades in quality but, as long as the packet loss isn't severe, you still get a picture you can see.

Interestingly, it's possible to connect directly to a StreamWorks site from the StreamWorks player without going through the browser, if you so choose. The player maintains a useful history file that can take you quickly back to sites you've previously viewed. Another feature I like about StreamWorks is the ability to switch Web sites after the program has loaded; the audio or video material will continue to play as you move around the Web. StreamWorks is shown in action in Figure 5.10.

The VDOLive player from VDOnet can be found at the company's home page: http://www.vdo.net/. VDOLive is well distributed on the Internet; in fact, VDOnet's technology is being used by such heavy hitters as CNN and CBS to display their programming. The program runs as a plug-in and can likewise run as a stand-alone application. One notable feature of VDOLive is the degree of control it provides over audio and video. Figure 5.11 shows VDOLive in operation.

Tip: Needless to say, the lack of standards for Internet-based video is one of its greatest detractions. It's as if my General Electric television could only pick up channels that were piped through General Electric's own licensed transmitters, while remaining unable to view programs being sent to Magnavox sets. What that means for you is that keeping up with the various video formats requires you to take up disk space with multiple programs, switching between them depending on what's available at the site.

There are some signs that this cumbersome situation may be about to change. A new standard called Real-Time Streaming Protocol is backed by many of the Net's major players, including Apple Computer, Progressive Networks (of RealAudio fame), Netscape, IBM, Macromedia, and Sun Microsystems. Standards like these aren't visible to end users, but they benefit them because they encourage developers to create more multimedia content. Similar standards processes have proven successful with both FM radio and television through the NTSC, or National Television Standards Committee, which established the basic ground rules for the broadcast of television signals.

Other companies are working on video technologies, both video players and streaming video applications. Their programs include:

Digigami's CineWeb, a plug-in player that handles most popular video formats (http://www.digigami.com/)

Iterated Systems' ClearFusion, a player for AVI files (http://www.iterated.com/)

FlatCracker Software's MediaSauce, a multimedia viewer for various formats of audio and video (http://www.flatcracker.com/)

Vivo Software's VivoActive, a player for compressed video (http://www.vivo.com/)

Vosaic Corp.'s Vosaic, an up-and-coming video player for compressed video streams (http://www.vosaic.com/)

Figure 5.10 Viewing TV station KSL in Salt Lake City through StreamWorks.

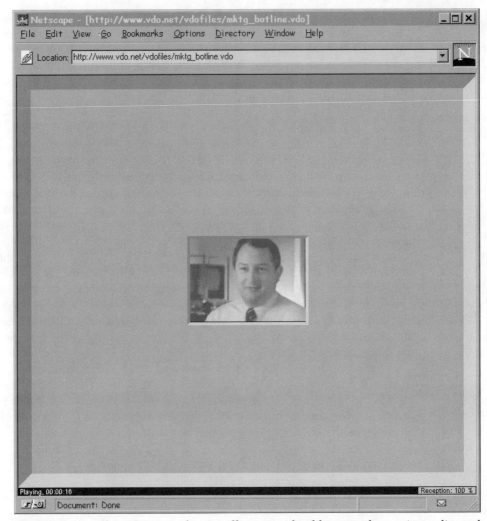

Figure 5.11 The VDOLive plug-in offers considerable control over its audio and video features.

Duplexx Software's NetToob, a multimedia player for video that handles multiple formats (http://www.duplexx.com/)

CU-SeeMe: Teleconferencing and Live Events

The advent of small and relatively inexpensive video cameras has brought two-way video into the range of possibility for Internet users. The technology offers something similar to what the old idea of a video telephone seemed to promise: You make a connection and both watch and talk to the person on the other end of the line.

A free software program called CU-SeeMe is one way to explore this new medium, and the good news is that even if you're not enamored of the idea of having a camera track your every move, you can still watch while other people take part in these sessions. And an increasing number of live events are being carried over the Internet using CU-SeeMe as the software of choice.

CU-SeeMe was developed at Cornell University, where you can acquire the free version (http://cu-seeme.cornell.edu/); the university has also licensed commercial rights to the product to White Pine Software, which has released a commercial variant (http://www.wpine.com/). The program works with CU-SeeMe servers, called "reflectors" in CU-SeeMe terminology. Having connected to a reflector, you can choose which connection you want to activate and click to view it. Participants are shown in small video windows offering a black-and-white image (the commercial version offers color), and a set of audio and video controls are provided. The program supports up to eight windows on a single screen. And CU-SeeMe is something more than a tool for hobbyists. Because companies can set up their own reflectors, it's possible to create a business reflector that broadcasts within a corporate-wide intranet, useful for company messages and video presentations. Organizations as large as The World Bank are using CU-SeeMe for conferencing.

You can download the program from a link on the primary CU-SeeMe page at Cornell or get Enhanced CU-SeeMe directly from White Pine Software. In addition to adding support for color, White Pine has boosted its performance and tuned up its interface. But be advised: a 28.8Kbps modem connection is the bare minimum for viewing CU-SeeMe sessions. Unlike the other plug-ins and helper applications we've looked at, CU-SeeMe won't configure itself automatically for your browser, so you'll need to make the adjustments yourself. Here's how:

1. Pull down Netscape's Options menu and click on General Preferences.
2. Click on the Helpers tab.
3. Click on the Create New Type button.
4. In the MIME Type: field, enter x-cu-seeme.
5. Click on OK.
6. In the File Extensions field, enter cu, csm.
7. Click on the Launch the Application button.
8. Click on the Browse button to find the CU-SeeMe executable file on your hard disk.
9. Click on OK.

CU-SeeMe deserves a place in your software library because of its importance in the developing world of Internet video. In Figure 5.12, you can see the program in action. Here, I am looking at a user engaged in conversation. You can see the audio and video controls adjacent to the video window.

Figure 5.12 CU-SeeMe at work. The program includes audio and video controls for the connection.

Reflector sites aren't always available, so don't be surprised if logging on takes more time than you would have thought; you may have to try numerous sites before making a good connection. But sitting in on a live videoconference for the first time is a thrill that will probably have you experimenting often with CU-SeeMe.

Tip: A good way to keep up with events carried by CU-SeeMe servers is the CU-SeeMe Event Guide page at www-personal. umich.edu/^johnlaue/cuseeme/default.htm.

What's ahead for videoconferencing are solutions from the major software players. Intel Corp. and Microsoft are already working together to add video capabilities to Microsoft's NetMeeting software (built into Internet Explorer), while making Intel's own ProShare software Internet-capable. Intel is also working with MCI on two protocols for improving bandwidth factors for such traffic. And Netscape, which supports audio conferencing already (as we'll see in the next chapter), has plans to add video to its CoolTalk plug-in to Navigator. The outcome seems clear: The Internet will increasingly be seen as a carrier for business and personal video applications, even if performance on today's network remains problematic.

Tip: Get used to a new set of acronyms when you deal with videoconferencing. One new protocol is RSVP—Resource Preservation Protocol; another is RTP—Real-time Transport Protocol. RSVP helps the application reserve bandwidth for its data needs, while RTP improves network response time. In addition, the International Telecommunications Union (ITU) has approved the H.323 standard covering voice, data, and video communication on networks. An adjunct to all this is ULS—User Location Service— which links a person's electronic mail address to his or her IP address, a powerful tool given how fast addresses can change on the Net today.

You may also find it interesting to look at another plug-in that offers a collaborative solution. It's called look@me for Windows (http://collaborate. farallon.com/).

The Printed Page On-Line: Adobe Acrobat

When it's necessary to put printed content into on-line form, publishers have always tended to roll their eyes. The problem in the Internet's early days was that the easiest way to reproduce content was to place it on-line in ASCII format, meaning that all the formatting, from boldfacing to font changes, was lost. An ASCII file was text and nothing more. The World Wide Web brought obvious graphical benefits to such content, including rich graphics and font capabilities, but there are still publications that can't easily be reproduced using HTML, even though HTML 3.2 has been beefed up with tables, style sheets, and frames.

Which is why Adobe Acrobat emerged. Using it, editors and publishers could capture the printed page with great fidelity. That makes the Acrobat Reader a useful weapon in your plug-in arsenal. Using it, you can read documents that have been posted in the PDF format that Adobe developed to represent documents, based on its PostScript language. PDF stands for Portable Document Format. Unlike HTML, PDF files require a separate, proprietary viewer for display, but they can display type designs and layout with greater precision than HTML. They can, for example, show text in multiple columns, wrap that text around graphics, display multiple typefaces and perform the old layout trick of curling text around a large initial capital letter. Nor is Adobe alone in offering such features, although Acrobat is probably the best known of these tools. Other names in the portable document field are Common Ground's Digital Paper and Envoy.

Tip: Ponder the design issue for a moment. If you're the editor of a printed journal, you can use a portable document format to reproduce your pages with great precision. For business, this may be a crucial need in distributing material to remote offices; it is likewise much easier to render archival publications into a portable document form than to adapt them for HTML. But the question of whether printed journals *should* attempt to reproduce themselves exactly in this medium is still up for debate. After all, while columns work on the printed page, they aren't necessarily optimum for reading on a computer screen; and hypertext itself takes standard text well out of the realm of conventional publishing. All these issues will have to be faced as we go through the coming shake-out in publishing. Some print publications will make a successful transition, offering both traditional paper versions as well as enhanced electronic texts, while others will fall by the wayside.

An Acrobat document can be seen exactly as it was originally created, giving editors and designers the ability to distribute worldwide without compromise to their editorial charter. The only requirement at the other end is that the user have a copy of the Acrobat Reader software. The link between Acrobat and the Web has tightened, with inclusion of links to Web sites within the Acrobat document, so that while the two formats pursue their own lines of development, Acrobat will maintain its links with Web pages. And unlike previous versions, Acrobat documents can now be viewed within your Web browser. What seems to be happening is not so much a battle between HTML and portable documents but a growing connectivity between the two, so that publishers can choose which works best for their situation.

You can download the Acrobat Reader by following links off the main Adobe page at http://www.adobe.com/. The program will install itself as a plug-in to both Netscape and Internet Explorer. When you've downloaded it, you'll be able to access pages created in its format. The beauty of Acrobat is that it allows users working on incompatible computer platforms to exchange documents without worrying about incompatible file formats. We should begin to see more documents appearing as PDF files as businesses see the benefits of distributing documents like internal reports, magazines, and brochures over computers. They'll especially like Acrobat's ability to share documents produced by spreadsheets, word processors, presentation, and page-layout packages. Figure 5.13 shows an example of the Acrobat reader at work. This is InterText Magazine, an on-line journal specializing in fiction (http://www.etext.org/Zines/InterText/).

The reader software gives you control over most aspects of the magazine's on-screen display. You can, for example, click on any portion of the text to

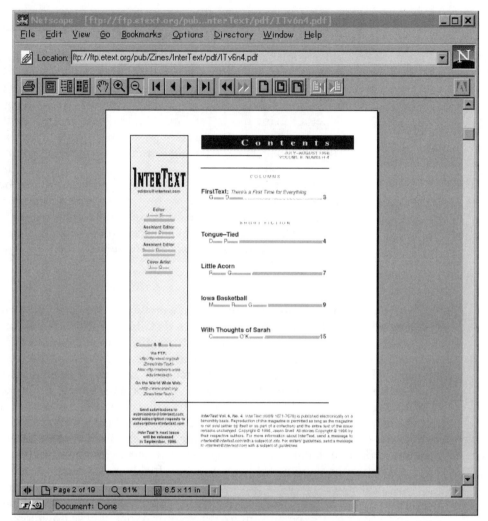

Figure 5.13 InterText Magazine brings fiction to a Web audience using Adobe's Acrobat format.

expand its size, as shown in Figure 5.14. You can move about in the text with a table of contents displayed in a split screen for easy navigation. Note, too, the icons along the top of the display window, which provide, like Netscape itself, basic movement commands—a click takes you to the beginning of the document, another to the end.

The Adobe home page is a good place to look for links to sites using the PDF format. Here are some interesting ones to get you started:

http://www.irs.ustreas.gov/prod/cover.html: This site provides IRS tax forms, an obvious instance where the on-line version of a text must exactly parallel the printed version.

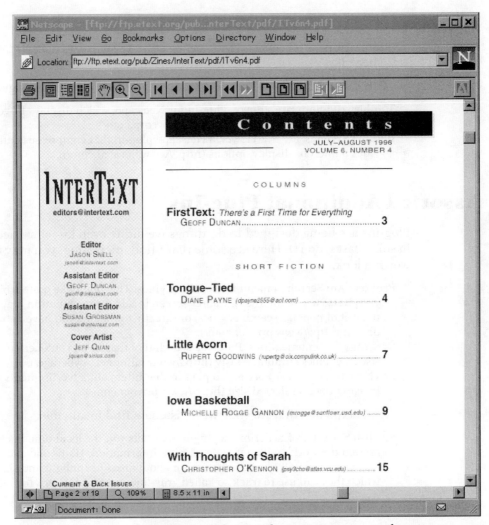

Figure 5.14 Using the Acrobat reader to enlarge text on-screen; the program provides numerous display controls.

http://www.windowatch.com/: WindoWatch Magazine bills itself as "The Windows Magazine of the Internet."

http://www.interink.com/escape.html: E-scape is an on-line magazine specializing in speculative fiction.

http://www.aas.org/ApJ/: The Astrophysical Journal is published by the American Astronomical Society.

http://www.si.edu/reader/acrobat.htm: This site houses on-line documents from the Smithsonian Institution, including exhibits like *World War II GI: The American Soldier's Experience* and *Underwater Photographs from the Belize Barrier Reef*.

http://www.cdsar.af.mil/air-chronicles.html: Air Chronicles contains journals published by the U.S. Air Force.

http://pathfinder.com/time/special/thefiles.html: Selected articles from *TIME* in PDF format.

http://www.pcworld.com/currentissue/toc.html: The current issue of *PC World Magazine*.

Other companies now working with intriguing display technologies include:

Tumbleweed Software's Envoy Plug-In for Netscape, which displays Envoy documents within the browser (http://www.twcorp.com/).

Iterated Systems' Fractal Viewer, a Netscape plug-in that compresses data and provides numerous display options (http://www.iterated.com/).

Assorted Additional Plug-Ins

Plug-ins are being designed to do things we didn't even know we needed (and in some cases, don't). Here are some that I find interesting; you may find them worth a look.

PrivNet's AnySearch, a menu for search engines. This one I like quite a bit; it alters your Netscape or Internet Explorer screen to add a search button that takes you to a list of popular search engines, or directly to the one you have defined as a default (http://www.privnet.com/).

CyberAge Communications' Raider, a search tool that helps you query multiple search engines simultaneously (http://www.miint.net/~cyberage/).

PrivNet's Internet Fast Forward, a plug-in that filters out advertisements and images above a selected size (http://www.privnet.com/).

And here's one that we shortwave listeners find invaluable:

Starfish Software's EarthTime, a plug-in that tells you the local time in cities around the world, with a variety of other information. Hams and shortwave radio listeners will like its information about areas of sunlight and shadow, which they can use to track so-called gray-line communications for maximum reception.

6

The Uses of Electronic Mail

The World Wide Web is always credited with putting the Internet into the public consciousness, but electronic mail remains the single most widely used of all network tools. I make a distinction between the two because the Web, strictly speaking, doesn't carry our electronic mail traffic. Instead, mail flows through its own set of Internet protocols. One of the many beauties of the browser model is that we can use it to read forms of content other than straight HTTP information, and the latest versions of both Internet Explorer and Netscape Navigator include excellent mail readers. In this chapter, I'll explain how to read mail inside Netscape, and the various ways you can use mail to communicate and learn.

Of course, you don't have to read mail with your browser. Although it's the place to start, since it's usually the first piece of Internet software that new users encounter, the browser has competition in the mail arena, just as it does in other areas of network use. I'll show you one such program, Eudora, later in this chapter. As always, the Net offers multiple choices, and a creative tension exists between the developers of specialized programs, including mail, newsreaders, and more, and the browser companies that are gradually adding these capabilities into their products. The best procedure is to get to know your browser's functions thoroughly, and then investigate on a case-by-case basis whether you want to extend them through a third-party program.

The power of electronic mail, as opposed to many other forms of communications, is that it's *asynchronous*. The term simply means that you can send mail at any time; if your recipient isn't on-line at the moment, the message will simply be stored at the remote site until he or she activates a mail reader there. Of course, the post office also handles mail asynchronously, but with a difference. Postal mail can take days to reach its destination; or, if it's sent with priority status, it can be costly. Electronic mail costs you only the price of your monthly Internet account, whether it's sent across town or across an ocean, and it can reach the person on the other end within minutes.

Nor is electronic mail limited to textual data. I routinely ship files in a wide variety of formats across the Internet, knowing that they can be quickly reconstructed at the other end as programs or spreadsheets or word processor documents. Moreover, Netscape makes it easy to work with World Wide Web pages and references to Internet resources. I can set up a mail message with an attached Web page; my recipient can choose to view the page within the browser, or to see a link to that page embedded within the mail message. And when someone writes to me about a new resource they've discovered, providing the URL to help me find it, that URL will itself appear as a hyperlink. Rather than pasting the information into my browser and then activating it, I simply click on the link within the mail message and go.

We think of mail as a one-to-one communications tool, and on that level it has remarkable powers. But it's also a broadcast tool that can reach out from a central site to numerous people. This is the model we use with the Internet's mailing lists. Here, messages about a specific topic are processed on a single computer and then resent to all subscribers to the list. We have the benefit of choosing from thousands of topics, ranging from archaeology to exobiology, and reading the comments of people with similar interests. Using these mailing lists and the computers that manage them will be the subject of the latter part of this chapter. We'll see that reading straight text on a computer screen has by no means been rendered obsolete by the Web. In fact, mailing lists are a wonderful tool for continuing an education or pursuing a hobby.

Configuring the Browser for Mail

Before you can use Netscape to read your mail, you will need to establish the parameters governing its mail operations. To do so:

1. Pull down the Options menu.
2. Click on Mail and News Preferences.
3. Click on the Servers tab.

You'll see the screen shown in Figure 6.1. To fill in the necessary information, you will need to refer to the materials supplied to you by your service provider when you opened your account. These include entries that tell Netscape which computer to connect to when it retrieves your mail and sends back your replies. To understand what's going on here, let's talk for a minute about how the electronic mail system operates.

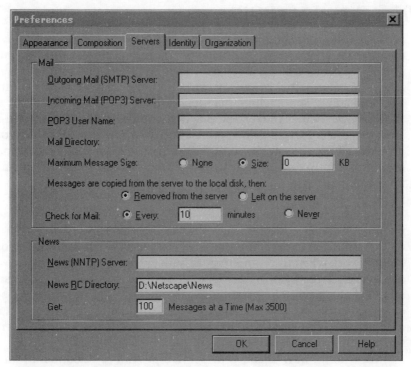

Figure 6.1 The Servers screen allows you to set up the parameters Netscape needs to manage your mail.

Simple Mail Transfer Protocol (SMTP)

We Internet users keep talking about protocols, those agreed methods used on the Net to make basic functions operate. TCP/IP is a collection of such protocols; it includes Internet Protocol and Transmission Control Protocol, both of which ensure that data will find its proper destination and be readable once reassembled there. FTP—File Transfer Protocol—is another major tool, allowing us to transfer files between computers, while Telnet is the protocol that lets us take control of a remote computer to use resources available on it. SMTP is the protocol that drives electronic mail. The fact that SMTP is understood globally means that we can use it to communicate not only with machines on the Internet, but also with computers on other networks.

When you send mail, your browser routes the message to your service provider, who maintains a server running the SMTP protocol. The traffic is then routed out onto the Internet. Examine your service provider's documentation now and insert the address of this server in the Outgoing Mail (SMTP) Server field on the Netscape Servers tab. If you are unsure which address to put here, check with your provider.

Post Office Protocol (POP)

SMTP is only part of the mail story. For modem users, getting on the Web means calling the service provider's computer, performing various network chores, and then exiting. Because you're not necessarily on-line at any particular time, your software can't assume that mail can be delivered directly to us 24 hours a day. That's where the second of the mail protocols, Post Office Protocol or POP, comes in (version 3 is in common use, so you'll see this abbreviated often as POP3). When you receive mail, it arrives at your service provider's POP server. The mail will remain on the server until you use your mail program to download it to your own machine. You are thus able to pick up your mail at a time of your own convenience. When you're ready to respond, your mail program can upload the traffic using the SMTP protocol.

So, as you see, there are two protocols at work in your mail traffic: POP3 for incoming mail messages, and SMTP for outgoing mail. Why not use just one? In fact, SMTP would be sufficient if we were on-line continuously, but it doesn't work when the computers at both end of the connection are not on-line at the same time. Electronic mail doesn't move in real time for most of us, and that's what makes POP3 necessary. In my case, letting the mail accumulate over the course of a day and then downloading and responding to it is the most efficient way to work. The POP3 protocol makes it easy to store my mail on the server until I need to see it.

You should now check your service provider's documentation and insert the necessary information into the Incoming Mail (POP3) Server field in the Servers tab. In many cases, this information will mirror what you've already added in the SMTP field, because many service providers use the same machine to handle mail traffic in both directions. Notice, too, that there is another field here, POP3 User Name. Enter your electronic mail user name here; this is the part of your electronic mail address to the left of the @ symbol (in other words, the address bbarkley@mullens.com would have a user name of bbarkley). If you have any doubts about what to put in any of these three fields, contact your provider's customer support staff.

Completing the Configuration

Several other items must be added to the Servers tab to complete your mail configuration. These are as follows:

Mail Directory   This is where Netscape will house your electronic
                              mail. You can accept the default setting in the
                              Netscape directory or store your mail elsewhere. I
                              always keep mine in a separate directory on the drive
                              where I store all my data files. The reason is that
                              when I run a data backup, I only need to back up the
                              data directory. Programs can always be reinstalled;
                              data can't. If you have any doubts where you want

| | your mail to be stored, simply accept the default setting. |
| Maximum Message Size | This field allows you to decide whether you want to place an upper limit on the size of the messages you receive. The default is None, meaning that you can receive any size message that is sent to you. I recommend that you leave the default in place initially. Should you decide to change it later, click on Size and choose a maximum message size in KB by typing it into the Size field. If you do this, any unsent lines from a given message will remain on the server until you dispose of them. |

The next two buttons govern what happens to mail once you have downloaded it to your machine. You have two choices:

| Removed from the server | Removes mail from the POP3 server after you have downloaded it. |
| Left on the server | Maintains your mail on the server even after you have received it. |

Tip: Why would you ever choose to leave mail on the server after you had seen it? I discovered the answer while traveling. I keep all my mail in a set of folders based on the projects I'm working on, and I wanted to keep those folders complete. But while overseas, I also wanted to check into my mail account to answer pending messages. I used Netscape at an Internet cafe in Scotland to check the mail, making sure to choose the option that would leave mail on the server. By doing this, I was able to return to the United States and download the complete set of mail that had accumulated during my absence, classifying messages as needed into the relevant folders. Once back at my office, I could let mail on the server expire since I already had it on disk.

The next option allows you to tell Netscape how often to check for mail on your service provider's POP3 server:

| Every *X* minutes | Click this button and enter a value in the minutes field. The default is 10 minutes. I check for mail every six minutes. |
| Never | Click here to turn off Netscape's mail check function, and the program will check for mail only when you give it a specific command to do so. |

Now you have to set the necessary default information that will appear on outgoing mail. To do this, click on the Identity tab after completing your work on the Servers tab. In case you already backed out of the menus, this tab is located on the Options menu under the Mail and News Preferences item, right next to the Servers tab. Here, you'll find several fields that need information. Fill in your name and e-mail address, including any organization name you'd like to appear on mail and news postings. If you want to receive replies to your mail at a different address than your e-mail address, you can list it here. The Identity panel is shown in Figure 6.2.

Before you leave this tab, note the Signature File field. Signatures are short statements that are appended to your electronic mail; Netscape will perform this function automatically if you have created such a file. Generally, signature files contain just a name, perhaps an address, and a favorite quotation. Here, for example, is a signature file I've often used:

```
Paul A. Gilster  Freelance Technology Writer  gilster@interpath.com
Author, Digital Literacy (John Wiley & Sons, 1997)
"I ve lost the name of the village, I forget the name of the girl, but the
wine was Chambertin."--Belloc
```

What you put in your signature file is up to you, and of course it's not necessary that you have one at all. But if you do decide to use one, be aware that

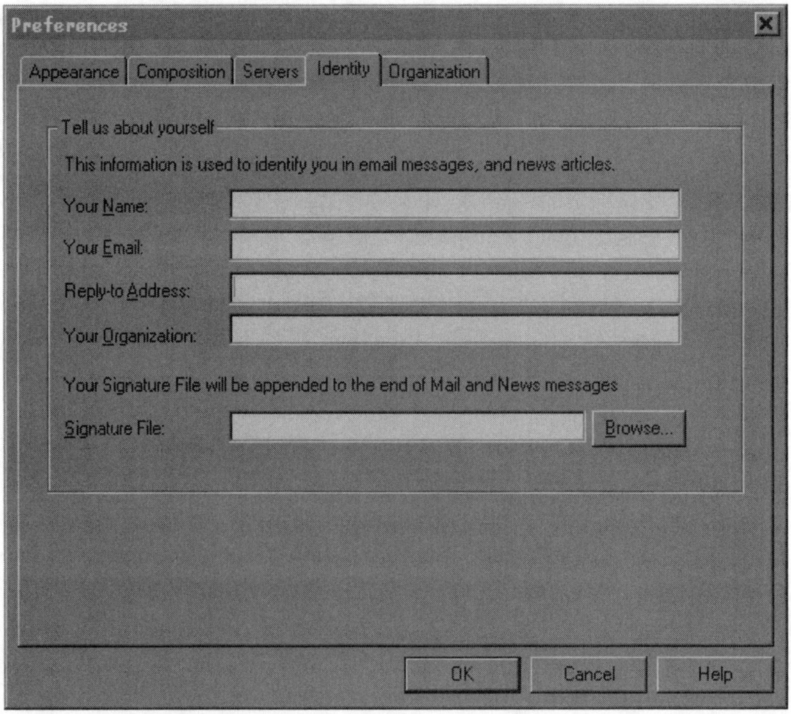

Figure 6.2 The Identity panel shows recipients of your electronic mail who you are.

lengthy signature files are considered bad form; they take up needless space and are regarded as showy. Generally, three or four lines ought to do it. Some people find it amusing to change their quotations often, and I've found some of the best quotes in my database (I collect these things) by seeing what other people have used.

You can create a signature file in any text editor. If you use a word processor, just be sure that you save the signature in a text rather than a proprietary format that will introduce odd characters when sent over the Net. ASCII text format is a universal standard, and all word processors have the ability to save files in it. Simply create the signature of your choice, then enter its location in the Signature File field on the Identity tab. Note that you can click the Browse button if you're having trouble locating the file in question.

Now turn to the Organization tab. Here you are given control over the way mail messages are organized. When messages are *threaded*, they appear adjacent to the original message, so that replies to a particular message, for example, will be clustered together. The default setting is to thread newsgroup messages but not electronic mail. I recommend that you change the default so that mail is threaded.

Click on The Thread Mail Messages Box

I find it very helpful in my own work to see the various parts of a correspondence grouped together, and I think you will, too. You can see the Organization panel in Figure 6.3.

Notice the checkbox at the top of the Organization panel. Your e-mail account doubtless requires a password to let you into the server. If you leave this box unchecked, you will have to supply the password every time you use Netscape mail. It would seem to make sense, then, to click this box, so that Netscape would automatically supply your password. But I am compelled because of security to urge you not to do so. If the box is checked, anyone who calls up Netscape on your machine can get into your electronic mail.

Two other panels are available for customizing mail.

Appearance	The Appearance panel lets you tweak the font you use in your message text and the text of any message quoted in your reply. By default, when you reply to a message, the original will appear at the beginning of your message, a useful way to keep the subject in mind for both sender and recipient. You also have control of the way Netscape presents the mail windows. I recommend staying with the default settings until you get used to working with Netscape mail.
Composition	The Composition panel lets you determine whether you want to use automatic quoting in replies. I recommend the default here as well, unless you find the presence of quoted text to be too obtrusive. Automatic quoting helps when you're engaged in a multipart mail conversation; it reminds your recipient of what he or she has said before.

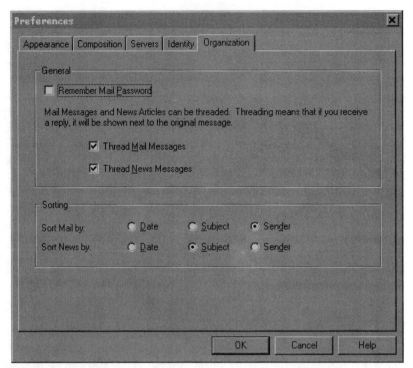

Figure 6.3 The Organization panel gives you control over how messages are presented.

Using Electronic Mail

Netscape is now fully configured to handle your electronic mail. To examine what's in your mailbox:

1. Click on the Window menu.
2. Click on Netscape Mail.

Netscape will produce a prompt for you to enter your password; once you've done so, the program will check with the POP3 server for any mail that is waiting for you.

Reading Your Mail

Netscape provides a number of useful features that make it easy to read and arrange your mail. When you bring up the Mail window, the program will produce a screen that shows any mail currently waiting for you. Figure 6.4 shows a typical screen with a message displayed.

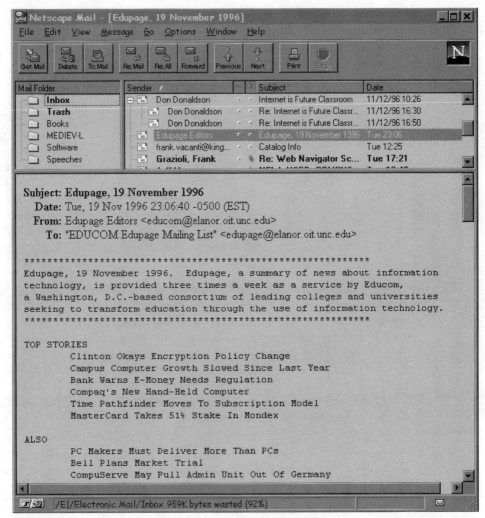

Figure 6.4 The Netscape mail screen, divided into separate panes to show your inbox, where newly arrived mail waits. Individual messages are visible in the bottom pane.

Notice that the screen is divided into three panes, each with its own scroll bar that you can click on to reposition yourself within the text. The top left of the screen is the mailbox pane; here you can see folder icons. Netscape stores your mail in these folders, the active one being the Inbox folder. There is also a Trash folder for messages you have deleted; this can be emptied periodically by choosing Empty Trash Folder from the File menu, but its presence serves as a check against accidentally deleting a message you meant to keep. If you widen the mailbox pane by dragging its right border with your mouse, you'll see that it also contains information as to how many messages are available in the active folder, and how many of these have been read.

Tip: The Mail window is easily changed by dragging with your mouse; simply position it on the boundary between two panes and drag to change the size of each pane. You can also set up changes that are larger in scope. By using the Options menu and choosing Mail and News Preferences, then the Appearance tab, you can choose to see the Mail page with a vertical orientation, or stacked, meaning that the three fields sit atop one another. In Figure 6.5, you can see what the Mail screen looks like when arranged vertically. It's your call, but to my taste, the vertical method is the best; it provides a readily viewable content area while maintaining everything I need to see about my inbox. In fact, I usually narrow the two panes on the left dramatically so that my content area is as large as possible. In most cases, all I need to see about the messages themselves is who their sender is. If I need more, I can always drag the mouse to expand the mail header pane.

Messages in the active folder are shown in the top right window, which is the message header pane. The active message is displayed across the bottom of the screen in the content pane. By clicking on a message in the top right window, you determine which one will be displayed in the content pane; you can also move between messages by using the Previous and Next buttons on the toolbar. Messages that have already been read are shown in the message header pane without bolding; those that have not yet been read are in boldface.

There are several other items of information available in the message header pane; they are shown as columns:

Sender	The person or organization from which the message originated.
Flag status	The flag status appears in the second column under the small flag icon. A red flag icon next to a message means that it has been flagged. You can flag important messages so you won't forget them by pulling down the Message menu and choosing the Flag Message item.
Read status	The read status appears in the third column under the small icon. Messages that have been read show no adjacent icon. Those that remain unread are shown with a green diamond next to them. You can change the read status by pulling down the Message menu and choosing either Mark as Read or Mark as Unread, depending on the message's current status.
Subject	The information in the Subject field of the message.
Date	The date the message originated.

You can use these columns to interesting effect in sorting your mail. A click on Subject, for example, will cause the mail in the message header pane to become sorted by subject; the same trick can be pulled by clicking on Date or Sender. Thus, no matter which defaults you've set for message sorting, you can override them during the current session to look at your mail in a new way.

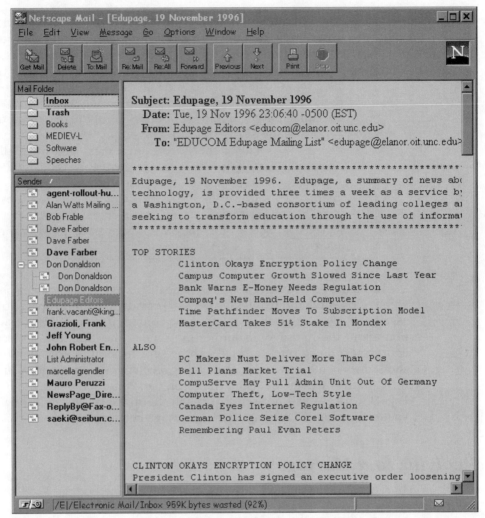

Figure 6.5 The result of changing the Mail window to display its three panes with a vertical orientation; this provides an arrangement some people find easier to work with.

The columns can be resized by moving the cursor over the boundary between two columns and dragging. For that matter, the three panes themselves can be resized by moving the cursor over a boundary between panes. You might do this if you weren't seeing all the necessary information in one of the panes.

Columns can also be rearranged in different order. If you place the cursor on the Subject bar and drag it to the left, for example, the program will show you your messages with the Subject field listed before the Sender field. Even the panes can be adjusted, placed adjacent to each other or stacked, by using the Appearance panel under the Mail and News Preferences in the Options menu. As you can see, Netscape provides ample opportunity for customization.

Tip: While you're working with your mail, Netscape will periodically check the server for new messages, according to the schedule you've set on the Servers panel. But the program will not automatically download new messages when it finds them. Instead, it alerts you to the fact that messages are waiting, and you have to retrieve them yourself. You can do so by clicking on the mail icon, the small envelope in the bottom right of the mail screen.

Netscape also keeps you advised of your mail status through this icon. As long as there are no new messages, the mail icon will remain as is. When new messages arrive, Netscape will insert an exclamation point next to the mail icon, prompting you to click the icon to retrieve them. If you see a question mark by the mail icon, it means that Netscape can't check for mail because you haven't yet opened the mail window, or have not yet supplied your password.

In Figure 6.6, you can see a message displayed in the content pane. I have all but closed the top two panes here to provide maximum space for the message itself. Notice that the top left of the content pane provides basic information about the message, including the sender, the date, the subject, and the addressees. Since Internet mail can be sent to multiple people at once, it is sometimes helpful to know who else is receiving the message. You can move through the message by using the scroll bar. Note that using the PageUp and PageDown keys will not scroll through the message; instead, they will move you to the adjacent message in the message header pane.

Replying to a Message

To reply to a message, you can use one of three methods:

- Click on the Re:Mail icon on the toolbar, which allows you to send a message to the sender of the original message.
- Click on the Re:All icon on the toolbar, which allows you to send a message to everyone who received the previous message, as well as the original sender.
- Right-click your mouse in the message pane to produce a pop-up menu. You can then click on either Reply or Reply to All.

I recommend using a right mouse click for the basic message commands, because it produces an instant menu and gibes with my previous advice to turn off the icons on the main Netscape screen and use right-mouse commands. When you turn off the main window icons, you do not affect the display of

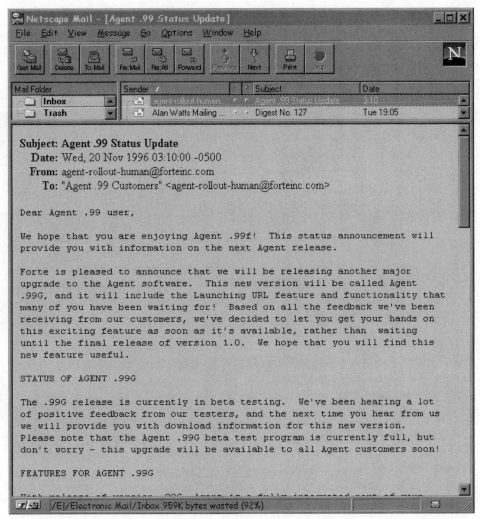

Figure 6.6 A message displayed in the content pane, sized for maximum exposure.

icons in the mail window. But developing the habit of right-clicking provides you with a consistent command strategy.

By clicking on Reply, you will cause Netscape to produce a separate message composition window, available for you to enter your comments. The message you are replying to will also appear with a greater-than symbol (>) before the quoted material. You can see such a message in Figure 6.7, along with my reply below the quoted section.

When you have completed your reply, click on the Send button or pull down the File menu and click on Send Now. You can also choose to defer delivery until you've completed replies to other messages. You might choose

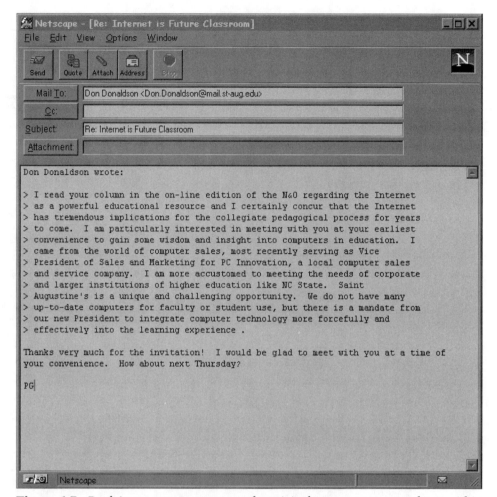

Figure 6.7   Replying to a message causes the original to appear as quoted text within the message composition window.

deferred delivery if you prefer to work with your mail off-line before sending all your messages in a single burst later. To do this:

1. Pull down the Options menu in the Message Composition window.
2. Click on Deferred Delivery.

With the deferred delivery option activated, messages you complete will be stored in the Outbox folder and sent at a later time. To send them:

1. Pull down the File menu.
2. Click on Send Mail in Outbox.
3. Use the Popup menu (see below).

Remember that using the right mouse button will produce a menu that is dependent on context. We saw earlier that you could position your cursor over an image and create a menu that offered various options for that image; if you position the cursor over a hyperlink, the options that appear on it will refer to the page specified by that link. Frame options are likewise shown when you right-click within a frame. In the Mail window, the options change once again, as they do in the Mail composition window. You should explore Netscape in its entirety with right mouse clicks to determine what you can do where. In my experience, using the pop-up menu is the fastest way to accomplish many on-line actions within the browser.

Here are the pop-up menu commands to use in the mail window:

Reply	Enables you to reply to the current message; the address of the sender will automatically be inserted.
Reply to All	Lets you reply to the current message, with copies sent to all recipients of that message, not just the original sender.
Forward	Sends the current message as an attachment. When you choose this option, the Message Composition window will appear, allowing you to send any comment you might wish to make along with the attached message being forwarded.
Forward Quoted	Sends the current message not as an attachment, but as a quoted message within the message currently being composed.
Add to Address Book	Adds the sender of the current message to your address book (see later).
Delete Message	Deletes the current message.
Unscramble	Lets you unscramble messages that have been scrambled according to a technique called ROT-13, in which letters are shifted so as to be unreadable. This method is sometimes used in newsgroups when, for example, a book is being discussed and the poster doesn't want to give away the ending except to those who have already read it. You thus have the option of deciding whether to see the message in plain English or not.

These commands are a subset of the total commands available through the Netscape mail menus, but they comprise the major actions you need to work with the mail program daily.

Deleting Messages

Your most useful command in electronic mail beyond those involved in creating messages themselves will be the delete function. This is unfortunately the case because of the huge increase in the amount of junk mail being propagated over the Internet today. To delete mail in Netscape:

1. Highlight the message you want to delete by clicking on it.
2. Press the Delete key.

Creating a New Message

To create a new message, click on the To:Mail icon on the toolbar, or pull down the File menu and click on New Mail Message (the right mouse button menu won't help you here). Several fields must be filled in here. These are as follows:

Mail To	The address of the recipient.
Cc	The address(es) of any additional recipients. With electronic mail, it's easy to add people here, rather than to send separate messages to each of them.
Subject	The subject of your message. Be as precise as possible in defining the subject, since many people have to deal with a great deal of e-mail and make decisions about what to read based on what they see in this field. In an era where junk e-mail is proliferating, your Subject field should be clear and on the topic.
Attachment	Allows you to attach a file to your message. In my own work, I frequently send articles and chapters back and forth to my publisher by attaching them in this way. Clicking on this button causes a box to appear that lets you search on your hard disk for the file you want to attach. More than one attachment can be made to any message.

One nice feature of Netscape is that you can attach a World Wide Web page to your electronic mail message. The box that appears when you click on the Attachment button will give you this option, and will enable you to send the page as an HTML file or as plain text. When your recipient opens the message within Netscape, the page will appear in his or her browser just as it did in yours. We've moved a world away from older methods of electronic mail, which used to be entirely text-based. Today we can find graphically enriched Web pages and share them with friends and colleagues with a mouse click.

If you prefer not to view a page attachment within the browser, you can set up Netscape to show you only a link to the attached page. Here's how:

1. Pull down the View menu in the Mail window.
2. Choose View Attachments as Link.

When someone refers to a URL in a mail message, the URL will appear as a live hyperlink in the Mail Content window. You can see an example of such a hyperlink in Figure 6.8.

When someone sends you news of an interesting Web page, you need only click on the hyperlink within the message to call up the page in the Netscape window. No cutting and pasting between windows or applications is necessary.

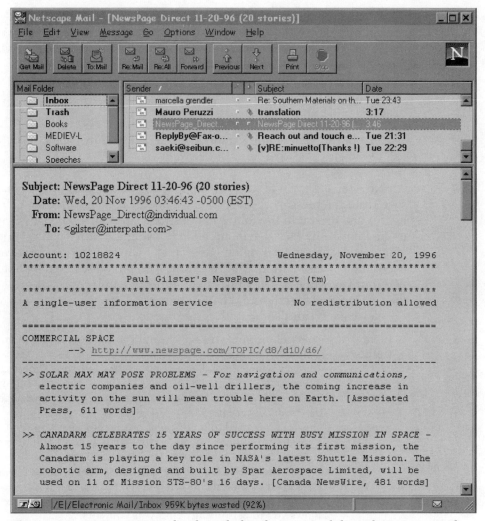

Figure 6.8   URLs appear as live hyperlinks when received through Netscape mail.

Using Folders for Mail Organization

Perhaps the greatest challenge of electronic mail is managing the flow of incoming messages. This is getting to be more of a problem as we move into a commercial Web environment, and our mailboxes begin to fill up not only with messages from friends, but with digital come-ons and advertisements. The best method for managing the mail is threefold: Go through your inbox messages in the message header pane, looking for those that, based upon sender and subject, are obviously not going to need a reply. Delete these using the Delete button, or by using the pop-up menu; you can also pull down the Edit menu and click on Delete Message.

For the remainder, the core of messages you do want to consider, reply as needed and delete those that are of no further use. There is no need to keep messages in your inbox once they've been responded to; if you want to file them for later consideration, go to the next step.

Set up folders for messages you want to keep, arranging them by topic so that they'll be useful markers to help you locate information later. Here's how to set up folders:

1. In the Mail window, pull down the File menu.
2. Click on New Folder.

Now the ease of a mouse-driven program comes into play. To move a message from the message header pane to one of your new folders, simply highlight it and drag it to the folder in question. This can also be accomplished by pulling down the Message menu and choosing the Move command, but dragging and dropping is so much easier that I can't imagine why anyone would choose the other method. Multiple messages can be selected by holding down the Shift key while highlighting them if they are adjacent, or by holding down the Ctrl key and highlighting them if they are discontinuous.

Netscape creates some folders automatically:

Inbox	Holds all incoming messages until you move or delete them.
Outbox	Contains messages you have created but not yet sent. You won't see this folder unless you have specified that Netscape should use deferred rather than immediate mail delivery. This is done by pulling down the Options menu in the Message Composition window and checking the Deferred Delivery item.
Sent	This folder is used to hold copies of the messages you send. You won't see it unless you have specified that such a file should be created by pulling down the Mail and News Preferences menu and choosing the Composition item. On the Composition panel, there is a field that allows you to state the location of the file for sent mail.
Trash	This folder holds any deleted messages. An item on the File menu allows you to periodically empty its contents.

Tip: The day will come when you look upon your Trash folder as the most important item in your mail window. All of us accidentally delete things we meant to keep, but more often, we delete things we felt safe in assuming were unnecessary, only to find out later that we have to use them. If you make it a practice not to empty out the Trash folder more than about once a week, you will be able to go back and retrieve messages like these. Moreover, if you've set mail up to arrange your messages in threads, it becomes easy to recover a complete correspondence. Be careful, then—once you delete the items in the Trash folder, they're gone.

Saving Messages

There will be times when you want to save a message, but not necessarily to store it in a folder in Netscape. You might, for example, want to simply create a text file of the message to save onto disk. If this is the case, here is the method:

1. Pull down the File menu in the Message Composition window.
2. Click on Save As.
3. Choose the directory where the file will be stored.
4. Enter a filename in the field provided.
5. Click on the Save as Type field to choose the format in which you would like to save the file.
6. Click on Save to save the file.

Working with the Address Book

Internet addresses are anything but easy to remember, so it's a good idea to set up an address book that will allow you to insert an address automatically. The Address Book can be found by pulling down the Window menu and clicking on Address Book. To add a particular address to it:

1. Pull down the Message menu.
2. Click on Add to Address Book.

The address of the sender of the current e-mail message will be added to the book. From this point on, you can simply double-click on a name in the address book when you want to send that person a message. This will cause the Message Composition window to open with the address of that person already inserted. You can also manually add addresses for both individuals and lists of users. The Address Book contains a pull-down menu marked Item that allows you to do this. You can see the Address Book in Figure 6.9.

And in Figure 6.10, you can see the result of pulling down the Address Book's Item menu and choosing Add User. As you can see, the Address Book gives you the ability to create an easy-to-remember nickname for the person in question; a frequent correspondent can thus be addressed merely by entering a first name, for example. You can also enter comments or descriptive remarks.

Eudora: An Electronic Mail Alternative

New users will want to master the electronic mail function inside their browsers, and for many people, what Netscape offers is all they will need. But the day may come when you decide to explore programs that have been specif-

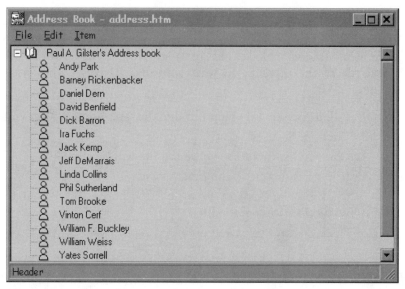

Figure 6.9 The Address Book appears in its own window and allows you to quickly insert an address into a new message.

ically developed with e-mail in mind. Some of these are quite powerful, and one, Eudora, is well worth your consideration whether you use e-mail for business or personal pursuits.

You can see the main screen for Eudora in Figure 6.11. As you can see, Eudora provides many of the same features offered by Netscape, including a

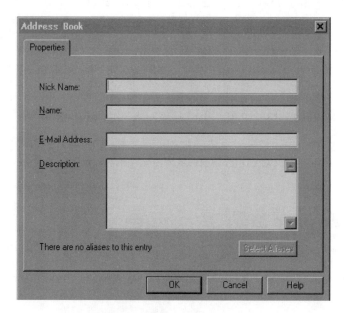

Figure 6.10 Adding a user to the Address Book allows you to create nicknames for the person and to enter descriptive remarks.

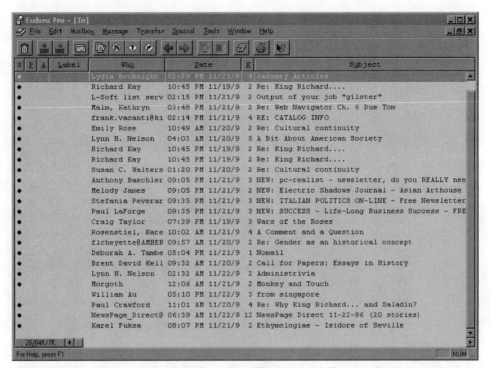

Figure 6.11 Moving beyond the browser offers you a different take on e-mail. Here, the Eudora program is shown displaying the contents of my inbox.

toolbar across the top of the display, and easily understood columns for showing inbox information. A click on any of the buttons—Label, Who, Date, Subject—causes the mailbox to be sorted according to that item. Thus it's easy to arrange a quick re-sort to cluster all the messages sent by a particular person; you can sort by Status, Priority, and Attachments, too.

But Eudora extends the mail program into new directions. One feature I prize is the ability to nest folders within other folders. I've created, for example, a central folder for messages relating to my books; within that folder, I've nested separate folders for each of the titles. The same is true for business projects; I maintain a folder for speeches and presentations that is subdivided according to the project at hand, and is easily changeable as I move through my schedule. The program also contains a range of filing options that can be used to filter incoming mail automatically; and, like Netscape, it allows you to click on hyperlinks within a mail message to activate the browser.

If you're interested in previewing Eudora, you can take a look at a freeware version, which is available at the company's home site: http://www.qualcomm. com/. Or you can download a trial version of the more sophisticated Eudora Pro. You can see a message displayed in Eudora Pro in Figure 6.12.

Attachments and various information items including urgency status of a particular message are shown with icons. Usefully, the program also makes lib-

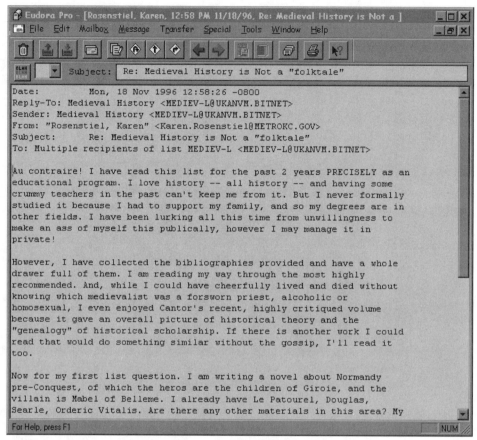

Figure 6.12   Eudora Pro's easily readable interface and useful filtering features make it an excellent choice as a third-party mail program.

eral use of that great time-saver, the right mouse click, to provide quick access to the major commands.

Electronic Mail Manners

You wouldn't think basic etiquette would have become such a hot topic in the high-tech world, but unfortunately, the easy availability of electronic mail has created a new set of issues for Internet users. The worst symptom is one I've touched on, the rise of the junk mailers, who broadcast their messages that hawk everything from million-dollar investments to baldness remedies to users who find themselves besieged with a daily barrage of such material. But e-mail problems go beyond marketing experiments and crude solicitations. This is a culture that has moved steadily away from the written word for decades, but the core of e-mail, despite its recent multimedia additions, is literacy—we use words to communicate. Thus we find ourselves in the uncomfortable position of using written language at a time when language skills have declined. The way to misunderstanding even among the well-intentioned is wide open. And until we've mastered the basic e-mail behaviors, the next sections offer some tips.

Beware the Ill-Conceived Joke

What sounds funny to your friends in person may not translate on the Internet, despite your best intentions. Remember that most of the people you'll be corresponding with don't know you personally; chances are you'll never meet them. Can you be sure they'll get your crafty allusion to an old Bogart line from *To Have and Have Not*, or will they just think you're insulting them? Caution is the byword until you get to know someone's personality.

For this reason, the Net has given birth to a whole range of so-called emoticons, symbols strung together to emulate an expression and thus give added point to a particular comment. You can create emoticons of all kinds by playing with the ASCII character set on your keyboard. Amusingly, in an era when various multimedia aids to comprehension have begun to flourish, emoticons continue to appear, presumably out of the sheer enjoyment of using them. Thus the primary emoticon (look at it sideways):

:-)

This one is understood as a happy face, or "smiley," and you can throw it in whenever you're making a joke that you think might be misconstrued. Ham radio operators do something similar when they use the term "hi," which means "humor intended," and is inserted to make sure that the person at the other end of the connection doesn't take offense at an innocent remark.

If you start playing with emoticons, you can suggest a wide range of emotions. The smiley emoticon can be tweaked with a single character change:

;-)

The use of the semicolon rather than the colon now provides what seems to be a winking eye (again, viewed sideways). Consider the range of suggestion covered in the following two sentences, each driven home by the quality of its emoticon:

I saw you and Linda at lunch today :-)

versus

I saw you and Linda at lunch today ;-)

The first sentence simply seems a happy response to a chance encounter. The second implies a relationship between the two parties that goes beyond what was on the table.

Some emoticons are inscrutable at first glance. I'm told that this one implies a person who has been up all night:

|-|

But I can't say I see the resemblance. And how about this one, which means a person's lips are sealed:

    :-#

Whether you use emoticons in your own correspondence or not, you're bound to encounter them in your Net travels. Their very presence reminds us that when dealing with people we don't know, it's not a bad idea to use whatever tools are at hand to clarify our remarks. If emoticons can help to do that, they're not a bad thing, but avoid overuse. There's nothing as tedious as a message with too many emoticons.

Keep the Word Count Down

This advice is offered not because the number of words you write presents major problems to the Internet, but because some correspondents, like some telephone callers, have a tendency to drone on. Since we're all getting more electronic mail than ever before (and a short stay on the Internet will see the same thing happening to you), now is the time to aim for conciseness in the messages you send. Bear in mind that, for many people, going through e-mail is a task squeezed in amongst other workaday chores. Unless you really know the person you're addressing, try to keep queries or comments short and to the point.

Use Descriptive Titles

An intelligent use of e-mail is to go through your inbox listings with an eye to weeding out anything that looks superfluous. This can mean that occasionally something good gets tossed out with the bad. To avoid this fate, your e-mail should be tagged with a short but descriptive subject line, so that it precisely states what you are talking about. Mail tagged with subjects like "Make a million dollars" go out of my mailbox without reading, but a message whose subject is "Internet access fees" is one I will probably read; it's on a subject I find both important and interesting. But what about a message marked "Hello"? The subject gives me no clue whether it's a query or a sales come-on. Obviously, I try never to delete a personal message, but given the number of mailing lists I receive, it sometimes happens by accident. A clear subject will help.

Use Obvious References

Electronic mail is so easy to send that we sometimes forget people may not remember what we said in our last message. On occasion, I've received cryptic e-mail from people I know, containing messages like "OK," or "You're right." What do these mean? In most cases, I can't remember what the reference is, and if it's a confirmation of a meeting or a friendly gathering, I'm absent-minded enough to want more. Netscape gives you the ability to quote from e-mail messages easily; use this capability to lift out the relevant portion of the

message you're responding to, following it with your own comment, as in the
following:

    <<How about lunch next Thursday at 12:30 at Simpson's?>>
    Sure, I'll be there.

Now the reference is clear and we'll both show up at the same restaurant.

Don't Waste Bandwidth

Quoting is obviously valuable, but I receive too many messages in which the
entirety of what I said earlier is parroted back at me, when all I needed was a
snippet. When you reply to a message and quote from it in Netscape, you can
easily edit the quoted section so that only the relevant part appears in the
returned text.

Be Conscious of Prying Eyes

It's highly unlikely that anything you send by Internet e-mail will be intercepted, but there is no way of knowing for sure. In the absence of encryption
(and we'll discuss encryption options in Chapter 11), follow this principle:
Don't put anything into electronic mail that you wouldn't feel safe saying aloud
to anyone you know. The medium is insecure enough that spilling too many
secrets onto the Net may bring you grief. The odds don't favor it, but why take
chances until Net security is airtight?

Treat Electronic Mail like Physical Mail

By which I mean, be mindful of the impression you're making with an electronic mail message. People who go out of their way to send a formalized and
carefully composed letter through the postal system sometimes send poorly
spelled and ungrammatical mail to the same people. This hardly matters
between friends, but it's interesting to learn that people in business receive
sloppy and ill-advised missives via e-mail from job candidates or potential
partners. It's as if, because e-mail is fast and can generate a quick response, it's
not taken seriously. But in today's world, this is a mistake. Electronic mail will
increasingly play a role in our communications—many companies, for example, advertise for workers *only* in cyberspace, the theory being that only those
people capable of reading the advertisement are qualified for the job. Treat
your e-mail seriously.

The Internet Mailing List

One of the great joys of electronic mail is that it gives us the capability to use
an Internet mailing list. Yet, for many, it's an unappreciated asset. New to the
Internet, we log on and begin exchanging messages with friends and acquain-

tances, gradually widening our sphere of interest as we run across people in newsgroups and through Web pages. Mailing lists tend to fade into the background in the graphical world of today's Web. And that's a shame, for the moderated discussion of ideas, with participation from experts in their respective fields, is the kind of resource the Internet was made to deliver. Indeed, mailing lists were among the earliest Internet communications, springing up to handle traffic on a wide variety of topics in the early days of ARPANET. They've only increased since.

Unlike a newsgroup, a mailing list is sent to your mailbox—you need no special mailing list software to read it. You subscribe to a list by sending mail to the computer that manages it. In most cases, the operation is automated; you send your message in a specific format that the computer can understand, and you are signed onto the group. In other cases, the list is managed by a human being, and you simply request that you be added to it, and shortly thereafter, you will receive a message giving you background and particulars about the group; and not long after that, the first messages will begin appearing in your mailbox.

Thousands of mailing lists are now available, covering a range of topics as comprehensive as those available through the USENET newsgroups that we'll discuss in Chapter 7. No matter what your interest, you'll probably find a mailing list frequented by people who share it. My interests are esoteric, but I've had no problem locating mailing lists that have become a valuable part of my working day and my hobbies. In general, because subscribing to mailing lists requires people to specifically request entry, they tend to be populated by relatively serious-minded people (which is not to say they don't enjoy themselves!). And the people who sign on and contribute tend to pursue more focused discussions than you'll find in the newsgroups. After all, it's easy to find yourself with a mailbox stuffed with messages, so those not committed to the topic tend to drop out rather than deal with the daily inflow.

And because it's just as easy to leave a mailing list as it is to get on one, there is no reason not to cast your net broadly, signing on to lists that catch your eye to take the measure of the participants and their discussions, signing off if you decide they're not what you're looking for or if the traffic levels are just too high to maintain. I go in and out of mailing lists all the time to check out ideas and to do research on projects I'm working on. There's nothing like being able to ask an expert how to handle a hard disk glitch or how to grind a telescope mirror, and there's no shortage of people who are willing to answer.

Finding and Subscribing to a LISTSERV

Mailing lists came into their own through the offices of BITNET, an attempt to link scholars in various disciplines through e-mail lists that grew up in the early 1980s. As BITNET expanded, the work of running the mailing lists became time-consuming for all concerned. A Paris-based BITNET user named Eric Thomas designed a software program called LISTSERV to automate the mailing list process, so that no human intervention was necessary. LISTSERV enabled all administrative tasks to be handled digitally. Thus the moderator was free to examine postings and work closely with the ongoing flow of information, rather than become submerged in a never-ending chore of administration.

Tip: BITNET is one of the great stories of the networked computer era. Begun in 1981, it grew out of the vision of Ira H. Fuchs, then vice chancellor for university systems at the City University of New York, and Greydon Freeman, who was director of the Yale Computing Center. Fuchs based his concept on work then being performed at IBM, where a network called VNET connected programmers, researchers, and managers around the globe through leased telephone lines. With experience CUNY and Yale had gained in connecting their own systems, Fuchs and Freeman decided that the IBM model could be extended to the universities. They encouraged schools with existing IBM hardware to join in the new network.

BITNET's approach was simple. Each school paid for its own communications link, and each made it possible for one more school to connect to BITNET. Traffic moved between participating institutions without charge, using a store-and-forward method that moved data files from one node to another over 9600bps leased lines. As the Internet model became increasingly robust, BITNET traffic gradually began to move to the TCP/IP protocols. By 1989, BITNET had begun to reorganize itself through a new high-speed backbone. Its corporate name changed to the Corporation for Research and Educational Networking (CREN), an organization Ira Fuchs now heads. CREN continues to encourage the growth of educational networking worldwide even as BITNET itself gives way to the Internet. Its work on new list management software has led to programs optimized for Internet traffic. You may want to check CREN's Web site at http://www.cren.net/ to have a look at current projects.

It is no exaggeration to say that BITNET played a crucial role in the development of the network concept. In a time when widespread computer communications was largely in the hands of the scientific community, BITNET connected scholars in all disciplines to each other and promoted the notion of networking as a cultural as well as scientific resource. The impact of a decade of solid growth in the educational arena was profound. Students took the principles they learned at school into the broader community, providing a base for subsequent Internet growth. If breakthrough technology can usually be traced back to a few people with vision, then Ira Fuchs and Greydon Freeman surely rank among the stellar figures of today's Internet.

Thomas took LISTSERV into the commercial arena in 1993 in the form of a company called L-Soft, producing a TCP/IP version of the software the following year. LISTSERV manages close to 30,000 mailing lists today, of which roughly 9,000 are public. You can see the L-Soft home page in Figure 6.13.

By sending a series of formalized commands to LISTSERVs, you can conduct all necessary mailing list business. Using them, you are able to look through descriptions of the lists and receive sign-on information about them.

Three good search tools exist on the Web for finding the right LISTSERV:

TILE.NET (http://www.tile.net/) provides a database that is searchable by topic or subject.

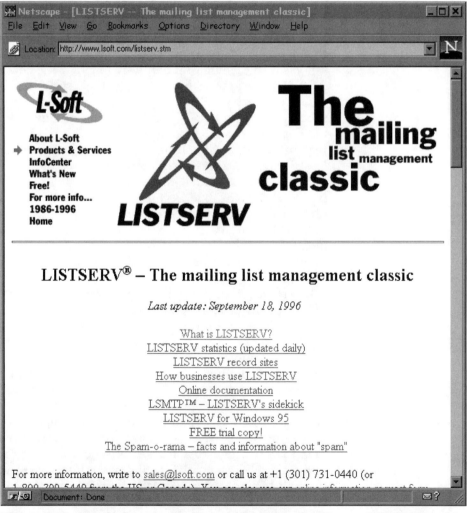

Figure 6.13   L-Soft's home page; this is the company that licenses LISTSERV and its upgrades.

CataList, the catalog of LISTSERV lists (http://www.lsoft.com/lists/listref.html) provides a sophisticated search engine for tracking down specific LISTSERVs.
The Liszt directory contains the largest number of mailing lists I am aware of, over
65,000; many of them use software other than LISTSERV. You can search this
database at http://www.liszt.com/.

In Figure 6.14, you can see the mailing list search tool at http://tile.net/.
This site maintains a searchable index of all mailing lists using the LISTSERV
software, but does not include those running the other major mailing list managers—ListProc, Majordomo, Mailbase, and Mailserv. Because each of these

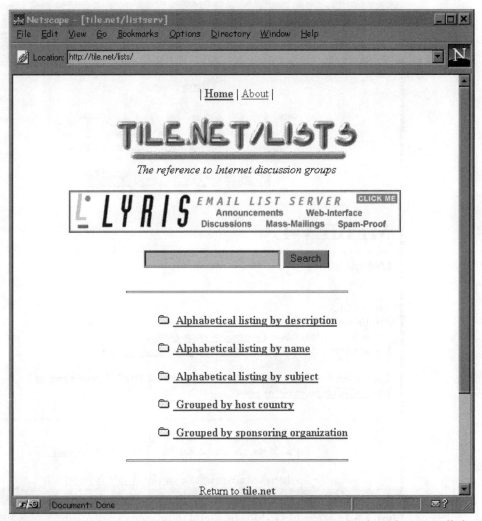

Figure 6.14   The searchable index at TILE.NET contains a database housing all the
LISTSERV mailing lists.

maintains a command set similar to, but not identical with, that of LISTSERV, you'll find that there are slight variations in procedures. We'll discuss how to use non-LISTSERV mailing lists shortly.

It's impossible to categorize all mailing lists under one banner, but in general, the LISTSERV lists are more likely to be those that have grown up out of the older BITNET system, and thus have roots in the academic, scientific, or government communities. Many of these have topics that are quite advanced, containing the work of leading experts in their fields. Figure 6.15 shows how to subscribe to such a list, this one specializing in medieval history. I called it up by looking under TILE.NET's alphabetical listing.

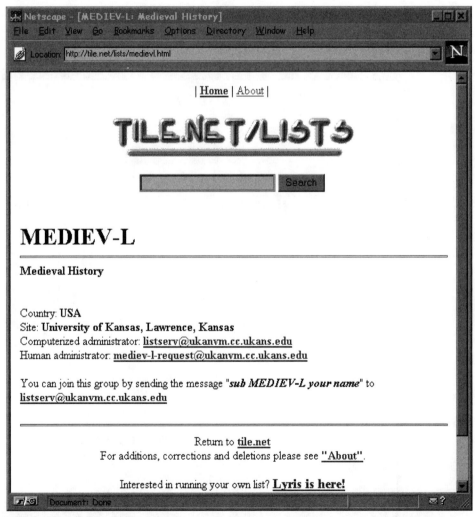

Figure 6.15 The LISTSERV lists tend to be more academic in nature and often contain the work of specialists. Subscription information appears in their descriptions.

Subscribing involves sending a precisely formatted message to the LIST-SERV. Here is how I subscribed to the Medieval History list:

1. I sent mail to the site listserv@ukanvm.cc.ukans.edu.
2. I composed my message to read "sub MEDIEV-L paul gilster."

Remember, the process here is automated, meaning that a single miscue in typing will result in an error message. Follow the directions precisely and be sure to send your message to the address specified for each list. You can see that the address in the figure is shown as a hyperlink; if I click on it, I am taken to Netscape's Mail Composition window with the LISTSERV address already inserted. I simply add my message and send. The message window with my command is shown in Figure 6.16.

With LISTSERVs, the turnaround time you can expect is relatively short. Being automated, the process does not require the intervention of a human being. A subscription request to a LISTSERV automatically generates a document that describes the mailing list in question. You should save this document, because it contains particular information about the list, its participants, its

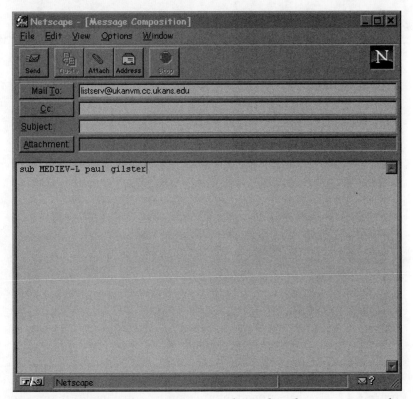

Figure 6.16 Using Netscape to send a subscribe message to the MEDIEV-L mailing list at the University of Kansas.

subject matter, and the major commands used to work with it. You can see the
backgrounder for the MEDIEV-L list in Figure 6.17. Notice, for example, that to
leave the list, you only need to send the command SIGNOFF MEDIEV-L to the
LISTSERV address. A series of other options are given that we will look at later.

You will also receive a second message that contains reference information
for the message that has just been sent to you. The material looks like this:

```
> sub MEDIEV-L paul gilster
You have been added to list MEDIEV-L.
```

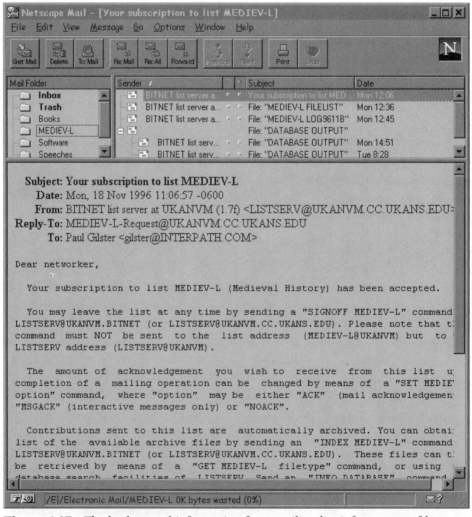

Figure 6.17   The background information for a mailing list informs you of key procedures for using the service.

```
Summary of resource utilization
CPU time:        0.978 sec    Device I/O:      439
Overhead CPU:    0.055 sec    Paging I/O:        5
CPU model:       5995         DASD model:     3380
```

This message is one you can safely discard.

> **Tip:** If you plan to be a regular user of mailing lists, I firmly recommend that you set up a folder for each list you plan to follow. Netscape's folder system makes it easy to catalog your retrieved postings this way. It's true that most mailing list messages won't be ones you'll want to save, but over the course of a few weeks, you'll doubtless find a few that merit further study. Placing them in a folder will keep your inbox uncluttered and provide order to your list work. Be sure to keep the introductory message for each mailing list in its folder. Then, if you decide to pause mailings or resign from the list for whatever reason, you'll have right at hand the commands you need to do this.

It's important to distinguish between two addresses when you use LISTSERV. One is that to which I just sent mail: listserv@ukanvm.cc.ukans.edu. An address with the term listserv in its name is the one to send subscription requests, sign-offs, and other administrative business; the listserv address exists only for this purpose. To send messages to the mailing list, you substitute the name of the mailing list for the listserv statement. Thus, listserv@ukanvm.cc. ukans.edu becomes mediev-l@ukanvm.cc.ukans.edu. This address is the one that handles messages; the former is strictly for mailing list business.

The distinction is an important one. One of the biggest mistakes a newcomer can make with a mailing list is to send a message properly directed to the LISTSERV to the entire subscription list. Obviously, requests to sign off or to suspend mail delivery are not ones that hundreds of list subscribers need or want to read; they just tie up traffic in everyone's mailbox. So remember the rules:

- Administrative commands go to the LISTSERV address.
- Messages go to the mailing list address, which is found by replacing the LISTSERV part of the address with the name of the mailing list.

You'll have noticed that other commands are available to help you manage your mailing list. Here for reference purposes is a listing of the major LISTSERV commands. Again, they are sent to the LISTSERV address only.

Subscribe   subscribe *listname your name*. Thus your message might
                            read subscribe twain-l john smith.

Resign from a list	unsubscribe *listname*. To leave the Medieval History list, my command would be unsubscribe mediev-l.
Ask for digest format	set *listname* digest
Suspend mail	set *listname* nomail
Resume mail	set *listname* mail
Get archive list	index *listname*

All these commands have an analog in the other mailing list management programs in common use. Once you're on a mailing list, you will receive in your introductory document a set of the primary commands, no matter what type of list management is in operation. So the question becomes, when do you use which command? Here are some thoughts:

Digest format will save you time if you find yourself becoming overwhelmed with the sheer volume of message traffic. In digest format, messages are combined into a single daily or weekly posting, thus consolidating your traffic. Unfortunately, many mailing lists don't offer the digest alternative, but those that do can help bring order to the incoming message flow. It's worth experimenting with this option when traffic is heavy enough that you can't keep up with it.

Suspending incoming mail is a wonderful tool when you're planning to be away from your desk. If you're on several active lists, then spending two weeks on holiday will find you returning to a mailbox totally stuffed with messages, most of which you'll doubtless simply discard because you don't have time to read them. By turning off incoming mail and turning it back on when you return, you'll save yourself time and aggravation.

Those mailing lists that *maintain an archive* will send you an index of the messages available there. In many cases, this archive can be searched, thus allowing you to pull up interesting material from before the time your subscription became active. Have a look at the archive by using the index command and see what interests you. For more information on LISTSERV's database capabilities, send the command info database to the LISTSERV.

Running a Sample Search on a LISTSERV Archive

Using LISTSERV as a research tool will highlight why Web-based search tools are so easy to work with. The LISTSERV commands are all textual and based upon a template. To use them, your first step is to retrieve the archival document for the list in question. Suppose I'm interested in learning more about Richard III, the English king who lost his crown during the War of the Roses, and has been condemned by history for the probable murder of the 12-year-old Edward V and his younger brother in the Tower of London. I'd like to find out what people are saying about this monarch on the Medieval History list, so I'll send the command index mediev-l to the LISTSERV. Figure 6.18 shows the document I receive in return.

Here as elsewhere with the LISTSERV system, it isn't necessary to supply a subject when you send your command message, although Netscape will ask you whether you want to or not. LISTSERV will ignore the subject header anyway, so it really doesn't matter.

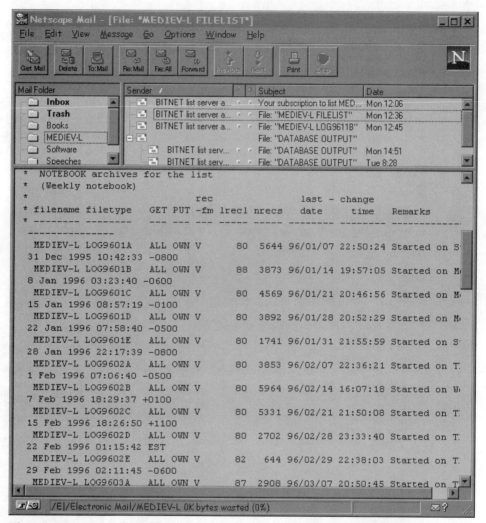

Figure 6.18 An index of archival files available at the Medieval History site.

Let's take a look at the index. Notice that the filename and type are shown with date information; we can assume, for example, that the first entry contains mailing list posts for the first part of January 1996, and so on. All the entries shown in the Medieval History index are logs; they are composed, in other words, of the collected messages of the group. Other mailing lists make various kinds of files available, including text files of interest to members, electronic editions of work discussed on-line, and so forth. The ALL statement tells us that anyone can have access to these logs by making the right request.

The request itself is straightforward. We send a command like this one: get mediev-l log9611b to the LISTSERV; this log houses messages for November 1996. The command syntax, then, is:

get *listname filename*

based on the filenames found in the list index. In a few minutes, the response should arrive in the inbox. Figure 6.19 shows this response, an example of what a log from a mailing list contains.

As you can see, this is simply a collection of the various postings to the mailing list. Imagine how much of a time-saver it is to acquire a log and run through it with Netscape's Find function (on the Edit menu), as opposed to having to print it out and search manually for a particular reference. Retrieving and reviewing logs is a great way to get up to speed with what has recently been said on the list.

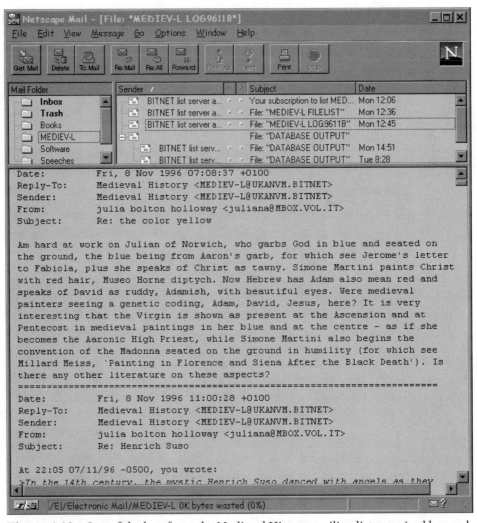

Figure 6.19 One of the logs from the Medieval History mailing list, acquired by sending a command to the LISTSERV.

> **Tip:** The Shelby Group provides a LISTSERV management program that makes it easy not only to track down and join various mailing lists, but to keep up with the arrival of new ones as well. Check out the home page for its Lyris software at http://www.lyris.com/.

Using the LISTSERV Database Function

Just reading an archival log isn't, however, the way to search for information about Richard III, or anyone else for that matter. For that, we need to use the LISTSERV database template, which allows us to search for particular text within the archives. Text-based, the LISTSERV search functions are complicated and hard to remember, but they function through a template that stays the same. All you do is insert the information required into the relevant slots.

> **Tip:** It's a good idea to keep a copy of the database template at your disposal for quick insertion and editing in the mail program. It's complicated enough that it becomes tiresome to look up its exact form each time you want to send a query. What I do is to maintain a copy in my note-taking program. I use Micro Logic's Info Select, but of course, you can use whichever program works for you, as long as you maintain the template in ASCII format for quick pasting into mail.

Here, I've inserted my information request about Richard III into the template:

```
//
Database Search DD=Rules
//Rules DD  *
Search Richard in MEDIEV-L
Index
/*
```

Of course, the search term you use will be specific to the mailing list archive you want to query. You can see that I have put my subject, Richard, in the search line; I have also specified which mailing list I am going to be looking at. The index command tells the server that after it has finished searching for my keyword, it should return an index of the results. Don't forget to send this command, or you won't hear anything at all from the server!

If we break the template out generically, here's how it looks:

```
//
Database Search DD=Rules
//Rules DD  *
```

```
command 1
command 2. . .
/*
```

The command lines are clearly the major ones; this is where you're telling the LISTSERV what to do. By sending the edited template, as here, to the LISTSERV, I cause it to run the search through the mailing list archives. In the case of my Richard III search, I retrieve a list of results as follows:

```
> Search Richard in MEDIEV-L
--> Database MEDIEV-L, 447 hits.


> Index
Item #   Date      Time    Recs   Subject
------   ----      ----    ----   -------
000772   96/02/08  10:37   33     Re: Medieval Anatomy (getting TAN)
000800   96/02/08  21:50   27     Re: drowning?
000812   96/02/09  22:23   58     Subject: Elite vs common language?
000822   96/02/09  12:06   17     Re: Martyrdom of John the Evangelist
000850   96/02/10  11:41   57     Relics, Politics, Democracy?
000860   96/02/10  15:48   35     Re: Relics, Politics, Democracy?
000866   96/02/10  19:34   24     Re: Wilton Dyptich
000900   96/02/13  17:59   38     Medieval anatomy
000902   96/02/13  09:27   33     joan of arc
000917   96/02/13  23:02   14     Re: Richard III s Hump
000918   96/02/13  20:57   59     Re: Medieval anatomy
000930   96/02/14  12:40   48     Re: joan of arc
000932   96/02/14  08:55   33     Re: Medieval anatomy
000936   96/02/14  14:30   61     Charles the Bald, Boleslaw Krzywousty an
000941   96/02/14  14:38   23     Re: Richard III s Hump
000943   96/02/14  10:09   36     Re: Richard III s "hump"
000945   96/02/14  15:22   19     Re: Richard III s "hump"
000947   96/02/14  11:04   24     Re: Richard III s "hump"
000948   96/02/14  11:25   30     Re: Richard III s "hump"
000949   96/02/14  11:27   32     Re: Richard III s "hump"
000951   96/02/14  15:48   24     Re: Richard III s 'hump'
000952   96/02/14  10:53   12     Re: Richard III s 'hump'
000953   96/02/14  11:51   49     Re: Richard III s "hump"
000954   96/02/14  08:54   36     Re: Medieval anatomy
000957   96/02/14  17:06   46     Re: Medieval anatomy
000959   96/02/14  12:17   19     Re: Richard III s 'Hump'
```

I've truncated the result here (there were 447 hits, after all), but you get the idea. One reason there were so many hits is that I used the term richard as my keyword, without specifying which one. Thus I called up hits about Richard the Lion Heart, as well as any other Richards mentioned in the Medieval History list. To avoid this kind of data overflow, a narrow specification of keywords is a good idea. When I ran the search again using Richard III as my keyword, the list of hits was reduced to 64.

But what if, after examining the index of hits, I want to read a specific message? The answer is to resubmit the query template with a number or numbers specified. Here's an example:

```
//
Database Search DD=Rules
//Rules DD  *
Search Richard in MEDIEV-L
Print all of 1046 1090 1092 1094 1122
/*
```

As you can see, I have left a space between the message numbers specified. Now the print command is the critical one; without it, the LISTSERV will run the search, but will not return any results. When I submit this request, I quickly receive another response, this time a customized set of messages containing only those I have requested. You can see the response in Figure 6.20.

A LISTSERV Search Methodology

Why is it so complicated to use these database functions with a LISTSERV? The answer is that we're working in so-called batch mode; we construct a search, submit it to the LISTSERV, and let the computer at the other end complete the procedures we have specified, sending us the results. We don't have interactive search capability with LISTSERVs, but must work through a sequence of commands and responses, all mediated by electronic mail. The LISTSERV Command Job Language Interpreter, or CJLI, is what you see at work in the template, and unfortunately, there's no way to get around the CJLI.

The good news is that thousands of mailing lists are available for archival searching, and in many cases, you don't have to be a member to search the archives. Here is a search procedure that will help you use LISTSERVs for research on any of the topics discussed on mailing lists. If you work through this methodology in sequence, you will quickly determine what's available.

1. Search for LISTSERV mailing lists about your topic by using the three addresses specified earlier: http://www.lsoft.com/lists/listref.html, http://tile.net/, and http://www.liszt.com/.

2. Read descriptions of the LISTSERVs on your topic to see which are the most likely to be queried.

3. Find out whether there is an archive at the site by sending the index command.

4. If an archive is available, create a keyword search around the specific issue you want to see messages about. Send the search statement to the LISTSERV.

5. If you receive a positive result, send a print request to the LISTSERV for the specific messages in question.

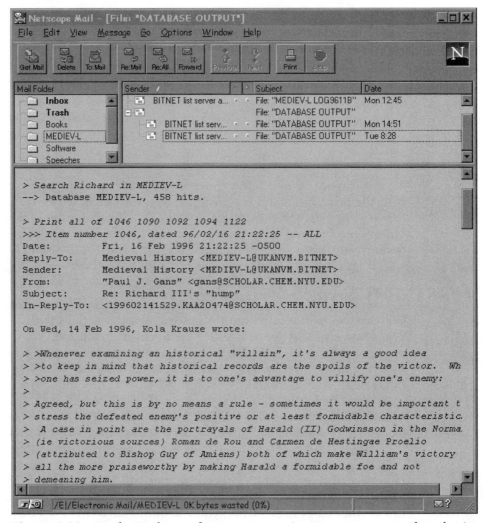

Figure 6.20 A tailor-made set of messages, sent in response to a search and print request to the MEDIEV-L list.

Tip: LISTSERV searching can use a variety of techniques including Boolean connectors for very precise searches. To get a complete rundown of how keyword strategies can be implemented, send for a document called Revised LISTSERV: Database Functions. It is available by sending mail to listserv@bitnic.bitnet. Leave the Subject field blank. In the content area, put this message:

   info database

The document is a lengthy one and contains all CJLI search parameters.

ListProc, Majordomo, Mailbase, and More

LISTSERV was one way of handling mailing list subscriptions, but others soon appeared. ListProcessor, or ListProc, is a UNIX-based system; it is now supported by CREN. Other tools are Majordomo, Mailbase, and Mailserv. The confusing thing about all this is that you may run into mailing lists managed by any of these programs, which means that the command set you need to use for message management may vary subtly from one to another. This would seem to be an insurmountable problem until you realize that most mailing lists will return to you a set of complete instructions explaining how to go about using their system when you sign on to the list. And if that's not enough, sending a help command to the server invariably results in a document with the basic commands explained.

Thus the question becomes less a matter of which mailing list software is in effect than of whether or not you can find the right list for your purposes. All will include some variation on the theme of sending a subscribe message to a central site; all will return some kind of response. This is why beginning your mailing list explorations with one of the Web sites mentioned previously is a good idea; you'll find complete subscription information there. But with the exception of Liszt, those databases house only LISTSERVs. The total number of mailing lists in the Internet universe is much bigger.

To begin exploring non-LISTSERV lists, go to Publicly Accessible Mailing Lists (http://www.NeoSoft.com/internet/paml/). It's a database of such lists created by Stephanie da Silva, whose contributions to the Internet and the world of mailing lists in particular are numerous and continuing. The da Silva list is actually available in several ways:

- It is posted regularly on the newsgroups news.lists and news.answers.
- It is available as a set of files at the FTP site ftp://rtfm.mit.edu/.

But the optimum method is to use the Web, because the da Silva site offers a searchable index that makes it easy to find what you want. You can search by the name of the mailing list or by the subject. In Figure 6.21, you can see the search page for this site, where I'm searching by subject.

Let's assume, for example, that I'd like to look at lists that specialize in philosophy. By clicking on the appropriate entry, I can call up a screen filled with mailing lists on that topic. Figure 6.22 shows the result of clicking on the list about Alan Watts, a philosopher and popularizer who did much to bring the writings of Zen Buddhism into the consciousness of the West.

Notice that the information contains a Web site address (fully clickable here) that takes me to the list's home page. This is a new direction for mailing lists—the early ones simply used mail as their vehicle and proceeded through text-only communications. Today, the Web simplifies archival searching, so that older lists can be cataloged and kept available for researchers. And you don't need a template!

By reading the description, I learn that this list is devoted to the study of Watts' books on personal identity, the nature of reality, and the fusion of East-

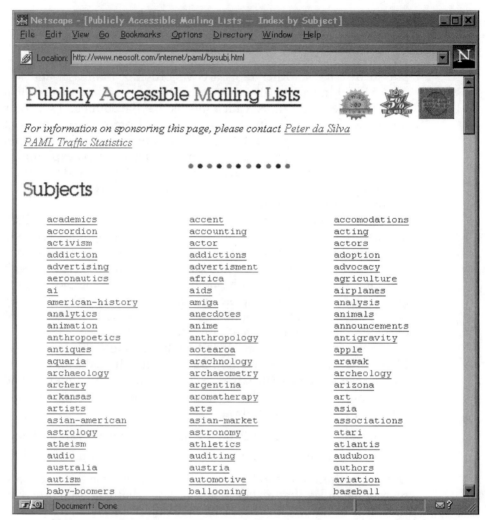

Figure 6.21 The Publicly Accessible Mailing Lists site makes it easy to search for a list by name or by subject.

ern and Western forms of religious belief. To learn more, I can try the Web site by clicking on its hyperlink. Figure 6.23 shows the result.

The various postings to the group are shown here in digest form; they have been edited and streamlined by the list moderator. A click on any of these hyperlinks takes me into the discussions themselves. Looking through previous postings in such an environment is a huge improvement over the old, text-based template method formerly necessary to search such archives. Many Web sites also provide convenient search engines for locating specific text in list postings.

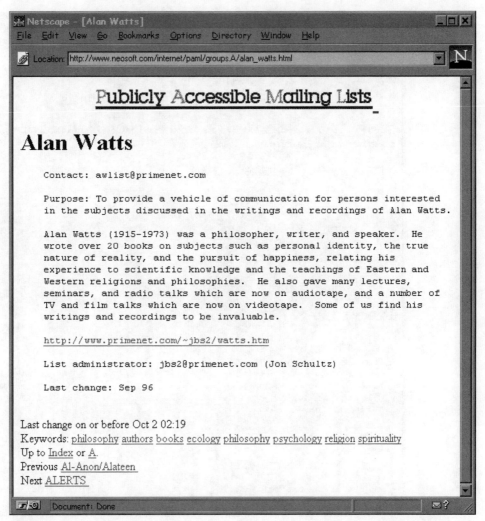

Figure 6.22 A description of the Alan Watts Mailing List, with full contact information and related Web site.

Notice that the Web page also contains a general information document about the list and Watts himself. A click on this calls up a helpful backgrounder, as shown in Figure 6.24. Prominent among the offerings of this document is information about how to subscribe to the list. I quote:

```
All communications to the list should be e-mailed to:

    awlist@primenet.com
```

```
If any message you send to this address is returned to you as undeliverable,
wait a day and send it again, and please notify the list administrator.
```

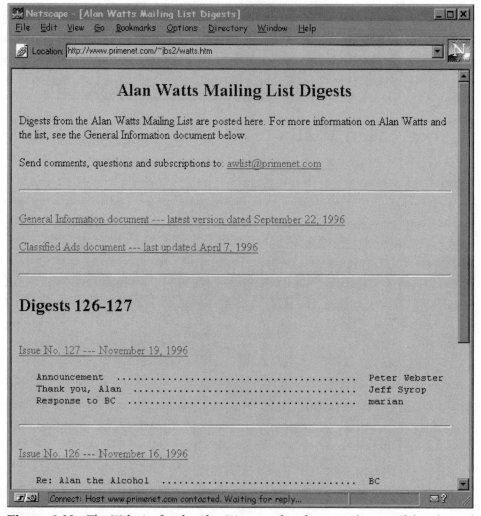

Figure 6.23   The Web site for the Alan Watts mailing list provides a useful archive of postings to the list.

```
To subscribe, send a message with the list command "SUBSCRIBE" on the
subject
line, as follows:

    Subject:   SUBSCRIBE

In the body of the message you must state the following:

    "I have seen the Alan Watts Mailing List General Information
    document and agree to the procedures outlined therein for the
    operation of the list."
```

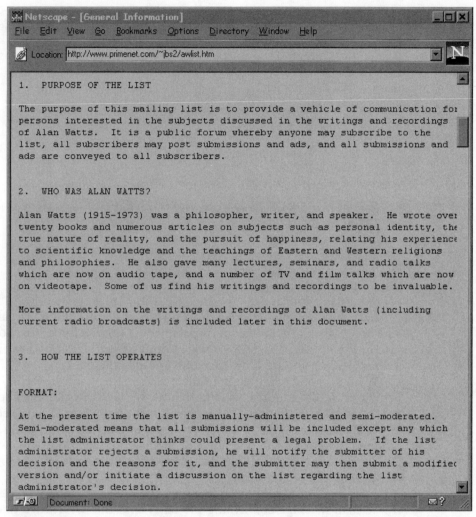

Figure 6.24 Always check background documents to gather information about the mailing list you're interested in; more and more lists are making these available.

The reason for this is that due to copyright law, your permission is needed for other subscribers to copy and share digests which contain submissions you
have posted. Note that you can post submissions anonymously, as described below.

If you just want to be able to post to the list but would rather read the digests on the World Wide Web than have them sent to your e-mail address, use:

    Subject: SUBSCRIBE BUT DON T SEND

```
including the "agreement" paragraph above in the body of your message. If
you choose this option you will instead receive a short e-mail message,
every
time a digest is issued, consisting only of the Table of Contents.

The digests are posted to:

      http://www.primenet.com/~jbs2/watts.htm

To quit the list, use:

      Subject:  UNSUBSCRIBE

For private messages to the list administrator which should not be included
in a digest, use:

      Subject:  PRIVATE

with the text of your message below.
```

Let's go through the procedure a step at a time. First, we are told the address: awlist@primenet.com. In fact, it's set up as a hyperlink, so that clicking on it will cause Netscape's Mail Composition window to open, with the address already inserted; we have only to write the message.

We're also told what to put in the message: the word subscribe, which is to be placed in the subject line. And finally, we have instructions about what to put in the body of the message, a canned text that reads: "I have seen the Alan Watts Mailing List General Information document and agree to the procedures outlined therein for the operation of the list." Having done this, we can send the message. You can see the Netscape Mail Composition window with my message in it in Figure 6.25.

A click on the Send button launches the message. Soon I'll receive an electronic mail message confirming my entry into the list. Notice that the entry into this list was handled differently than the LISTSERV techniques I ran previously, but the instructions I received took me through the process one step at a time. Be sure to learn everything you can about the list you're interested in before proceeding.

Tip: If you're looking for a master list of major commands for the various mailing list programs, James Milles of Saint Louis University Law Library has constructed a Web page that can help. The address is http://lawlib.slu.edu/training/mailser.htm. Here you'll find information about all five of the mailing list managers, and the variations in commands used by each. Some of these differences are significant. Consider the methods used to subscribe using the five different programs:

LISTSERV	subscribe *listname your name*
Listproc	subscribe *listname your name*
Mailbase	join *listname your name*
Mailserv	subscribe *listname your name*
Majordomo	subscribe *listname*

Sources of Mailing List Information

Fortunately, there is no shortage of information about mailing lists. Here are some sites that will round out your knowledge. The best procedure is to search for a topic that you know you'll find interesting, read the description, and sign up to see what the list is like. Avoid signing up to more than one or two in the beginning. Many lists contain huge amounts of message traffic, and you may find yourself so overwhelmed by the sheer number of messages you receive that you'll wish you had never subscribed. As with any form of electronic mail, proper mailing list management is important. Thus the importance of the Sub-

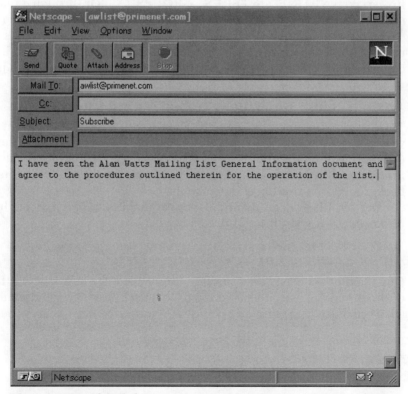

Figure 6.25 The Mail Composition window appears when you click on the mailing list address; here, I've inserted the necessary information to subscribe to the list.

ject field; when you subscribe to numerous lists, you'll often delete messages wholesale depending on whether the subject catches your eye.

The Global List of LISTSERVs

The first comprehensive list of LISTSERV mailing lists was created in 1987 as part of the BITNET network. Interestingly, it did not reach the 1,000 list mark until the following year, whereas today, tens of thousands of such lists exist, about a quarter of which are available to the public. If you simply want a list of the public sites, you can send e-mail to any LISTSERV address, including the message "lists global" in the Contents field. For example, send mail to listserv @kentvm.kent.edu, including "lists global" as the body of your message. A short description is provided for each list.

The List of Lists

Maintained by Vivian Neou, this is one of the oldest of the mailing list documents. You can retrieve it in two ways: via anonymous FTP on sri.com in the NETINFO directory in the file INTEREST-GROUPS.TXT; the URL is thus ftp://sri.com/NETINFO/INTEREST-GROUPS.TXT. Or through e-mail by sending a message to mail-server@sri.com with "send interest-groups" in the body of the message. One of the most useful features of the List of Lists is its comprehensive descriptions of the various features of each list. The List of Lists can be searched at http://catalog.com/vivian/interest-group-search.html.

The Directory of Scholarly Electronic Conferences

This list is maintained by Diane K. Kovacs and a team at the Kent State University Libraries. The URL is gopher://gopher.usask.ca/. Follow these menus: Computing, then Internet Information, and finally, Directory of Scholarly and Professional E-Conferences. The list is broken down into topics and contains background information about each list.

Dartmouth College maintains a searchable directory of mailing lists at http://www.nova.edu/Inter-Links/cgi-bin/lists.

Announcements of New Mailing Lists

One mailing list exists only to serve as a vehicle for announcing the creation of other mailing lists. To subscribe to this useful service, send mail to listserv @vm1.nodak.edu. Your mail should read subscribe new-list *your name*.

Read before You Post

A final thought about mailing lists. A mailing list is a community, a group of people clustered around a common interest. While many of these people have never met face to face and probably never will, they've become accustomed to each other's eccentricities and they have evolved a culture particular to their group. When you sign on to a list for the first time, the thing to do is to look around and learn. Read messages, see where the discussions are going, look at past discussions. All of this will give you a feel for how this particular group likes to conduct itself. Once you have learned the rules of the road, you can contribute.

Probably the worst way to make an entrance into a mailing list is to simply appear, demanding answers. In many cases, you're dealing with people who are experts in their field. Asking them to give you a complete history of the late Roman republic or for a breakdown of current thinking in quantum electro-dynamics is a bit presumptuous. Chances are, list participants will be more than willing to direct you to sources that can help in your research, provided you ask politely and are willing to find out for yourself what is available in the list archives. But plan on spending at least a week reading messages before you think of posting.

Tip: One of the best ways to keep up with events affecting the Internet is to subscribe to Edupage. A newsletter put out by Educom, a Washington, D.C.-based consortium of colleges and universities supporting information technology, Edupage comes out several times a week and contains brief summaries of major news stories. To subscribe, send e-mail to listproc@educom.edu. Your message should read:

   sub edupage *your name*

You can check Educom's home page at http://www.educom.edu/.

7

Interpreting the Net: Newsgroups, Telnet, and Gopher through the Browser

By now, it should be clear that the Internet and the Web are not synonymous. Electronic mail moves according to its own set of protocols, and can be viewed either within or outside of the browser. But it's equally clear that a good browser is an excellent way to portray Net-based information, whether it moves in the form of Web pages or not. And today's full-featured browsers have increasingly begun to incorporate the major Internet programs so that they can all be displayed within the same comfortable interface.

As with electronic mail, the question you face is how you want to handle the Net experience. A Web browser can perform most of the functions you'll ever need to use, and in many cases, it will do so with as much efficiency as a stand-alone program. Adding other client programs takes up space on your hard disk, but such programs sometimes extend the browser's functionality. We'll have to watch these issues as we explore what the browser can do, and I'll alert you to the presence of third-party programs where necessary.

The goal is to equip you with an Internet computer that can handle any major Net task. We'll see how Netscape handles USENET newsgroups, those ongoing conversations on thousands of topics that are so similar to, and in other ways so disparate from, the mailing lists we just examined. We'll also use Netscape as a display tool for Gopher. Despite rumors of its demise, Gopher still has a place, particularly in a text-based world like that found in many developing countries. Gopher was the first major program that seriously advanced the idea of displaying information in an intuitive way. It widened the Net's user base and foreshadowed the later emergence of the World Wide Web. And we'll download two other add-on programs, tools that Netscape uses to launch Telnet sessions. You'll be able to get into data collections like the catalog at the Library of Congress, and submit queries to it. Telnet is one of the Internet's oldest tools, and enough sites still use it that it belongs in a fully equipped browser.

Reading USENET Newsgroups

The Internet is all about introducing people with similar interests to each other, in this way forming on-line communities. USENET grew up as a way of doing this in a particular environment, the network of connected UNIX machines. Computers using UNIX have always been common in academic and research institutions, where their powerful processing capabilities have been used for specialized tasks. UNIX contains all the network tools it needs to connect computers across a room or across a continent. Two graduate students at Duke University created USENET as a way of exchanging messages back in 1979, and the network has mushroomed since then. Tens of thousands of newsgroups on all conceivable topics are now available.

Tip: USENET actually grew out of Net deprivation. ARPANET required that participating sites be working on projects for the Department of Defense, and usage at those sites was limited to those active in the project. That left quite a few institutions out in the cold, including the University of North Carolina at Chapel Hill and Duke University, just down the road in Durham. Duke graduate students Tom Truscott and James Ellis worked with UNC student Steve Bellovin to create at least limited networking capability using UNIX-based computers. Traffic would be exchanged the low-cost way, through the telephone system and modems. The three created a program called Netnews in 1979 to manage this traffic, and USENET quickly spread. Soon it became possible, thanks to the work of Mark Horton at the University of California at Berkeley, to funnel ARPANET mailing list traffic through USENET connections. From this point forward, the growth of the newsgroups was unstoppable.

Today, we tend to speak of "the newsgroups," and the term USENET is gradually diminishing in use. But the distinction between USENET and the Internet itself was there for a purpose. The original USENET traffic moved by means of

UNIX's UNIX-to-UNIX Copy Protocol, or UUCP; messages could move without reference to ARPANET or the later Internet. But today, most USENET traffic flows over the Internet itself using Network News Transfer Protocol (NNTP), so the distinction is becoming less important. For the end user, no real difference is evident; you can read and participate in newsgroups through a Web browser or a stand-alone program without reference to their origin.

How the Newsgroups Work

Newsgroups are places where people talk about the things that interest them. Most newsgroups are thus collections of people with a hobby or a common profession. You will find trout fishermen talking about their methods, or computer marketers discussing the latest software. You'll also find groups that specialize in news from particular countries, while an increasing number of groups are used for supporting customers of particular computer products. There are newsgroups for classical music enthusiasts and hang-glider pilots, and people who want to follow the latest news in Wake County, North Carolina. Not to mention hard news sources, debate areas, file and photographs groups, and collections of facts in the form of Frequently Asked Questions documents.

To read a newsgroup, you have to subscribe to it, but unlike the mailing lists we just looked at, newsgroups require no e-mail message to a central site. Instead, you use your browser or newsreader software to call up a list of the newsgroups available from your service provider. When the complete list appears, you choose which groups you'd like to subscribe to, and join each with a simple command. From that point on, headers for all messages that arrive for that newsgroup will be shown to you. When you want to read a particular message from the newsgroup, you can call it up, usually by clicking on it, and your newsreader will contact the server to retrieve the message. At the end of the session, you can mark all messages read so you won't see them again.

Are the newsgroups organized? In one sense, they are organized about as well as the Internet itself, which is to say, there is no overall structure being imposed from a central organization, but the infrastructure that keeps the whole thing flowing continues to work through approved methods. The newsgroups in most cases are unmoderated, meaning that whatever anyone decides to post on them stays there, subject only to the pressure exerted by the audience. Newsgroup etiquette attempts to keep conversations on track and exhorts against individual attack, with greater or lesser effect depending on the nature of the group. Occasional gems and insights are often surrounded by invective or off-topic postings, but you can find the good stuff if you know how to look.

Newsgroup Hierarchies

The newsgroups use a hierarchical structure within which to place their topics. Hierarchies should be familiar by now; we're used to seeing with electronic mail addresses. There, the principle is to read from the left to the right in order to move from the most precise to the broadest level of information. Thus jjackson@monterey.surf.com refers to a specific individual, jjackson, at a specific computer at a company; the latter is shown by the familiar com designation. Newsgroups function much like this, except that they go from broad to specific. The newsgroup alt.classics, for example, uses the broad alt category to designate its family of newsgroups, and the classics designation to tell you what it's about.

Newsgroups can become exceedingly specific, too. The newsgroup rec.collecting.books is obviously a subset of the broader rec.collecting category. And then there's alt.animals.felines.snowleopards, and the extremely precise alt.building.insurance-bonding-surety. As you can see, the principle is to be as accurate as possible at labeling the newsgroup and placing it within a broader topical structure. A number of hierarchies have been established for basic newsgroup postings, but the popularity of the medium has given birth to numerous regional and even local newsgroups. One called ba.jobs.resumes, for example, provides job resumes in the Bay area around San Francisco, while nyc.announce is a newsgroup catering to New York City residents.

Tip: Sometimes you'll see newsgroups referred to with wildcard characters, such as the asterisk. If you see something like comp.infosystems.*, the statement tells you that there are newsgroups available within the comp.infosystems hierarchy. Newsreaders will often show groups this way; you can then click on the statement to call up the list of newsgroups within the hierarchy.

What follows are the major categories of newsgroups and a brief description of each:

comp   The comp hierarchy contains messages of interest to computer professionals as well as amateur users. Subjects can range from particular hardware systems to software from various developers. Some newsgroups are more theoretical in their approach, others highly practical. Here are some examples:

comp.ai	Discussions of artificial intelligence
comp.archives	Descriptions of public access file archives
comp.compression.research	Ongoing work in data compression algorithms and theory
comp.forsale.computers	Messages about computers for sale
comp.laser-printers	For users of laser printers
comp.lang.c++	The object-oriented C++ programming language

sci   The sci groups specialize in research and discussions about ongoing scientific issues. Some of these groups are followed by professionals in their fields; others are mostly devoted to the work of amateurs. Some examples:

sci.bio	Biology and related sciences
sci.engr.biomed	Biomedical engineering
sci.nanotech	Studying nanotechnology, engineering at microscopic levels
sci.space.science	Related to the space program and scientific experiments therein
sci.virtual-worlds	The realm of virtual reality
sci.psychology	A series of groups devoted to psychology and human consciousness

soc   The soc newsgroups are a fascinating mix of conversation and cultural information. They contain numerous groups devoted to particular countries, for example, and broader groups devoted to the social scene in all its forms. Examples include:

soc.culture.celtic	The culture of the Celtic lands of Ireland, Scotland, Cornwall, and Wales, with nods to other Celtic outposts
soc.college.gradinfo	Graduate schools and how to get in them
soc.politics	The great issues of the day as seen through a political lens
soc.roots	Discussions about genealogy
soc.veterans	For military veterans and those interested in their welfare
soc.women	Women's issues, feminism, and so on

talk   This hierarchy is devoted to debate, particularly about issues as contentious as gun control and abortion. If you're looking for a good argument (and sometimes pure aggravation), wade into some of the more feisty of these. Examples:

talk.environment	Pollution and how to avoid it
talk.politics.animals	The group to visit for animal rights issues
talk.politics.medicine	Health care and national policy regarding Medicare, and so on
talk.rape	The crime of rape and what we can do about it
talk.rumors	A great place to hear the latest wild speculations about virtually any event
talk.origins	A group for the discussion of evolution versus creationism

news   This is one of the most important of all newsgroups; it deals with the Internet, the newsgroups themselves, and issues involving policy and administration of network sites. For new users, a number of groups provide excellent help by posting Frequently Asked Questions documents. Examples:

news.announce.important	The group where announcements of interest to all newsgroup readers are posted
news.announce.newgroups	Announcements about the creation of new newsgroups and discussions about the need for same
news.answers	A repository for Frequently Asked Questions documents from many different newsgroups
news.groups.reviews	Information about the content of various groups
news.future	Where newsgroups are headed and the technology that will take them there

news.newusers.questions	A good place for asking introductory questions about USENET

rec   The rec groups are for hobbyists and the arts, with niches for collectors of all kinds and other groups simply devoted to life's amusements. Such as:

rec.arts.animation	Discusses the art of animation
rec.arts.comics.info	Reviews, news of conventions, and other information about comics
rec.arts.fine	The fine arts from a variety of perspectives
rec.arts.sf.written	Science fiction of the written kind
rec.audio	For audio enthusiasts
rec.collecting.stamps	The latest news from the world of stamps

misc   Everything that won't fit in the other newsgroups find a home here. As you would expect, the range of topics is wide, and most of them have nothing to do with computers. Here are some examples:

misc.education.language.english	A group focusing on teaching English as a foreign language
misc.forsale.computers.mac	For postings regarding Macintoshes for sale
misc.invest	The place to go if you want to talk about your investments, including stocks, bonds, and other vehicles
misc.kids	A group about children and their behavior
misc.taxes	For discussions of the tax system
misc.writing	A group that talks about writing of all kinds; a hangout for would-be writers.

The preceding newsgroups could be considered the primary newsgroup hierarchies; they're circulated worldwide and show up at most service providers' sites. But they're hardly the whole story. Each provider must decide which newsgroups to make available, so that while the average provider will be sure to include the groups just listed, there is also a wide choice among alternative sources of information. Here are some of the most widely followed hierarchies, most of which will be available through your provider.

alt   The so-called alternative groups are an interesting variation on the standard newsgroup theme. In the other hierarchies, creating a newsgroup is a formalized process requiring discussion and a vote to see if the group is justified. The alt groups fall under no such restriction, which means that virtually any kind of group can be created here. If a given topic is so unusual that only a few people might find it intriguing, it's more likely to show up in the alt hierarchy than anywhere else. And if someone wants to create an entire newsgroup devoted to him or herself, this is the place; anybody can create a group here on any topic. Examples include:

alt.abuse. transcendence	The spiritual route to overcoming abuse of all kinds
alt.animation.warner-brothers	Discussing the cartoons of Warner Brothers

alt.barney.dinosaur.die.die.die	Perhaps the most famous alt newsgroup, focusing on shared aversion to the television dinosaur from which it gets its name
alt.history.what-if	Studying the possibilities of alternative history
alt.paranormal	Anything connected to the realm of the psychic
alt.smokers.pipes	For pipe smokers and lovers of aromatic tobacco

biz   This is the hierarchy for the business-minded. The newsgroups found here began with a completely computer-oriented slant, focusing on products and services, but they have expanded to include many other forms of commercial activity. The growth of the biz groups is one more indication of how much the Net has changed since the days of its research and academic adolescence. Examples:

biz.dec.decnews	News from the world of Digital Equipment Corporation
biz.marketplace.international	For those with an interest in marketing and selling products overseas
biz.oreilly.announce	Announcements of new titles from a major computer book publisher
biz.zeos	A newsgroup for users of Zeos computers

clari   ClariNet is actually an electronic publishing service rather than a set of user-defined newsgroups. News from Reuters, United Press International, and a number of features and columns from various sources including financial information is converted into newsgroup messaging format before being posted here. ClariNet is not offered by all service providers, but for those who do have ClariNet access, here's a sample of the newsgroups available:

clari.biz.currencies	News from the world of currency speculation and central bank dealings
clari.biz.industry.travel+leisure	An industry-specific newsgroup, one of many offered by ClariNet
clari.living.movies	News from the world of cinema
clari.usa.briefs	The major headlines from news in the United States, condensed for quick reading
clari.news.europe	Events in Europe

gnu   Here's a whole hierarchy devoted to the work of the Free Software Foundation, which was created to remove restrictions on copying, redistributing, and modifying software. The Foundation's primary activity is to replace proprietary software with free, and often quite powerful, replacements. Its work centers around GNU, an operating system that provides compatibility with UNIX. GNU, another Internet acronym (and a recursive one at that), stands for GNU's Not UNIX. Examples include:

gnu.emacs.news	Announcements about the popular emacs program
gnu.misc.discuss	Miscellaneous talk about the FSF and GNU
gnu.utils.bug	Problems with and solutions for GNU utility programs

k12   This hierarchy is devoted to discussions among elementary students in various grade levels.

bionet   High-level professional discussions among biologists.

bit   Many BITNET mailing lists have been made available through the newsgroups for those who chose not to subscribe to the mailing lists themselves. Using the bit groups is a good way to get an overview of list traffic before you sign up for one.

Again, all of these are major hierarchies that will probably appear among the newsgroups offered by your service provider, with the possible exception of the clari hierarchy, which is a subscription service that not all providers carry. But the range of newsgroups is remarkably wide and includes a host of other classifications, which are described next.

Regional or Statewide Newsgroups

Newsgroups can be set up to carry information only to specific regions. Here in North Carolina we have such groups as nc.general and nc.charlotte.sports that fulfill a precise function. Other providers may or may not carry such groups. In Raleigh, for example, I can read many groups devoted to issues on the West Coast through the ca (California) hierarchy. Similarly, my provider carries many ne hierarchy groups; the ne stands for Northeast, and denotes groups of interest in that part of the United States. You'll need to scan your provider's offerings to see which of these are carried.

Local Newsgroups

Newsgroups can be carried down to the local level. In central North Carolina, we have the triangle newsgroups, which carry announcements and postings concerning Raleigh, Durham, and Chapel Hill. Similarly, we can read ba postings for the Bay area, or the nyc hierarchy for New York news. Local groups can be helpful not only in tracing events close to you, but in learning more about an area you intend to visit.

Language-Defined Newsgroups

The de hierarchy contains postings in German, through newsgroups such as de.alt.ufo and de.comp.databases; the fj groups do the same thing for Japanese; other languages are likewise available.

And be advised that numerous companies and other organizations have set up newsgroups for their own internal use. If you work inside a large company, you might want to check with other workers or the system administrators at your workplace to see if any company groups are available. They can be handy for scheduling meetings and working on common projects.

Tip: Like other Internet information, newsgroups use URLs. The newsgroup rec.collecting.books, for example, sports the URL news:rec.collecting.books. Notice that a newsgroup URL contains no double-slash after the colon.

Configuring Netscape to Read the News

As with electronic mail, reading the news in Netscape requires a small amount of configuration. Here's how:

1. Pull down the Options menu.
2. Choose Mail and News Preferences.
3. Click on Servers.

You should see the screen shown in Figure 7.1.

You're already familiar with the top of this panel. But note the three fields at the bottom:

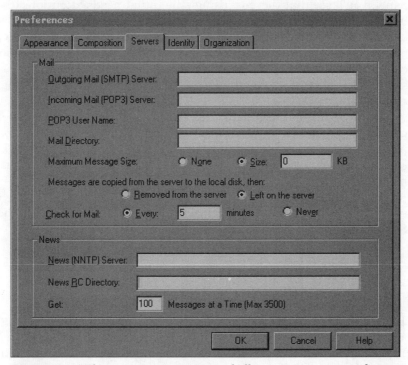

Figure 7.1   The Netscape Servers panel allows you to enter configuration information for your newsgroup reading.

News (NNTP) Server	This is the computer that handles your newsgroup connection. Netscape will pull message headers off this machine and retrieve from it the full text of any messages you request. Check the documentation sent by your service provider to learn what server name to put here.
News RC Directory	This field specifies the location of newsgroup subscription and information files. These tell Netscape which groups you are subscribed to, and provide other information relating to your use of the newsgroups. The statement here should default to a subdirectory of Netscape, although you can change it if you choose.
Get	This field specifies how many messages Netscape should retrieve at a time. The default is 100 and I recommend you leave it there, at least for now. The value can go as high as 3,500, but choosing a larger number increases the length of time it takes the browser to download the necessary information.

With this information in place, you have armed Netscape to handle your news traffic. But let's finish with a few other configurable options.

From the Preferences tab, choose Composition. On the Composition panel, you'll see that there is a single field that needs attention. It's under the heading "By default, copy outgoing message to the file," and it offers you the chance to save anything you want to send as newsgroup traffic to a file. The field is labeled News File. You can leave this field blank if you choose, or you can put in a directory path telling the browser where to put copies of your messages. If for any reason you think you'll want to have such copies for reference, enter a value here now.

Finally, click on the Organization tab from the Preferences panel. Note the checkbox: Thread News Messages. I recommend you check this box, so that news messages are presented to you in logical fashion. Doing so makes it much easier to follow ongoing discussions without jumping around in the list of message headers.

Below this, one last field needs a look: Sort News by. You have the option of sorting messages by date, subject, or sender. I recommend checking the Subject field to get the most logical order for your messages.

Netscape is now configured for using the newsgroups.

Reading the Newsgroups

The newsgroup option in Netscape is found by dropping the Window menu and clicking on Netscape News. You will see a screen like the one in Figure 7.2. You can see that the screen is divided into three panes, just like the mail screen. At the top left is the News Server panel, where the server you listed on the previous Servers panel should now appear. Double-click on this item to command Netscape to contact the server and retrieve the newsgroups to which

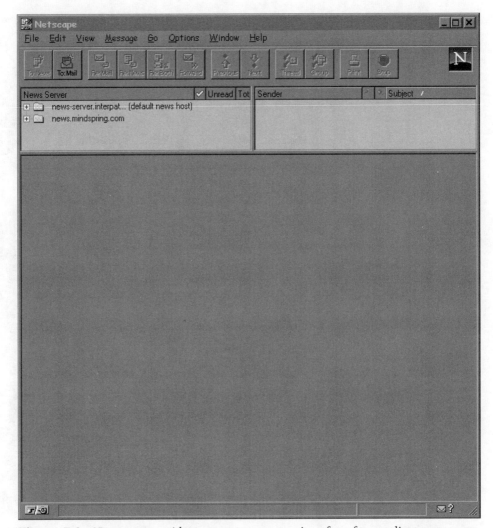

Figure 7.2 Netscape provides an easy-to-master interface for reading your news-groups.

it has subscribed by default. They will appear in the News Server pane below the server itself.

If you click on one of these newsgroups, you will be able to call up a list of the messages currently available in it. Clicking on news.announce.newusers, for example, produces a list of message headers in the pane on the right. The message header pane includes information about the sender of each message, its date, and its subject; it is similar in this respect to the mail pane, and like it, includes icons telling you when a message has been read and when it has been flagged for special attention. Double-clicking on any message will cause that

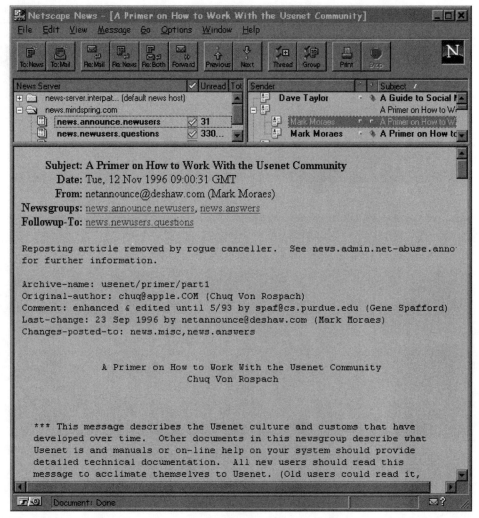

Figure 7.3 A newsgroup message as displayed by Netscape; note the three panes, divided into the same areas as the Mail window.

message to be displayed in the message pane. You can see a message on display in Figure 7.3.

To move through the messages, you have several options. You can scroll through what's available by using the scroll bar in the message header pane, and then click on any message you want to see. Alternatively, you can use the toolbar, clicking on the Previous or Next buttons to move through the list of available messages.

As with your electronic mail window, I recommend rethinking how information is displayed in the newsgroups. You can follow the same procedure to change the window to a vertical orientation, thus providing a content area that is easier to read while still retaining newsgroup data and message headers. To do so, pull down the Options menu, choose Mail and News Preferences, and click on the Appearance tab. At the bottom of the Appearance panel are the controls that allow you to change the display of news. Click on Split Vertical to change the display, following this with a click on the OK button. You will have to leave the newsreader window and then return to it to see the changes take effect. In Figure 7.4, you can see a vertically split screen adjusted for maximum content. Here I've enlarged the screen display by dragging the right boundary of the news window with my mouse.

Notice how the newsgroup information is displayed in the server pane. You'll see a folder for each news host you can access; unless you use multiple

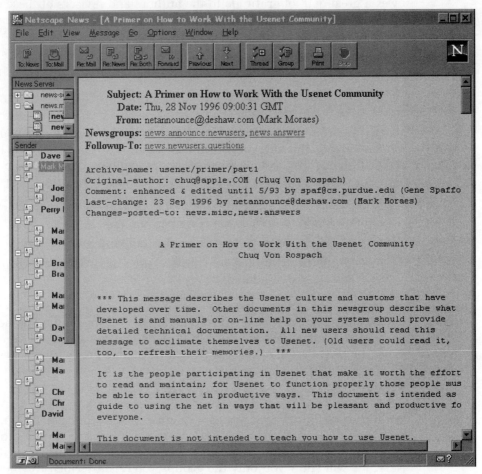

Figure 7.4 Changing the orientation of the news window and resizing the panes provides maximum content area while retaining control over newsgroup information.

service providers, you should see only one folder here. This folder then opens to reveal the newsgroups to which you are currently subscribed. Next to each are three items:

A checkbox	A check in the box indicates you are subscribed to the group in question.
Unread messages	This column shows how many messages you have not yet read are available in the newsgroup.
Total	The total number of messages available in the newsgroup.

Depending on how you arrange the panes, you may see only part of the Total or Unread field, but you can always move the boundary between the panes with your mouse if you need to check this information.

The news.announce.newuser group is a wonderful place to start because it's stuffed with documents about the history and culture of USENET. The Net owes a great debt of gratitude to the authors and revisers of these core documents, which have been assembled from years of newsgroup experience, and are essential reading for anyone getting involved in cyberspace. You should plan to spend some time reading through the postings in news.announce. newusers to gain insight into newsgroup operations.

Marking Groups Read

When you've finished with a particular newsgroup for the day, you'll want to mark it as read. This tells your software that the next time you log on to the news server, it should display only those messages that have come in since the time of your last logon. If you don't do this, you will wind up reading through many of the same message headers in search of new material. To mark a group read:

1. Highlight the group in the newsgroup pane.
2. Click on the Group button on the toolbar icon.
3. Alternatively, pull down the Message menu and click on the Mark Newsgroup Read item.

Notice, incidentally, that you can also mark particular threads as read by highlighting a message in the thread and then clicking on the Thread button in the toolbar. This allows you to skip threads that don't interest you while still using the Next button to work your way through a group's messages.

Setting Up Newsgroup Subscriptions

With thousands of newsgroups available worldwide, you'll soon want to branch out into your own areas of interest. It's important, then, to retrieve a list of all the newsgroups available from your service provider. Remember, Netscape will show you only the groups you're subscribed to when you first call it up. All newsreaders operate this way, and they also make it easy to see the entire list when you want to expand your subscriptions. Here's how:

1. Pull down the Options menu.
2. Choose Show All Newsgroups.

Netscape will now contact the server and retrieve the complete list of groups. News hierarchies are shown with asterisks. For example, the alt hierarchy is shown in the newsgroup pane as a folder, and it is followed by an asterisk and the notation (3,111 groups). This tells you that you're dealing with a set of nested newsgroups; double-click on the folder to open it and reveal the hierarchies of newsgroups inside it. Some of these are quite lengthy paths to a specific newsgroup, as each branch of the hierarchy is similarly represented by another folder with an asterisk.

You don't, incidentally, have to be a subscriber to a particular group to see what's in it. Clicking on any newsgroup shown in the newsgroup pane will cause the message headers within it to be revealed, and a click on any one of these will in turn place that message in the content pane. Subscriptions are only necessary when you decide you want to see the contents of a newsgroup regularly, and don't want to have to wade through messages you've already seen each time you log on. The subscription process is easy:

1. Find a newsgroup to which you want to subscribe.
2. Click on the newsgroup's Subscribe box in the newsgroup pane.

In Figure 7.5, you can see the news window with a newsgroup called alt.internet.services displayed. I have been examining the group while deciding whether or not I want to subscribe to it. Notice that I have pulled the boundary between the newsgroup and message header panes to the right to reveal the subscribe boxes for each group (in the column under the check). I can now click on the Subscribe column next to the alt.internet.services group to subscribe to the group.

Tip: Which newsgroups should you put on your subscription list? In the beginning, I recommend subscribing to the groups that propagate background information about the Net and answer basic questions. These groups include:

comp.internet.net-happenings	Updated news about new sites and interesting destinations on the Net.
news.announce.newsgroups	Announcements of the formation of new groups.
news.announce.newusers	Basic questions for new users answered and discussed.
news.answers	The place where many newsgroups place Frequently Asked Questions documents.
news.newusers.questions	The place to ask questions about how to use the newsgroups.

> alt.internet.services   Useful discussions of Internet issues
>   from a variety of perspectives; a good
>   place to eavesdrop on what old
>   hands are saying about the Net.
>
> As you build your expertise, you'll obviously want to explore
> the groups your provider offers to find those that suit your own
> interests.

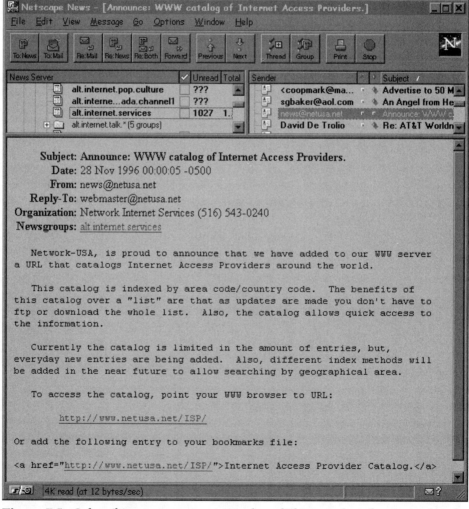

Figure 7.5   Subscribing to a newsgroup involves clicking on the subscription box for that group.

Searching for Messages in a Newsgroup

If you're looking for targeted information within a newsgroup, you can search the message headers or the content field of the available messages. To do so:

1. Pull down the Edit menu.
2. Click on Find.

The Find window will appear, as shown in Figure 7.6.

Responding to Articles

If you read a newsgroup message to which you'd like to respond, the quickest way is by using the toolbar. There are three options there:

Re:Mail   Allows you to reply to the current message's sender through mail rather than the newsgroup itself.

Re:News   Allows you to post a reply on the newsgroup, to be seen by all subscribers.

Re:Both   Enables you to create a mail message as well as a reply that will appear in the newsgroup.

You can perform the same actions by using the Message menu and clicking on either Post Reply, Post and Mail Reply, or Mail Reply; and all three actions can likewise be performed by right-clicking in the content pane to produce a pop-up menu.

Responding to a message produces the Message Composition window we looked at previously with electronic mail. The message to which you are replying is quoted in the window. As with e-mail, using quotes from the message is a good idea because it helps people remember what you're talking about; but

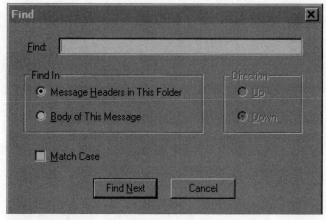

Figure 7.6 The Find window lets you search for keywords inside message headers or text.

be vigilant to edit the quoted material to delete anything that is not precisely on topic. The surest way to make people avoid your reply is if it contains unnecessary amounts of quoted text. You can see a message inserted as quoted material inside a reply in Figure 7.7.

And consider whether you want to send your reply by mail or through the newsgroup itself. While the essence of the newsgroups is communications, the last thing you want to do is to tie up an already overloaded group with messages that may be of interest to only a few. Consider whether your message is genuinely useful and interesting to the entire newsgroup population, or

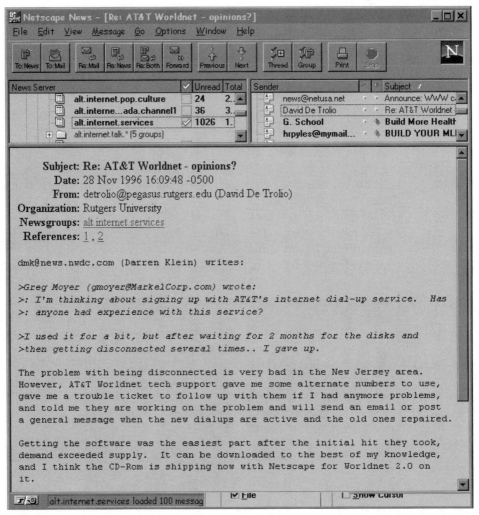

Figure 7.7 Quoting from a previous message enhances the clarity of your reply, but don't overdo the length of the quoted material.

whether it's really targeted at the individual to whom you're sending it. If the latter is the case, send the message by electronic mail.

Posting a New Message

To start a new thread in a newsgroup, either of the following methods will work:

1. Click the To:News button in the toolbar.
2. Pull down the File menu and click on New News Message.

This will produce the Message Composition window with the relevant information already inserted.

Saving Interesting Newsgroup Postings

In the absence of a folder system like the one it uses for mail, Netscape requires that you save postings via the menus. The method:

1. Pull down the File menu.
2. Click on Save Message(s) As.

You will then be able to choose a destination on your hard disk for the messages you want to save.

Decoding Graphics and Photographs

USENET has always been laden with graphics and photographs, but until recently, the process of downloading and decoding them has been a difficult chore. This is because the newsgroups travel across the network in the form of ASCII text. If you want to take binary information and send it through this medium, it's necessary to encode that information using various software programs and to decode it at the other end. The principal tools have always been a program called uuencode to handle the encoding and uudecode for rebuilding the binary file and thus displaying the image (or re-creating the program, or whatever type of binary data was being sent). Each download required separate work to decode it. Netscape allows us to forget about the whole encoding/decoding process because it happens in the background.

The alt.binaries hierarchy is a good place to look for images. Let's take a look at a group called alt.binaries.pictures.fractal. In this newsgroup, you'll find quite a few images generated by various computer algorithms; think of a fractal image as a graphical representation of mathematical data. Fractal geometry, derived from the work of the Polish mathematician Benoit Mandelbrot, can describe many of the irregular shapes found in nature that cannot be depicted using Euclidean geometry.

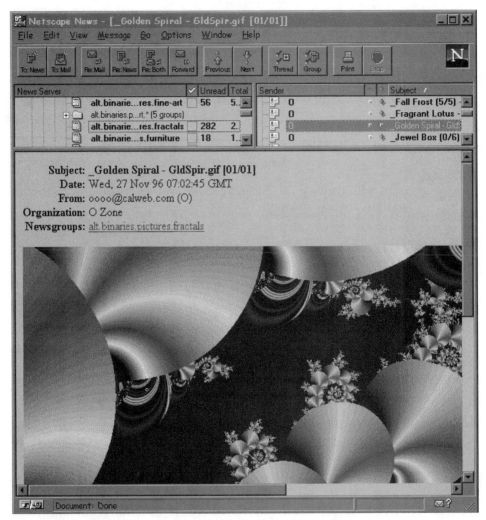

Figure 7.8   A fractal image shown in Netscape's content pane.

To see a fractal image, we can go into the newsgroup and click on the message we'd like to display. Netscape displays the image as part of the content pane. You can see one such image in Figure 7.8. The display was automatic; all I had to do was to choose the appropriate message and Netscape handled the rest.

Incidentally, images are not the only thing that can be coded and decoded in this way. Numerous groups exist for the posting of programs. One of these is comp.binaries.ms-windows, where programs can be found and decoded. You'll also find newsgroups focusing on programs for OS/2 and the Macintosh and various other platforms. Many of these binaries are made available in

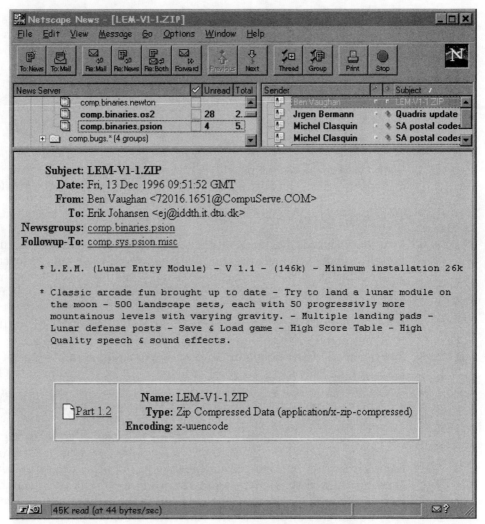

Figure 7.9 A compressed program is shown in the content pane; a click on the item allows you to save it to disk, where it can be decoded using the WinZip software.

compressed form, usually through the .zip format. To download such a file, it's necessary to save it to disk and decode it there. You can see how Netscape displays such information in Figure 7.9.

Tip: If you think you'll be downloading programs from the Internet, you need a copy of WinZip, a software program from Nico Mak Computing Inc. that handles all compression and decompression chores within an intuitive, windows-based environment.

You can check the WinZip home page out at http://www.winzip.com/. WinZip supports almost all Internet file formats, so it allows you to decode information no matter where you find it. The program's uninstall feature allows you to install a program found in a zip file and, if you choose not to keep it, to uninstall the program and return your system to its original state.

Newsgroup Do's and Don'ts

Your use of the newsgroups will be more enjoyable and productive if you heed a few basic rules. Here are some tips from my own USENET experience.

Read the FAQ

Frequently Asked Questions, or FAQs, have begun to enter our culture—they're questions that everybody needs to have answered when they're learning about a new topic. They're also questions that so many people ask that newsgroup regulars don't want to keep answering them. You can see a sample FAQ in Figure 7.10.

The core of newsgroup etiquette is to familiarize yourself with the FAQ for your newsgroup before you ask such questions. If, after reading this document, you still don't know the answer, you're justified in posing your question to the group. Who knows, it may wind up in the next version of the FAQ; these things are revised on a regular basis.

There are several ways to find the FAQ for a particular group. The easiest is to start reading the newsgroup and stick with it for a short while. If the group maintains a FAQ, it will be periodically posted as a message. Another possibility is to join the news.answers newsgroup, where most groups' FAQs regularly appear. This has the additional effect of providing you with some fascinating FAQs about topics you might not otherwise have considered, but it's less targeted than looking for the FAQ within the group itself. You can also find FAQ documents at an FTP site: ftp://rtfm.mit.edu/pub/usenet/news.answers/, but this may be the least effective way, given how busy this site stays, and the limitations it places upon the number of concurrent users.

Stick to the Subject

Years of experience with newsgroup reading has convinced me that the biggest problem the newsgroups face is the tendency of its subscribers to wander off the subject. An on-line community can maintain an ongoing conversation that benefits all its members, or it can break down into a series of disconnected comments and verbal snipes that do no one any good. Too many newsgroups have taken the latter course, and because so many of them are unmoderated, the breakdown tends to perpetuate itself. As with most Internet features, we'll get from the newsgroups what we put into them.

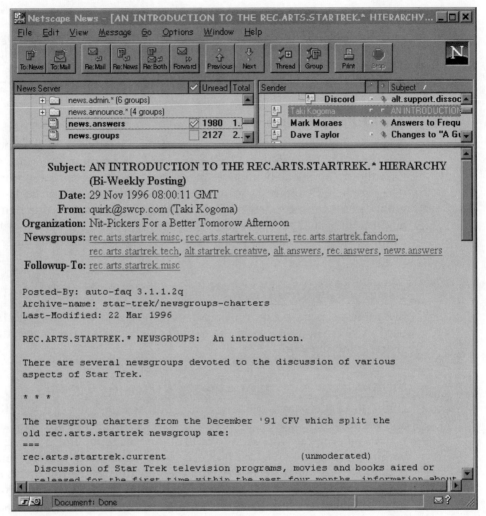

Figure 7.10   A FAQ displays answers to the basic questions about the newsgroup and the subject it discusses.

Pick Your Newsgroup Carefully

When you post, make sure you've targeted the right newsgroup for whatever it is you want to say. Messages that are cross-posted indiscriminately have a perverse effect upon USENET as a whole; people tend to stop reading groups that are filled with irrelevant material. Local or regional messages should be placed in the appropriate hierarchies, and not blasted around the globe. Given that there are now tens of thousands of newsgroups available, the beauty of the system is that it allows precise placement of commentary. Posting to the wrong group diminishes that capability.

Use Descriptive Titles

Most of us read our newsgroups by going through the message headers and deciding which threads seem interesting. Poorly chosen titles confuse everybody and result in lost time. Always try to make your titles clear and descriptive.

Avoid Flame Wars

"Flames" are messages stuffed with invective, usually aimed at somebody who has committed a gaffe or voiced an unpopular opinion. A certain amount of flaming isn't necessarily undesirable, since they can keep newsgroups on track when some individuals try to steer conversations off topic or decide to use the group as a forum for self-promotion. But it's all too easy for flame wars to develop, in which people who have never met trade insults about everything from spelling mistakes to political beliefs. Flames contribute little to debate and can poison the atmosphere of the group.

Use a Short Signature

Signatures can be posted in newsgroup messages as readily as they can be used in electronic mail, and the same advice applies: Use a signature that is short and to the point.

Summarize Messages about Particular Topics

Often the best way to use a newsgroup for research is to ask a specific question and request that answers be sent to your electronic mailbox. The assumption is that not everyone will want to read about this topic. But if you find yourself with a set of useful answers, it doesn't hurt to put them together into a single document, editing as necessary, and then posting the result; this is something like the digests that many mailing lists use to avoid cluttering people's mailboxes. A summary will be most appreciated if you delete unnecessary header information and cut messages down to their most significant parts.

Tip: The newsgroups have truly evolved into a culture of their own, one that is best understood by spending some time in them and learning how the regulars go about their business. To learn more about netiquette on the newsgroups, you should look for two documents in the news.answers postings. Both Rules for Posting to USENET, by Mark Horton, and A Primer on How to Work with the USENET Community, by Chuq Von Rospach, are helpful walk-throughs of the principles that keep daily life on the newsgroups at least semi-sane.

The Newsgroups through Forte Agent

A third-party newsreader offers some functionality not yet supplied by your browser. Forte's Agent program, for example, includes a variety of filtering mechanisms that enable you to remove from your message list any postings by people whom experience has taught you not to read. It also provides a bevy of helpful features that include integrated e-mail, cross-posting control (so that you can avoid messages that have been sent to more than one newsgroup automatically), import subscription list files to keep multiple copies of the program in sync, and archival features including folders and automatic filing. You can see Agent at work in Figure 7.11.

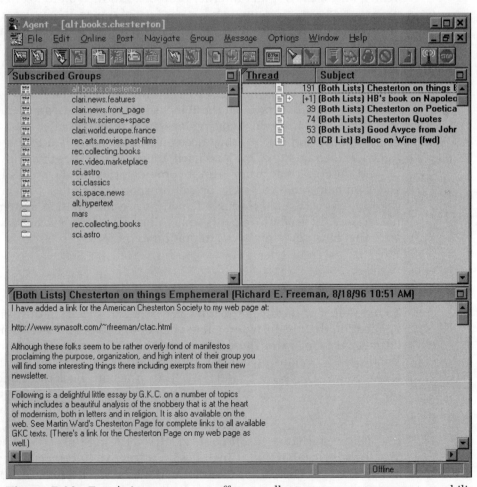

Figure 7.11 Forte's Agent program offers excellent message management capabilities and includes integrated e-mail.

Moreover, a freeware version of Agent called Free Agent is available to give you a taste of what the product can do. You can download Free Agent at the company's Web site: http://www.forteinc.com/. In most cases, your browser can handle all necessary Internet functions, but after you've gotten familiar with how to read the newsgroups in Netscape, I think you'll find Free Agent and its commercial counterpart well worth a look, particularly if your interest in USENET continues to grow.

Telnet: Logging In to Remote Computers

Telnet, one of the original Internet protocols, allows you to log in and use the resources on remote computers. On the face of things, it may seem that that is what you are doing every time you access the Web, but in fact, the model is different. A Web page is sent as a transaction; it crosses the network to you and is then displayed on your machine. What Telnet enables is a real-time user session, meaning you connect to a computer and, for the entire time you are connected, have access to whatever programs are made available on that machine. As long as you are involved in the Telnet session, you have an open connection to that site, meaning you are using its system resources.

While the number of Telnet-accessible tools has failed to grow with anything like the rapidity of the Web itself, there are still sites that allow you to log on and do everything from search commentaries on the works of Dante to check on ham radio call-signs or call up sports schedules. Numerous library catalogs are accessible through Telnet, as are information systems at many universities. In general, Telnet is something of a stopgap; it helps you use services that have yet to make the migration to the Web.

Downloading a Telnet Client

To use Telnet within Netscape, it's necessary to specify a third-party Telnet application that the browser can use. That, of course, means finding a Telnet client. A good many of these are available for various operating systems; for Windows 95, options include CRT for Windows 95, HyperTerminal, MrTerm for Windows 95, NetTerm, and QVT/Term. You can check these and other Telnet clients at sites like http://www.shareware.com/ and http://www.tucows. com/, both of which provide extensive lists of readily downloadable programs. For my purposes, NetTerm, from InterSoft International, works just fine (http://starbase.neosoft.com/~zkrr01/netterm.html). It's available in a Windows 95 version and it includes an attractive interface. The program is shareware, but comes with a reasonable $20 tariff; you can download an evaluation copy at the company's Web site. Installing NetTerm is a matter of running the set-up program, just as we did with the various plug-ins in Chapter 5.

Tip: It's a good idea to bookmark the major software sites for Windows-based shareware and freeware. Here you can search through lists of good Internet programs and experiment with different clients. The major sites are:

Stroud's Consummate Winsock Apps List (http://www.stroud.com/)
Windows95.com—32-bit Shareware Collection (http://www.windows95.com/)
Jumbo (http://www.jumbo.com/Home_Page.html)
The Ultimate Collection of Winsock Software (http://www.tucows.com)
PC Win Resource Center (http://pcwin.com/software.html)
Shareware.Com (http://www.shareware.com/)
Snoopie (http://www.snoopie.com/)
SoftwareSite-Dot-Com (http://softwaresite.com/index.html)

Or you can search for sites at FTPSearch (http://129.241.190.13/ftpsearch/)

Configuring Netscape for Telnet Use

Netscape must know where your Telnet client is to function. Here's how to tell it:

1. Pull down the Options menu.
2. Click on General Preferences.
3. Click on Apps.

The screen in Figure 7.12 should appear. The field in question is the one marked Telnet Application. In this field, enter the path to your Telnet client. Now click on OK to close the Apps panel and accept the changes.

Tip: Whenever forced to specify a path and filename for a new application, I've always found it easiest to use the Browse button provided by Windows 95 next to the relevant field. By clicking on this, you call up a visual display of your hard disk's contents and can quickly navigate to the executable file you need. This methodology is especially necessary given the ability of Windows 95 to use long filenames, which can be as confusing as they are helpful, depending on context.

Telnet and Terminal Emulation

With Netscape enabled for Telnet, we can choose an Internet resource and go. I've decided to look at FedWorld, a collection of governmental services and

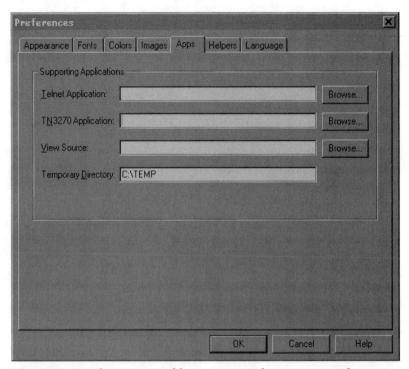

Figure 7.12   The Apps panel lets you enter the necessary information to tell Netscape where to find the Telnet client.

databases whose URL is telnet://fedworld.gov. To get there, I enter the URL in the Location field of Netscape and press a Return. The screen shown in Figure 7.13 then appears.

Notice that I'm prompted for a user name and password; or, in the event that I'm not familiar with the system, I'm given the opportunity to enter as New and be walked through the login procedure. By following the prompts and working my way through a form that asks for name and address, I choose a user ID and password and then am shown the main screen, as in Figure 7.14.

First of all, take note that the Telnet client appears in its own window; remember, this is a separate application that can't run inside Netscape itself. NetTerm's interface is full-featured, with icons governing major functions and a complete range of pull-down menus. This is quite a change from the days when we had to enter precise commands at a UNIX prompt!

Notice, too, that we're given the opportunity to enter commands within the NetTerm window. The command structure at each Telnet site will vary depending on what's being offered there. No single set of commands can therefore be surmised about any particular session, but you can count on most sites having information provided about available options. Be sure to follow these carefully, particularly the logout options. It's considered bad form to leave a Telnet session without going through the standard logout process at that site.

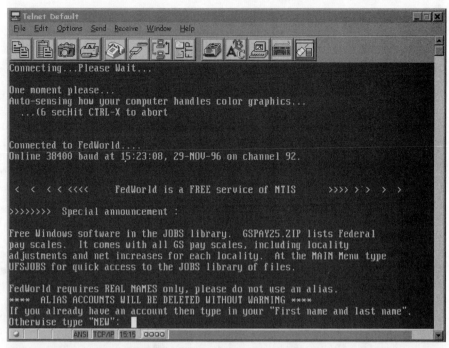

Figure 7.13 The FedWorld system walks new users through setting up a new account and then provides access to a variety of services.

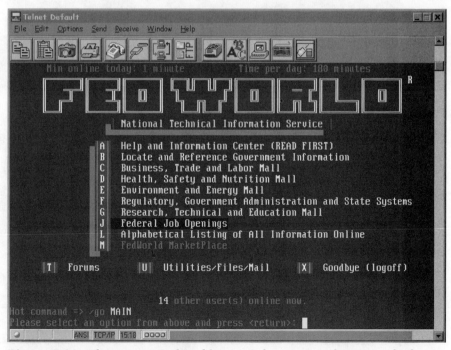

Figure 7.14 The primary FedWorld screen, showing you the range of information, from job openings to government databases, available here.

At FedWorld, I've been given the opportunity to display my data as straight text or through the enhanced ANSI method. The remote system needs to know what kind of display I'm using so that it can format its data properly. Many systems will use VT-100, a standard for displaying information in Digital Equipment Corp.'s terminals. ANSI graphics provide bolding and underlining as well as color; they make for a more interesting screen display. In Figure 7.15, you can see the range of government information available at this site, which I accessed by following the menu structure here. Using FedWorld turns out to be similar to using any bulletin board system.

But why worry about types of screen display? Certainly that's not something we've had to consider with standard Web pages. The answer is that Telnet treats our computer as though it were a terminal; the proper term for what the computer is doing is *terminal emulation*. The Telnet protocol comes out of the era when the most common way to compute was to connect terminals up to large centralized computers. A terminal is simply a display; it contains no processing power to speak of, but must show the information the mainframe sends. By asking us what kind of terminal we are using, the computer is determining what special features our terminal has, from color or graphics to full-screen editing capabilities and command keys.

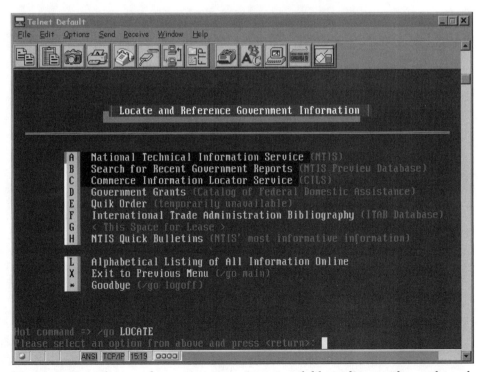

Figure 7.15 A listing of government resources available on-line, as shown through the NetTerm interface.

Of course, you're running a real computer and not just a terminal, but the remote machine doesn't know that. ANSI stands for American National Standards Institute, the group that developed the set of standards that made it possible for enhanced features to work over such a display. VT-100, the standard for Digital Equipment Corporation terminals, enables your system to display everything the Telnet server can send. Later, if you get adventurous, you can try out some other terminal emulation modes. NetTerm supports not only VT-100, but also VT-102, VT-220, and various other terminal emulations, giving you the ability to see boldface and underlined text, optional colors, and various other features.

One feature I like about NetTerm is that it provides a handy directory of Telnet sites, which you can see in Figure 7.16. You can easily add new sites to the list. Quite a few databases are available, as are various games, university directories, and miscellaneous services offering everything from backgammon to weather. Figure 7.17 shows the search screen at the largest of the library catalogs, the Library of Congress in Washington, D.C. Its address is telnet://loc. locis.gov, which can be entered directly into your browser or accessed through a hyperlink on the Library's Web site (http://lcweb.loc.gov/).

At both these sites we have come a long way from the graphical and fully formatted pages of the World Wide Web. Here, we're dealing with text, monospaced and, after the kind of typeset-quality pages we're used to on the Web, rather uninteresting. You can see why Telnet is fading before the power of the Web; given that we can now offer powerful search tools through gate-

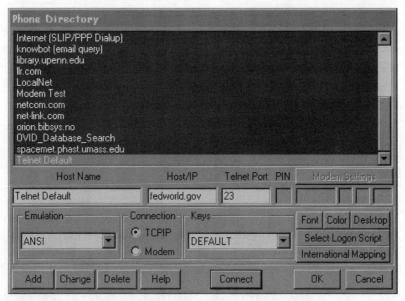

Figure 7.16 NetTerm's directory of Telnet sites is a great way to see what's available and to explore.

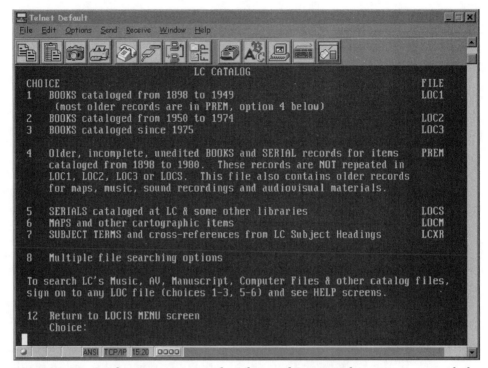

Figure 7.17 A Telnet connection to the Library of Congress; here, you can search the catalog by subject, author, or title.

ways and provide forms capabilities in our Web pages, the need for Telnet seems to have passed. But many services continue to be offered, including numerous bulletin board systems. You can check out an index of these on The Guide to Internet BBS home page (http://dkeep.com/sbi.htm/), maintained by Richard Marks.

Tip: Remember, when you are using Telnet, you are involved in an active user session. That means that for every minute you spend on-line at the site, you are taking up time and processor cycles on the remote computer. That's quite a difference from the Web, where you can simply pull up a page and let it sit for hours without causing any further traffic at the remote site. So don't waste your time when using Telnet. Be sure to locate what it is you're interested in and use it; then log off to allow other people their chance. Like an FTP site, a Telnet site can accommodate only so many people at any one time.

Another user issue: You'll run into links to Telnet sites on the Web, but often, simply calling up your Telnet program and picking out an address from its directory is the best way to go. Once I know that a given resource, like the Library of Congress catalog or, indeed, my own local library's catalog, is available only through Telnet, I simply find the NetTerm program and launch it, using it to connect quickly to the site. The linkage between Telnet and the Web is minimal.

HYTELNET: A Directory of Telnet-Accessible Resources

For years now, HYTELNET has served as a unique resource providing access to sites on the Internet that are accessible by Telnet. And that's no trivial matter. In fact, if you start looking around the Net by category of tool, it's quite difficult to locate information about Telnet sites, especially now that the Web has garnered the lion's share of press attention. But I've been using HYTELNET for a long time to get into library catalogs, Free-Nets, Campus Wide Information Systems (CWIS) and diverse other offerings including accounts with commercial on-line services and databases. If you get hooked on Telnet, you need to understand HYTELNET.

There are two primary ways of accessing this tool:

- By logging on to a HYTELNET server.
- By downloading the software and running it on your own system.

To track down background information about HYTELNET, try going to the source. In Figure 7.18, you can see the server at Northern Lights Internet Solutions in Saskatoon, Canada. This is where Peter Scott, old Internet hand and creator of HYTELNET, provides updates and information about the product. The address is http://www.lights.com/hytelnet/.

And in Figure 7.19, you can see a HYTELNET server at work. This is the one at Cambridge University in the United Kingdom. In the figure, I am viewing a page devoted to Free-Nets and community-based systems. These are bulletin boards with Internet access of one kind or another; all have been established through volunteer effort and fund-raising on the local level, and many provide interesting connections to their communities. Just as users in the Free-Net area can use the service to gain Net access, so Net users can log on to ask questions or follow discussions. All HYTELNET data is broken down on the Web into hyperlinks. Thus Figure 7.20, which shows you a listing of Internet-accessible library catalogs in the Netherlands.

Tip: Accessing a library catalog through Telnet is reason enough to download a Telnet client. Many local libraries are on-line, for example. When my son needs books for a school project, I can search the library catalog at home to find out what the options are without standing in line at the limited number of terminals available in the building. I can then print out a list of exactly what he needs and give it to him, letting him make the trip only after he has discovered what's on the shelf and where to find it.

However, HYTELNET needs a thorough revision. It's probably a symptom of the decline of Telnet that it has been such a long time since the last one; it's also an indication that the people who have been providing useful software for

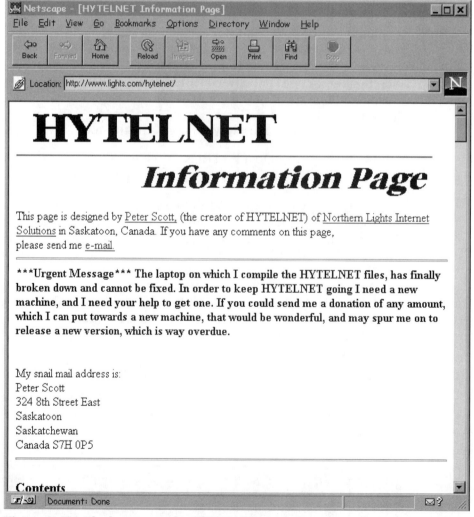

Figure 7.18   The home page for HYTELNET, with directions on accessing updates and using HYTELNET servers.

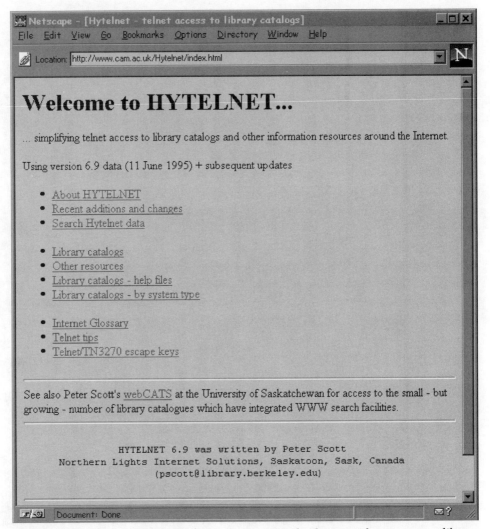

Figure 7.19 The HYTELNET Web server at Cambridge provides numerous library catalogs available by Telnet, as well as fee-based services, freenets, bulletin boards and more.

so many years on the Net can't go on forever making information available without expecting remuneration. I recommend adding HYTELNET to your bookmark list for those times when you do need a library catalog or a fast logon to a university that doesn't yet provide Web access. You can also look through older, but still occasionally useful, services like Netfind and the X.500 materials at PARADISE, a directory service used more in Europe than the United States.

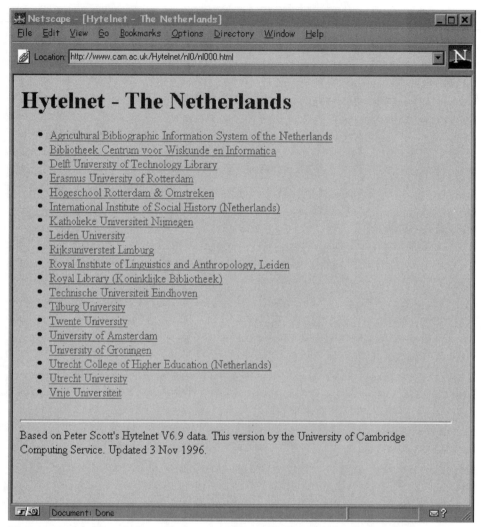

Figure 7.20 One click in HYTELNET lets you log in to various library systems around the globe.

Tip: One of the frustrations of HYTELNET is that you are often asked for a user name and, sometimes, a password. This is because not all the Telnet-able systems on the Internet are open to the general public, and thus wish to restrict access to a particular group of people. But in many cases, user names and passwords are freely available, which is where a program like HYTELNET can help. If, for example, I try to log on to the Netfind server at Imperial College in London (Netfind is a directory service to help you track down Internet addresses), I would come up against the need for a user name unless I went through HYTELNET. The latter program provides me with a link to the site and tells me the user ID to insert as well as the top-level menu choices I'll see once I log on. Other good sources for Telnet user names and passwords are the thick "yellow pages" directories that list Web sites and other destinations. But be sure to get one that provides more than just Web sites; Telnet, after all, is not part of the World Wide Web.

tn3270: Terminal Emulation for IBM Connections

Various interesting Telnet sites are available only in a special format. The IBM series of 3270 terminals, designed to work tightly with that company's mainframe computers, doesn't display information like other terminals. These screens offer blanks that users can fill in; they also use so-called programmed function, or PF keys. All of which means that a Telnet client that tries to access such a computer will retrieve unreadable results unless that client has been optimized to handle the right codes. The version of Telnet that does this is known as tn3270. In many cases, even with IBM computers, a normal Telnet client will be all you need, as the computer you connect to will recognize your client and supply the correct emulation. But if it doesn't, a good tn3270 client becomes the only way you can proceed.

Few Telnet clients offer tn3270 capability, which is why Netscape sets up a separate application field for this type of software. But if you browse in some of the software archive sites, you'll find several programs that can handle the chore. One of these is QWS3270, a freeware program written by Jim Rymerson; its URL is ftp://ftp.ccs.queensu.ca/pub/msdos/tcpip/qws3270.zip. You'll need to download and unzip it before you can run the program, but the installation is straightforward. Then it's time to configure Netscape:

1. Pull down the Options menu.
2. Click on General Preferences.
3. Click on Apps.
4. Enter the path name and filename in the TN3270 Application field.

At this point, when you try to log on to a tn3270 site, you'll be able to retrieve a screen you can read. But you'll rarely find direct links to tn3270 sites. Instead, you'll often have to open a connection directly, by calling up the QWS3270 program and inserting the proper address.

You can see an example of such a screen in Figure 7.21. Notice that this is not the usual Telnet screen. Instead, you're shown information in fields. You can enter a user ID and then press the Tab key to move to the Password field, and so on. The 3270 is a full-screen application, meaning that it expects you to move around on the screen for data entry with the Tab key. This site offers a database with information from the Harris organization relating to poll

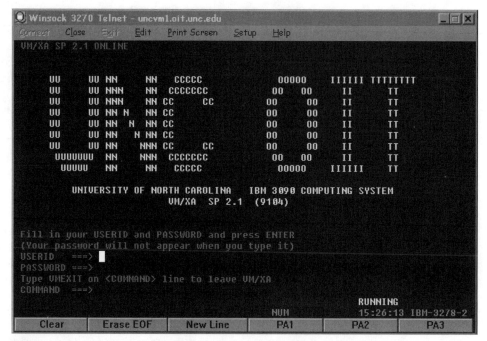

Figure 7.21 The QWS3270 client being used to access a tn3270 site.

results, but the identity of the database isn't the key. What counts is the way the 3270 system works with input and output commands. The screen, for example, does not scroll; instead, it goes blank and then reappears as you work your way through the system. If you page through a site like this, you'll also see reference to the function keys, like F1 or F2. It's impossible to specify which keys will have what effect, because tn3270 relies on a file called map3270 to list how the various keys are mapped to your keyboard. Remember: You're trying to convince the remote computer that you're using a 3270 terminal, even though you don't have all the necessary keys! Trial and error is often the best technique at a 3270 site, but if you get stuck, try either a Ctrl-C or a Ctrl-] command to get out of the system.

Gopher: A Trusty Tool Soldiers On

In the days before the World Wide Web had taken off, people who wanted to use the Internet without learning complicated UNIX commands or relying on their system administrators for constant advice turned to Gopher. This text-based, menu-driven tool was created at the University of Minnesota by Mark McCahill and a team of programmers who wanted to open up the resources of the Net to nonspecialists. The Gopher interface was simplicity itself—a menu with a movable pointer. You could use the Up or Down arrow keys to put the pointer on whatever item you wanted to see and press a Return to call up the document. Moreover, Gopher could easily link to information on other Gophers, so that the system of interlocked information became worldwide.

While the information available on Gophers started out as text alone, it quickly grew to encompass many of the same formats we're used to seeing on the Web—images, sound files, moving video, programs. Gopher could be used to access an FTP site, and many people found that moving around in that site's directory structure was easier using Gopher than with traditional FTP methods. Gopher also provided easy-to-use indices that could be searched by entering a keyword. Thus you could find out what was available on the Gopher you were using without hunting through the menus; or you could search through the worldwide "Gopherspace" by submitting the search term and viewing a menu of results.

Today, you can easily use Gopher through a Web browser; in fact, the browser interface only adds flexibility to your Gopher work, so that no other client is necessary, although a variety of programs are available. In Figure 7.22, you can see the Gopher site at the University of Minnesota, where Gopher was born. The address is gopher://gopher.micro.umn.edu/. At this site, you'll find the amusing definition of Gopher:

gopher   n. 1. Any of various short-tailed, burrowing mammals of the family Geomyidae, of North America. 2. (Amer. colloq.) Native or inhabitant of Minnesota: the Gopher State. 3. (Amer. colloq.) One who runs errands, does odd-jobs, fetches or delivers documents for office staff. 4. (computer tech.) Software following a simple protocol for tunneling through a TCP/IP internet.

In fact, Gopher was named after a combination of the preceding, the team name of the University of Minnesota being the Golden Gophers. And, of course, the software does precisely what the definition implies—it goes out and fetches things, in this case computer documents and files, and brings them back to you.

Tip: The beauty of using a common interface for network tools like Gopher and the newsgroups is that it allows you to stick within a single framework of menus and commands. If you used a different Gopher client, for example, you'd have to master its own menu structure for doing things like creating bookmarks to mark useful sites. In Netscape, you can use the same bookmark list for Gopher sites as you use for Web pages, all through the magic of URLs.

The Gopher methodology is obvious. Each of the menu items on the browser screen is a hyperlink. Click on it to call up information. The folder

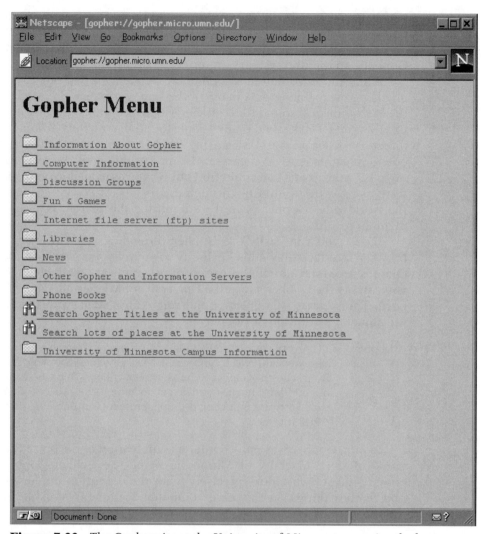

Figure 7.22   The Gopher site at the University of Minnesota remains the best source of Gopher information.

icon tells you that there is more to be found within the hyperlink, and indeed, when I click on the News item, I call up the screen in Figure 7.23.

A click on the Other Gopher and Information Servers item from the main Gopher menu calls up links to Gophers throughout the world. This is a good way to browse through Gopher holdings. You'll find that while use of Gopher has tapered off dramatically in the United States and Western Europe thanks to the spread of the World Wide Web, the text-based interface Gopher provides nonetheless offers powerful advantages in areas where bandwidth and equip-

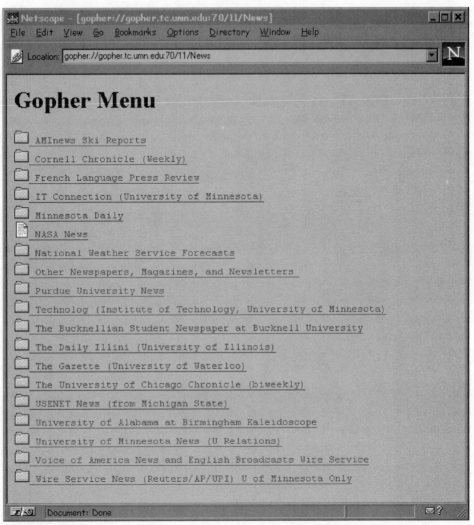

Figure 7.23 Gopher nests menu within menu; using it with a browser is a matter of point and click.

ment constraints make using the Web less feasible. Figure 7.24, for example, shows a listing of Gophers in South America.

If you become interested in the resources available through Gopher, I recommend checking into the Gopher Jewels site. The Web page is at http:// galaxy.einet.net/GJ/; there, you'll find Gophers conveniently broken down by topic, so you can drill down to the particular type of Gopher you're looking for. In Figure 7.25, for example, I have asked to see Gophers dealing with politics and government.

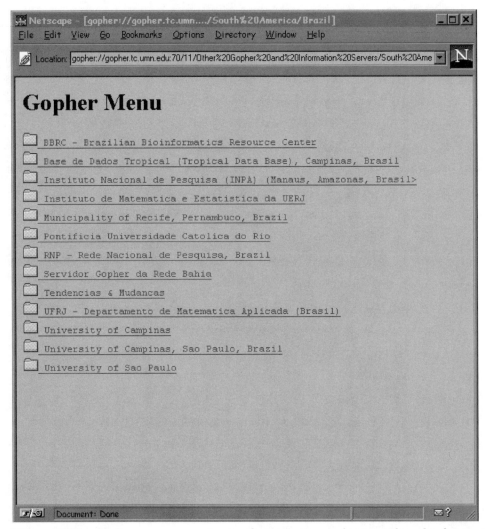

Figure 7.24 Gopher servers remain significant in areas where text-based information is still the norm. These Gophers are found in Brazil.

Notice the search button at the top of this screen. Entering a keyword here helps me home in on specific information. The Web interface simplifies the operation, but Gopher Jewels is also available in traditional Gopher format (gopher://cwis.usc.edu/11/Other_Gophers_and_Information_Resources/Gopher-Jewels. And if you'd like to keep up with happenings in the world of Gophers, you can join the Gopher Jewels mailing list. To subscribe, send mail to listproc @EINet.net with the message "subscribe gopherjewels *your name*." A final suggestion: the newsgroup comp.infosystems.gopher tracks Gopher events and issues, often from a technical perspective.

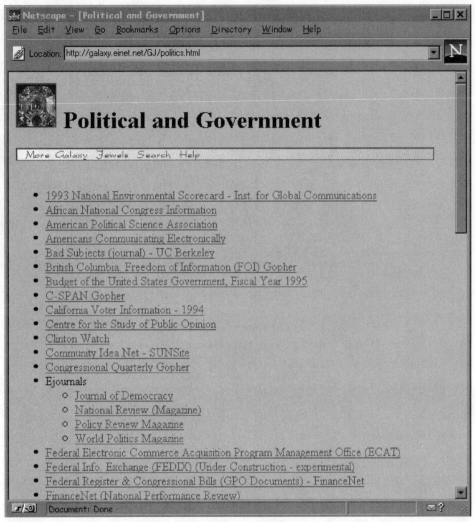

Figure 7.25 Gopher Jewels is an excellent way to get an overview of Gopher information.

Tip: You'll run into the term Veronica at some time during your Gopher travels. Veronica is a system that was developed by Fred Barrie and Steve Foster at the University of Nevada to search Gopher menu titles. In the days before we had Web-based search engines, Veronica was the hottest research tool in town. It allowed you to connect to a remote server and specify a keyword search that could take in Gophers all over the world. The results would be returned as another Gopher menu. Thus you could quickly build up a clickable menu of all Gopher items mentioning the term "italy" and including the word "politics," and so on. Then you could select one of these items and call it up.

But as the Internet grew, the search capabilities of Veronica ran into difficulties. There weren't enough Veronica servers to handle the immense traffic load, and as word of the system's utility spread, it became common to attempt logging in to multiple sites with no success. Veronica is still available through numerous Gopher menus, but when you reach a Veronica server, the wait can be interminable. More likely, you'll receive a message that the server has too many connections, and that you should try again later. Needless to say, this is a frustrating experience, and the growth of Web search engines has likewise contributed to Veronica's decline. Several of the Web engines, as we'll see in the next chapter, perform Gopher searches as well, so the need for a separate search tool like Veronica has rapidly diminished.

8

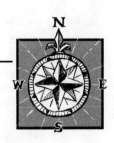

Breakthrough Web Technologies

No other medium has grown as fast as the World Wide Web—not television, not radio, certainly not the cinema. The pace of development keeps even industry professionals confused, requiring that they monitor developments daily if not hourly, and sometimes reverse the courses of company projects and overhaul ideas that were themselves innovative just a month or two before. You have only to look at Microsoft, which transformed itself to embrace the Internet with a rapidity that most observers thought impossible for a company of its size. But Microsoft CEO Bill Gates could see that the Internet was where the future of computing was pointed, and suddenly Microsoft was a browser maker; and The Microsoft Network, originally an on-line service comparable to CompuServe or America Online, evolved into a Web-based content provider.

But if the pace is furious, it's becoming clear that certain key themes are emerging. The Internet, and by extension the Web itself, has become so pervasive a factor in modern communications that many of its newest technologies are destined to become household items within the next few years. We are moving beyond question to a Web that is more interactive than its present model would suggest. Pointing in this direction are tools like Java and ActiveX, from Sun Microsystems and Microsoft respectively, both of which tie your computer closely to Web content. Rather than dealing with the Web as a thing that is "out there," accessed by a computer that reaches out and pulls in content, the new Java and ActiveX models create content on your screen through downloadable and updatable programs that work seamlessly with the Web site. In this model, the network becomes an extension of your hard disk, with immense ramifications for how we conceive of stored software, and indeed, how we view the nature of computing itself.

Both Java and ActiveX are available now, even if their early implementations are nowhere near as fully featured as the tools we'll routinely use in a few years. Java is built into both Internet Explorer and Netscape, while ActiveX, an integral part of Internet Explorer, is accessible to Netscape users through a plug-in. Neither technology will leapfrog the other, in my judgment; both the major browser players will have to build in the necessary hooks to keep the twin Net tools functional, for more and more Web sites will begin implementing content in one or the other format.

But beyond the exciting possibilities of Java and ActiveX, we also see developments in areas that would have boggled the minds of early network pioneers. A new language, Virtual Reality Modeling Language (VRML), has been developed to create content in imaginative on-line environments. Virtual reality is all about simulating self-contained worlds, using your mouse to control your movements. Your range of action is three-dimensional, so you can explore a building, move through a corridor and open a door, or walk outside and around a structure. We'll doubtless see all sorts of experimentation with this model, producing databases in which, instead of entering keywords into a blank form, you enter a room and type in a request to a virtual librarian. Such environments are being built into browsers right now, through technology folded into both Internet Explorer and Netscape Navigator; and though the number of virtual worlds available today is small, those that we do have point to a future filled with alternate digital realities and revisions to our current interfaces.

Internet telephony is in the cards as well, pushing voice through the Net's long-haul communications channels and connecting people around the world through their desktop computers. Pointcasting is turning the Web into the equivalent of an extremely targeted television station, one that can be customized to reflect your needs and accessed on a schedule you determine. Agents are being designed to run basic Web searches and perform other network chores for you, while off-line readers and downloaders cope with the limitations of today's modern connections by giving you time- and money-saving alternatives. Indeed, the issue quickly becomes not whether you can perform this or that new task, but which task you want to take the time to perform, and which set of software tools you'll download to handle it.

Modes of Interactivity

What exactly does it mean to make content come to life? Isn't one of the great virtues of the Web the fact that we can view data in so many different ways, surmounting the old limitations of text-only display? The answer is certainly yes, but in important ways, most Web pages we can view today have only begun the trek into genuine interactivity. The reasons have to do with the way Web information is handled through standard HTTP methods.

Consider what happens when you access a Web page. You make a choice and click on a hyperlink with your mouse (or else type in a URL in the Location field, or choose it from among your bookmarks or history list). Your mouse click causes your browser, the client, to send an information request to a server, which processes it and returns the desired Web page, including whatever text, graphics, and other forms of content the developer of that page has made available. The result, returned to you via HTTP, displays on your screen—a magazine page, a moving video, an animation, a sound file, viewed from within your browser.

What's missing here is a continuous presence. Although it may give the impression of maintaining a live connection to the remote site, your browser is actually displaying content in a one-shot fashion. Once the request has been fulfilled by the server, the page in front of you does not change. The software has handled a transaction—you've asked for something that has been sent. When you want to see an update of that page, you must ask for it again. This might not be a problem with many kinds of sites. You probably wouldn't worry about reloading the pages of a classic novel, for example; they're unlikely to change due to work at the site upgrading their page environment. But the Web has become a prime mover of news—financial news, world events, company information, personal sites—and when it comes to fast-breaking stories, you want some way to stay on top of them. You don't want to go to a CNN Interactive, or a Washington Post On-line, only to find that while you were reading the page, a major news story broke that you missed because you accessed the page a minute too early.

So what we need is a way of creating a Web *session*. A session is a continuous on-line presence, so that once you've logged on, changes at the site can be reflected in what you see on the screen. That crisis in the Formosa Straits or that sudden uptick in your stock's price now reaches you because the screen updates itself according to what the system administrator at that site—the Webmaster—has added there. Now the Web is truly alive, and the reach-and-acquire methodology of standard Web access changes. It becomes more analogous to tuning in a broadcast on either the radio or the television, with the significant difference that the Web provides sites, or channels, to continue the metaphor, in the hundreds of thousands. You can pick your content with great precision, and having done so, you can keep up with what's happening there by staying connected.

 Tip: Don't plug-ins also make the Web interactive? The answer is yes, but technologies like Java and ActiveX significantly extend that interactivity. Plug-ins require users to download software for their specific operating system and to install it, a nontrivial task for many. Both Java and ActiveX move beyond the plug-in model by creating tight integration between the Web and your own software. As far as the end user is concerned, Java transcends the operating system limitation, and applets downloaded in the Java environment run without user intervention, so no tricky installation is required. ActiveX can link not only Web sites and browsers in interactive ways, but can also work closely with standard desktop software like spreadsheets and word processors. While plug-ins will remain a vital force in browser development, it's safe to say that the real action will increasingly be found with Java and ActiveX.

Java: Toward an Interactive Web

Java grew out of work at Sun Microsystems in the early 1990s that was originally devoted to the consumer electronics market. By 1993, features that would make the language shine in the Internet environment were added, but it was really when Netscape announced that its Navigator version 2.0 would include support for Java's interactivity that the language took off. Intriguingly, its rapid rise from "beta" version (an early release for testing purposes) in the latter half of 1995 to fully activated Web tool points to changes in the plug-in model we examined in the previous chapter. Plug-ins are a way around a problem, meeting the need to add functionality to the browser. Plug-in technology arose because a browser couldn't be all things to all people; adding particular programs that worked seamlessly with the browser was a good way to provide those who needed it with the chance to add particular services to their software, while avoiding tools they didn't need that would just take up space on their hard disk. Thus the plug-in tool could recognize file formats that the browser could not. Earlier add-ons and helper applications did precisely the same thing, though without the programming hooks that enabled them to be so tightly integrated with the browser.

By contrast, Java works with a so-called Java Virtual Machine, which basically 'wraps around' the operating system. The Java Virtual Machine is ported to each operating system, allowing the same set of code to work on computers running Windows 95, OS/2, UNIX and more. A Java-equipped browser and its Java Virtual Machine receives content over the Web, the content being the actual code necessary to run a specific application. Along with the virtual machine is a set of basic routines (or libraries) which every application downloaded can depend upon to facilitate the operation of the program. The Java *applets* we use today are small applications that can be programmed to view or process particular kinds of data. Unlike plug-ins, Java does not require special installation of applications. As a complete programming environment, it allows the development of almost any application that can run on an operating system supporting the Java Virtual Machine. For the end user, programs will be able to be distributed as soon as they are developed, without having to await the user's upgrade to particular file viewer plug-ins.

Java is significantly different in that it comes without the standard baggage of operating systems. By that I mean that we're used to functioning with software written specifically for the type of computer we use. Thus my Windows 95 version of Netscape Navigator works fine in that environment, but to get Netscape up and running on my Power Mac, I have to procure the Macintosh-specific version of the program. In one form or another, the limitations of operating systems have kept computer users apart for years, effectively isolating Macintosh and OS/2 users from the huge user communities of DOS, UNIX, and Microsoft Windows.

Java circumvents that limitation because of the way it's built. A browser that works with Java turns the Java instructions the browser receives from the server into an executable program that runs on your computer. When the browser is confronted with a Java applet, it is able to run that program through the Java Virtual Machine. The program will run as long as the virtual machine designed for your operating system is present.

The process is a five-step activity:

1. By clicking on a hyperlink, you cause your browser to request an HTML page from a remote computer.
2. The browser then receives the HTML page.
3. The browser encounters a tag within the HTML file that specifies a Java applet; this requires a separate applet file.
4. The browser sends a request to the server for the applet file.
5. The browser receives the file. The built-in Java Virtual Machine checks the code for correctness and then executes it.

Crucial to the Java model is that the program is executed on the user's machine, which steps neatly around some of the Internet's bandwidth restrictions, though not all; the applet code, after all, must still be downloaded.

The Java Virtual Machine can be created for any type of computer. When the browser queries the server for the Java applet and downloads it to the user's machine, the browser recognizes the Java data type and hands off the Java instructions to the interpreter. It's the fact that the code is running locally, on the user's machine, that distinguishes Java and enables it to avoid the operating system trap. The Internet itself has been a conciliator in the operating system wars, since it too is platform-independent; I can view a Web page created on a Macintosh or UNIX server as readily as I can view one created in some version of Windows. But Java extends that cross-platform capability into the realm of programming itself; we begin to foresee a day when operating system questions fade before the power of the network.

Tip: We've seen that Web developers use the Common Gateway Interface (CGI) to produce interactive forms, clickable maps, and other types of user-oriented pages. CGI, often written using the Perl programming language, creates scripts that require processing on the server to function. Java is different in that the processing happens locally, based on the data the server sends to the client. That makes Java a more efficient means of creating these user-interactive pages. Rather than moving huge amounts of data from server to client, Java moves only its own set of instructions. User interface elements are then displayed by the Java Virtual Machine.

Notice that I said when the Java code arrives on your machine, it is checked before being executed as a program. This is for reasons of security. You can imagine what would happen if it were possible to download programs into your system without any sort of oversight; the makers of computer viruses would have a field day writing malignant code that would crash systems and destroy data. To circumvent this problem, the creators of Java built a variety of safety mechanisms into the language. A Java file being transferred to your machine will be checked to make sure that its requested operations are legal. Java also supports other security mechanisms that we'll discuss in a later chapter, including RSA public-key encryption; the program is likewise compatible with Netscape's own Secure Sockets Layer (SSL) and the Private Communications Technology (PCT) developed by Microsoft and VISA. Java programs, in other words, work within a tightly controlled environment, and their code is continually rechecked to make sure it follows the standard format.

Tip: Needless to say, all the security in the world can't induce a complete sense of safety about any software; people have broken into computer systems thought to be invulnerable, even some belonging to the military. Sadly, we're beginning to see a number of applets specifically designed to cause trouble, everything from crashing your browser to trashing your data files or, even worse, corrupting your hard disk's boot sector so that it can't be used at all. One possible solution has been suggested by Microsoft, which built a system called Authenticode Secure Technology into Internet Explorer 3.0. The idea is that software authors can certify their code as tamper-free, and the corresponding programs can be validated by third-party companies. It's a new technology, but in theory it could provide an additional layer of protection into Java applications. We're also beginning to see the development of Java-specific anti-virus products. Finjan Software's SurfinBoard 1.0 is the earliest of these.

For a look at what a prankster can do to a Java applet, take a look at:

www.math.gatech.edu/~mladue/HostileApplets.html.

The beauty of Java is that anything that can be programmed using the C++ programming language (a standard development tool for programs of all kinds) can be written in Java. Thus the Internet can become a globally distributed delivery system for new software, a kind of virtual hard disk that pulls in programs as necessary. These programs could be database search engines or spreadsheets armed with a variety of analytical tools, or word processors hooked to dynamically updating dictionaries, thesauri, and libraries of clip-art imagery. Hit a button at the top of the screen and your program connects not to a disk-based (and disk-filling) database of words or formulae, but to a Web site optimized for delivering such data. Today's Java effects, which are largely visual demonstrations like animated icons or scrolling ticker tapes of text, will give way to larger, more sophisticated programs that will be transferred over tomorrow's broader bandwidth data pipes, and optimized for particular uses according to the Web site you access. Java's modular approach means that it will be possible to load just those portions of a particular program that you need; if you want to load a chart into a document, a Java applet could handle the job without the overhead of downloading an entire graphics display program. These advantages hold true not just for the Web, but also for electronic mail and other types of Internet data with which Java makes a natural fit.

What can be done with Java in the real world?

Newt Pong is an unusual paddle-based game with a familiar contestant (http://www.metamor.com/pages/_play_pages/newtpong.html).

The National Geophysical Data Center offers a Java-enabled interface to its database (http://www.ngdc.noaa.gov/mgg/test/mggdevelopment.HTML).

The Bahasa Pages offer several Java-based language tutorials, including English to Mandarin Chinese (http://www.bahasa.com/).

Mountcomp Applied Software provides a interesting Java-powered currency converter (http://www.mountcomp.co.uk/currency/).

You can find links to these and many other applets at the Gamelan site: http://www.gamelan.com/index.shtml). Here you can see Java in all its interactive glory. Numerous applets are on-line, making it a good place to survey the possibilities. But bear in mind that true functionality with Java awaits the arrival of a better network infrastructure. Many of today's applets are more proof-of-concept demonstrations than anything else.

Tip: One interesting feature about Java is that it recognizes two types of programs: applets and applications. An applet, as we've seen, is designed to be referenced inside a Web page and run inside a Web browser like Netscape or Internet Explorer. An application can be a stand-alone program that runs outside a Web browser. Remember, Java is very similar to C++, a major programming tool for the development of software of all kinds. This means that a particular program could be written in Java and stored on your hard disk. When you run the program, it functions. But it would still contain the other Java features we find so intriguing, including the ability to be revised on the fly by accessing the necessary network site with your browser. Java applets could be used to tweak its parameters and incorporate new features. One aspect of Java, then, is that it blurs the distinction between programs stored on your disk and programs stored on the network.

Finally, Java changes the upgrade scenario. In today's world of shrink-wrapped software, upgrading a program means buying new disks from the developer or retailer, which you then install on your system. Unless you make the effort to seek out the upgrade, your software remains the same. With a Java application, every time you access a site housing it, you are getting the latest version; in the case of Java applications already running on your system, new features can be absorbed directly into them. The software works tightly with the interpreter, so you the user don't have to worry about the intricacies of installation, and you upgrade only when you need the revised software, as demonstrated by your accessing the program site. The upgrade process—everything from enhanced versions of major programs like spreadsheets and word processors to fixes for minor system glitches—becomes more effective and virtually transparent to the user.

Using the Java-Enabled Page

With Java now built into Internet Explorer and Netscape, using Java in your own work is a simple matter. You simply click on the page you want to see, and if a Java-enabled program is available on the server, it will begin to be displayed on your screen. Small applets won't take long to transfer; you'll see jumping icons and animated logos, and hear sound effects and music almost as soon as the page begins to load. Larger applets will take longer to download, a problem that awaits the widening of the Net's infrastructure to include faster communications links (it's also a reminder of your need to keep up with the fastest modem speeds possible). When the applet is present, it will run continuously until you exit its page, depending on how it has been designed, and how well it has been programmed. And be aware that in these early days of the Java revolution (the language was only introduced in May 1995, at the SunWorld conference), numerous relatively untested programs will be making their way across the network in this way; system crashes may result from some, while others will serve as potent demonstrations of how Java can enhance a Web page. For the next few years, patience will be the order of the day as developers push the limits of the Java medium.

Tip: In technical terms, we call Java an object-oriented programming language. It's also said to be an interpreted language, and a multithreaded one. You don't need to understand these terms to work with Java on-screen, but if you're curious, let's run through the concepts:

Object-oriented: Rather than viewing them as procedures that operate on data, object-oriented programming considers the parts of a program as "objects" that can exchange information. Each object is a combination of data and program code that is self-contained; the program includes the object, among other objects, as part of its overall structure. Object-orientation implies modular programming. Because each object can stand by itself, it can be copied to another program rather than having to be re-created in that program. Furthermore, because objects, once created, are complete in themselves, they can be interchanged to create new programming structures. You can see that this model works nicely with graphical user interfaces. An icon can represent an entire object, and can be moved on the screen to be copied elsewhere. The ability to hide the object's complexity is the key benefit of object-oriented technology. The most popular object-oriented programming language today is C++; Java is more object-oriented than C++. You may also have heard of Smalltalk, from Xerox's Palo Alto Research Center, which played such a large part in the evolution of the Macintosh and its graphical interface.

Interpreted language: An interpreted language is one that does not create an executable version of the program itself, but uses a so-called interpreter to run the program. This feature allows Java to run on many hardware platforms. Rather than being compiled into machine code, Java applets are downloaded in so-called bytecode format to the interpreter on your computer. It is within that interpreter that the instructions conveyed by the code are actually executed, which means that the interpreter can adjust as needed for differences in the hardware on which it will run the program. Without this ability, Java would not be able to offer cross-platform capability. Users working with different operating systems can run the same Java program as long as they have an interpreter on their machines. As you can imagine, software developers like this capability, as it means they don't have to write new code for each type of computer that their program may encounter on the Internet.

Multithreaded language: Multithreading means that in a single Java applet or program, numerous different instructions can be executed at the same time. Thus a database query can take place even as a communications session is occurring.

Here are some Java-enabled pages that you will want to explore in search of further information:

http://java.sun.com/: This is Sun Microsystems Java page, which contains links to a motherload of Java information and demonstrations that showcase the potential of the language.

http://www.acl.lanl.gov/~rdaniel/classesJDK/PickTest2.html: An intriguing use of Java to display medical imagery.

http://reality.sgi.com/grafica/impression/: The Impressionist is a Java-based paint program that lets you create a painted representation of a photograph.

http://www.hotwired.com/java/: The HotWired site is always a good place to keep up with network developments. Here you can get Java news and see various animations and other effects created by the language.

http://www.servonet.com/javaStuff/: A useful site for multimedia applets, including some interesting applications of sound.

http://www.intrepid.com/~robertl/index.html: A variety of financial applications that highlight Java's capabilities.

Java and the Network Computer

Java's many virtues make it a potentially transforming technology. Today, we have accepted a model of computing that puts individual processors on the desktop, but that model is a recent one. It wasn't that many years ago that most computing occurred through terminals connected to mainframe machines, thus spreading the computing muscle of a company by offering access to people other than the computer staff. And if the Internet can be treated by Java as a huge hard disk, is there some sense in which we are returning to that model of centralized computing? Some people think so, but it's a centralized model with a difference.

Companies like Sun Microsystems, Oracle, IBM, and Apple Computer, among others, are exploring the concept of the so-called network computer (NC). In its purest form, the NC takes on many aspects of the old terminal connecting to a mainframe—it houses just enough processing power to get you connected to the computer resource, in this case, the Internet, and to display what you find there. Storage could be local on a hard disk or network-based, depending on configuration. Software, given the expected expansion in network bandwidth in the next few years, could be stored on the Net itself. When you needed to write a document, for example, Java could create the necessary text editor through a quick network connection. When you needed to manipulate financials to check out a new home loan, Java could supply the necessary spreadsheet, expandable as needed, modular, and updated to the latest version every time you accessed it.

When first debated, the NC won points on price; the idea was to make it cheap enough that people who would not otherwise buy a computer wouldn't hesitate to buy an NC. But that price point—around $500—is now seen as the least of the NC's advantages. After all, computer prices continue to drop as power continues to increase, so it's not at all out of the question to expect a fully featured, network-compatible computer to sell for that same $500 in the near future, and it would include things an NC did not, such as a large hard disk and the power to run applications while off-line. But the NC competes more effectively in terms of its simplicity. For home as well as corporate users, the Java model would mean the end of difficult, user-installed upgrades. Especially where the operating system is concerned, such upgrades frequently leave novices frustrated, who often work with less than optimized machines because the complications of the upgrade are too great. Java sidesteps that problem by updating itself every time a particular applet is run; the user's machine is always running up-to-the minute software and is always optimized.

The Java model can be described as "thin clients" and "fat servers"—thin clients because the network computer has been minimized to house only the essential components for its tasks; fat servers because the servers that feed it data will have to hold both host programs for the NCs and enough storage space for user files. The third key element is the high-speed network; many business offices already support speeds adequate for the task, while for home users, the Internet's bandwidth will continue to increase. Whether the Java model can succeed in the average home is questionable; home computers rely on local storage and software from portfolio managers to games that have yet to migrate to Java. Whether the NC takes off in the home depends largely upon how effective Java becomes at supplying programs that will serve it, and upon the necessary infrastructure improvements that will make its use advantageous.

But network computers may take off in the environment most receptive to their advantages—the large corporate computing office. Here, system administrators will welcome this ease of installation and use, and they will appreciate their ability to maintain control over a large and diverse group of computer users, particularly in terms of such problems as virus control and standardized applications. Here, too, cost remains a huge factor. Studies by the Gartner Group have estimated that the total cost of running a personal computer linked to an office network runs between $8,000 and $13,000 per year, including such factors as maintenance, support, depreciation, and user training. By contrast, Sun estimates that the cost of running one of its JavaStation thin clients is roughly $2,500 annually. Key to the savings is the fact that the NC returns administration functions back to professionals, thus avoiding lost productivity as workers try to figure out how to manage their own machines.

The ActiveX Alternative

Although it was first out of the gate, Java isn't the only technology being marketed as a way to make the World Wide Web more interactive. Microsoft, which has announced its support for Java, has nevertheless also produced an alternative called ActiveX. Where Java works with applets, ActiveX works with so-called controls, which can either be stored locally on the user's machine or on a remote server on the Internet. Internet Explorer 3.0 includes ActiveX as part of the browser; Excite Corp.'s NCompass Labs division is also making a plug-in available for Netscape that handles ActiveX. Using the technology, Web sites have greater ability to include user input in their presentations; in a sense, they can offer many of the same features that standard desktop programs offer, but with the difference that these applications are networked. Once again, we are pointing to a merger between the desktop computer and the Internet.

ActiveX draws on Microsoft's Object Linking and Embedding (OLE) technology, which is supported not just in Internet Explorer, but in standard desktop applications as well. OLE is a way to embed information and create links to it. A document can be linked to another in this way, so that when the information in the first program changes, the data in the linked document also changes. Moreover, OLE can work between two different programs. For example, I might be using spreadsheet data in Excel to create a graph of the performance of a particular stock. And perhaps I have embedded that graph in a letter I send out once a month to my clients. When the information in the spreadsheet is updated every month to reflect changing prices, the OLE link to the letter will ensure that its graph is also updated. In its updated ActiveX form, OLE offers a model of networked computing where the local computer and files on the remote server work together in a seamless way, much as Java offers applets and applications that can function either by being downloaded through the Internet and executed locally, or by running as independent programs on your own machine.

Tip: Why do we refer to ActiveX "controls?" The answer goes back to 1991, when Microsoft brought out its Visual Basic 1.0, an object-oriented programming language. The Visual Basic Custom Control, or VBX, was a component that could be added to a programming project as an object. For example, an entire routine for talking to a modem could be built into a program by adding the right control. The benefit, of course, is simplicity; programmers saved time by not having to reinvent the wheel every time they wanted to add a new feature. When Microsoft folded this control model into its OLE system, we wound up with the OLE custom control, or OCX. ActiveX works off this model of object-oriented, modular procedures. For Microsoft, the history of control development means that numerous programmers already understand what controls are and how they function. The result should be quick development of new controls.

All of this fits nicely with the Microsoft model, in which the Internet becomes tightly integrated with the operating system. Future versions of Internet Explorer will be designed to maximize the blending of remote and local computing; you will use the same interface for accessing local files that you use for pulling in material from the Internet (think of the operating system interface as itself a Web page). Thus ActiveX takes the Microsoft OLE formula and extends it to the browser and, by extension, the operating system itself.

ActiveX controls can be embedded in Web pages just as data from one document can be embedded in another; the control can thus create a variety of interactive effects on the local machine from the Web. Moreover, the OLE technology, being widespread in terms of applications, offers a host of intriguing uses linking Net content to the desktop. Spreadsheets, for example, could be shared and edited within the browser. Unlike Java, however, ActiveX requires a different version for each operating system. But the approach is comprehensive, including the integration of a variety of security features and mechanisms for filtering Web sites according to user-defined criteria.

And ActiveX is already beginning to affect the major software programs we use daily. New versions of Microsoft Office will provide the appropriate ActiveX hooks that will allow you to edit an Excel or Word for Windows document inside your browser; the converse—viewing a World Wide Web page from within a word processor document, for example—is also being provided for. The fact that Java can also tie documents to the Internet is pointing to a continuing development battle between the two platforms, enhancing the power of each (and Microsoft is extending Java to work with ActiveX controls). Corel's office suite is a case in point; it includes the capability of turning Word-Perfect and Quattro Pro documents into Java-enabled files that can be posted on the Internet. The long-cherished dream of consistency between major applications seems within reach.

To use ActiveX-enabled Web pages within Internet Explorer, it's necessary only to click on the appropriate Web page link. Netscape users can download the ActiveX plug-in at http://www.ncompasslabs.com/binaries/index.htm/. And here are some sites you may want to examine for ActiveX news, as well as a selection of ActiveX controls:

http://browserwatch.iworld.com/activex.html: This is the ActiveX page at the BrowserWatch site, which contains links to all the ActiveX controls now available on the Net, divided by category. The BrowserWatch page also contains useful news articles about the technology.

http://www.activex.com/: This is C|NET's ActiveX site, containing a major software library and useful information about security and standards. You can see the ActiveX site in Figure 8.1.

http://www.microsoft.com/activex/: The Microsoft ActiveX page contains press releases, product information, and links to numerous ActiveX sites. It includes a useful component gallery that gives you an overview of work being done with controls from various vendors.

http://www.windx.com/scripts/homepage.epl: The Development Exchange archives ActiveX controls and contains much information for the technically minded.

http://netday.iworld.com/devforum/axfiles.html: A column from Internet World that tracks the fortunes of ActiveX and its relationship with Java. The archive of past columns at this site is particularly helpful.

http://www.partbank.com/activex/: A superb site from PartBank for tracking ActiveX in the press.

http://www.techweb.com/activexpress/: TechWeb's site for news and ActiveX software.

Figure 8.1 C|NET's ActiveX page keeps pace with developments and offers a comprehensive ActiveX library of controls.

The Internet Telephone

Internet telephony is an idea whose time seems to have arrived. Viewed largely as a toy not so long ago, the technology points to a future in which computers connect not only to other computers but also to the global telephone infrastructure. New developments, including the emergence of necessary standards, are causing the long-distance carriers to reevaluate their position with regard to the uses of the Internet to carry voice transmissions. For the end user, while the technology is in its infancy, it is still possible to experiment with it by talking to people around the world through a variety of different programs.

What is Net telephony? Simply, the digitization and packetization of data. The Internet doesn't care what goes into the packets it carries, which is why it can become such an intriguing mix of media. On the Net, voice can travel in the form of packetized information. The sound is recorded, digitized, compressed, and sent through the network, then reassembled at its destination and converted back into familiar analog soundwaves. All that's needed to accomplish the task is a properly equipped PC, which in this case means a machine with a sound card, the necessary telephony software, and a microphone.

While some telephony programs can operate at speeds as low as 9.6Kbps, you'll find a 14.4Kbps modem is far superior and will handle most of the major products, though 28.8Kbps is best. You speak into the microphone and someone talks back; recent versions of the major telephony programs support *full-duplex* transmission, meaning that both parties can talk at the same time without switching off, just as you do in an ordinary telephone conversation, this also requires a full duplex sound card. *Half-duplex* means you alternately talk and receive; phone products that support full-duplex also support half-duplex.

At the core of an Internet telephony product is the codec, the coder-decoder software that compresses the digitized audio data and decompresses it when it arrives at its destination (codecs were discussed in use with video traffic in the previous chapter). The quality of voice sent over the Internet is related to the degree of compression in the codec; as you might suspect, the lower the compression factor, the higher the quality of the output. That emphasizes the need for a fast modem, one that does not require the high compression ratios that produce distortion and delays in the received voice; 28.8Kbps is optimal.

The sound card and microphone are necessary because there has to be some way to get your voice into the computer so that the software can digitize and packetize it for transmission. But once this is done, your options grow exponentially. Suddenly, a transoceanic telephone call is available for no more than the standard Internet access charges you're paying anyway, which represents quite an end run around the rates charged for such calls by the long-distance carriers. The downside: A wide range of companies are working on the necessary software, each with its own format and each requiring that you connect with users of the same product, which makes it necessary to choose programs that are widely distributed. You can consult a list of other users of the software and can be talking to them over the Net within minutes, but the list of users remains small.

Tip: Why is it so difficult to track down an Internet address for Web telephony? Because many on-line services have more customers than they have IP addresses. The result is that when you log on to such a provider, you're given a different IP address each time, depending on which is available. Such addresses are said to be *dynamically assigned.* This is the reason why many Internet telephony products require that you connect to an Internet Relay Chat (IRC) server, where you can connect more easily with other users of the product. In this case, the distance between using Net telephony and the phone on your wall couldn't be greater. Your phone number, after all, is a constant, and finding that number in the phone book requires only a telephone directory. The directory problem will remain a hurdle for the spread of Internet phone traffic as it grows out of the hobbyist world and into business.

Net Telephony and the Search for Standards

It's not a list that connects you through your PC to the conventional telephone system, although as we'll see, such sets are coming. So, the Internet telephone will really take off when you can use the Net to call any telephone number that would be accessible through your standard telephone. The technology today suffers from audio distortion and the effects of packetization, not to mention the bandwidth question, which causes some packets to arrive at different times than others, and thus creates noticeable problems with what you hear on some calls (Net technicians refer to this problem of packet delay as *latency*). That calls for innovative fixes by software developers, but a coalescing of the standards used by telephony programmers should help.

Intel Corporation, for example, maker of the processors that power the vast majority of today's desktop computers, has produced a program called Internet Phone. While the software is fully featured, perhaps its greatest significance is that it embraces a standard called H.323, which unifies Net telephony so that products from different vendors can work together. Supported by Microsoft and other major players, H.323 lays the groundwork for a Net telephony industry that is fully interoperable among the major products. IBM and Microsoft are among those who plan to add support for H.323 to their programs.

But even in the absence of completed standards, major companies like AT&T, MCI, and Sprint are studying this technology with interest. They know that it provides an alternative to conventional rate structures, one that they may be able to use to their advantage. How? Local telephone companies normally charge an access fee for connecting a long-distance call in their jurisdiction. In fact, in 1993, such access charges accounted for more than 50 percent of the Bell operating companies' profits, according to EDS Management Consulting Services. A robust traffic in Net telephony could cut the charges the long-distance carriers pay, while perhaps causing problems for the regional Bells now competing for Internet revenues. An influx of voice traffic over the Internet could also stimulate the demand for leased lines sold by the long-distance companies. Remember that the Internet backbone runs on circuits provided by these carriers.

And that raises another difficulty with the software: its audience is limited. In most cases, it can only connect you to someone else using a computer and modem. Net telephony specialist Jeff Pulver has formed a coalition called Voice on the NET (VON), which is trying to promote and defend the interests of Internet telephony developers (http://www.von.org/). Pulver estimates that the number of calls carried over the Net probably doesn't exceed 55,000 per week, not much when compared to the $73 billion long-distance business. If the person you're trying to reach has a network connection and the necessary program and equipment to use it for telephony, you can reach him or her, but only with a bit of searching.

And options for connecting to someone who isn't on the Internet are only now being developed. Network Long Distance, a Baton Rouge-based carrier, is developing a telephone-to-telephone service using the Internet to carry the calls, which would open any telephone globally to the Net-based medium. Other players in this game are IDT Corp. of Hackensack, New Jersey, which connects PC users to telephone customers through a product called Net2Phone, and Labs of Advanced Technologies International in Rockville, Maryland.

But using services like these may change the equation, for Net-to-phone and phone-via-the-Net calls will not be free. Although IDT plans to charge significantly less than current telephone company rates for its service, introducing a fee creates two levels of access. It's easy to imagine a future for Net telephony that includes a customized, fee-based service for business, with various kinds of service guarantees, and free (but inferior) uses for hobbyists.

Making Phone Calls from Your Browser

Netscape has made Internet telephony available for version 3.0 in the form of a utility from InSoft called CoolTalk, which also includes text chat features and data-sharing options; Microsoft's Internet Explorer offers NetMeeting, with whiteboard capabilities for workgroup data sharing on a project, and chat utilities that support multiple users. You can download CoolTalk from the Netscape home page at http://home.netscape.com/. The program installs through a software wizard that helps you configure it for your system. You can see the program interface in Figure 8.2.

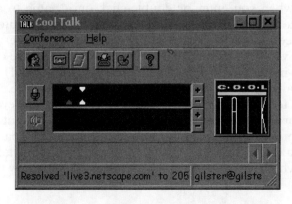

Figure 8.2 Netscape's CoolTalk is a voice telephony product that includes whiteboard capabilities for textual conferencing as well as voice.

Tip: CoolTalk is an extremely interesting way to extend Netscape's powers, but it does not come bundled with the minimum download version of Netscape, nor does the Live3D virtual reality plug-in we'll discuss later. If you don't already have CoolTalk or Live3D on your hard disk, you can download both from Netscape's home page by following the links to Netscape plug-ins. At the time of this writing, the URL was http://home.netscape.com/comprod/mirror/navcomponents_download.html.

CoolTalk works through the conference model. When you want to talk to someone else, you either start a conference with that person or you accept an invitation to join one. Once the conference has been started, you can either use audio, the whiteboard, or the chat tool to communicate. CoolTalk works with a directory of users that is set by default when you download the software. You can check to see which server this directory runs on by pulling down the Conference menu, clicking on Options, and choosing the Conference tab, where you'll see the server listed in the Host Name field. Using the list of users provided by this server is the quickest way to get started with CoolTalk.

To start a conference in CoolTalk, take the following actions:

1. From the Conference menu, choose Start.
2. If you have already talked to the person before, his or her address should be on the Address Book page, in which case you need only double-click on the name.
3. If the person's name is not on the Address Book page, you can check to see if it is listed on the 411 Directory listing, accessible from the tab of the same name; if so, a double-click will initiate the conference query.
4. If the person you want to talk to is not listed either in the Address Book or the 411 Directory, you can type his or her Internet address in the field at the top of the Address Book page.

What happens when you enter or double-click on a name to activate a CoolTalk conference? The software contacts the host computer at the addressee's site to see if a copy of CoolTalk is running (remember: Net telephony requires that you use the same software at both ends of the call). Your party will receive an invitation to join a conference with you if CoolTalk is running and that person is not already involved in another conference.

Like other Net telephony products, CoolTalk attempts to leverage the power of the microprocessor not only to deliver voice telephony but to extend its functions. The program includes an answering machine capability that operates much like a conventional telephone answering machine, taking messages from people who have tried to call you while you were away from your desk. The "machine" includes a counter to tell you how many messages you have waiting. In addition, information about the caller will appear when you play back the message, including a sort of digital business card that can feature a photograph chosen by the user.

Or consider the whiteboard, which is accessible by clicking on its icon on the CoolTalk toolbar. A whiteboard is an example of collaborative computing at its best. It allows you to share information in ways not possible through conventional telephony. If you and I are working on a project and need to make alterations in a house plan, we could talk about it over a standard telephone and perhaps fax our suggestions back and forth. But with a whiteboard, we can talk about the situation and then use the digital technology to draw our suggestions in real time, with all the additional tools supplied by a full-featured drawing program. What I see on my screen would be visible to you, and vice versa. Whiteboards are becoming widespread in digital teaching environments, where distance learning classes supplement video and audio from a physical classroom with a shared workspace. Adding this capability to our Internet toolbox extends it in useful and intriguing directions. You can see the CoolTalk whiteboard in Figure 8.3.

Figure 8.3 The whiteboard uses digital drawing tools to support a shared workspace for conference participants.

The chat tool, meanwhile, includes textual information, so that we can type messages back and forth, a slower model of talking, but one that has proven its popularity in years of on-line use. Overall, Net telephony points to a collaborative model of computing rather than one-to-one communications, with the potential for evolving into a videoconferencing tool with sufficient bandwidth.

Tip: A major issue at play in the development of Internet telephony is the question of universal access. Built into U.S. telecommunications policy is the notion that people in rural areas and low-income environments should receive telephone service at prices they can afford; making this possible requires that the cost of local telephony should be subsidized by higher rates in the long-distance sector. Net telephony could encourage a movement away from this long-distance traffic as currently tariffed onto the Internet, in which case the pool of funds available for universal access is diminished. This is the argument, at any rate, made by an organization called the America's Carriers Telecommunications Association, which is made up of small carriers and telephone service resellers. ACTA has petitioned the Federal Communications Commission to review the implications of the Internet phone, in particular, querying whether vendors of Net telephony software be considered communications carriers. If they are, then they fall under the same regulatory framework as the ACTA membership. The FCC's position with regard to phone technology will be important to watch, as it could determine whether this category of software continues to grow unimpeded by government restriction. The swift response to this petition by the Voice on the Network coalition and the growing interest among the long-distance carriers in Net telephony mean that the government is unlikely to heed ACTA's pleas.

Here are some sites that you will want to add to your bookmark list if you're following developments in Net telephony:

http://www.vocaltec.com/: This is the home of the Israeli company that made Net telephony into the growth industry it is today. Its Internet Phone product is available for a free evaluation period. This company is also actively pursuing options for connecting Net telephones with the regular phone system.

http://www.planeteers.com/: This is the home site for Camelot's DigiPhone, an intriguing program with three-way conference calling capabilities; it includes a speed dialer.

http://www.microsoft.com/: NetMeeting is Microsoft's group collaboration software, now built into the company's Internet Explorer. The program allows you to share program data while you discuss what's on the screen. It supports application sharing, text chat, and file transfer.

http://www.freetel.com/: FreeTel lives up to its name; it's a freeware product with an enhanced commercial version available for download here.

http://www.mit.edu/network/pgpfone/: Check here for the latest information on encryption and Net telephony. An encrypted call is one that can't be overheard by someone else trying to monitor your conversation.

http://www.netspeak.com/: This is NetSpeak's Web site, where you can download WebPhone. The product supports multiparty conferencing, call blocking, voice messaging, and answering machine functions.

http://www.jabra.com/: Jabra offers a bundled set of software tools for Net telephony and a microphone and speaker unit that fits in your ear.

http://www.quarterdeck.com/: Quarterdeck's WebTalk includes a copy of Quarterdeck's Mosaic, although you'll probably find both Netscape and Internet Explorer to offer superior interfaces.

Tip: Internet phone enthusiasts put up with a lot of problems that you and I wouldn't tolerate in a normal telephone conversation. It's much like the early days of amateur radio out there, as voices break through in a tiny and sometimes disjointed fashion, but the thrill of the communication takes the edge off the problematic audio. Remember, we're on the cutting edge of this technology, pushing it through an Internet not yet optimized for voice communications. The sharp rise in the quality of audio tools like RealAudio presages a continuing improvement in sound quality on the Net.

As the industry develops, it's likely that we'll see two distinct types of Internet telephony emerge. The first, business-oriented and high-bandwidth, will provide the best quality in audio and reliability, most likely delivered by the telephone companies themselves. The second type will resemble Internet telephony today—ideal for setting up test connections and for experimenting with the tools, but hardly optimized for mission-critical work. The first option, needless to say, is where the phone companies will look for revenue opportunities.

The Virtual Web

Virtual reality is perhaps the most promising, and the most confounding, of Internet developments. It offers designers the ability to create not just Web pages, but entire digital universes in which the rules of the road are whatever can be imagined by people and executed by computer processor. But with such power comes a major problem in design. Developers have worked for well over a decade to bring a menu-based, mouse-driven graphical environment to computers so that people could work with common objects on-screen and not be confused by myriad choices when they moved from machine to machine. Virtual reality will require deftness on the part of developers to ensure that we're not going back to an idiosyncratic model in which each VR site requires the user to figure out a new set of rules.

How does virtual reality work? Think of it as a digital extension of metaphor and simile. Suppose we want to create an on-line travel agency, complete with the ability to buy tickets and to pull up information about flights, travel times, destination hotels and restaurants, and so on. At the level of raw information, we could do this through a series of databases, linking to them through a basic Web page interface with clearly marked hyperlinks. But if we wanted to do the same thing through virtual reality, we could create the on-screen representation of that travel agency, an environment that could be explored by the user with a mouse: Move the mouse forward while holding down the left mouse button to walk into the agency; move it to the side to turn left or right. Above all, virtual reality is a three-dimensional experience, and it operates in environments that look like the real world.

The reservations desk at our travel agency might be pictured as a physical object, in which you go to request ticketing information. Perhaps a digital version of a rack of brochures is set up to the right of the desk; browsing there, we can find photographs, telephone numbers, rates, and other information about possible hotels. Because this is the World Wide Web, we can likewise link to remote sites that give us background on the destination in question. We can interact with the staff at the virtual travel agency, who take the form of avatars—on-screen figures that move in response to mouse movements. In today's audio- and video-enabled Web, we may be able to talk to these people directly through Web chat, or type in our information requests.

The virtual reality travel agency, then, would be a combination of the physical travel agency that we walk into from the street and the digital agency that draws on computer databases, hypertext links, electronic mail, and the whole panoply of Internet tools. The key benefit of constructing it this way is that people who are not comfortable with computers can understand what they have to do readily. Anyone who walks into a physical travel agency knows to go to the reception desk and state his or her needs. In the virtual agency, the user does precisely this, but with a mouse movement to set up the motion through a computer-generated space. What might be a forbidding database interface becomes simplified through a basic search field and a surrounding context of directions. Virtual universes are understandable—or they can be—and they can be constructed so as to reduce user intimidation.

But of course, they can be more than this. We can also conceive of virtual reality as a marvelous education and training tool. Obviously, some environments don't lend themselves to putting people inside for purposes of study. We can't, for example, put every Boeing 747 pilot through realistic emergency procedures without endangering the lives of the crew, whereas with a completely modeled virtual environment, we can re-create all the sensory inputs necessary to train that pilot, including accurate instrument readings and visual displays that capture the scene outside. The same is true for high-risk situations like bomb disposal, nuclear power plant emergencies, railroad disasters, and any other environment endangering life.

And what about modeling environments that we otherwise could treat only hypothetically? As a former teacher, I would love to have the ability to create a virtual Chartres Cathedral, allowing my students (and myself!) to wander through the structure at leisure, exploring works of art, studying building design, exploring the foundations, and analyzing the workmanship in the stained glass windows. I can't fly a class to France for that purpose, but the right software could model the cathedral down to the paving-stone level. Software could simulate galactic formation, geological accretion, quantum-level particle interactions, and even social relationships in user-defined settings.

The Language of VR

Computers force us to become familiar with their languages, the tools they use to interpret Net data on our screens. If the language of the Web is HTML (Hypertext Markup Language), the language of virtual reality is VRML, or Virtual Reality Modeling Language. You can think of a VRML document as a plan for creating a virtual world, one in which you can move using your mouse; rotate your point of view, go through digital doorways, and explore hypothetical structures. By adding plug-ins to your browser, you can explore worlds like these, of which there are a growing number on the Web. Both Microsoft and Netscape have built support for virtual reality into their respective browsers, Microsoft in the form of the Intervista VRML viewer, Netscape with its Live3D plug-in. Folding virtual reality into browsers adds further impetus to the development of VR-enabled sites.

VRML files are made up of plain ASCII text, just like their HTML equivalents (although serious developers now use 3-D modeling programs to develop these files), and contain the file extension .wrl (for "world"). VRML describes environments through text codes that represent not only objects within those environments, but also light sources and other, still more complex features of an interactive landscape. The language grew out of the realization that Net-based virtual reality would require a language that could describe scenes as well as set up links between VR-enabled sites. Its origins go back to a conference held in Geneva in 1994, in which Tim Berners-Lee, the creator of the World Wide Web itself and one of its most important figures, co-chaired a session with David Raggett that was designed to set forth basic VRML requirements. By late 1994, the language was developing around principles drawn from Silicon Graphics' own work in 3-D modeling.

The language's first official version appeared in April 1995, but development on future features continues apace, with VRML 2.0 appearing in August 1996. The latter upgrades the relatively static VRML 1.0 by providing for greater user interactivity. The earlier version, for example, did not allow for sound or animation, and users could only move through the on-line space and examine it. VRML 2.0 sets up richer standards for 3-D content on the Web.

Tip: If you start getting drawn into virtual reality, you'll run across a group known as VAG—the VRML Architecture Group. These are the people who published VRML 1.0; they are behind the development of standards for the language.

Creating a virtual reality language for network use poses no small number of challenges to programmers. Consider that each virtual world must possess enough analogies to the world we inhabit to make it recognizable, while including the metaphorical function that makes it useful as a commercial, educational, or scientific tool. As VRML creator David Raggett wrote in a seminal article on the language: "Sound can be just as important to the illusion as the visual simulation: The sound of a clock gets stronger as you approach it. An aeroplane roars overhead crossing from one horizon to the next. High-end systems allow for tracking of multiple moving sources of sound. Distancing is the technique where you get to see and hear more detail as you approach an object. The VR environment can include objects with complex behavior, just like their physical analogs in the real world, for example, drawers in an office desk, telephones, calculators, and cars. The simulation of behavior is frequently more demanding computationally than updating the visual and aural displays."

You can read Raggett's fascinating discussion of VRML challenges on-line. The article is "Extending WWW to Support Platform-Independent Virtual Reality," and it's found at http://vag.vrml.org/www-vrml/concepts/raggett.html. Perhaps the most useful site for keeping up with VRML and the world of virtual reality browsers is The VRML Repository, at the San Diego Supercomputer Center. The address is http://www.sdsc.edu/vrml/. You can see the home page for the Repository in Figure 8.4.

Here you'll find browser plug-ins, user guides, Frequently Asked Questions documents, links to other VRML sites, and more. The complete VRML specifications are also on-line. And you'll probably want to set up a bookmark for http://vag.vrml.org/www-vrml/. This is The VRML Forum site, created after the 1994 World Wide Web Conference in Geneva, to support VRML development. Here you'll find useful articles like Raggett's and mailing list archives.

VRML development is leading to a wave of activity among software companies and on-line services. Worlds Inc., for example, has produced a groundbreaking site that allows you to set up virtual chat sessions. You choose an avatar from a set of possible representations, and when you move into the chat space, you interact with the avatars of other users. AlphaWorld is a Worlds Inc. production that sets up a virtual reality city on-line, including shopping malls and various urban features such as a tour of San Francisco's Market Street.

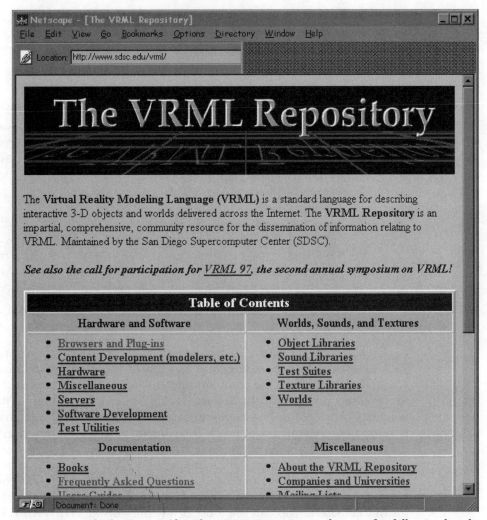

Figure 8.4 The home page for The VRML Repository, a key site for following breaking developments in the field of virtual reality.

Netscape, Intel, Silicon Graphics, Virtus, Template Graphics, and Microsoft have all been active in virtual world implementations, the latter with its V-Chat; CompuServe has also moved to support VR-based chat.

The key question with VRML is the same one that haunts HTML: How will developers choose to implement their virtual worlds? The choices are several. A company can choose to create its own proprietary virtual tools, as Worlds Inc. has done with its Worlds Chat system. It can use VRML version 1.0, which is now available but limited, or VRML 2.0, which extends the language in significant new directions. As you can see, these questions resonate through all Internet development; it's the old issue of Netwide standards versus proprietary development. A company that brings out a superior product might find that its success paves the way for the acceptance of its technology as a de facto standard. Or it might find that proprietary standards leave it in a dangerous backwater as development surges past its work.

Tip: What happens when you try to access a VRML site that's not compatible with your browser? In some cases, you won't have access to advanced features at the site; usually, these are based on extensions to VRML that are supported only by some other variety of browser. The worst-case scenario is that the site may simply crash your browser as it tries to download and display the VRML coding it finds there. In this case, it may be necessary to reboot the machine to get out of the predicament. Such snafus will become more uncommon as stable standards for VRML emerge, but for now, they're part of the price of keeping pace with emerging technologies. The best bet for a stable browser experience with virtual reality is to stick with Live3D and Netscape until you're ready to explore more proprietary worlds.

Today, Netscape's Live3D technology is the most common approach to VRML worlds, but its extensions can cause problems with other VRML-enabled sites, much as the company's extensions to HTML can cause problems for browsers not specifically designed to take advantage of them. The problem is hardly restricted to Netscape, however; VRML is in such an early stage of development that most companies focusing on virtual reality have either opted for the proprietary solution or have moved to additional extensions to VRML to enhance its capabilities. Thus the list of VRML plug-ins is huge; for Windows 95 alone, we have Cosmo Player, NAVFlyer, Pueblo, VR Scout, WIRL, CyberGate, Live3D, WebSpace, WorldView, and about 10 others that compete for market share. You can see a list of VR plug-ins at THE VRML Repository site: http://www.sdsc.edu/vrml/browsers.html.

Enabling the Browser for Virtual Reality

Netscape's Live3D plug-in (once known as Web-FX) allows you to access many virtual worlds through your browser. The plug-in is not provided with the minimum download version of the browser, however, so you'll need to download it from the Netscape home page. Follow the link to Netscape plug-ins, where you'll find Live3D. The plug-in installs through a set-up wizard and works seamlessly; when you encounter a 3-D site, it enables you to control movement with your mouse. Using Live3D means traveling to a Web site that has been created with VR in mind. Such a world is Duke's Diner, which you can access at http://www.marketcentral.com/vrml/duke.wrz. Letting the virtual world load, the first thing you will see is the home page, as shown in Figure 8.5. The initial image is of a diner floating eerily in a field of stars.

To move into the diner, simply hold down the left mouse button and move the mouse forward. The movement takes a moment to get used to, but once you realize that you can control your forward, backward, and lateral motion with mouse movements, it will come easily to you. Move the mouse over the images shown here and you will see pop-up messages depending on where the cursor is. Since this is a game, they will point to the location of clues; the object here

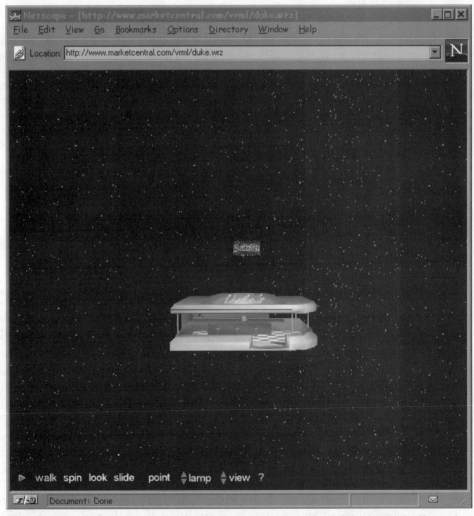

Figure 8.5 The home page for Duke's Diner shows the kind of visual effects that make VR so fascinating.

is to find Duke, the owner of the place. Clicking on the Duke's sign on the top of the diner causes the RealAudio player to pop up with audio clues inviting you to explore the diner and advising you where begin the search.

Notice that there are controls at the bottom of the screen that explain the modes of movement available. This navigation bar shows the available viewpoints; they help you adjust the way you view the virtual world. Clicking on one of these will cause the menu item to change color and become the active mode. By clicking on the Question Mark (?) on the menu bar, you can cause a set of possible commands to pop up advising how you can use these controls. The commands vary depending upon which mode is selected, as you'll see:

walk	Walking is controlled by the left mouse button; hold it down and slide the mouse to simulate walking into the landscape. In walk mode, you can make the scene spin by dragging with the right mouse button.
spin	This mode rotates the scene. In spin mode, left dragging (holding down the left mouse button as you drag the mouse) activates the spin control.
look	Look mode can be controlled with the left mouse button. It is a relatively quick way to get an overview of an object or a landscape. While the spin command rotates the scene itself, the walk, look, and slide commands move you through the scene.
slide	Slide mode allows you to move the virtual object without rotation. It is controlled by the left mouse button.
point	Point allows you to move directly at the thing to which you are pointing. Ctrl-click will make it happen.
lamp	Clicking here will allow you to use the lighting control. Clicking on the up arrow will increase the lighting; the down arrow will decrease it.
View	View restores the virtual object to its prior position on the screen.
<Green Triangle>	The green triangle on the far left of the navigation bar controls animations. You can click it to pause the display of the animation.

The right mouse button has a purpose here, too. A right mouse click with the cursor in the virtual world will cause the main Live3D menu to pop up, offering a range of additional, more finely tuned options controlling viewpoint, lighting, detail, and more.

The Live3D navigation controls definitely require some getting used to, but once you have worked with viewpoints and caused virtual objects to spin and slide around your screen, you'll begin to feel comfortable in this new environment. In Figure 8.6, you can see the view now that I have moved completely into the diner in search of clues about the missing Duke. The program has already clued me in that by examining the salt and pepper shakers on the counter I can learn something new. When I click on them, I get another RealAudio file, telling me another place in the diner to look for Duke.

You can see several things by looking at this virtual reality environment. In the first place, the settings aren't nearly as graphically interesting as a complex HTML page. This has to do with the limitations of computers on the client side of the equation. Simply put, our machines (at least, those on the average desktop) lack the graphical sophistication to render complicated three-dimensional environments with the kind of detail we'll see one day in the future. It's for this same reason that text generally displays in difficult-to-read format in the virtual space. Moving about a simply drawn virtual space is fun at first, but it's clear that the next generation of processors will be required to provide truly effective 3-D modeling.

Figure 8.6 The viewpoint after I've moved into the diner by using the Live3D navigation controls.

Exploring the Virtual World

Here are some intriguing virtual worlds for your exploration. Note that some of these require that you download VRML software other than Live3D:

http://popularmechanics.com/vrml/VRML.html: Popular Mechanics has put up a unique front end to its Web site that allows you to move through a star-filled space to zoom in on the content you need. Once past the VR entrypoint, your site exploration proceeds conventionally, but the front end shows how we may be constructing database interfaces for specialized uses in days to come.

http://www2.blacksun.com/pointworld/index.html: This is the PointWorld site, developed by Black Sun Interactive, that models the company's Web site reviews in 3-D format. Rather than clicking on links to get to a particular site, you move about in a landscape and choose a virtual building as your destination. Black Sun is a major player in the area of avatars; it is working with Sony and Paragraph to create a set of standards called Living Worlds to provide universal support for avatars. You'll need to download the company's CyberGate browser plug-in for full display capabilities here.

http://www.rlspace.com/: An interesting use of panoramic image technology from RealSpace. RealVR uses wraparound images that provide a 360-degree rotation. Apple's QuickTimeVR is another take on panoramic files, which provide unique realism in VR.

http://www.ch.ic.ac.uk/VRML/: Check this site, at the Department of Chemistry at Imperial College in London, for an example of how virtual reality can be used in data visualization.

http://www.itp.tsoa.nyu.edu/~student/yorbClass/Web/hotel/: This is a murder mystery in which you work through a series of clues to try to figure out who killed the mayor of New York. You explore a hotel lobby and various rooms in search of clues. The site is audio-enabled through RealAudio.

http://www.onlive.com/: Onlive Technologies has worked out a way to add sound to the virtual reality experience, although you'll need a microphone to use it. The experience goes beyond conventional text-based chatting and points to a collaborative Net environment for 3-D conferencing.

http://vrml.bigbook.com/bb3d/index.html: An interesting take on a three-dimensional database, starting out with an experimental presentation of San Francisco.

http://webspace.sgi.com/Repository/SGI-Depot/: An on-line assembly manual for a computer workstation desk from Silicon Graphics, which uses illustrations and three-dimensional modeling to help the user build the workstation on-line.

http://www.worlds.net/: Worlds Chat is one of the oldest virtual reality implementations on the Web, and it remains one of the best. You'll need to download the proprietary Worlds Chat software, but the experience of on-line chatting with avatars is worth the trouble. So is the company's AlphaWorld community that models a modern city.

http://www.planet9.com/vrsoma.htm: The first virtual city on the Internet, complete with sound and animation enhancements. The VirtualSOMA on-line city is a community complete with businesses, art galleries, and community-based organizations.

Tip: An interest in virtual reality should lead you to Apple Computer's QuickTimeVR, a photographic take on the experience. QuickTime is Apple's software for viewing video, text, and animation; it is normally used as a plug-in for a World Wide Web browser to display files stored in this format. QuickTimeVR extends the idea by providing a complete, panoramic world that you can view through the QuickTimeVR window. By using mouse commands, you can work your way through a lifelike image with three-dimensional movement.

Such scenes are created by taking a series of photographs at varying camera angles, which are then combined to form a montage of the scene. The software will blend these photographs together, to give the effect of a single, continuous environment. The virtual reality experience thus takes on photographic definition, a boon in a VR universe that has thus far been dominated by relatively crude graphics. QuickTimeVR is an add-on to the QuickTime package that is built into Netscape; both are available at the Apple Computer site: http://qtvr.quicktime.apple.com/.

Browser Tips for the Virtual Reality Experience

Using today's VR-enabled sites poses challenges not found on simple HTML pages. Here are some tips that may ease your way:

• A three-dimensional world has to be downloaded to your system before it can be displayed and explored. This process can take time, depending on how large the necessary files are; even a well-compressed 3-D landscape could take several minutes to download. But the problem is not only one of time. Because VRML is not HTML, it's not always possible to tell how far the browser has proceeded in downloading the virtual reality world. When nothing seems to be happening, it's still a good idea to give the download several more minutes to see if it will run. Clicking at the wrong moment may simply abort the download, or freeze your browser, requiring a reboot.

• Explore the site well before following links to other sites. The reason: Should you decide to return to the original VR site, your browser will have to reconstruct that world from scratch, which means running through the entire download process a second time. Until VR gets faster on our machines, you'll want to explore these environments one world at a time.

• Remember that the world you're examining may possess odd features, like letting you get stuck inside a virtual wall, seeing nothing on the screen but the color of that wall. Nothing prevents a virtual world designer from creating an alternate reality that defies conventional laws of physics (although there are compelling reasons why this is a bad idea). Jump off a cyberspace building and you may fall to the "ground" without mishap, or the program may simply fail. Walk into a wall and you might pass right through it, or bump off it, depending on how the developer has set up the virtual rules of the road. Some browsers let you move back immediately to your initial position in the VR world, but for those that don't, navigation can be tricky.

A major question faced by VR developers is how best to use their technologies. Creating a virtual world as a demonstration is unquestionably a fascinating experience, but how do you translate this virtual environment into something genuinely useful? A database, for example, can be set up with a virtual reality front end, but end users are bound to ask what additional benefits they receive from being able to choose a destination by entering a virtual building as opposed to clicking on a straight textual hyperlink. If the additional burden of virtual reality is that it slows down the data acquisition process by insisting upon modeling it, we may see business users regard the technology as nothing more than a novelty. Their need, after all, is for repeated entries into information sources; once they've seen the VR effect, they may opt to turn it off in favor of the standard keyword data query procedure.

What does seem likely is that virtual reality will develop quickly in those areas where people who are networking create new user communities. We can see the development of Net-based games as a prime beneficiary of this technology, allowing users to play against each other in a vividly realized virtual environment. VR capabilities also make sense in the conferencing arena, but their utility beyond this will have to be demonstrated by Web site developers, too many of whom seem content to wrap a virtual reality experience around a Web page that could more simply, and more effectively, be modeled in straight HTML format.

Numerous corporate experiments with this technology are underway in the areas of three-dimensional design (imagine being able to construct a building in VR, then tour it to check for design flaws before the first nail has been driven into the physical structure); simulations range from aircraft cockpits to ships' equipment; shopping applications that allow you to customize a car's colors on-line or play with furniture choices within a VR-enabled house; and interfaces for databases and other data structures. The latter are particularly interesting, in that data visualization is well suited for working with large amounts of simultaneous information. A collection of database results could be viewed in virtual reality in such a way as to point out quickly the major areas of interest, as opposed to working through a long list of text-based "hits."

Tip: With bandwidth creating bottlenecks all over the Internet, particularly where complex graphics are concerned, it's natural to wonder whether virtual reality will become the application that forever jams the Internet's pipes. The answer, perhaps surprisingly, is no. When virtual reality is properly implemented on today's Net, the virtual world can be downloaded to the user's machine, while actual movement through that world in the on-line environment can be managed by update information provided by a remote site. That means that while virtual reality may clog your hard disk, it doesn't have to be a burden on an overstressed network. Of course, proper design is everything; a poorly created VR world has the potential for serious bandwidth mischief if its developers don't take these factors into account.

VRML 2.0, recently finalized, includes a number of specifications that enhance the earlier version of the language. One interesting aspect of these changes is the inclusion of binary encoding in VRML 2.0, which provides the format necessary to compress virtual worlds for downloading over the Internet. The result is a wholesale speed-up of virtual reality, turning what can be an agonizingly slow process at some sites into a usefully interactive experience. This is the step virtual reality must take if it is to move past its present experimental status.

Agent Technology

The average new user, overwhelmed by the choices available on the Internet, may justifiably wonder how to keep up with news. The non-networked world makes it relatively simple: turn on the television or read the newspaper and you can quickly gain an overview of what's happening in the world. But the Web, with its myriad sources of specialized data, raises the question of where to look for what you need. Nobody can click on every possible link to find information, or know which site to visit at the right time to dig out that specialized bit of arcana that will solve a puzzle or add a point to a presentation. That's where *agents* come in.

An agent is a software tool that can be customized to fit your needs. Unlike you, software can operate 24 hours a day to monitor breaking developments, and it can be sent out on its own to search through sites you would never have time to examine. This model of agent system is now being developed in conjunction with search engines to provide ever more precise tools for information gathering; we'll look at several of these in the next chapter. But agents don't necessarily have to work with search engines. They can also be used to filter and analyze any kind of computer database using user-determined criteria.

With bandwidth constraint slowing performance at many sites, an agent is also a way to off-load search projects that might otherwise tie up your desktop for hours. You can be working on another project while your agent searches, effectively doubling your productivity with the help of the intelligent software. The agent is in some implementations an add-on to a search engine; in others, it is more like a traveling personal information manager, crossing network boundaries to update your files and keep your calendar on target. In today's world, the former is the standard; agents basically live on the server and work in conjunction with its operations. In a few years, agents on the desktop will be ubiquitous, helping us manage tasks and make choices among alternative sources of information.

At the MIT Media Lab, agents are being developed that can play a role in your work life. Imagine a software tool that can connect buyers and sellers of particular products. You instruct the agent in what you need and it goes out onto the network to compare prices; when it finds your commodity in the price range you've specified, it returns that information to you. A young company called Agents Inc., created to explore MIT's work, has produced a proof-of-concept product called Firefly, now operating as part of the newly developing Firefly Network.

Firefly (http://www.firefly.com/) has built a database of its members' tastes in music and movies, and is able to link it to a wider database of discographies, reviews, and film credits. By teaching the software what you like in the world of entertainment, the Firefly agent can match up your interests with those found in its database, learning from you each time it makes a choice. It can also connect you to other users of the technology who share your profile. The notion is to connect people and then build a community of common-minded customers, a sort of intelligent chat service.

On a broader level, Firefly mimics what we all do when we verify information. An information filter is something that allows us to decide how much weight we give to what we hear. I might believe a close friend who told me that the president was in town unannounced, but I would demand more evidence if I simply overheard that statement on a bus. What Firefly can do is to link people of common interests and thought processes, so that a pool of users who tend to share similar ideas is formed. This idea could, of course, be extended into the scientific and business worlds. The technology could alert scientists at one location to the presence of similar work being performed somewhere else, thus allowing the two teams to avoid reinventing the wheel. You can see the Firefly home page in Figure 8.7.

Tip: What the world of agents really needs is a tight definition. The problem: Everything from enhanced database searches to customized news delivery is being referred to as agent software, because the term has developed a certain cachet among developers. If we use the term agent to refer to software that handles a particular task for us, like delivering personalized news after searching a central database, then the definition is obviously a broad one. If we become more specific, we may want to reduce the concept to one of autonomy. If the agent operates on its own and learns from what it discovers, including by monitoring our own on-line behavior, then perhaps it is more deserving of its name. I don't make that distinction here because so many different companies are referring to what they do under the rubric of agent software, but the definition will doubtless be clarified as genuine agents gain in power.

The agent concept applies readily to news gathering. Consider NewsPage, from Individual Inc. This company (http://www.newspage.com/) offers a personalized news service coupled with a search engine. The database, constantly updated, includes 700 business magazines, trade journals, wire services, and

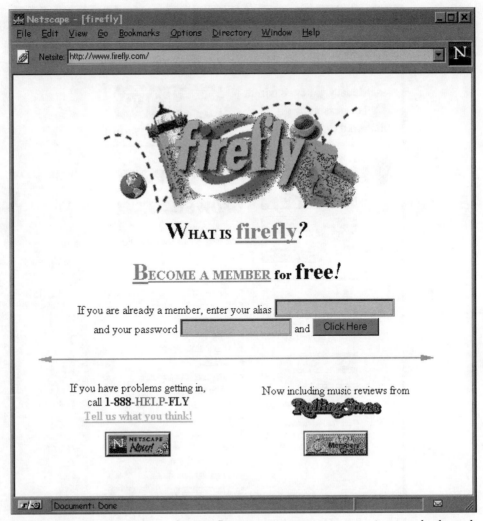

Figure 8.7 The home page for Firefly, an experiment in connecting people through agent software.

newspaper business sections, divided into 1,700 specific topics, along with information about public and private companies. By filling out a personal profile, a customer can create a personalized newspaper, delivered by e-mail every morning. The stories are shown as links to the company's Web site, where they can be read in full. The user sees only what is in his or her profile, so that the information is precisely targeted. You can see the Individual Inc. home page in Figure 8.8.

What we're seeing in both Firefly and NewsPage is the evolution of the agent concept. It is a legitimate question to ask where the boundary between intelligent agents and simple database searching is to be found. Any list of

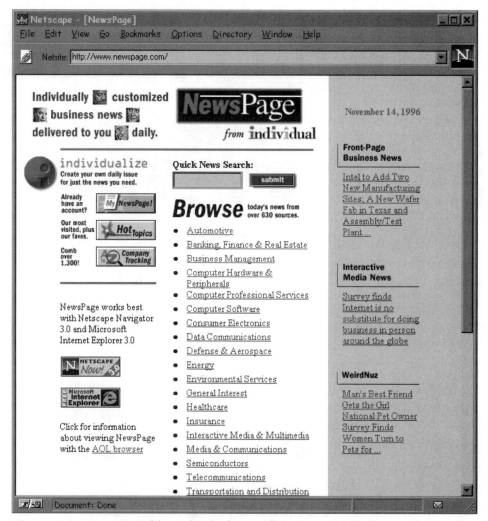

Figure 8.8 Companies like Individual Inc. offer customized information by using server-based agent technology.

"hits" from a database search can be seen, in some sense, as a personalized news source—it is information produced by running user-selected keywords past a mass of data. Is Individual Inc. producing an agent-mediated newspaper or simply the results of a specific search request that it can deliver to your mailbox? Whatever the answer, there is no question that the true agent software that is coming will be an active tool that observes what you do and learns from it. These agents will refine their searches as they proceed, having determined the parameters of your search need. Within five years, most major software programs will use them.

And they'll be more than Web tools. For the true agent breakthrough may be the linkage between desktop applications like word processors and spreadsheets and agent software. Everything points to an outcome where you will be able to instruct an agent to harvest data found on the Internet itself or on a corporate intranet; the agent will return the required information and feed it directly into the application of your choice. Already, products like Edify's Electronic Workforce and Alpha Microsystems' Alpha Connect point to this scenario. Edify automates information retrieval through agents that can work directly with corporate databases, while AlphaConnect's agents can journey out onto the Web and map its findings to a spreadsheet.

Tip: A key breakthrough in agent technology will be the introduction of standards governing how agents communicate not with other applications, but with each other. As things stand today, all the agent products can talk only to other agents from the same company. But we'd like to see agents that can distribute information more broadly, so that someone else's agent can transfer data to yours, thus saving time. The standard now in formation is called Simple Agent Transfer Protocol (SATF). An industry group formed by General Magic is now working on developing the necessary protocols. Once industry-wide standards have been created, interesting security issues will need to be addressed. How secure is your agent, and with whom will it share its secrets? A variety of authentication measures will doubtless be created to prevent corporate espionage and hacker attacks.

PointCast: The World of User-Defined News

From the end-user's perspective, agents are all about extending the range of choice. They are tools that allow us to decide what we want to see and personalize the dataflow. Such technologies are inevitable, because the Internet is so diverse a medium. With World Wide Web pages numbering in the millions, we need to be able to specify what kind of data we need on the desktop, to set up the best filters for our work, and to work with information that is relevant. Thus, the agent is nothing more than a software program that runs on a remote news server to match up our personal profiles with what it finds in the server's database. News delivery can be by electronic mail, personalized Web page, or independent program, displaying results upon demand.

If we think of television as a broadcast medium, we can see that the Internet drastically changes the experience of acquiring knowledge. The Net is demand-based; we must decide what it is we want to see, and acquire the necessary skills to find it, which is why our work with search engines is so significant a part of the Internet experience; we'll examine these engines closely in the next chapter. The demand-based Web requires that we master the skills to search, and if we can leverage the power of our computers to run searches while we perform other work, then agents will have come into their own as personalized data harvesters.

PointCast, a program from PointCast Inc., is a demonstration of how the Internet model changes the way you read the news. It is a filtered news service that lets you choose from among a variety of data sources and types of story. You download the client software to your machine and personalize it by working though a series of choices. When you go on-line, PointCast will contact its server and update the news. What you see when the software runs is a customized news ticker. You can check out the weather for only those areas you specify; you can pick out stocks and market indicators that fit your own financial profile; you can follow the fortunes of baseball but choose to ignore the NBA.

PointCast isn't a browser plug-in; like the Worlds Chat software discussed previously, it runs as a separate program. But it has tight connections with the Web. In fact, you can set it up so that when you click on a particular story with a Web connection, it will launch your copy of Netscape or Internet Explorer, which you can then view in a separate window. While it is optimized for use over a dedicated network connection, you can use it just as readily with a modem, updating the news on whatever schedule you choose. Figure 8.9 shows the home page for PointCast, where the free software is available for downloading.

The genius of the PointCast concept is twofold. First, by allowing you to tailor the news, it saves you time and helps you focus on the information you need. But the company also understood what numerous rivals did not: the battle for software dominance is all about space on the screen. PointCast melded the screen-saver concept, in which you run a program that provides constantly changing images on screen for entertainment and hardware protection, to the concept of the newsfeed. Leave your keyboard untouched for a preset time and the PointCast software will pop up, an eye-catching and useful display of the latest news, weather, and sports.

Figure 8.10 shows PointCast at work. You'll quickly notice that the software subsidizes its newsfeed service by offering advertising, usually linked to background Web sites at the home of the advertiser. Companies understand the value of screen space, too; they know that having their image and news of their products flashed before the eyes of millions of users can have a positive impact on sales and corporate image. Time will tell just how viable this viewer

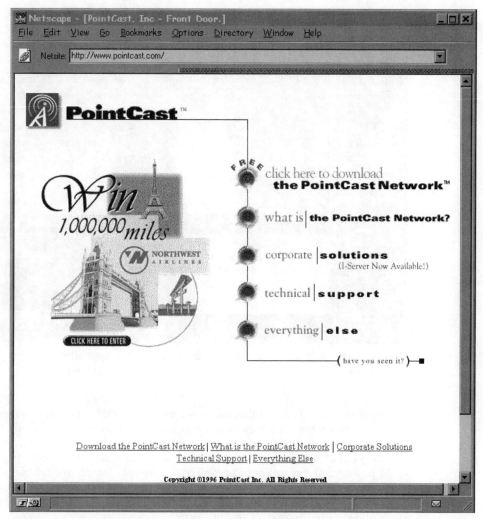

Figure 8.9   The PointCast home page, from which you can download a customizable news program that also doubles as a screen saver.

saturation is, but for now, enough companies are experimenting with such advertising that developers like PointCast remain financially sound.

PointCast, of course, isn't the only company experimenting with personalized news technologies. We've already mentioned Newspage, which provides access to hundreds of news sources and offers e-mail updates of stories under the topic you select. Other sites to watch for news dissemination through agents include these:

> http://www.desktopdata.com/: The NewsEDGE service offers over 500 news and information sources delivered according to user profiles, with full search capabilities. The company specializes in news delivery to networked corporate sites.

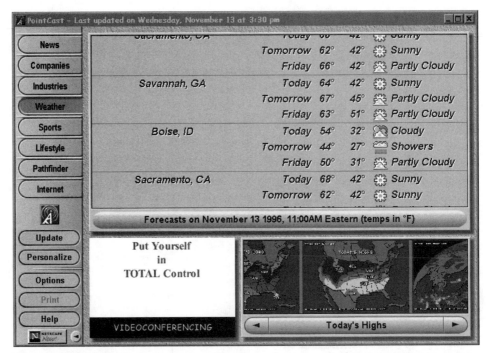

Figure 8.10 As PointCast operates, the flow of news and advertisements is nonstop; many of these items are linked to Web sites that can be reached through a mouse click.

http://www.farcast.com/: Farcast uses agents to cull information from newsfeeds and return their findings to you via electronic mail. Sources include the Associated Press, United Press International, PR Newswire, BusinessWire, and a variety of business sources. Retrieval is full-text at a flat rate of $9.95 per month.

http://interactive.wsj.com/: The Wall Street Journal Interactive Edition offers the complete newspaper as well as links to information in its regional and overseas editions, along with financial capabilities, including a simple portfolio manager and a search engine for recent stories.

The capability for tailoring news through user-determined profiles is becoming commonplace. Consider what The Microsoft Network does (http://www.msnbc.com/). In addition to its regular sources of news, it also allows you to customize what you see through a profile that can be filled out on-line. Figure 8.11 shows the profile page.

A similar, although industry-specific, example of this is the Ziff-Davis site at http://www.zdnet.com/, which searches through a database of computer periodicals to track down items that correspond to your personal profile. It will be interesting to see how these various providers work out their financial models. Will subscriptions prevail? Can an advertising-backed source survive without other income? As with so many Web experiments, only time will tell.

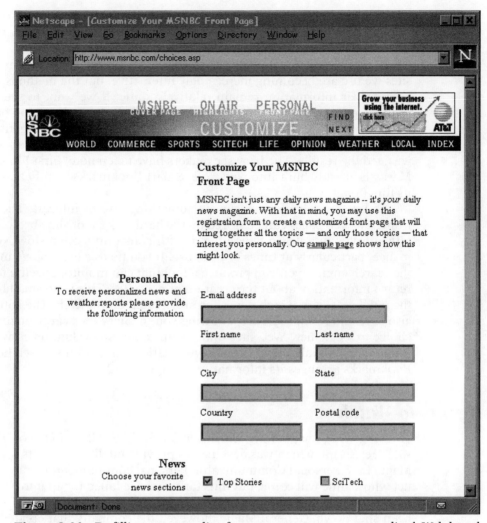

Figure 8.11 By filling out an on-line form, you can create a personalized, Web-based delivery of news to your desktop.

Smart Bookmarks: A Clientside Agent

Bookmarks are an indispensable part of the browser experience; they allow us to return quickly to sites of interest without typing in lengthy URLs. And they're organizers, too, providing the tools to arrange our Web sites according to subject and add them to folders. Smart Bookmarks, the creation of First Floor Software, provides an extension of this basic concept. A smart bookmark is one that stores information about your Web travels and saves it into a database. The bookmark tracks where you have been, and what you found there.

Then, at a time chosen by you, the software can go back out onto the Web to see whether these sites have changed. If they have, it will alert you to the fact according to a profile you create.

Keeping up with changing sites is becoming critically important. The Web sites we use are becoming increasingly interactive, but the methods we use to access their information remain relatively static. If we want to see what has changed on a particular site, our only recourse is generally to log back on to that site, even if we have just looked at it a few hours before. Agent software can handle this chore for us, running the entire process behind the scenes until we need the results. The browser makers have taken note: First Floor's Smart-Marks is already built into Netscape; Smart Bookmarks significantly extends its functionality.

And a smart bookmark can do something else of interest. The contents from new Web pages can be stored on the hard disk for off-line browsing, a significant plus in a world where bandwidth constraints often slow Net performance, particularly at times of peak use. If you tie this technology into that of the search engine, you can produce a tool that can monitor specific topics and return information about the creation of new sites. This is no small feat, given the quickness with which new sites are created on the Web. The software can also save and rerun searches, allowing you to query the search engine of your choice to locate new Web sites under your topic. An evaluation copy of Smart Bookmarks is available at http://www.firstfloor.com/. You can see how Smart Bookmarks arranges its information in Figure 8.12.

Agents to Watch

Tracking what's happening with agents can be bewilderingly complex. Consider Telescript, which was designed to provide intelligent agents for the Sony Magic Link Personal Communicator. Personal communicators may be a product whose time will come, but thus far they have failed to tap into a significant market; indeed, the Personal Link network AT&T built to carry such traffic has been shut down. General Magic, however, the company that created the Telescript agent technology, continues to be an active force in the agent wars; it is investigating how agents can negotiate tasks like those involved in portfolio management and investing, which require the monitoring of incoming data and the matching of action to information. You can check General Magic's technology, now called Tabriz, at http://www.genmagic.com/.

Now we are in the realm of the mobile agent, a software tool that not only searches but also performs actions for us depending upon our instructions. The Tabriz tools work on servers enabled with the software. The idea is that you contact such a site and set up a search request, filling out the information necessary for the agent to do its work. The agent is then launched onto the network, traveling between Tabriz servers armed with our query. When we need material from sites that are not Tabriz-enabled, the home site server for the agent will contact them to extract data. Tabriz agents also work after we have

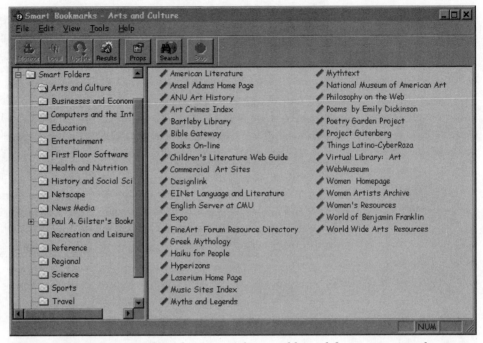

Figure 8.12 Smart Bookmarks is an indispensable tool for monitoring changes at multiple sites.

gone off-line. The software is able to conduct transactions, buying at preset price limits or matching buyers to a set of sellers.

Another company with a technology of interest is Verity (http://www. verity.com/. The firm specializes in search and retrieval software, including the SEARCH97 tool that uses agent techniques to monitor sites and find new data. And Banyan Systems' Coordinate.com produces BeyondMail, an electronic mail program that uses agent technology to set up filters for filtering and filing incoming messages (http://www.coordinate.com/). IBM is in the hunt, too. The company has developed an agent called Web Browser Intelligence that examines your actions at a Web site and simplifies the way you retrieve information from it. You can check out this work at http://www. raleigh.ibm.com/iag/iaghome.html.

And check the following sites, where two other programs for monitoring Web activity are being developed:

http://www.cs.cmu.edu/~webwatcher/: Look here for a link to WebWatcher, a program that observes your Web behavior and highlights links that may interest you as you continue to browse.

http://www.empirical.com/: WiseWire provides personalized information based on your interests, drawing on newswire articles and sources of on-line information, and learning from your input what kind of article you want to see.

Tip: The biggest problem in agent technology is the element of serendipity. When I read the morning paper, three-quarters of what I find interesting tends to be material for which I would not have known to set up a search. This kind of extraneous information, while it doesn't fit any user profile we might construct, nonetheless catches our attention. Even the best of today's agents can make the kind of serendipitous judgments we'd like them to so that we don't miss articles that might intrigue us. Figuring out how software can distinguish among the myriad possibilities in the daily newsflow is a huge challenge. In the absence of such an agent, we'll continue to use both the physical newspaper as well as the digital, agent-enabled search tool to generate the material we need. In that sense, agents are helpers, but they cannot replace the activity of the human brain as it engages the multimedia world of sound and sight.

9

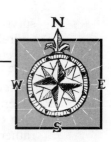

Searching the Internet

If the Web gave us a way to visualize the Internet, the search engines that followed provided a means of exploring it. The problem with hypertext is the mirror of its strength—it is a self-referential medium, built up by a series of interconnected links. The model we used in the early days of the Web was more akin to browsing in the conventional sense than searching. To find something, you followed one link, then another; eventually, if you were lucky, you got to the document or file you needed, but retracing that same path the next time might take you through an entirely different set of connections. It was like looking through a large bookstore whose books were shelved in no particular order. Serendipity was the order of the day.

The Web's search capabilities contrasted sharply with other early tools for finding things on the Internet. One of these, called archie, was a text-based solution for finding files. You typed in a command and followed it with a keyword, adjusting any number of variables through the unique archie command syntax. When you ran the search, archie would check for your keyword and parameters in one of its databases, which were made up of listings of files at numerous popular FTP sites. This search tool could look only for filenames, and they had to be accurately stated. If you needed a program called scrncap.exe and that program was listed at the site as scrncp.exe, your search would fail. For all its promise, archie was a frustrating and inefficient way to search.

Numerous other search techniques followed archie. Veronica was used with Gophers to track down specific menu items on Gopher sites. Again, the tool had its own command syntax, so that if you wanted to run something other than a simple keyword search, you had no choice but to master yet another set of commands. Both Netfind and WHOIS were developed to search for people on the Net, but both drew on databases of existing users that were limited in scope; the odds of actually finding the person you were looking for were relatively small. WAIS created a quick way to search databases, but foundered as an independent search service when relatively few such databases were produced. Today, WAIS

319

survives as an integral part of numerous sites, having been folded almost entirely into the Web's technology. When you see a keyword field and click on a search button, chances are you're running a WAIS search behind the scenes.

Thus the Web, with its unique browser architecture, once again subsumes the technologies that preceded it. But tools like archie, Veronica, and Netfind haven't disappeared; you can still run searches through their systems by logging on to the right site with your browser and using a graphical front end rather than a command prompt. But the biggest news in recent years has been the development of the Web search engine, specifically designed for the demanding world of Web linkages. Using such a site, you can run your keyword(s) past current databases that house information on Web sites and other Internet tools. Many of these engines can search Gophers and FTP sites as well, and the number of directory services for people and products is growing.

All of that is a long way from where we started. But I find that the prospect of searching the Internet is the major driver of Net use; after all, what good is a universe of connected information if you can't do anything with it? Enter a keyword or two and go—that's the model of today's Net searcher, and it's a flexible and powerful model at that. Incumbent upon all of us who intend to get the most out of Net searching is the need to understand how to find the best search engines, and just as significantly, how to interpret the results they give us. This chapter will look at how search engines work, suggest some trustworthy strategies for using them, and explain what to consider, and what to reject, when you evaluate their findings.

A Sample Search through AltaVista

Any search, of course, begins with a well-defined topic, so let's choose one and run a quick search through AltaVista, a major Web engine. The address is http://www.altavista.digital.com/. Entering it in the browser, I come up with the screen in Figure 9.1.

This is the model for the search engine—a keyword field, a Submit button, and a set of parameters. I can search the Web itself; or, if I click on the Search box, I can pull down a different option, that of searching the USENET newsgroups. I have some control over how results are displayed by pulling down the Display the Results box at the top right of the screen. There I can choose to see a standard listing or opt for lesser or greater detail. Usefully, the site also provides background information about Web searching, including a helpful Frequently Asked Questions document.

Tip: When you first visit a search engine, always look at the background documents available there. Sure, it's easy to run a simple search at any site by entering a keyword. The problem is, you don't always know how complete the search is because you

Figure 9.1   The AltaVista search engine's home page.

don't know enough about the database involved. Nor do you necessarily know how to view the results. Are they being presented in a particularly filtered form, and if so, how? These are issues that should make you wary. I print out any FAQ or other backgrounder I find at a search site and house these documents in a separate notebook. When I run searches, I've learned which engines complement each other's databases and which significantly extend my search horizons. With new engines coming on-line all the time, methods like these can help you stay current.

Let's assume for the moment that I'm looking for Web pages about Edgar Rice Burroughs, the creator of Tarzan, John Carter of Mars, and a host of other adventures set on Earth and other worlds. To see what's available at AltaVista, I enter his name in the search field and click on the Submit button. The results appear swiftly, as shown in Figure 9.2.

Already I've struck paydirt. The top entry is a site that houses a collection of Burroughs' literary works. As you can see, the site is set up as a hyperlink. I can read a short description of the page and then click on the hyperlink to visit it. The site houses everything from *The Gods of Mars*, a wonderful John Carter title, to most of the Tarzan books in on-line versions. But by scrolling through the list

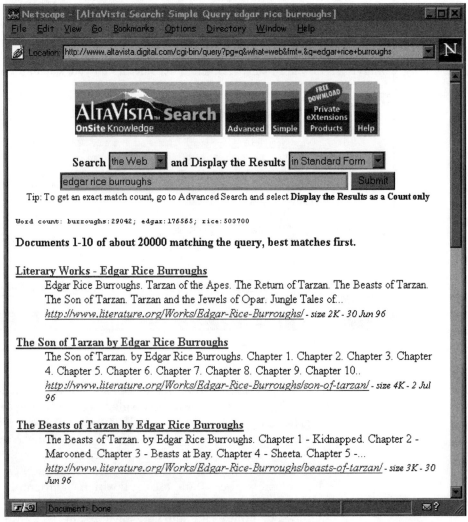

Figure 9.2 Results of a search for information about Edgar Rice Burroughs.

of hits, I also find sites like the one shown in Figure 9.3, a page devoted to Burroughs that includes a bibliography, links to related sites, information about publications for Burroughs aficionados, and photographs from Tarzan movies.

Notice that these are hardly the only results from the search. In fact, AltaVista tells me at the top of Figure 9.2 that I am looking at a list of 10 hits from a search that netted roughly 20,000! I'm also given the inscrutable statement "best matches first." Presumably, this means that the results I'm most interested in will be at the top of the list, so that as I page through it, I will descend progressively into less interesting information.

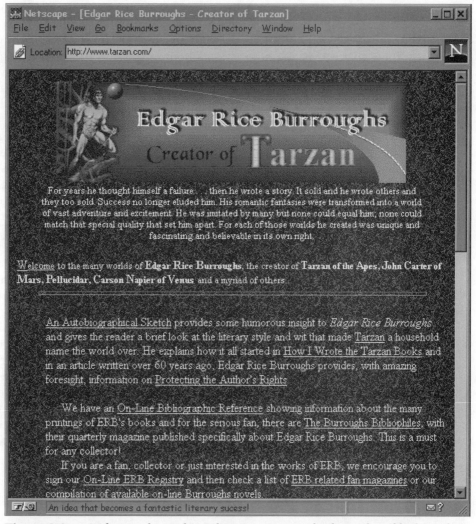

Figure 9.3 A Web page devoted to Edgar Rice Burroughs, located swiftly through an AltaVista search.

How does AltaVista know what I'm looking for, and how accurately can it present its information? These are the kind of questions that should preoccupy any Web searcher, for they have much to say about how we integrate the World Wide Web into our research process. To answer them, let's look at how AltaVista works internally, and then we can generalize from AltaVista to other Web engines.

The Anatomy of a Search Engine

What exactly do we know about the AltaVista search engine? Well, for one thing, we know it houses a big database. You can search through over 30 million Web pages housed on almost 300,000 different computers; you can also examine several million newsgroup articles from over 14,000 groups. We also know that this is one busy site; its home page says that AltaVista gets 21 million access every weekday. The FAQ adds further information: AltaVista's database is updated once a day, usually at night, processing results that have been sent directly to the site by Web page authors along with results that have been automatically generated.

And the word automatic is the key. It's easy to retrieve Web page information by asking people to send you recommendations; these can then be checked and folded into your database. But suggestions aren't sufficient if what you're after is a comprehensive search facility. What you need is an automated way to search as many Web sites as possible. A search engine like AltaVista does this with a so-called software robot, a program that ranges widely throughout the Net looking for Web pages, adding new ones to its list of results, and looking for changes in old ones. After all, Web pages change constantly as authors add new information; a good search engine has to be able to track these changes, so that when we click on a site, we don't simply get an error message telling us the server no longer exists, or a page that houses nothing of interest.

Think of a search engine as divided into three parts: the software robot that prowls the Internet; the database into which that robot puts all its results; and the search engine interface you use through your own browser. With the latter, you submit your search queries directly to the database, and the results are then returned via conventional HTTP methods. All manner of sophisticated search techniques can be added to this process, and all sorts of variations on how the keyword(s) must be submitted, but the three-step method of finding Web information is the standard across all the search engines we'll discuss here.

Methods of Indexing a Site

Complicating our use of search engines is the fact that they don't all work the same way with the data they generate. Some engines, like OpenText and

AltaVista, record the full text of every page their software robots encounter. The most ambitious can lay claim to mapping the entire Internet, although at this point, that grand project seems impossible given the rate at which new sites keep appearing. Other sites go after a subset of Web pages based on factors like user popularity (this can be approximated by finding how many pages offer links pointing to particular pages). They then develop tight indices of those sites. And what any engine pulls off a site can be as comprehensive as its full text or as skeletal as its title information and URL, or perhaps its title, headers, and any table of contents. Lycos is an example of an engine that works with headers, titles, links, and words in key paragraphs.

All of this has ramifications for what you get when you run a search. Send the same keyword query via five different search engines and you will retrieve five different sets of results. More and more people are encountering this phenomenon as developers release search software that queries multiple search engines simultaneously. A full-text search engine will find your word(s) no matter where they appear on the Web page, even if buried in the most inconsequential paragraph on it. Engines that work with summaries and abstracts, on the other hand, may not locate many of the same pages, but their results will often be more concise and, depending upon how they display their results, easier to rank in order of relevance.

The general rule, then, is: Use a full-text database for the most comprehensive searches, but always be aware that in sifting through the results your work will be more demanding. Use an abstract or title-based engine if you're after only those pages on which your keywords are major aspects of the page's subject matter. And as we'll see, you can also use one of various directories that rank Web sites to choose among a limited universe of reviewed pages.

The Art of Relevancy Ranking

Most search engines factor in a way to present their results so that what you want to see isn't lost in the middle of a huge list. Thus AltaVista ranks its results through a sophisticated computer algorithm that grades the items in its list against the original keyword statement. Factors it looks at are how many of the search terms are contained in the Web page, where these words occur (do they, for example, appear in major headers on the page, or only in a relatively insignificant part of the text?), and how close to one another the various keywords are in the document. In this way, the engine tends to cluster information, so that if you've entered three keywords, your results will show pages most likely to meet your criteria at the top. The general term for this kind of arrangement is *relevancy ranking*.

Does it work? Sometimes. As you would imagine, no computer has become completely adept at understanding what we want when we run a search. I've often found items that were exactly on target far down in the list of results, which can be a frustrating realization when you realize that nobody is going to go through a list of 20,000 hits examining each one for possible use.

The answer is to understand first of all how each search engine ranks its findings, and to use a keyword strategy that reduces the possible number of hits. If you can reduce the list of results to manageable size, you'll be far more likely to go through it in its entirety to make sure the computer hasn't missed something.

Another factor you should consider with any search engine is not only how the results are ranked, but how they are displayed. Most engines display the URLs of all hits they retrieve, a seemingly essential service. You should also check to see whether the engine you're evaluating displays the page's title, a relevancy ranking score (usually expressed as a percentage), the size of the page, and summary information that helps you make a choice between pages. Summaries are constructed by stripping out computer code and attempting to present essential contents, though in many cases a page summary will still appear inscrutable.

Tuning Up the Burroughs Search

What we need, then, is a way to fine-tune our search statements. Having decided that 20,000 hits is simply too great a number, I return to my work on Edgar Rice Burroughs. The first question to ask is, how does AltaVista run my search? I've entered three keywords: edgar rice burroughs. And AltaVista has produced results this way: It has found 28,900 documents containing the word burroughs; another 176,433 containing the word edgar; and some 503,076 containing the word rice. It has then looked for sites containing as many of these words as possible, in either upper- or lowercase. And while the early parts of the list of results are helpful, the sheer number of hits makes the search inconclusive. The key fact: The search engine does not guarantee that every keyword will appear in every hit.

I need to find a way to tell AltaVista how to run my search. Specifically, I want to show the engine that the three keywords in question must all appear together, in the form of a name. To do this, I construct the statement this way: "edgar rice burroughs". The quotes tell the search engine to treat the words as a phrase. When I submit this phrase to AltaVista, I immediately see a major change in my search findings. Instead of 20,000 hits, I'm down to roughly 1,000, as shown in Figure 9.4.

Now 1,000 hits is still too many, but by reducing the list by a factor of 20, I've clearly moved in the right direction. The problem now is to figure out exactly what I want. Since Burroughs is mentioned so many times on so many different Web pages, I choose to go by book references. I'd like to know about pages that talk about Burroughs' Martian novels featuring the character John Carter. There are several ways to set up such a query, and the more specific ones are the best. For example, I could use this keyword phrase: *burroughs and mars*, except that AltaVista would then return results with either of the terms listed, and I'm certainly not looking for all pages where that precise phrase appears. So I phrase the query this way:

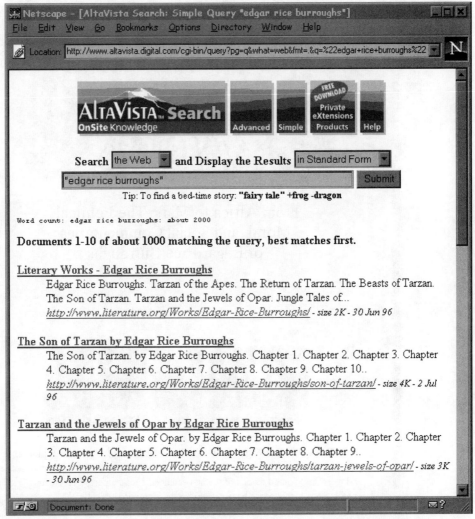

Figure 9.4 Results of changing the three keywords into a phrase marked by quotation marks.

   +burroughs +mars +carter

This tells AltaVista to look for any page containing the term burroughs and to match it against any page containing the words mars and carter. Notice how I've used the plus (+) sign to make this distinction; putting it in front of each term specifies that any page I locate must have that term on it. I wind up with about 300 hits, a more than manageable number. You can see one such hit in Figure 9.5.

     Here I'm given an interesting essay on Burroughs' place in American culture. Writing in the early part of the twentieth century, his work often serial-

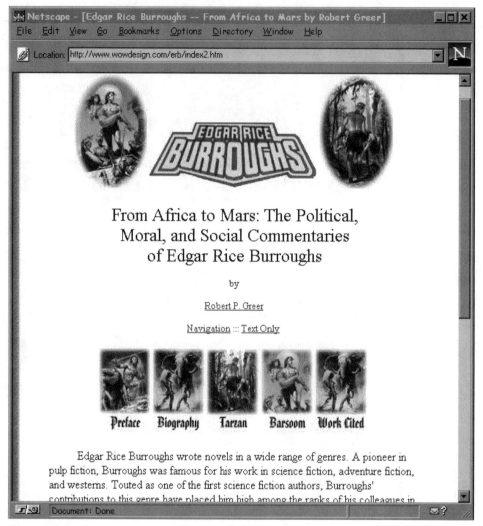

Figure 9.5   A commentary on Burroughs' Mars novels. AltaVista has zeroed in precisely on my subject.

ized in adventure magazines like *Argosy* and *All-Story,* he was easily dismissed as a pulp novelist whose works were pure escapism. Robert Greer's view is that his books have a more serious underpinning, providing case studies of citizenship within American culture. Greer is also interested in understanding Burroughs' description of contrasting political systems, and sees him at his best as a social commentator. That strikes me, a lover of the Martian books, as a bit of a stretch, but the Web gives me the chance to size up Greer's views and, if I so choose, easily make contact with the author.

> **Tip:** AltaVista will rank its documents so that the ones matching
> the most words and phrases in your query will be shown at the top
> of the list. But do not assume that even the top hits will contain all
> of your search terms. If you want to force the search engine to find
> only those pages with all your terms on them, you must specify
> this at the time of your search. And remember, search engines vary
> in how they treat your keywords. The HotBot engine we'll examine
> next displays only documents containing all your search terms by
> default. You can then choose to search for any of the words (not
> all) by using the engine's menu. Always find out how your engine
> processes its requests.

HotBot: Adjusting the Search with Menus

The simple search I just ran shows how important it is that you develop a keyword strategy of your own. Most people use search engines simply by inserting
one or two words and going with the top 10 results, as if computers were better at making the subtle distinctions of research than people. A good keyword
search will take you to the place *you*, and not the computer, decide you should
go. But search engines present a further complication—they're all different.
There being no set of standardized keyword methods and no universal database solution to the search engine question, you must go from one search
engine to another, learning how each works and mastering its system. What
works with one engine may fail with another, or succeed with judicious tweaking of the parameters.

Case in point: I just used a plus (+) sign to tell one search engine to include
specific words on any page it finds. AltaVista uses the plus sign because that's
the way its designers have built it. If I were to go to another engine, like
HotWired's HotBot (http://www.hotbot.com/), I would find a different way to
proceed. You can see the home page for HotBot in Figure 9.6.

HotBot, running on software produced by Inktomi Corporation, claims to
consult a huge number of Web pages, and it does so in ways different from
AltaVista. I can enter a search term like my previous statement in its search
field, but when I want to specify how it should treat those keywords, I can simply pull down the for box on-screen to get these, among other, possibilities:

all the words	HotBot looks for pages containing all my search terms.
any of the words	HotBot pulls up any page that includes one or more of my search terms.
the exact phrase	Equivalent to using quotation marks in AltaVista, this checks for phrases exactly as they appear in the search box.
the person	Checks for keywords listed as complete names.

This is an interesting situation. I can run my AltaVista search (*+burroughs
+mars +carter*) without using any special markers. Simply entering *burroughs*

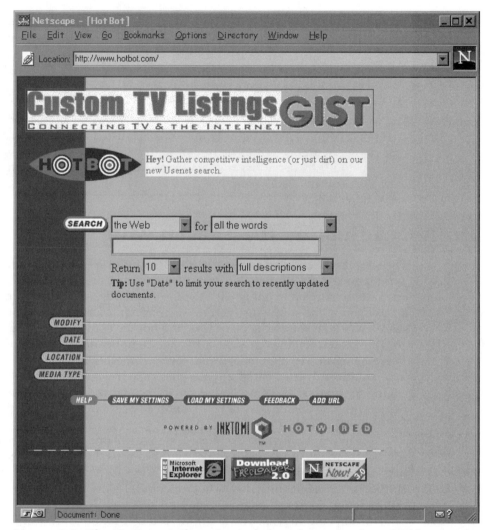

Figure 9.6 The HotBot search engine includes a larger number of Web pages for searching than most other engines and an alternative keyword strategy.

mars carter as is in the HotBot search field and choosing the all the words option, I produce 888 matches, all of them meeting my criteria (HotBot would also allow me to accomplish a phrase search by using quotation marks, just like AltaVista). HotBot is in that sense easier to use than AltaVista, but you'll notice that of the many conceivable search strategies available, only the most popular are fixable by menu, meaning you'll still need to explore the unique search possibilities at HotBot when you want to move on to a more advanced search.

So the initial steps of any search strategy are these:

1. Learn to use a single search engine well by mastering all its capabilities.
2. Choose a second engine and learn how it runs the same kind of searches.
3. Examine the difference in results to determine which engine more closely suits your style and research needs.

Is HotBot all that different from AltaVista? In many respects, the answer is yes. You've already seen the primary HotBot search screen, but consider now the various ways you can modify any search you run there. As you can see by examining Figure 9.7, the HotBot screen can be expanded by clicking on the various options found there.

Here are the fields you can implement:

Modify   This field allows you to specify a further term or terms that can be added to your first search statement. You can do this as well with other search engines, though in some cases you will have to use various methods specified by the engine to string the additional phrases onto your first set of keywords. HotBot's virtue in this case is that it's easier to use. My search for *made in tibet,* for example, could be expanded by adding the term *china,* which reduces the total number of hits while focusing on a more precise topic.

Date   The Date field allows you to search through the entire universe of Web documents, or to limit the search to pages that have been posted within a specified period of time. A third alternative is to choose a specific date as the launching point of your search. This is useful if you want to look for information, say, about a new product. Knowing that the NetPC, for example, really didn't gain notoriety as an idea until 1996, I could start all my searches by specifying that they query only those pages posted after January 1 of that year.

Location   The location field allows you to specify a particular Web address or range of addresses. If you want to search every university site for a file pertaining to education, you could specify .edu here; HotBot would then cruise through those sites with an .edu extension, while ignoring all the .com, .org, and other sites. The same method can be used for geographical location, restricting your search to all educational institutions in France, for example.

Media Type   Although not visible in the figure, this is a useful field indeed, for it lets you search by type of file. If you knew that you needed to find a document that was in Adobe's Acrobat format, you could specify that with a mouse click; HotBot would ignore all other types of files, leaving you with a much smaller list to work your way through. The same can be done for audio and video files, as well as files formatted for VRML, Shockwave, Java, and other file types.

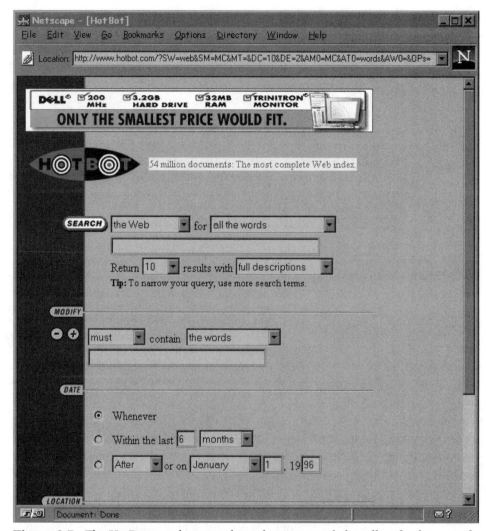

Figure 9.7   The HotBot search screen, here shown expanded to allow further specifications to the original search.

HotBot uses a program called Slurp as its automated search engine; the robot downloads millions of Web pages every day to build its database and keep it up to date. HotBot's indexing engine creates a page abstract that houses all the keywords used in fielding search queries. Like most search engines, HotBot supports so-called Boolean operators, referring to terms like AND or NOT that appear in traditional database searching. Boolean searches can be remarkably complex and allow tight specification of search parameters. Here's an example:

("science fiction" AND (barton OR "transmigration of souls"))

Notice the nested parentheses; these separate out the various parts of the query, telling the search engine in what order to run the search. Thus we're asking it to find sites using the term *science fiction* (note the quotation marks), and then to track down, from this list of sites, any additional ones that use either the word *barton* (for William Barton, one of my favorite science fiction authors) or *transmigration of souls* (the name of one of Barton's novels).

The advantage of Boolean operators is that most search engines use them; they thus constitute a kind of universal search language, which is no mean feat in an era when every search engine insists on its own way of doing business. The disadvantage of Boolean terms is that they're difficult to master, and most Web engines haven't been optimized for them. What you see when you log on is a keyword field that is more often designed for ease of use; thus HotBot's pull-down menus that allow you to tighten up your search. My view is that you're better off mastering several key search engines and their various techniques rather than working on an entirely new set of search parameters.

As for results, HotBot gives each hit a set of scores. Let's see how this works by running another search. In this case, I'm going to try to find out something about archaeology; specifically, I'd like to find sites that focus on work done in Egypt in the last hundred years relating to the pharaoh Akhenaten. He, you may recall, was an early monotheist who would later be considered a heretic by Egyptian priests. I can construct a keyword search for this remarkable man like this: *egypt archaeology akhenaten*. And because I've run my search terms together in a nonphrasal way, I can let HotBot search for all the included words. The screen in Figure 9.8 shows the results.

The HotBot screen must be scrolled through to check each entry, but that's not a problem here, because I've retrieved 114 matches, not too many for a quick scan of each. Notice the rankings to the left of each site; HotBot has declared a value for its results, the higher percentages being those it considers most likely to meet my needs. It does this by using a set of criteria, among which are these:

Word Frequency	A good search engine like HotBot looks not only at how often your keywords appear in the Web pages it finds, but also how differentiating they are. An obscure word will have more weight than a common term (you can imagine what HotBot thought about the term akhenaten!).
Title Words	Titles are obviously significant, and HotBot will rank the page higher if your keywords appear there.
Length of Document	If your keywords appear frequently in a short document, HotBot will rate that document more highly than if the words appear in a longer document. You can see that this is an arbitrary call; a high number of keywords in a short document should indicate focused attention on that subject, but you can lose much good information in longer texts if it weren't for the other criteria.

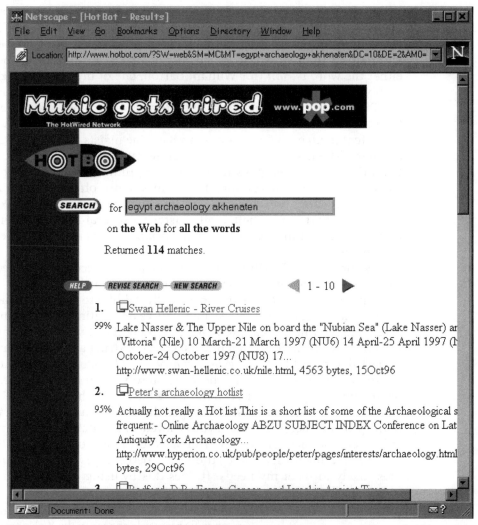

Figure 9.8   Results of a search for information about the Egyptian pharaoh Akhenaten.

Tip: Another way that HotBot qualifies its findings is by filtering out so-called spoofing, which is a technique that pranksters use to create false hits by search engines. They insert duplicate words thousands of times, or add characters in a font that matches the background color of the page, so that you can't see them on-screen. If HotBot recognizes such spoofing, it will lower the page's ranking dramatically.

Figure 9.9 shows one of my major finds with the Akhenaten search, a site at the University of Cambridge devoted to Egyptology. Here I found resources as diverse as a searchable archive of mailing lists related to Oriental studies, a multilingual Egyptological thesaurus, an index of scholars in Coptic, Demotic and related studies, the Prosopographia Aegypti database with search engine, and links to both the Oxford Classics page as well as the Papyrology home page at the University of Michigan. As to Akhenaten, one variable in my search turns out to be the spelling of his name, which is variously transcribed as

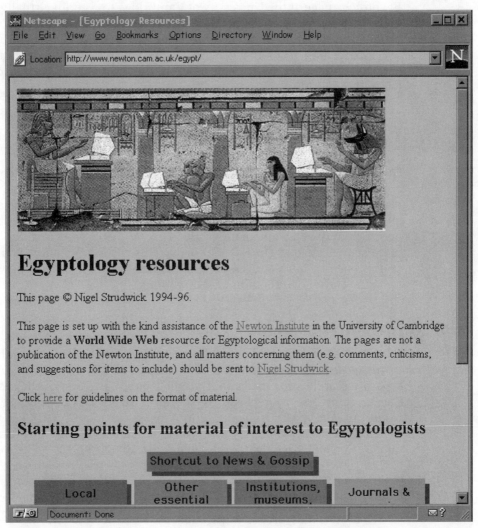

Figure 9.9 A major find—a site that collects Egyptological references and links, pointing to specific information about the subject of my search.

Akhenaten, Akhnaton, or Ikhnaton; he was also called Amenhotep IV, or Nefer-kheperure Amenhotep, and in Greek, Amenophis. His brand of monotheism, if it is correct to call it that, centered around the worship of the Aton, the disk of the Sun. His mummy has never been found.

Tracking down all this required clicking back and forth to various sites, but I found abundant resources. One of the most effective routes you can take when you're on a data hunt is to locate a major site for the study of whatever discipline you want to know about, then branch from it; if it is competently structured, there should be major pages devoted to your subject. I found the Egyptology page at the University of Cambridge to contain virtually everything I needed to home in on Akhenaten; but I could also have explored the HotBot listings further to focus directly on pages at these sites. One method is deductive, proceeding from the general to the specific by way of building your knowledge of the subject. The other is inductive; it offers a direct path to focused information.

Typical Search Issues

Given the sheer number of databases, it's obvious that not all searches will proceed alike. But certain themes will arise again and again. What follows is a listing of various keyword possibilities that reflect how you might approach a given search. I'll often refer to the AltaVista search engine here because it's both fast and well implemented. But I recommend you consider how to run these searches using HotBot. Following this section, I'll show you how other search engines have addressed basic search techniques, and how several of them have extended them in new directions.

Search for Phrases Where Possible

All search engines provide ways for you to search for phrases, so that the keywords *made in tibet* produce a search on that specific phrase, rather than three separate searches for pages that might contain any one of the search terms. The more precise your phrase is, the more likely it is to produce a targeted result. In AltaVista, using quotation marks to identify the keywords as a phrase, a search on *made in tibet* yields 10 hits, as opposed to taking out the quotes, in which case the search yields over 30,000.

Use Capitalization to Restrict Searches

AltaVista runs all searches as case-insensitive as long as they are typed in lowercase. Case-insensitive means that no matter how the word appears in the Web document, the search engine will be able to find it—the search term *washington* will pull hits mentioning Washington, a proper noun. If you want to force a case-sensitive search, you can do so by using one or more capital letters in your search statement. This tells AltaVista that the search should follow case exactly. A search for *Washington* thus pulls up only references to the capitalized word.

Make Certain Keywords Mandatory

A given search will not necessarily pull up pages that contain all your keywords. Many search engines simply search for as many of your terms as possible, so that as you move further down the list of ranked items, you will find pages that bear only a marginal relationship to your query. This can be confusing, and it certainly adds to the total number of hits. To get around it, with any search engine you use, make sure you understand how to direct the engine to produce pages with a specific term in them.

Let's assume, for example, that you want to search for news about a coup in the Comoros Islands, so often the scene of government takeovers in the Indian Ocean. Your keywords might be *coup comoros*. The word coup might be optional, but you must have hits that mention comoros. In AltaVista, you would set up the search phrase this way: *coup +comoros*. This forces the search engine's hand; you will get no pages without the terms marked by the plus (+) sign. If you wanted to include the word coup in all pages, your statement would be: *+coup +comoros*. The search for *coup comoros* yields over 20,000 hits. The search for *coup +comoros* yields 19.

Use Wildcards When Necessary

Wildcards are symbols that tell the search engine to substitute any letter or letters after the root. For example, suppose you were trying to find information about uninterruptible power supplies, those useful gadgets that protect your computer from power outages and voltage variations. If you use the keywords *uninterruptible power supply,* you run the risk of losing a page called Uninterruptible Power Supplies (note the plural). To get around the problem, you could search for *uninterruptible power suppl**. Here, the asterisk tells the search engine that it should look for any variation on the root *suppl*—thus it will pull supplies, supply, supplying, and so on. In this case, I would also require that the three keywords be searched for as a phrase; in AltaVista, this would require quotation marks: *"uninterruptible power suppl*"*. In HotBot, I could force the issue by picking the appropriate item on the pull-down menu.

Tip: A word or phrase does not have to be grammatical or even spelled properly to appear in a search engine's list of results. The only requirement is that it occurs in a document that has been posted on the World Wide Web. You will be amazed at what you'll find if you search for common verbal gaffes. Try a search on *tradgedy,* a frequent misspelling of tragedy, and see what you get. Or try *acronymn* (for acronym—a word I constantly misspell). And if you've forgotten the old "i before e except after c" rule, run a check on the keyword *recieve*—this common spelling error pulls up over 20,000 hits! Searching for the word as properly spelled—*receive*—pulls 1,000,000 hits. Can it be that we've identified a new Internet statistic? Is the ratio of properly spelled to misspelled words on Web pages really 50 to 1?

Targeted Searching within the Document

Most search engines make it possible to get specific about particular types of information inside a given document. For example, it's possible to specify that you want to see pages that contain a particular title, or that house a link to a particular URL. The methods used will vary, so you'll need to check the documentation at the engine you're using. In AltaVista, you can use options like these, substituting your own terms for the sample ones I use:

anchor:recipes	Searches for pages that use the word recipes in the text of a hyperlink.
host:interpath.com	Searches for pages that use the term interpath.com in the host name of the Web server. You might do this if you were interested in what a particular site housed.
image:eagle.gif	Searches for pages that contain eagle.gif in the HTML coding for that page. This can be useful if you happen to know a specific filename for a given image, or if you want to search for what will probably be a generic image of the subject in question.
link:mindspring.com	Searches for any page that contains a link to a page with mindspring.com in its URL. This will tell you how many pages are pointing to a particular site.
title:"The Economist"	Searches for pages that contain the title you specify. Notice that I've used quotation marks to tell AltaVista that this is a phrase.

Major Web Search Engines

Both AltaVista and HotBot are excellent tools, but they're joined by a wide variety of other engines. In the pages that follow, I'll examine the major sites, with the caveat that there are more engines out there than can be satisfactorily reviewed. Again my recommendation: Learn one engine backward and forward, then master a second. From that point on, having built up a basic set of skills, you can try new engines on a case-by-case basis. You may find one that fits your needs better than others; my discovery of Excite, for example, added greatly to my ability to group my findings and saved time in my research.

Lycos: *Hunting for the Right Image*

One of the useful things about the old Veronica search tool was the flexibility it gave in finding specific types of information. Web-based search engines have begun to move in the same direction, but perhaps none has so extensively categorized the Net's content by data type as Lycos (http://www.lycos.com/). You can see the Lycos home page in Figure 9.10.

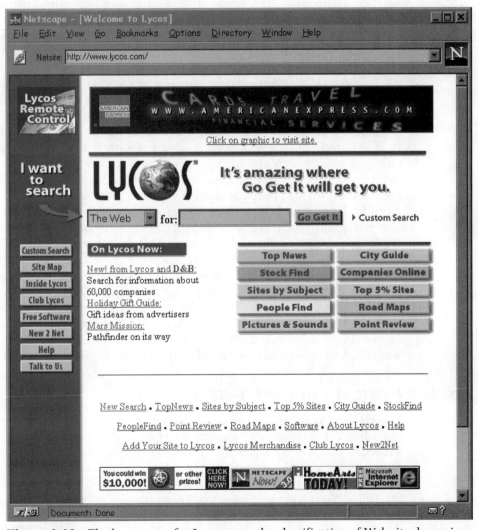

Figure 9.10 The home page for Lycos; note the classification of Web sites by various sorting criteria.

Here you can see that sites are ranked according to subject, city, pictures, and sound. You can move quickly to a search for news topics or look up people using the Lycos directory service; there's even a way to examine road maps. Which is not to say that Lycos prevents you from running more orthodox searches; the search field is at the top of the screen, and can be used to search the Web in its entirety, or as a subset of pictures, sound, or subject listings. Assume for the moment that I'd like to find a photograph of a scene in Thailand. To do so, I can simply click on the Pictures & Sounds button. I am taken to a search box that will run my query past a restricted database, thus cutting my search time substantially. I can choose between pictures and sounds on this page. Entering *thailand* as my keyword and clicking on Pictures, I call up a list of 43 images. They range from a Thai flag to a photo of rush hour in Banghok and shots taken around various mountain villages; there's even a shot of a Thai Ovaltine label! You can see one of these images in Figure 9.11. This figure of the Buddha from Sukothai, Thailand, was available with a mouse click off the Lycos search page.

Lycos makes an interesting attempt to serve as the bridge between the older directory-type services and state-of-the-art search engines with keyword entry. In Figure 9.12, you can see the search page for news topics.

Yahoo!, to be examined later, was one of the first Internet directory services; it, too, has now moved to incorporate direct keyword searching, although its directory structure is still intact. The directory format allows you to start with a generalized knowledge need and work your way through a set of categories until you've focused on your topic. But at any time, you can also jump to the keyword field to search across the entire site. Lycos also provides context-sensitive help, a useful and all too uncommon feature that spares you the tedium of paging through a lengthy FAQ document for a specific question. Clicking on Help calls up the feature, no matter where you are on the site map.

The Lycos database is not based on the full text of the Web pages its robot searches. Instead, it is cumulatively updated from information found in the titles of these pages, their major headers, their links, and their key paragraphs. Usefully, your key term will be highlighted in the list of citations, which also include percentage-based relevancy ranking. Customized search options allow you to adjust how results are displayed and how keywords are matched.

Excite: Using a Concept Search

The Excite engine is an interesting variation on the basic search idea. While providing a searchable database of Web pages, this engine also lets you search a directory of reviewed sites. Its concept searching is a great way to find pages that meet your needs, even if your specific keywords don't appear on them. For example, suppose you are searching for information about television stars of the 1950s. You might enter a set of keywords like television, fifties, or perhaps the names of particular stars. Like any other search engine, Excite can feed these keywords through its database and produce a result. But it can also fig-

Figure 9.11 A figure of the Buddha from Thailand, located for me by the Lycos search engine.

ure out that television is related to telecommunications and media, two terms that aren't in your keyword list.

The result: Excite gives you a flexible search tool that can help gloss over an inefficient keyword statement. As with site ranking, you can't expect the Excite software to figure out every connection you may have in mind, but it's remarkably thorough at linking to related sites, and as it indexes your documents, it can draw more terms from them. Excite searches some 50 million Web URLs in its hunt for the right match, and allows you to hunt through USENET newsgroups. It even offers a USENET classified ad option that lets

Figure 9.12   The Lycos page for news searches; notice how the subjects are broken into categories for specific searching.

you look for merchandise and check prices in those newsgroups dedicated to connecting buyers and sellers.

In Figure 9.13, you can see a screen full of Excite results from the search on television stars I just ran. Notice that next to each of the results, there is a link marked [More Like This]. Click on this link if you want Excite to run another search, this time focusing on what it finds in the first hit and trying to match up keywords so that it pulls up similar pages. The More Like This function helps you group related sites and provides what seems to be the most efficient way of ranking results I have seen.

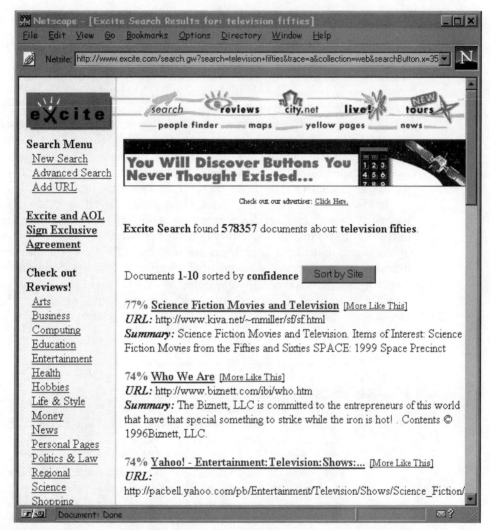

Figure 9.13 Excite's concept search strategy draws in sites that are related to your keywords but that don't necessarily mention them.

Excite's database is a full-text collection of information drawn from sites that are known to be attracting numerous readers. This engine offers the aforementioned Boolean search capabilities, meaning you can search using terms like AND, OR, and AND NOT; thus a search might read *clinton AND NOT white-water*. The engine uses a plus sign (+) just as AltaVista does as a way of marking a keyword as essential. You can also use a minus sign (–) to tell the search engine to exclude a particular term. Thus *clinton –whitewater* will perform the same function as the Boolean statement just shown. Excite's concept methods, still evolving, foreshadow interesting developments in tomorrow's agent software.

Infoseek: Text and Precision

Infoseek (http://www.infoseek.com) has indexed over 50 million URLs in its database, and claims, with its Ultra technology, to have eliminated redundancies and dead links, meaning you're not likely to run into many links that repeat themselves or simply no longer exist. Its database is based upon the full text of the Web pages its robot visits. Infoseek is also a confusing service, with various offerings that, put together, provide you with a comprehensive way to search the Net, if not a totally integrated one. In Figure 9.14, for example, you can see how the engine handles complex queries. Here I'm using separate fields for specialized queries. These include the ability to search for images, particular sites, the hyperlinks themselves, to URLs, and page titles.

Infoseek offers Ultraseek, a search engine, as well as Ultrasmart, a directory of Web sites broken down into topics with natural language search capabilities. The site includes a handy news center with easy access to major events of the day, including a search option for USENET that summarizes ongoing discussions in various newsgroups. Finally, Infoseek's SmartInfo provides directory services for people and companies, and includes links to a variety of references sources. I've used Infoseek's various tools for longer than almost any other search engine, and I continue to find it the most accurate in terms of returning hits that I can use.

Tip: The term natural language is one that's assuming renewed importance as search engines make a pitch for the average user. As opposed to Boolean statements, with their complicated syntax, or other site-specific query options, natural language is the ability to phrase your query simply by typing in a question. Instead of sending a phrase like *hayes tilden 1876 election* to the engine, you could type *how did rutherford hayes become president?* The good news is that natural language queries make it easier than ever to use search engines. The bad news is that this kind of query is more likely than Boolean searches to generate misleading hits. Advances in software design should help natural language systems refine their techniques, but we always fall back upon the difference between what a human can conceptualize and what a computer can understand. Don't let anyone tell you that the gap doesn't remain a wide one.

Open Text: Full Text, Full Power

Open Text draws on a full-text database to offer a range of search options for the experienced researcher. You have the option of choosing a simple search or going to the power search mode, which includes Boolean operators and the ability to focus your search on anything from the full text of the site's Web

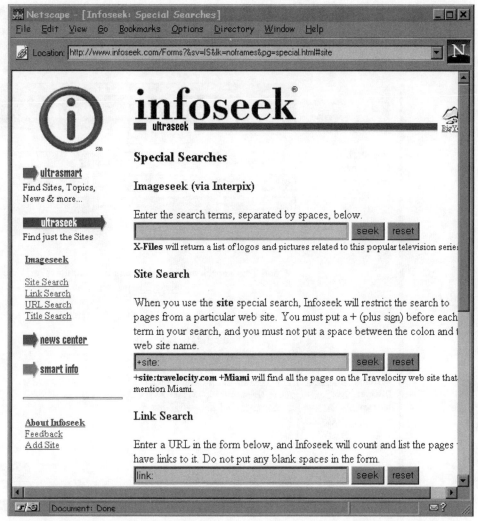

Figure 9.14 Infoseek's Special Searches page provides options for setting up special-ized queries.

pages to their titles, URLs, summaries, or headers. Usefully, Open Text includes FTP sites as well as Gopher pages. Lycos is another search engine that does this, but many do not, a reminder that you need to be careful about what goes into the search engine's database. A great deal of helpful information can be found in the world's Gophers, much of it hidden to the average engine.

In Figure 9.15, you can see the Open Text search screen set up for power searching; the URL is http://index.opentext.net/. The Open Text index is updated on a continuous basis; the site claims to add or update over 50,000 pages per day.

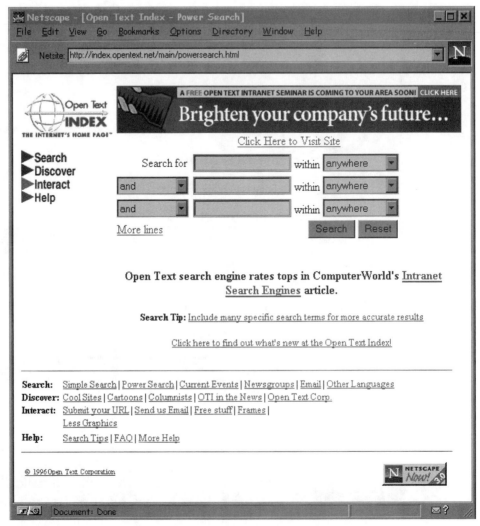

Figure 9.15   The power search screen at Open Text can use Boolean operators and target title, URL, or full text.

Because Open Text makes it easy to narrow your search from the full-text option to header, title, summary, or URL, it's quite easy to change your search on the fly and keep experimenting until you retrieve the necessary results. Suppose you launched a search that turned up 10,000 hits on the keyword *shakespeare*. With many engines, you'd then need to start adding to your keyword phrase, hoping to make it more specific. With Open Text, you can decide that what you want to see are Web pages whose primary focus is Shakespeare. Asking the engine to search only for pages that have your search term in the title, you narrow the list to 347 hits, each of which merits a closer look. If 347 is still too many, you can narrow this universe down to a workable dozen or so by tightening up your query with Boolean operators. Add *macbeth* to the query, for example, and you pull down 27 hits. What I did in this case was to keep the *shakespeare* keyword in the title search, but added a search for *macbeth* within the full text of those pages.

WebCrawler: The America Online Solution

WebCrawler, now operated by America Online, searches an index of Web sites that is updated daily. While the engine supports natural language queries, it also offers Boolean operators for the more experienced searcher, and provides a variety of ways of displaying your search results, from a list of titles or more complete summaries. The engine also makes this puzzling statement in its Frequently Asked Questions document: "Adding advanced search operators will not fundamentally change your top results, it will just limit the total number of results you get back." Which seems to be a concession that if you don't find what you need the first time through with WebCrawler, your chances of tightening up your search are relatively slim. You can see the WebCrawler home page in Figure 9.16. Its URL is http://www.webcrawler.com/.

DejaNews: Looking for Newsgroup Messages

Several of the major search engines allow you to run keyword searches against a database of newsgroup messages; both AltaVista and HotBot, for example, make this an option by dropping down a menu and offering a USENET choice. DejaNews is a site that specializes only in the newsgroups, and it's probably the place to start if you plan on doing intensive newsgroup work. The URL is http://www.dejanews.com/. As you can see from its home page in Figure 9.17, the site is set up with a standard keyword field in which to enter your query; alternatively, you can run the search by topic by looking for the right newsgroup.

As a mystery fan, I'd like to see if anyone is discussing the works of Ellis Peters, the wonderful author of the Brother Cadfael books. Set in medieval Shrewsbury, these novels follow the erstwhile Benedictine monk and sometime detective through a series of adventures against the backdrop of the bloody wars of King Stephen and the Empress Maud. To run the search, I simply enter the keywords *ellis peters*. DejaNews will run the search past 15,000 newsgroups. The result is shown in Figure 9.18. A click on any of these items will call up the complete message. Usefully, DejaNews has searched across the entire universe of mailing lists, allowing me to run a search that would be impossible through my own newsgroup software.

DejaNews also provides a power search tool that lets you refine the search and create a query filter. You can search by newsgroup, date, author, or subject, sorting the results in various ways and searching either a current database (DejaNews works with 500MB of new information daily) or the newsgroup

Figure 9.16 The home page for WebCrawler, a good beginner's tool, but not one that's optimized for power searches.

archive. Bringing the power of a search engine to bear on newsgroup postings is a helpful expansion of the Net's power. I often find useful advice on equipment purchases and ongoing industry stories here.

For another take on newsgroup searching, try:

Reference.COM (http://www.reference.com/), which allows you to search both newsgroup and mailing list archives.

TILE.NET (http://tile.net/), a favorite engine for mailing list searches as well, but helpful with the newsgroups.

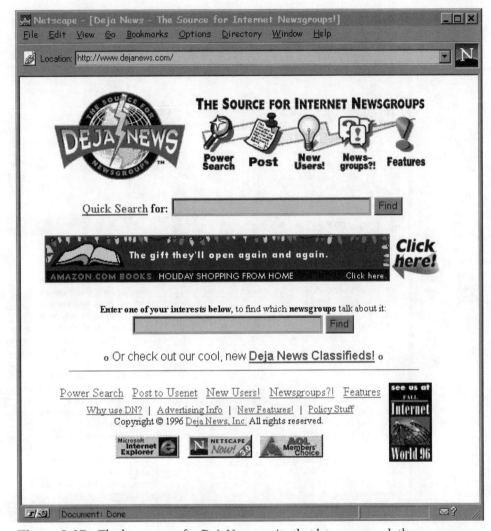

Figure 9.17 The home page for DejaNews, a site that lets you search the newsgroups.

Search Engines versus Directories: A Meeting of the Ways

In their purest form, search engines and directories are two different kinds of tool. Think search engine and you should visualize a database with a query in front of it; when you call up an engine, you invariably have to feed it a keyword or phrase to make things happen. Directories, by contrast, are more like listings of sites broken down into categories that are usually based upon subject.

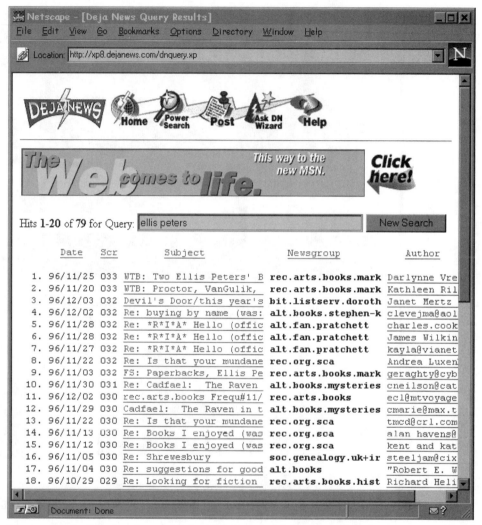

Figure 9.18 Results of a search for Ellis Peters. Multiple mailing lists are represented here.

Instead of constructing a set of keywords, you pick the topic closest to yours and click. A second set of topics, subtopics of the first, then opens up, and so on. You delve ever deeper into the nested topics until you find the one you need.

The type of thinking required by search engines and directories is also different. With a search engine, you need to have a fairly clear idea of what you're looking for. If you don't, your search will turn up so many hits, in so random an order, that you are little better off than you were before you ran the search. Starting with a precise idea of your need, you sift through hits and misses, looking for the ones that will target your question. With a directory, the process is the reverse. If search engines require inductive thinking, directories work from the general to the particular, a form of deductive analysis.

It makes sense that directories were the first real sources from which to find things on the Net. Gopher, after all, was menu-based, constructed in layers of nested information. The problem in searching such a database is that you can't move *across* the menu structure; instead, your data hunts begin as a descent into a particular knowledge tree; you explore there, and then ascend the same structure to start over. In that sense, a Gopher hunt was among the least efficient data searches you could run, and the early Web-based directories like Yahoo!, which offered topic-driven lists of sites on the Web, suffered from the same problem.

An efficient search tool is one that lets you move freely within it in all directions. You should be able to find a set of possible hits, look through each, return to the search page, check another, and, in general, not be encumbered by the restrictions of the search software. Thus it was that the early Web directories quickly began to include search features among their offerings. With a built-in search engine, you could run a keyword search past the site's database to go directly to the site you needed, bypassing the menu structure. But if you wanted the topic targeting offered by a directory, that function was also available.

Another difference between directories and search engines is the way the site retrieves its information. If a site uses a robot or Web spider to troll the Net for database information, it's a search engine. If it builds its database with user-submitted URLs, site descriptions by Webmasters, or has its own staff review the contents of particular sites before putting them in its database, it's a directory. In between are the sites that perform both functions to a greater or lesser extent—Infoseek now does this, as does Excite; so, too, does the latest version of Yahoo! Today, with engines trying to outgun each other in an ever more crowded field, the merger between straight search engine and enhanced directory is a fact of life. To survive, developers have to offer search functions as well as value-added services like reviewing of sites, presentation of news, opinions columns, and the like.

Tip: One problem searchers invariably encounter is that after exploring a site that has been suggested by a search engine, they want to return to the search results page without backing out through an entire sequence of cached pages. Although not all search engines allow you to do it, setting up a page of search results as a bookmark is an excellent way to solve the movement problem. Click on a hyperlink to explore a page. If it's not what you want, just click on the bookmark to return to your search page.

Yahoo!: A Classic Directory Revisited

It wasn't so long ago that Yahoo! was almost the only Web-based directory service available. The work of two graduate students at Stanford University, Yahoo! quickly seized the imagination of Net users and grew out of its early parameters into a full-service search engine. But fortunately, it still returns its results to you in directory form, meaning it's easy to see in what general topic the site's software has placed each entry. This is especially helpful when you're dealing with a Web page whose title is ambiguous.

You can see the primary Yahoo! screen in Figure 9.19. Notice that you're given a search field at the top of the screen, which can be used like that of any other search engine by filling in the appropriate keyword and clicking on the Search button. Or you can work your way down through the various topics, attempting to home in on what you need without worrying about going through lists of hits. Yahoo! breaks down its topics into numerous submenus, and if what you need is fairly clear-cut, it becomes easy to find promising Web sites. Notice that Yahoo! also offers yellow-page listings for businesses, people searches, news features, city maps, stock quotes, and sports. It's obvious that engines like these are trying to become full-service information providers rather than just database front ends.

Magellan Internet Guide: Web Sites Rated

Magellan was one of the first sites to begin regular reviews of Web pages and incorporate them in its findings. Now the site (http://www.mckinley.com/) combines directory-like features and original editorial content to serve as a kind of base camp for new Internet explorers. You can browse topics from Education and Law to Mathematics or Travel, choose between a guide to Net events and a directory to e-mail addresses, and run straightforward Web searches with the Magellan search engine. Moreover, sites you pull up through such a search are rated for content and possibly objectionable material.

You can see Magellan in action in Figure 9.20. Here, I've generated a list of results on the query *internet news*. I've also asked Magellan, by clicking on the appropriate button, to search only those sites its staff has reviewed.

Magellan produced ratings and reviews for each of the sites, along with the page's title and URL. Magellan puts a green light icon next to sites that contain no sexually questionable content. It's also possible to exclude any sexually oriented materials from a Magellan search altogether.

The Web pages rated by Magellan are studied by editors and writers, and sites are selected based upon their usefulness and utility. The ratings are based on issues like depth, ease of navigation, and basic appeal, with a four-star system in which four stars is the highest rating. Magellan also provides links to related topics. Search options include simple search as well as plus (+) and minus (–) sign options for forcing a word to appear in each document or excluding a particular word. By default, the database searches for records that contain one or more of your search terms.

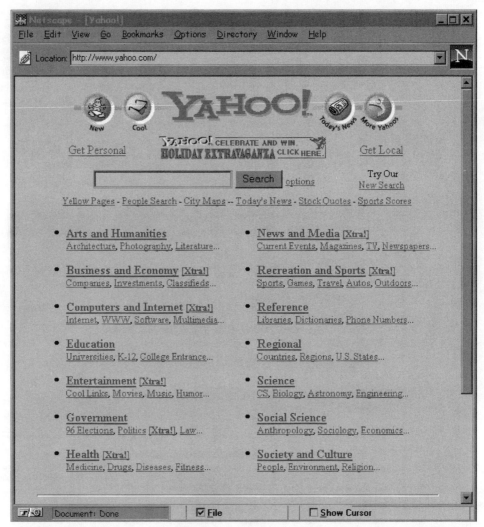

Figure 9.19 The Yahoo! search screen betrays its origins as a topic-based directory.

Tip: Given the rush into the search engine arena, what's in store for the companies that operate these tools? Probably a shakeout. Advertising is the key to keeping a search engine afloat; indeed, according to a report from Jupiter Communications, the top five search engines—Yahoo!, Lycos, Infoseek, Excite, and Magellan—generated combined advertising revenues of approximately $14 million in the first half of 1996. But the amount of advertising dollars and the number of possible users is limited, and the search engines are in competition with specialized and local sites. As is

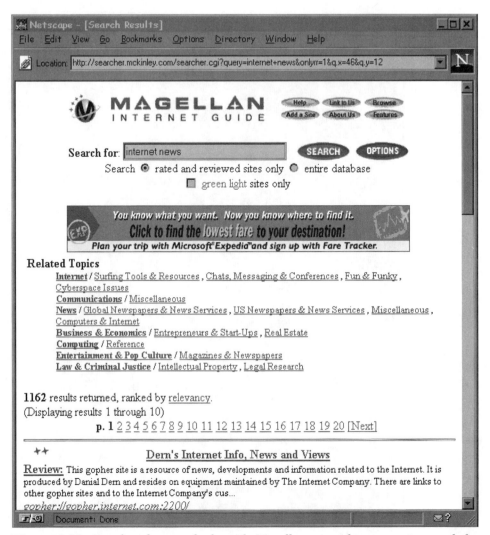

Figure 9.20 Results of a search through Magellan; note the star ratings and the reviews.

the case in the Internet service provider (ISP) market, we may see a weeding out of all but the most robust companies.

The analogy between search engines and ISPs works on another level as well. Smaller ISPs are looking for ways to survive in a crowded marketplace; many are choosing to become conduits of local content, under the assumption that these are the services that national providers will be unable to match. Search engines are likewise changing their format. Many engines that grew up as little more than a keyword search field feeding a large database now include a host of directory options that could be considered value-added services. The attempt is to catch casual searchers who will be attracted by their ability to find information in a multitude of different ways. Only the best (and best-funded) will survive, but the battle should be fascinating.

Four11: Finding People

The most intractable of all Internet search problems has been that of finding people. In the early days of the Net, locating a person required that he or she already have an Internet address. It was also hampered by the kinds of software available. The WHOIS program, for example, allowed you to search through listings at a particular site, but you had to know where the person in question was and then access the server there to find them. Recently, Web search engines specializing on finding individuals have begun to emerge, and Four11 (http://www.Four11.com/) is one of the best.

Figure 9.21 shows the search screen at Four11. The site's directory contains 8 million listings from voluntary registrations, public sources like the newsgroups, and automatic registration through Internet service providers. You can search by name, geographical location, or electronic mail address.

Switchboard: Locating Physical Addresses

Switchboard allows you to enter a name and city/state information to track down an address. Listings are compiled from published white pages directories, so you're likely to find yourself here whether you intend to be or not (although listings can be hidden or removed). The URL is http://www.switchboard.com/). You can use Switchboard in conjunction with the handy Yahoo! Maps site (http://www.vicinity.com/yahoo/) to first find the address of a person and then construct a map of that address.

Other Web Directories

Here is a listing of other Web directories that may be worth a look. My general rule is to bookmark all such sites as they appear and run sample searches on them as part of my regular work. A few searches at a site will quickly tell you whether it is going to prove useful.

Apollo (http://apollo.co.uk/): A directory of Web-based advertising.
Argus Clearinghouse (http://www.clearinghouse.net/): Internet-based topical guides to information resources.
AT&T Toll-Free Internet Directory (http://www.tollfree.att.net/dir800/): Listings of 800 numbers.
Database America (http://www.databaseamerica.com/html/index.htm): Business information from a marketing company.

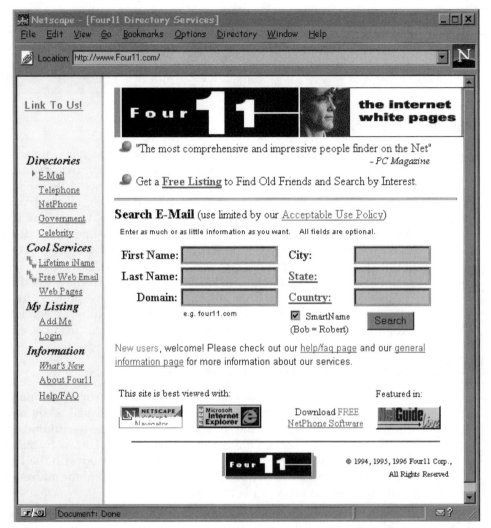

Figure 9.21   The search screen at Four11, the best of the people finders.

Galaxy (http://galaxy.einet.net/): Directory of Net resources divided by subject.

InfoSpace (http://www.infospaceinc.com/): Telephone directories for the United States and Canada, as well as e-mail directories for people and companies.

Internet Address Finder (http://www.iaf.net/): Pulls up electronic mail addresses.

LinkStar (http://www.linkstar.com/): Corporate information through a proprietary system called e-Card.

LookupUSA (http://www.lookupusa.com/): White pages and yellow pages.

The Stalker's Home Page (http://pages.ripco.com:8080/~glr/stalk.html): Devoted to people-finding software and the issues it raises.

Phonebooke (http://www.phonebooke.com/): Links to phonebooks as well as other search sites.

Starting Point (http://www.stpt.com/): General information by topic.

Telephone Directories on the Web (http://www.contractjobs.com/tel/): Directories from countries all over the world; the only site I've found that allows you to look up telephone numbers from places as diverse as French Polynesia and the Isle of Man.

Virtual Yellow Pages (http://www.vyp.com/): Another business and corporate directory.

Web Interface to WHOIS (http://rs.internic.net/cgi-bin/whois): Here's how we used to do it—the WHOIS databases, now accessible through a Web interface.

WhoWhere? (http://www.whowhere.com/): Directory of e-mail addresses.

World Wide Yellow Pages (http://www.yellow.com/): Business listings.

WWW VirtualLibrary (http://www.w3.org/pub/DataSources/bySubject/Overview.html): One of the earliest directories (once found on the CERN server where all this got started).

Yahoo! People Search (http://www.yahoo.com/search/people/phone.html): Finds people by telephone number alone.

Metasearching: Combining Your Tools

A metasearch is one that includes more than one database at a time. Theoretically, you save time; a site that offers metasearching lets you enter a keyword and run that keyword past however many databases it can contact. In practice, the story is somewhat less rewarding. Supposing you get a list of the top 10 hits and 10 different search sites. But by now you know that search engines aren't precise enough in their relevancy ranking to guarantee a solid hit among those top 10. Hence you may wind up with 10 different lists of irrelevant material, and need to go to the search engines one by one to dig deeper. By the time you're through, you would have been better off using one well-chosen engine and using it with precision.

But let's take a look at some of these metasearch engines. They point to new ways to harness computer power in searching, and if they're only beginning to show their stuff, we can expect solid advances as the software is improved. The one to start with is SavvySearch (http://www.cs.colostate.edu/~dreiling/smart-form.html), a tool that does something that other metasearch engines can only dream of: It integrates its findings so you don't wind up with duplicates. Its context-sensitive help and variously adjustable query capabilities make it easy to use, although demand at the site often results in slow performance. Searching for information about the connection between William Shakespeare and fellow playwright Ben Johnson, I retrieved results from WebCrawler, Yahoo, and Lycos. But other engines can be consulted in sequence. A click sent me into Excite, Galaxy, and DejaNews, and I could have kept clicking to add other engines as I used the SavvySearch search plan.

Other meta-engines include:

All-in-One Search Page (http://www.albany.net/allinone/): A huge number of search engines on a single page, though each must be searched individually.

The Internet Sleuth (http://www.intbc.com/sleuth/): Search engines of all kinds, with opportunities to find specialized tools for subsets of the Internet community. The topic menu helps you locate the appropriate engine.

IBM InfoMarket (http://www.infomkt.ibm.com/): A fee-based service (you pay per document) for Internet-based databases and private information collections.

MetaSearch (http://metasearch.com/): Searching for software, Web pages, and reference items in dictionaries and thesauri.

Intelligent Software and Off-Line Browsers

Metasearch engines can begin to simplify your search process, but real advances in the area of metasearching are more likely to be found in the realm of agent software. Indeed, a number of companies are bringing tools to the market that consult multiple databases, integrate the results, run update checks, and pull up new material, all while you work on other things. As with the metasearch sites themselves, these programs are in their infancy, and serious issues remain to be addressed, but you can try many of them out without charge to see if they produce results.

Autonomy: An Intelligent Search Tool Using Agents

Let's look, for example, at a program called Autonomy (http://www.agent-ware.com/). What agents promise, and Autonomy tries to deliver, is intelligent searching and presentation of results by means of automated tools. Autonomy breaks into two functions, the first of which is the engine that conducts sweeps through Web sites, the second the program that studies the documents returned by the search and makes judgment calls about its key concepts and usefulness. And here is the novel part of the exercise: As you use Autonomy, the software begins to focus more tightly on the concepts and keywords that are found on the pages you use the most. It's an overstatement, to say the least, that the software has become "smarter," but that at least is the impression the program gives. An intelligent agent is one that "learns" from its experience.

Of course, agents have other benefits that are not inconsiderable. A good agent can be sent out onto the Net and allowed to operate while you're away from the computer. Finishing up a long workday, you may decide to continue research overnight. Arming Autonomy with the appropriate information, you can send it through the Net and let it work while you sleep. In the morning, you have a set of search results, usefully sorted by a variety of criteria, and you can be sure that the more you run such searches and choose from among their results, the tighter your next search will become. You can build a database of useful results, or create a daily newspaper relevant to your own interests.

Autonomy calls its agents Web Researchers. They can be armed with a keyword or phrase, or you can paste in a particularly relevant bit of text that contains the sort of information you're looking for. The agent will visit Web sites and retrieve those that match your keywords; it will also follow links off the pages it retrieves to see which of these are most relevant to the search. In that sense, the agent acts much like a person, the bulk of whose Web time is spent following leads to related material. By automating this part of the process, Autonomy has the potential for saving you considerable time. When you want to view the software's results, you call them up in Netscape; you have the option of accepting or rejecting a given document, thus refining the list for further searching.

Autonomy comes with another interesting feature, a tool called Press Agent, that can use many of the same search techniques to scour electronic news sources—newspapers, magazines, wire services, and press releases—to find stories that fit your profile. Usefully, the software is not confined to working within predetermined categories, which can be an unusually restrictive feature of news services like Individual's NewsPage. Instead, the agent works through whatever topic you give it, highlighting concepts rather than third-party clusters of information. In Figure 9.22, you can see the Autonomy program. Each of the dog icons represents a search agent.

The program comes with a helper agent that walks you through the basic procedures. To create an agent, you simply pull down the File menu and click on New. Autonomy then allows you to name the new agent and specify what you're looking for in plain English. The agent can then be launched in search of your material. My first Autonomy search was for material about Peru, a country where I have investments, and in which I therefore have an interest in political developments. When Autonomy's agent scoured the Web, it quickly pulled up a series of Web pages and documents that answered my queries. I was then able to teach Autonomy which pages were the most relevant by adding them to its library.

I could also create a personalized news page by using the Press Room function. Doing so, I had my choice of any combination of sources including CNN, the Associated Press, *The Financial Times*, *The Daily Telegraph*, and more. Add to this the capability of setting up multiple searches for relevant information and you can see how useful a tool this is. A site that demands you choose categories for your information fails to acknowledge the fact that, in many cases, our information needs vary from day to day. Autonomy is readily adjustable depending on your circumstances.

Tip: One of the first things you'll notice about intelligent agents like Autonomy is that they tend to take longer to run than you would expect. Bear in mind, of course, that the search can be run in the background, so it's plausible to argue that you're still saving time by using them. But if you intend to simply log on to the Net and run an Autonomy search, you may be in for quite a wait. The same holds true for the agent software to be discussed next, Web Compass.

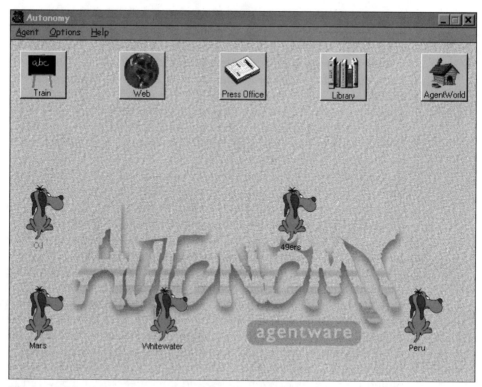

Figure 9.22 Autonomy provides powerful intelligent agent capabilities and allows you to build personalized news pages.

Autonomy joins the Net software crowd with some impressive credentials. Its parent company is Cambridge Neurodynamics, a pioneering force in the development of the neural network technology that attempts to mimic the actions of the human brain and replicate them in software. The latter firm is a commercial affiliate of Cambridge University. And while Autonomy still has a great deal of work ahead to improve the speed of its searches and refine its reporting, the software is among the most provocative agent-based programs on the market. Its 30-day free trial gives you the opportunity to sample neural networking.

A Sample Search Using Web Compass

Quarterdeck's Web Compass (http://www.quarterdeck.com/) was one of the first fully featured commercial search agents to hit the retail shelf. But the program is both more complex and more problematic than I might wish, and it reveals the limitations as well as the possibilities of this technology. The program works in two ways. First, it can access a variety of different search engines, running the same keywords past them all in a single sweep. You can add search engines as well, so that you're not limited to a particular subset of this universe. In the second part of the process, Web Compass can categorize your results, producing document summaries and clustering similar sites. When this system works, it can dramatically reduce search time, but the software has a steep learning curve, and the results I've achieved with it have been mixed.

A recent project involving the nature of Internet content seemed like a good place to test out Web Compass Professional. My keywords were extremely general, but I couldn't figure out how to fine-tune them. I was looking for articles involving how we evaluate Internet documents and Web sites. In other words, in a world where anyone can use sophisticated (and often free) software tools to create Web pages, how do we make reliable judgments about their content? What tricks can we use to verify what a Web page says, and what should we look for by way of supporting documentation in an on-line discussion or publication?

My normal procedure would be to set up a fairly complex Boolean search at one of the engines that accept such strategies, linking terms like evaluate, content, resource, and critique, coupled with a demand that any documents fitting these criteria should all include the words *internet* and *network*. Boolean searching is demanding; you have to know how to structure the query, and besides, not all search engines support Boolean methods. But I've found those that do allow me to bring pinpoint accuracy to my searches.

A search like this one would return a list of hits, ranked (depending on the search engine) according to their relevance to what the software assumes to be my purpose. But search engines are not very good at making this inference; I often find the ideal document far down on my list of hits, and having to page through 896 documents to locate the one I need never ceases to be daunting. This is where Web Compass Professional tends to shine. The software can run this search past multiple engines and cluster the results in the background, while I work on other things. I can then go off-line and examine the results, and when I need to update, Web Compass will examine what I have and locate any new sites meeting my criteria.

Don't be misled by the so-called lite version of Web Compass that's available at the Quarterdeck site (http://www.quarterdeck.com/). While it allows you to search multiple engines, it lacks the reporting features of the Web Compass Professional product, and these are its strongest suit. It's interesting to see how variable are the results between a search at different engines, but after you've run it, you're still left to point and click your way to the various sites to decide whether they're useful. The Professional product makes it easier to make that call, and while it takes longer to gather its data, as noted, it runs in the background so you can keep working on other things.

I launched a topic-based search with Web Compass Professional using the same keywords I just mentioned. I then minimized the program and proceeded to work on other projects. In the corner of my screen, the flashing modem lights told me that the software was continuing to search and retrieve information. When I finally got curious enough to check, I saw that Web Compass was in the midst of a great categorization. Using my keywords, it had produced a list of hits, sites that included all my terms. It had then generated an index and had begun to rank the sites according to methods of its own. Thus I found a hyperlink marked "5 documents about plan, systems, students, activities, goal," and another hyperlink marked "6 documents about experience, syllabus, ability." A click on either link took me to an synopsis of each site; I could also access an abstract, which included a summary, a list of keywords found on the page, document statistics, and a place for annotations.

The method seems promising; it's much easier to work with documents that have been gathered into subtopics than with several hundred documents laid out in no particular order. Where the problem arises is with the subtopics. What, for example, do documents marked "experience, syllabus, ability" have in common? I haven't a clue, which means that I have to investigate each of these topics one by one, forgoing the supposed usefulness of the product in the first place. Some of the topics make little sense. What do the nine links clustered under the title "part, contents, systems, macgyver, week" have in common? MacGyver?

I finally decided, after culling 672 documents and letting Web Compass Professional cluster them as it would, that its topic system was taking more time than it was worth. Fortunately, there are alternative ways of searching using this software. I went back in and ran a straight search under my keywords without asking Web Compass to summarize my findings. I then scrolled through the list and checked off the documents that fit my criteria and created a new topic that held them. The program proceeded to go out on the Web and generate summaries of those documents. This method yielded much more precise results.

The ability to generate summary documents about individual sites is useful, because it can save you the need to visit a site. But I'm still uncertain how to rank Web Compass Professional in terms of its flexibility. The program's manual is clear about one thing (and little else): If you want to use the advanced searching techniques available at a specific search engine, you have to go directly to that engine and run your search. You do the same thing, in other words, that you would do if you didn't have Web Compass.

This also means that you have limited flexibility in choosing keywords. I finally discovered, after much trial and error, that I was better off using just a few well-chosen and relatively general keywords than trying to get too precise. What I lost by way of keyword control I made up by letting the software categorize its results. The search procedure using Web Compass Professional is thus considerably longer than it would be using other methods, but it's also more comprehensive. If there are topics that you follow on a regular basis and want to update, this software is probably a good choice. And when you simply want to run a quick check to see what's out there, you can run one-time-only searches without building the database of supporting documents or clustering the search results.

My take on not only Web Compass Professional but the entire range of agent-style software for the Internet is that the category is in its infancy. The concept is sound, but the practical results of letting your computer attempt to generate information clusters are as likely to be wide of the mark as they are to be helpful. Web Compass Professional can become a valuable tool if you're willing to live with the product's eccentricities and work with it long enough to fine-tune its procedures. But it may take an upgrade or two to make the software as powerful as Quarterdeck claims. Version 2.0 should be available by the time you read this; perhaps it will be better.

Other Web Search Tools

Other agents that can improve your search results include the following. In most cases, you can download a trial version with limited functionality or a time limit on its usage. Some companies provide light versions that are free and can be upgraded to more powerful commercial programs.

Go-Get-It (http://www.hpp.com)

From Home Page Press, this program runs background searches based on your keyword lists and is extremely fast. Pages are downloaded into folders you create inside the Go-Get-It program. The software finds updates and retrieves new information. It can download pages for off-line reading and is capable of searching the USENET newsgroups.

The NetFerret Utilities (http://www.vironix.com/)

A group of products from FerretSoft that searches various kinds of Internet information. The newsgroup search tool (NewsFerret) enables you to run searches across multiple newsgroups. Binary attachments can be automatically decoded, and you can use your regular news client to view search results. WebFerret searches multiple engines to answer keyword requests, while EmailFerret locates addresses of companies and people through publicly accessible databases.

MoreLikeThis (http://www.morelikethis.com/)

A helper application from KDL Interactive that searches multiple search engines and allows you to progressively refine your queries. You can find sites that are relevant to your search even if they don't include the keywords you specify through "concept" and "wide-angle" intelligent searching.

WebTamer (http://www.agentsoft.com/)

AgentSoft's automated search tool and off-line browser can be programmed to run searches any time of day; it provides task-specific agents for retrieving particular types of information.

CompassWare Development (http://www.compassware.com)

This agent uses an intelligent search tool called MagnetFind that learns from each search to refine future results.

Off-Line Browsers: Search Filters and Automated Downloads

The distinction between intelligent search agents and off-line browsers is in some cases relatively trivial. Many search agents, for example, make it possible to pull in complete pages, or summaries of same, that you can analyze on your own time. Some off-line browsers include sophisticated search functions, so that you can update pages in the background and produce a compendium of new material every day. And the benefits of browsing off-line are many. Rather than working through a site slowly during peak usage times, you can schedule that time-consuming process for off-hours, or do it in the background while you work on other things. Once downloaded, the site is easy to use; moving between its pages is not dependent on network conditions.

One day soon, increased bandwidth to home and office will make off-line browsing products seem like antiques. But that day may be years away, and until then, this category of product can produce robust results without the aggravation of waiting for lengthy downloads. Another benefit: If you do presentations, your weakest link is the Internet connection you use to illustrate your points. An off-line browser lets you download entire sites for exploration whether or not the phone system is working at the time. Here are some off-line browsers for you to consider:

Net Attache (http://www.tympani.com/)

Available in light and commercial versions, Net Attache runs background searches and Web page retrievals and allows you to view pages off-line. Net Attache Pro provides a wider variety of search options and archival tools. You have control over whether you want to download such features as Java applets, multimedia files, or various inline plug-ins.

WebWhacker (http://www.on.com/)

This program captures Web sites for off-line reading, allowing you to retrieve as many levels of hyperlinks as you choose. It can download an entire site or selected pages, and enables you to home in on new pages only. Useful filtering options give you control over downloaded content so that you can, for example, screen out advertisements.

Netriever (http://www.metz.com/)

Metz Software Inc.'s automated delivery program works in the background and can display Web pages as screen savers or desktop wallpaper. It works independently of your browser.

Freeloader (http://www.freeloader.com)

From Freeloader Inc, this program lets you download Web pages on your own schedule and updates them automatically.

Web Retriever (http://www.folio.com)

Folio Corp.'s off-line reader can also convert HTML files into a separate database, allowing you to run sophisticated search routines on your results; it also offers editing and annotation features.

WebEx (http://www.laplink.com/)

Traveling Software's off-line reader is optimized for laptop and notebook computer users who want to read complete Web sites while on the road. The program is fully customizable, allowing you to choose what to download from a given site and offering complete update options. WebEx supports Java Applets, image maps, sound and video clips, and animation files, while maintaining all hypertext links. Perhaps its best feature is that it retains original URLs, rather than only pointing to a file's position in the local cache.

Teleport Pro (http://www.tenmax.com/pro.html)

Teleport Pro provides off-line browsing and keyword searching through a full-featured Web spider. From Tennyson Maxwell Information Systems, the program allows highly targeted file retrieval and search filters.

10

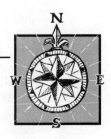

Publishing on the Web

The Web can be considered a great experiment in the art of publishing. Countless newspapers, magazines, brochures, essays, and personal jottings populate its precincts, as a quick browse through almost any network neighborhood will confirm. Perhaps most startling to old-time network hands is the degree to which the Web has been embraced by individuals. The personal home page, filled with favorite restaurants, or photographs of family, or links to good books and collections of music, is beginning to attain cult status. "Check out my home page at the following URL . . ." reads an e-mail signature, and the page in question is a kind of personal testament from a private Web publisher.

Of course, all Web pages could in some ways be considered "published" material, for they've been put out there in a publicly accessible way for people to mine their resources. In this chapter, though, we focus on publishing in its more traditional sense, the great migration of newspapers, magazines, and book publishers into cyberspace. We also look at the personal home page and the tools that can be used to build Web content and get it on-line.

Why the interest in publishing per se? Surely it's because we've made it so easy. Thirty years ago in the days of my unchastened youth, I published a whole series of science fiction "fanzines" devoted to my favorite authors—J. G. Ballard, Cordwainer Smith, Poul Anderson, and whomever else had caught my eye in the book and magazine scene of the time. My tool was a mimeograph bought through Sears Roebuck, a messy drum with handle that required frequent fillings of ink, and invariably stained whatever I was wearing. Turning out an issue took patient cutting of stencils on a ribbonless typewriter, weeks of composition, long hours of printing and collating. I felt like Gutenberg.

Today I could do all that with a software tool that I picked up as shareware on the Internet, or I could use any number of commercial programs. Publishing software for the Web has become big business, as companies like Soft-Quad, Anawave, Claris, Macromedia, and Adobe Systems have discovered. Both Netscape and Microsoft have weighed in with significant entries as well,

367

and hosts of tools supporting the publishing enterprise are in the pipeline. All must work around a central fact of the Web—HTML, the language that conveys Web information and displays it on our screen. Manipulating that language lets anyone create high-quality layouts, complete with mixed fonts, graphics, moving video, audio, and special effects.

We've moved, if you will, into the desktop publishing era on the Web. The original desktop publishing revolution meant that people in their offices could create brochures and newsletters without having to send the material out for fine-tuning by a professional designer. Completing complicated chores in-house saved money; it also extended the capability of at least limited publishing to countless groups, like hobbyists, clubs, church organizations, and others, which would not have ventured into print without its cost-saving features. Web publishing tools now make it possible for anyone to propagate ideas on the cheap, and to reach a global audience at a relatively trivial cost.

Needless to say, serious content issues are thus raised. If desktop publishing made the process easier, it also resulted in countless poorly designed and implemented documents in a bewildering array of fonts. If Web publishing has democratized the printing process, then we must ask who the editors are, what their qualifications happen to be, and how to evaluate their pages when we find them. Moreover, the new publishing software means that we can easily be deceived; high-quality in design is no longer a marker for reliability, and people with today's low-end computers can create pages that possess the impact of professional work. Reader beware is a caution worth heeding; for Web publishers, the motto is: present it, validate it, and link it to corroborating materials.

Who Publishes on the Web?

A survey of Web publishing takes in everyone from the individual with an idea to the international magazine with a new audience in mind. It encompasses book publishers who are experimenting with on-line versions of popular titles, authors who are renewing older books by making them available in revised hypertextual formatting, and newsletter editors who are either offering their work for free or making it available at nominal charge. And we can't forget the lively effort to promote classic works of literature and history that continues through Project Gutenberg, The Online Book Initiative, and several other venues. University libraries have also begun to play a role in converting existing manuscript collections into provocative Web sites.

The On-Line Print Magazine

Any editor of an existing publication moving into cyberspace has to confront the question of how best to adapt the print publication to the medium. Consider *TV Guide*, the national weekly that compiles television schedules and offers articles on the entertainment industry. *TV Guide*'s Web site (http://www.

iguide.com/tv/index.sml) offers content drawn from the print edition; click on the story and go. But it also diverges from print by providing a searchable database of weekly programming. You can see its home page in Figure 10.1.

Content here is significantly enhanced by cyberspace tools. Thus a column on science fiction programs and gossip about the stars therein is enhanced with links to a bulletin board on which fans can discuss the shows; the various categories of *TV Guide* content all offer such user communities. Even the seemingly narrow science fiction area offers forums on *Star Trek, The X-Files,* and a larger Sci-Fi/Fantasy newsgroup. In the print version, the sense of com-

Figure 10.1 The *TV Guide* Web site adapts print feature stories to cyberspace, with columns and television listings.

munity can be fostered by letters to the editor only, a relatively distant way of communicating with other TV zealots. In this medium, communication becomes interactive.

And there's more. News and feature stories are also enhanced with a movie database that lets you run searches through over 30,000 movie reviews, with cast and credit information as well as filmographies on half a million people connected with the industry. In Figure 10.2, you can see the results of my search for the movie *Unknown World,* an odd 1951 tale about a team of scientists that drills its way deep into the Earth's crust in search of a refuge from atomic war.

Figure 10.2 The *TV Guide* on-line database offers interactive searches and ratings on thousands of movies.

The television listings are likewise searchable. This is a powerful feature; how often have you been stymied by a schedule change or simple forgetfulness, finding yourself unable to track down a favorite show? The search engine here will quickly find it for you; it allows you to search not only by title but by type of listing. You can, for example, search for all science and nature shows during a particular week, narrowing your search with the addition of descriptive copy or other keywords.

The point made by the on-line *TV Guide* is that to be successful, a print publication has to take advantage of the digital, hyperlinked format. As many an editor has discovered to his or her discomfort, simply putting content on-screen will not in itself draw readers. A computer screen is not an optimum place to read long stretches of content, and most magazines are offering articles and columns that require the reader's attention to text. What the Web compels publishers to do is to leverage their computer connection by linking to databases, chat sessions, bulletin boards, and related sites. The best Web publications are those that bring significant interactivity to a previously static publication.

Figure 10.3 shows the home page for *Science* magazine at a site called Science Online. This weekly publication is a respected venue for scientific research in many disciplines. At the site, I am given the capability of reading the articles in the current as well as past issues of the magazine; I can choose to see them either in full-text or abstract form. Thus I find articles on subjects like carbon in space, the effect of the Internet on scientific research, the solar wind and its perceived causes in displacing dust around the planet Jupiter, and the enigmatic discovery of ice on the moon.

Would I read an entire issue of *Science* by clicking to call up the full-text of such articles on-screen? Assuredly not; in any case, *Science* is not a cover-to-cover reading experience, but a journal designed to be browsed in search of specific information. What value, then, does the on-line version have that the printed version does not? One answer is that it can provide hypertextual linkages not found in print. In Figure 10.4, for example, you can see the article on the aforementioned moon ice.

Notice the footnotes, each of them set up as a hyperlink. With such links, I can quickly check references and move back and forth in the article, without the usual displacement caused by checking notes at the bottom of pages or the end of an article.

And there's more. *Science* makes an archive of its past issues available. I can search by author, title, subject, or keywords found in the abstracts of the articles. Thus, if I read about an interesting story in *Science* (as I did yesterday when I learned about ice on the moon), I can quickly go to the site to pull up the article; and if I need to refer to that article three months from now, I can search for it with a few keywords like *moon* and *ice*. Obviously, such capabilities go beyond what is available even in a good research library; they extend the definition of the print magazine and provide powerful research tools for the computer literate.

And how about *The Wine Spectator?* For years, I've been using it as a resource for news from the world's vineyards. Its articles track the industry

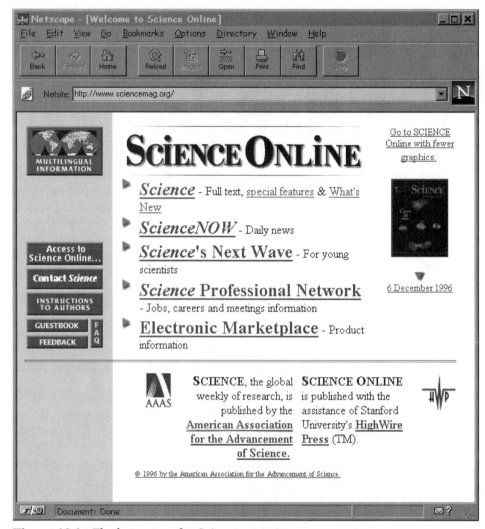

Figure 10.3   The home page for *Science* magazine.

globally, and its reviews offer expert analysis of retail offerings. Its on-line site (http://winespectator.com/) is a successful venture into the digital arena, one that includes forums for the discussion of various wines, along with a search-able database of the magazine's wine reviews, complete with wine ratings, descriptions, score, price, and other information.

Tip: Almost any magazine that's serious about expanding its readership is at least examining the possibilities in cyberspace, although as mentioned, some do a significantly better job than others. To browse through the universe of available titles, your

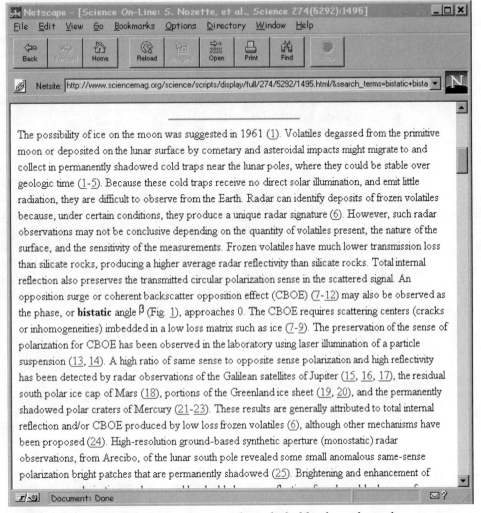

Figure 10.4 A printed article cannot use hyperlinks like those shown here to connect article text with footnotes.

best bet is to use a search directory. A search engine lacks the topic layout that a directory provides, and thus will take longer to provide your results unless you have a specific magazine in mind. Try the Yahoo! directory (http://www.yahoo.com/) for a nicely arranged overview of magazines of all kinds.

The significance of on-line publishing has yet to be determined, for we're still awaiting an answer to the crucial question: Does an on-line edition add to or diminish the print publication's readership? If the former, it's because people can use additional tools like search fields and archives to get more out of the publication. If the latter, it's because people opt to save subscription money knowing they can find the same content on-line. A key factor driving on-line publications will inevitably be the subscription model itself. A subscription is fixed; you pay a set amount for a certain number of months of service, whereas on-line, many publications are available on an as-needed basis; numerous magazines make their content available without charge. That happy state of affairs can't last long, but small user fees may support such sites while still maintaining a healthy base of readers.

If magazines can surmount subscriptions by the month or year and move to a microtransaction model, then readers will be able to log on to whatever journal suits their fancy, download stories at nominal cost, and avoid being locked into lengthy subscription services they don't need. Ultimately, this could benefit magazines by providing a class of reader they currently lack—researchers and browsers who find mentions of their articles in Web search engines and are curious. Some of these readers will doubtless take out a subscription after experiencing the magazine's content on-line, while others will stay long enough only to do their research; but in either case, the magazine can benefit if we can work out a stable way to provide payment for its content.

Here are some magazines that have made a successful transition to print. Your own Web travels will quickly reveal others.

BYTE (http://www.byte.com/): One of America's premier computer magazines, with in-depth and highly technical coverage of industry breakthroughs.

Discover (http://www.enews.com:80/magazines/discover/): The journal of popular science site.

The Economist (http://www.economist.com/): Some people, including myself, think that *The Economist* is the best journal of news and financial information there is.

The Electronic Newsstand (http://www.enews.com/magazines/tnr/): Links to thousands of on-line journals with helpful breakouts by category.

Fortune (http://www.pathfinder.com/): Tips from the rarefied world of the wealthy, with plenty of sound investment advice.

Money Magazine (http://www.pathfinder.com/): Stock market techniques and general financial information for the individual and small business owner.

The New Republic (http://www.enews.com/magazines/tnr/): The journal of moderate to left political opinion, with lively reviews and features.

Outside Online (http://web2.starwave.com/): News and equipment reviews for the outdoor-minded.

Popular Mechanics (http://popularmechanics.com/): Excellent take on moving this well-established magazine into cyberspace, but you'll need a fast connection.

Time Magazine (http://www.pathfinder.com/): An early entry into the field, and still one of the best.

Independent On-Line Magazines

Of course, one of the beauties of cyberspace is that you don't have to be working with a print counterpart to publish your ideas. Consider *The Transom*, a magazine that appears only in cyberspace and takes advantage of its Web format to offer frequent updates. A recent issue included stories on *The X-Files*, pop culture trends including movie reviews, and hip commentary with a youthful slant on cyberculture. Or how about *FEED*, which describes itself as "a leading journal of thought and opinion on the Web." Having recently signed an agreement with The New York Times Electronic Media Company, this on-line journal intends to continue creating its own innovative content while providing interactive services for *The New York Times*. Hyperlinks off the paper's Web site can point, for example, to discussion areas, as was done recently with a special issue of *The New York Times Magazine* and an article on heroine worship and its cultural roots.

What's available on *FEED?* Anything from discussions on Web site design to drug policy in America and commentaries on politics and the media. *FEED* specializes in electronic roundtables, which are discussions from experts about controversial topics. Subscriptions are free. You can see the *FEED* home page in Figure 10.5.

Interestingly, *FEED* is a customizable magazine. When you subscribe to it on-line (http://www.feedmag.com/), you choose from a set of topics and can be notified by the magazine's editors when an article appears that suits your profile. Topics cover everything from Annals of Academia, Notes from Abroad, Pop Frontier to Technopolitics and Weird Science.

The new term for the exclusively on-line magazine is *Webzine*. A good Webzine will update its site on a regular basis, and will often use interactive multimedia tools as a key part of its publishing enterprise. Many are excessively personal, often designed around pet peeves and oddball hobbies, but the best of these magazines look at larger issues of politics, culture, and the future of cyberspace. Some of them weigh in with powerful financial backing. *Slate*, for example, offers political commentator Michael Kinsley the chance to tap the Microsoft money coffers while presenting debates on issues of the day. You can see the home page for *Slate* (http://www.slate.com/) in Figure 10.6.

Another magazine with money and imagination is HotWired (http://www.hotwired.com/) a regular review of culture, politics, Web personalities, and reviews of popular media. As is customary with Webzines, the tone is bright, often pointedly irreverent, and sometimes naive.

Tip: Most Webzines come free of charge, raising the question of how they intend to support their original content. Writers and artists both like to get paid; Webmasters are even more demanding. Advertising is one way to pay the bills, but subscriptions can't be far behind. *Slate*, for example, now comes via subscription, while *Playboy*, which faces huge demands on its server, has moved to the same model. There will always be a place for the individually produced, published-on-a-shoestring Web journal, but the major players are quickly replicating in the on-line world the same

Figure 10.5 The home page of *FEED*, a Web-based journal of commentary and opinion with customizable features.

kind of publishing battles they've fought on the newsstand. We can only hope that a stable base of subscribers continues to raise the level of quality.

And don't forget that the Web is only one venue on the Internet for original content. Shown in Figure 10.7, for example, is *Seidman's Online Insider,* a regular publication that covers events on the Net. Author and editor Robert Seidman is interested in covering events surrounding the big consumer ser-

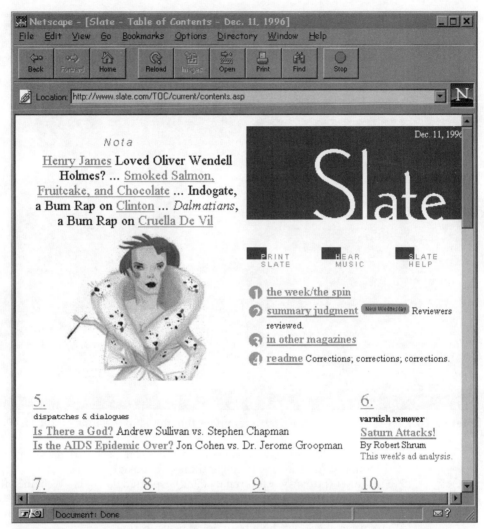

Figure 10.6 *Slate*, a magazine that appears only on-line, is an example of how major corporations are exploring publishing in cyberspace.

vices—America Online, CompuServe, and Prodigy. He also analyzes Web developments such as the browser wars between Netscape and Microsoft and events that have an impact on how people access cyberspace. You can reach Seidman at listserv@peach.ease.lsoft.com, where he maintains the magazine in the form of a mailing list. Subscribe by sending the message **subscribe online-l** *your name.*

On-line magazines provide you with an opportunity to take the editor's chair, but you should examine current offerings carefully to see what's being done. Here are some journals that may intrigue you:

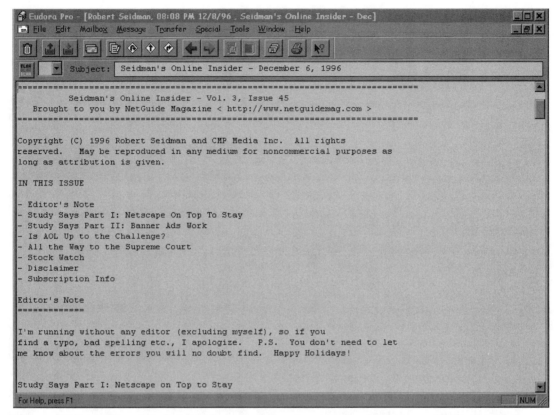

Figure 10.7 *Seidman's Online Insider,* a reminder that not all publishing on the Net is Web-based.

Addicted to Noise (www.addict.com/ATN/): Cyberspace with a modern music emphasis (at least my teenager thinks it's music).

FutureNet (http://www.futurenet.co.uk/): Updated daily, this Webzine offers news, computer features, reviews of videogames with a European slant.

The Onion (http://www.theonion.com/): For a liberal dose of on-line humor (be sure to check out the international news section).

Stim (http://www.stim.com/): A wildly interactive journal offering observations on pop culture.

Salon (http://www.salon1999.com/): One of the best of the Webzines, with solid content of the literary kind supported by comics and audio.

Urban Desires (http://www.desires.com/): The urban scene stylishly analyzed, with reviews and occasional fiction.

ZuZu's Petals (http://www.lehigh.net/zuzu/zu-link.htm): Poetry, fiction, commentary, and book reviews.

The Cyberspace Newspaper

Delivering news to your computer is an idea whose time has obviously come, but how, and in what format? Newspaper editors around the world are pondering questions like these as they venture, however uncertainly, into cyber-space. Among the key issues to be resolved for both magazine and newspaper publishers is this: If content appears on-line, does that mean that readers will stop buying the print version? The problem is especially acute for newspaper editors, since they've been facing declining readership for years, assaulted first by television and now by the advent of personalized news delivered to the desktop.

But many papers have clearly opted to join the cyberspace revolution rather than trying to resist it. As with magazines, the job of the newspaper editor is to factor in interactive content to make the site a sound alternative, and a complement, to the print publication. The advent of the search engine—often a WAIS-driven database working behind the scenes at the Web site—can provide this content, as can innovative use of hyperlinks to create user communities or to link to archives. In Figure 10.8, you can see the on-line edition of *The Los Angeles Times*.

The *Times*, for example, offers news from the AP Online service for registered users. Registration is free, although to use the paper's archival capabilities, you will be subject to a fee for each story displayed. Various search options are provided. The *Times* also offers searches of its site (no fee required) and a movie database, as well as a Los Angeles restaurant guide. Using the latter, you can search by cuisine, area, pricing, and other factors.

If the *Times* has found creative ways to present its content on-line, it has sharp competition from papers like *The Financial Times, The Wall Street Journal, The New York Times,* and *The Washington Post,* all of which provide links to current stories and additional content through archives. *The New York Times* offers site searches, while *The Financial Times* offers an archive of news stories for the previous 30 days, along with a battery of stock information for companies worldwide. *The Wall Street Journal*'s Interactive Edition pushes these strides even further. You can see its home page in Figure 10.9.

Among the significant additions to print content made by the *Journal* is the addition of a personalized version of the paper. You can pick and choose from among the various features and home in just those that appeal to you. You can also select stocks that will be updated in a portfolio; news about any of them will then appear on your personal page. Or, as with the other newspapers, you can choose to go into the paper's content from the top, without customizing filters, and simply browse what's available. Figure 10.10 shows a personal page from *The Wall Street Journal*.

My personal journal includes a variety of stocks that I follow on a daily basis. I have also alerted the system to flag certain keywords no matter in what section they appear. Thus the *Journal* will provide me with stories about the transition of power in Hong Kong as well as the fortunes of Internet providers as they attempt to expand bandwidth.

Here are the URLs of some newspapers to watch. They've proven they understand the medium, and will doubtless lead the way as newspapers adapt to the Net.

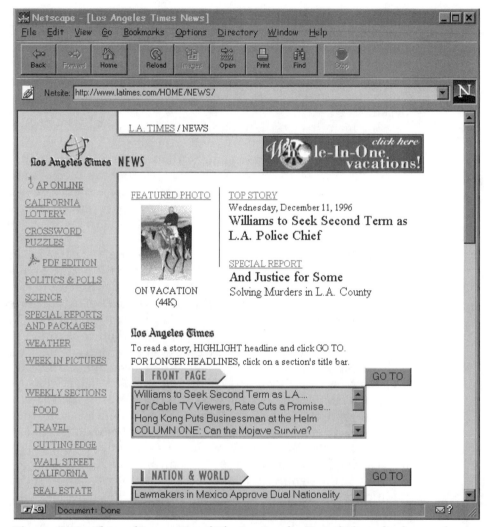

Figure 10.8 The on-line version of *The Los Angeles Times* links to background news such as AP Online, and offers quick links to the major news topics.

The *Albuquerque Journal* (http://www.abqjournal.com/): Excellent take on how to bring a regional newspaper on-line. Numerous interactive features.

The Financial Times (http://www.ft.com/): Europe's best financial newspaper now offers complete coverage of world financial markets on-line, along with updated stock prices and company information.

Jerusalem Post (http://www.jpost.co.il/): Israel's premier newspaper offers an excellent set of features for keeping up with developments in the Middle East, including a useful search engine.

Le Monde (http://www.lemonde.fr/): Current issues and archives of the French newspaper.

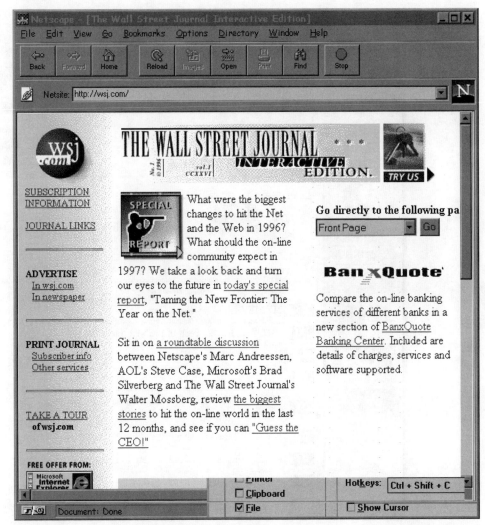

Figure 10.9 *The Wall Street Journal*'s Interactive Edition, one of the most advanced newspaper sites in cyberspace.

The New York Times (http://www.nytimes.com/): Uses a clickable image map to provide access to its major sections; emphasis on Internet news, but you can also get the major stories as well as editorials, letters, and more.

The News & Observer (http://www.nando.net/nt/nao/): One of the best U.S. newspapers for showcasing local news, but offering extensive national and international coverage as well.

San Francisco Chronicle/Examiner (http://www.sfgate.com/): News with a Bay Area slant.

Times of London (http://www.the-times.co.uk/): The world's oldest broadsheet newspaper in an interactive edition that includes the *Sunday Times*.

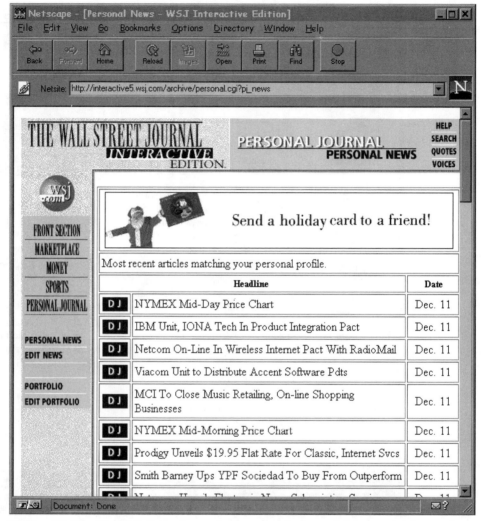

Figure 10.10 *The Wall Street Journal* offers singularly useful customization tools as part of its news presentation.

The Wall Street Journal (http://www.wsj.com/): Subscription-based, and offering a superb range of customizable features.

The Digital Book

If the Internet changes the way we present magazines and newspapers, what do we do with books? The book presents unique problems because of the way we read it. Unlike newspapers, we don't tend to browse a book, skipping huge chunks, focusing tightly on a few paragraphs here and there, and then moving on. Instead, we read in sequence; nobody picks up *Bleak House* or *The Hunt for Red October* without planning to go through it page by page.

But computer screens aren't optimized for this kind of work, and in any case, we've seen that hypertext offers abundant opportunities for linking the various parts of a text to other materials. So the question becomes, what is the best way to present a book, and which books should we present? Numerous on-line collections attest to the fact that books of various kinds are being placed on-line, but their formats differ wildly, and the debate over their proper form continues to intensify. Meanwhile, we have significant issues of copyright and revenue generation to address. If a publisher digitizes a book on which he or she holds the copyright, does that mean the publisher loses money? Or have we simply expanded the potential audience for the book?

A huge amount of material is already on-line, and it's not by chance that most of it is material on which no copyright restrictions apply or are being enforced. Consider a work by James J. O'Donnell, a classics professor at the University of Pennsylvania. In 1979, O'Donnell published a book about Cassiodorus, a remarkable figure in the days following the fall of the Roman Empire whose efforts were instrumental in preserving manuscripts and building libraries. As the copyright holder, O'Donnell has made the decision to place the entire book on-line for the benefit of the scholarly community. You can see a screen from Chapter 2 of this book in Figure 10.11.

Study this figure and you may notice that hypertext does appear here, in the form of a footnote about halfway down the page. Click on this hyperlink and you move immediately to the note. Other than that, however, the information is purely textual, a reproduction of this very useful volume that can be accessed by anyone with an Internet account. If you have a classical bent, the URL is http://ccat.sas.upenn.edu/jod/texts/cassbook/toc.html.

Books that aren't currently in print are obvious candidates for this kind of treatment, and it's possible to locate examples all over the Internet. Eric Drexler, for example, wrote a remarkable study of nanotechnology—engineering at atomic levels—in 1986. The book, called *Engines of Creation,* has now been placed on-line at http://www.asiapac.com/EnginesOfCreation/, and you can see a page from it in Figure 10.12.

Note here that we've moved beyond the standard footnote; the hyperlinks are more conceptual, and serve to point to background fillers that explain key points Drexler is making. In fact, footnotes here are stuffed with hypertext, often to the works referred to in the note. Thus you could check a comment by Drexler that referred to an article called "Biological Frontiers" in *Science* magazine and then click on the footnote itself to jump to the original note.

Or consider what's going on at Open Book Systems (http://www.obs-us.com/obs/english/top.htm). At this site, Laura Fillmore works with content of all kinds, convinced that books in the on-line environment should be surrounded by discussion groups, commentaries, links to related sites, and all the panoply of digital multimedia. A book in this sense, no matter its provenance, is a living thing; it grows over time as more and more people connect to it.

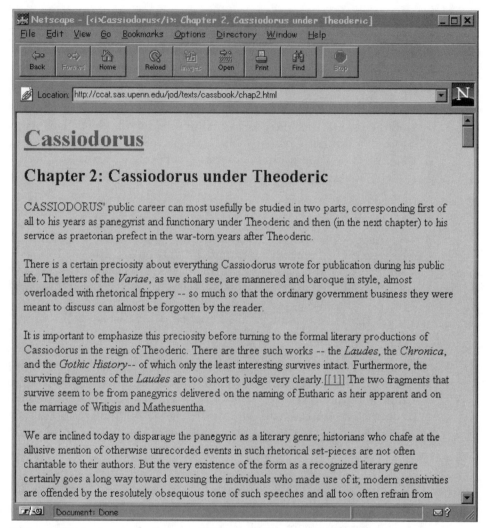

Figure 10.11   A page from James O'Donnell's book on Cassiodorus.

Ultimately, the book site becomes a constellation of connected information with significantly enhanced value over the printed volume. Few on-line books are like this yet; we're still learning as we go, and publishers are pondering the economics of such extensions to their print content.

But Open Book Systems (OBS) continues to publish actively. In Figure 10.13, you can see one OBS project, a book by Gregory Rawlins called *Moths to the Flame*. The text is eye-catching; as you can see, it's surrounded by a visual field that makes it attractive, and includes a table of contents with built-in search engine. The current chapter is broken down into its constituent parts in the contents table, with a marker to show just where you are in the text. By

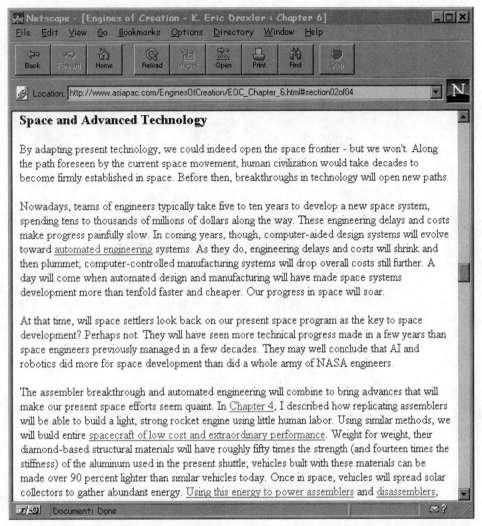

Figure 10.12 Drexler's *Engines of Creation,* in a new hypertext version created by Russell Whittaker with Drexler's permission.

clicking on the Search button, I can race through the index of Rawlins' book to locate specific information. Or I can page sequentially through it by following the links that appear at the end of each section.

Rawlins' book is current, a publication of MIT Press. But what of older titles? The beauty of the classic works of literature, history, and philosophy is that copyright is no longer an issue. Thus we can generate a wonderful site like the Shakespeare archive shown in Figure 10.14. The site, http://the-tech.mit.edu/Shakespeare/, contains the full text of all the plays and sonnets, with a search engine that lets you easily track down a favorite passage, and a

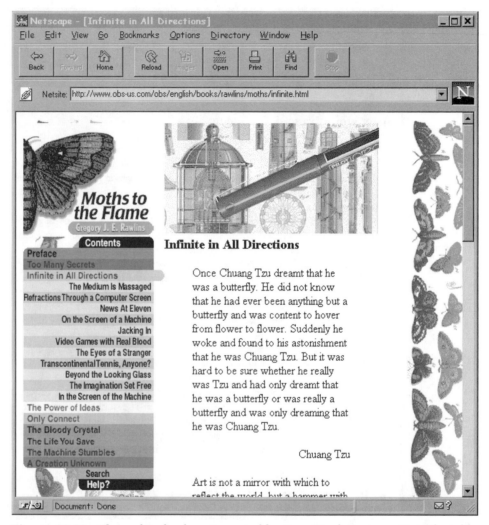

Figure 10.13 The on-line book as presented by Open Book Systems. Note the table of contents on the left side of the screen.

glossary that helps you figure out the occasional obscure term. Similar sites exist for classical authors including Aeschylus, Euripides, and Aristophanes, while those with a more modern taste can read on-line versions of everything from George Bernard Shaw to Samuel Beckett.

Among the names most closely connected with putting books on-line is that of Michael Hart, whose Project Gutenberg is a volunteer effort to digitize as many works of literature as possible and make them available over the Internet. The project began in 1971 with a typed-in version of the Declaration of Independence, and today includes hundreds of books of all descriptions.

Figure 10.14   The Shakespeare archive at MIT, a repository of the Bard's works with powerful search features.

You can check the Project Gutenberg home page at http://www.promo.net/pg/. Here, too, you'll find the archives, housing works ranging from Saint Augustine's *De Dialecta* to Hawthorne's *The Scarlet Letter*, and selected works of Edgar Allen Poe; for the truly dedicated on-screen reader, Gibbon's *Decline and Fall of the Roman Empire* has made a recent appearance.

Who will read these books? Michael Hart has labored for years to make the point that plain ASCII text should be the foundation of the on-line library. Formats like HTML and other markup languages add capabilities that many can benefit from, but it's also true that changing standards and equipment requirements limit their users to a subset of the total audience. Thus the attempt is to produce an ASCII version of the text before any other; this can later be enhanced in any format that may prove useful, while preserving the original text in as close to universal a form as computing technology seems to allow.

By following this approach, Hart ensures that readership for any of these titles can include those with the latest Pentium processor and 17-inch screens as well as people running a now antique 8088 computer with a single floppy disk drive. Storage costs have dropped so significantly over the past 10 years that the ability to put a book on a disk makes these works accessible to people who might otherwise not be able to afford them. Couple the on-line book with the kind of search engine found in any browser or word processor and you can see that Hart is also creating a library that can be used for research.

But wait: Aren't these titles available anyway through any of the hundreds of libraries now connected to the Internet? Absolutely not. If you start examining libraries around the globe, you'll find that in almost every case, what is available on-line is the library's catalog and nothing else. You may be able to locate the title of Hardy's *Return of the Native* in a library, but you won't be able to read a word of it without resorting to an electronic library project like Project Gutenberg. That's why Hart's work in putting older works onto the network is so critical. In our rush to modernize and hypertextualize our information, we run the risk of overlooking those parts of our culture that have yet to make the transition into the new environment.

It's the irony of on-line publishing that with all its obvious benefits, the great bulk of the world's literature remains in paper form, often disintegrating as the various acids eat through ever more brittle pages. In whatever form we choose to take the on-line book, its future as a way of preserving and studying knowledge seems assured. In the next chapter, I'll discuss an economic model that may convince publishers that even current books bearing copyright and being sold in the bookstores can benefit from being placed on-line. For now, here are some other collections of on-line literature that may interest you:

ALEX: A Catalog of Electronic Texts on the Internet (http://www.lib.ncsu.edu/staff/morgan/alex/alex-index.html): A database of over 2,000 electronic titles.

Electronic Text Center (http://www.lib.virginia.edu/etext/ETC.html): An on-line archive from the University of Virginia.

The Electronic Wiretap (gopher://wiretap.spies.com/11/Books/): Books arranged alphabetically on a Gopher server.

Labyrinth Library (http://www.georgetown.edu/labyrinth/library/me/me.html): Books and treatises in Middle English.

Online Book Initiative (gopher://ftp.std.com/11/obi/book): Diverse collection of classic works mixed with modern titles.

Project Libellus (http://osman.classics.washington.edu/libellus/libellus.html): Greek and Latin texts.

The Personal Web Page

Individuals as well as companies can be publishers. In fact, some of the more interesting material on the Web today is being posted by people who are collecting archives of their own writings, or producing new essays, reviews, and reflections. The dramatic reduction in the cost of publishing that technology has produced means that you and I can stake out a claim in cyberspace for only a moderate cost. I'll explore how to establish that claim—and where to file it—in a moment. But first, let's look at how some innovative authors are turning the cyberworld to their advantage.

One such writer is David Bennahum, whose home page can be found at http://www.reach.com/matrix/welcome.html. Like all good page designers, Bennahum is careful to provide solid attribution for what he does. Thus a link on the bottom of his home page goes directly to a backgrounder on the man and his work. Bennahum is, we learn here, a graduate of Harvard with a degree in history and literature who now makes his living as a New York-based writer. His work has appeared in *The New York Times*, *Harper's Bazaar*, *New York*, *The Economist*, and *Wired*, among others. He is also a consultant to numerous companies in the uses of the new media and the expansion of telecommunications. And he uses the personal information link on his home page to explain why he does what he does:

> Why did I create this Web site? Its central mission is to pursue a theme I'm passionate about—exploring how technology and social change fuel each other. Why do the tools we create get put to certain uses and not another? Why is it that momentous change is often brought on by a series of accidents, usually inventions which were never intended to have the impact that they had? The Web is one such example. What better medium then to explore these issues? I also want to test this theory that on the Net the writer becomes publisher and distributor all in one—and that somehow it can work out. I want to believe it can work: that I can provide quality information which is accentuated and enhanced by appearing in this medium. I also respond well to the quick turnaround of this medium, and the feedback which develops with readers. That's also why I enjoy writing for magazines and newspapers. I have no idea how this site is going to turn out, or what it might lead to. That's the best part about it.

The writer as publisher and distributor all in one—this is precisely what the Web offers to anyone with an idea to convey. And Bennahum does indeed have ideas. Another link off his home page leads to an archive of articles he has written, in full-text form with clickable hyperlinks. You can see this archival page in Figure 10.15.

Bennahum is also an active interviewer; his forum is a biweekly journal sent in mailing list form to subscribers. The journal is called *MEME*, the word for a contagious idea that spreads like a virus and is passed from mind to mind. Examples of memes include melodies, icons, and phrases. Within the pages of *MEME*, Bennahum speculates on where technology is leading us and

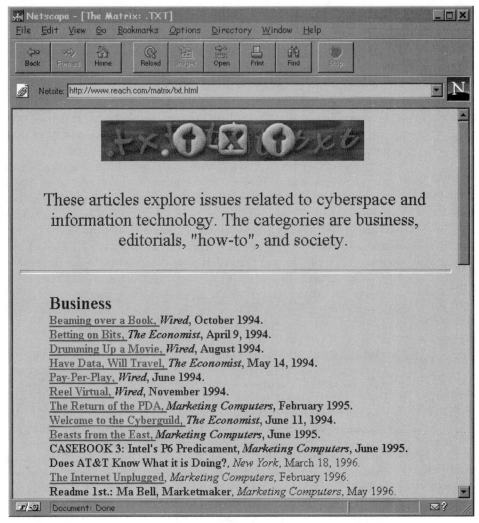

Figure 10.15   David Bennahum's archive of articles about technology and society.

conducts interviews with leading figures in cyberspace. These interviews are then archived with the complete run of *MEME* issues on Bennahum's site. You can see one such interview, with VRML inventor Mark Pesce, in Figure 10.16.

Other interviews, with the likes of MIT Media Lab director Nicholas Negroponte and former Secretary of Labor Robert Reich, can be read on-line, while Bennahum encourages comments about *MEME* and his other work through a hyperlinked e-mail address.

How difficult would it be to set up such a site? In terms of the technical aspects of Web page development, not difficult at all. The challenge—and this has always been the challenge of the Internet—is to generate worthwhile con-

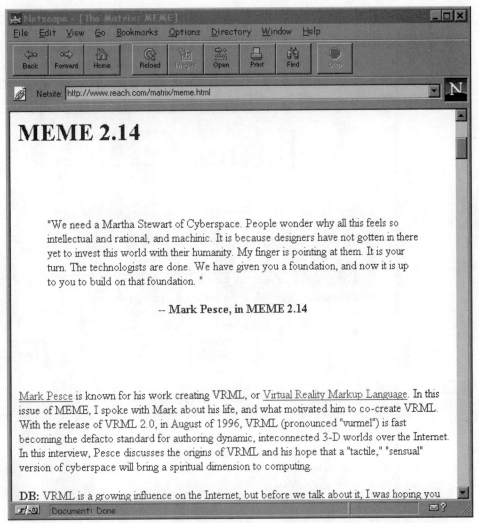

Figure 10.16 An interview with Mark Pesce in *MEME*. Personal publishing brings high-quality content like this to light. The trick is knowing where to look for it.

tent. And if you start looking around at what some of the Net publishers are doing to propagate their works, you'll see that a surprising amount of high-quality information is available, even if it can be difficult to find. In Figure 10.17, for example, you can see the Web site of James Gleick.

You'll notice immediately that a personal Web site can become a vehicle for whatever ends you seek. Gleick, the highly regarded author of *Chaos: Making a New Science* (Viking Penguin, 1987) and *Genius: The Life and Science of Richard Feynman* (Pantheon, 1992), can tell you about his new book, and even solicit comments that might prove useful in it, by posting his e-mail address

Figure 10.17   James Gleick's Web site, with archives of his writing.

prominently on this page. He also includes links to some of the provocative articles he has written for *The New York Times Magazine*. If you're like me, you don't have time to track down everything a favorite author writes in such venues, but if you know that the author has a Web site, then you can keep up by checking the site on a regular basis for new material. Thus I can read Gleick's thoughts on Microsoft as monopolist, America Online's fortunes, the coming problem with computer dates in the year 2000, the end of cash, and bugs in major software programs.

George Gilder is accessible in much the same way. His Web site (http://www.discovery.org/ggindex.html) promotes his technology report through a toll-free number and e-mail address, and includes interviews and articles he has written for *Forbes ASAP, The Wall Street Journal,* and other venues. But here, the publication comes secondhand. The Gilder site is maintained by the Discovery Institute for Public Policy, established in 1990 to promote free markets, voluntarism, and the use of technology to improve society. You can see the Gilder site in Figure 10.18.

Whether you're promoting your own work or trying to advance the ideas of others, the Web is a superb publishing vehicle. Speaking as one who has clipped all of Gilder's 'telecosm' articles out of the various issues of *Forbes*

Figure 10.18 George Gilder's articles about the impact of digital communications are gathered at the Discovery Institute site.

ASAP over the years, I value the ability to call any of these up on-screen from this archival site. Many people have content they'd like to publish, from catalogs of their favorite stamps to essays about their latest trip to France, not to mention small business uses such as publishing a brochure for a product or a list of new offerings. We turn now to the question of how you can create pages and post them on-line.

Creating Web Pages

Web publishing is a multistep process that begins with the creation of your pages. This involves planning, usually aided by a diagram or flowchart of the site in question. If you do the necessary work now, you won't find yourself in the awkward position of having to go back through your pages, revising URLs when a better plan suggests itself. Take the time to think through your project. Your diagram doesn't have to be detailed, either. A large block to indicate the home page, with branching blocks to indicate the major content groupings will suffice. Be thinking, too, of the kinds of content you'd like to link to: Are there images you plan to insert, and if so, into which page? Mastering such questions may involve going onto the Web to look at sites you admire. See how the developers there did the work.

When you're ready to make pages, you have to work with HTML itself, or with an HTML editor. Manipulating HTML isn't as difficult as it sounds. The Hypertext Markup Language is created in straight ASCII text, a job that can be managed in any text editor, as I learned by creating my first home pages in Windows Notepad. True, there are numerous codes you have to understand and place properly, but the major ones, such as location of headers, their font and point size, and the images they surround, are relatively easily mastered. Plus, the Web is littered with sites that specialize in teaching you how to program in HTML, so learning the rudiments can be done with nothing more than your existing Web connection. Those who want to dig deeper will profit from books like Ian Graham's *The HTML Sourcebook* (John Wiley & Sons, Inc., 2nd ed., 1996).

Figure 10.19 shows an example of HTML coding at work. As you can see, HTML may look like a programming language, but it is just a textual document that includes specific tags that tell the browser what to do with the information specified. You can learn a great deal about how HTML works by coding it line by line in a text editor.

But it's only fair to add that HTML is not as easy to code as it used to be, because the language has undergone considerable evolution, with strings of difficult additions brought about by the continual evolution of standards. Today's Web page may feature any variety of video, sound, background features, image maps, and other applications. Whereas the earliest version of HTML, in use since 1990, dealt primarily with issues surrounding character formatting, headings, lists, image placement, and the creation of hyperlinks, today's version 2.0 adds commands for interactive features like forms and menus. Version 3.0

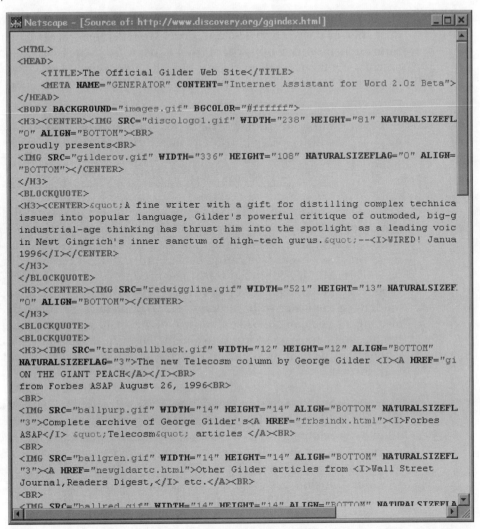

```
Netscape - [Source of: http://www.discovery.org/ggindex.html]

<HTML>
<HEAD>
    <TITLE>The Official Gilder Web Site</TITLE>
    <META NAME="GENERATOR" CONTENT="Internet Assistant for Word 2.0z Beta">
</HEAD>
<BODY BACKGROUND="images.gif" BGCOLOR="#ffffff">
<H3><CENTER><IMG SRC="discologo1.gif" WIDTH="238" HEIGHT="81" NATURALSIZEFL
"0" ALIGN="BOTTOM"><BR>
proudly presents<BR>
<IMG SRC="gilderow.gif" WIDTH="336" HEIGHT="108" NATURALSIZEFLAG="0" ALIGN=
"BOTTOM"></CENTER>
</H3>
<BLOCKQUOTE>
<H3><CENTER>&quot;A fine writer with a gift for distilling complex technica
issues into popular language, Gilder's powerful critique of outmoded, big-g
industrial-age thinking has thrust him into the spotlight as a leading voic
in Newt Gingrich's inner sanctum of high-tech gurus.&quot;--<I>WIRED! Janua
1996</I></CENTER>
</H3>
</BLOCKQUOTE>
<H3><CENTER><IMG SRC="redwiggline.gif" WIDTH="521" HEIGHT="13" NATURALSIZEF
"0" ALIGN="BOTTOM"></CENTER>
</H3>
<BLOCKQUOTE>
<BLOCKQUOTE>
<H3><IMG SRC="transballblack.gif" WIDTH="12" HEIGHT="12" ALIGN="BOTTOM"
NATURALSIZEFLAG="3">The new Telecosm column by George Gilder <I><A HREF="gi
ON THE GIANT PEACH</A></I><BR>
from Forbes ASAP August 26, 1996<BR>
<BR>
<IMG SRC="ballpurp.gif" WIDTH="14" HEIGHT="14" ALIGN="BOTTOM" NATURALSIZEFL
"3">Complete archive of George Gilder's<A HREF="frbsindx.html"><I>Forbes
ASAP</I> &quot;Telecosm&quot; articles </A><BR>
<BR>
<IMG SRC="ballgren.gif" WIDTH="14" HEIGHT="14" ALIGN="BOTTOM" NATURALSIZEFL
"3"><A HREF="newgldartc.html">Other Gilder articles from <I>Wall Street
Journal,Readers Digest,</I> etc.</A><BR>
<BR>
<IMG SRC="ballred.gif" WIDTH="14" HEIGHT="14" ALIGN="BOTTOM" NATURALSIZEFLA
```

Figure 10.19 HTML coding is nothing more than text documents with inserted tags that instruct browsers on how to display the page.

added a raft of new tools, including tables; version 3.2, the current proposed standard, adds Java applets, superscripts and subscripts, text wrapping around images, and more. All of which makes for exciting developments in Web page viewing, but difficult times for you the designer; using advanced features is far more challenging than juxtaposing basic graphics and text.

HTML Editing Tools

To help, you need an HTML editing tool. Here, too, there are options. Most word processors have begun to offer conversion facilities that let you take a standard document and quickly turn it into HTML. Word 7.0 for Windows 95 does this, as do Word Pro 96 and Corel WordPerfect 7.0; we can assume that future generations of our programs, not just word processors but spreadsheets and other content creation engines as well, will provide HTML capabilities. We can expect Internet links inside all major applications before long.

 Tip: To check whether your word processor has been augmented with HTML publishing capabilities, pull down its File menu and select Save As. If HTML is listed as one of the document types there, your software is Web-enabled.

Anyone serious about HTML, however, will want to use a full-fledged publishing program, one that supports advanced features and includes tools that simplify the posting of your pages. And while the earlier versions of many of these programs were frustrating because they didn't keep up with the frantic pace of HTML development, most new products do provide both HTML versions 2.0 and 3.0 tags. That gives you access to cutting-edge techniques without having to master truly complex HTML procedures. Using a dedicated tool also means you can choose pull-down menus instead of requiring painstaking typing. Some tools go so far as to shield you from the actual HTML code altogether; you work only with the external interface. Others provide access to both formats.

Look through any computer magazine today and you'll see that these tools comprise one of the hottest categories in the software business. Microsoft has waded in with a powerful product called FrontPage that simplifies page creation by providing a WYSIWYG ("what you see is what you get") editing environment; the product includes a personal Web server that makes it easy to check out your site on the local level and to upload it when ready. SoftQuad's HoTMetaL includes a graphical editor and support for the latest HTML 3.2 standards. WebEdit Professional Edition includes Java and ActiveX support and is optimized for those who want to work directly with HTML coding. Macromedia's Backstage Designer Plus includes Shockwave multimedia applications and Java support, plus tools for remote site management. Sausage Software (no kidding!) produces HotDog Professional, one of the best of all Web page editors, and it's shareware.

The list could be extended considerably. How do you make the best choice? The answer is to read reviews and consider the nature of the tool. Some HTML editors hide all coding from you so that you never need to see HTML itself; Microsoft FrontPage is the most prominent example. Other editors are designed for professionals; they give you sophisticated utilities and assume you'll want to work with coded HTML on your screen. Programs like Claris Home Page give you the option of going back and forth between the two formats, previewing your work in the browser. Netscape's own Navigator Gold offers close ties to the browser. Almost all these programs are now stand-alone tools; the days of add-ons, most frequently to word processors, seem to be numbered (although as integral parts of word processors, HTML editing options will definitely survive, just as most word processors have incorporated desktop publishing features).

Using Claris Home Page to Publish on the Web

The choice of tools is a complicated one, as much determined by your own eccentricities as by the power of the individual programs. The category is still so new that significant changes can be expected with new versions of each. I will use Claris Home Page to demonstrate basic composition issues because the program offers most everything the novice might expect. You work within a graphical interface that always keeps in front of you what you will see on the screen; HTML coding is kept in the background, but it's directly editable if you choose to go to that level. Table and frame editors allow for sophisticated effects, and updating can be quickly effected throughout a set of documents. Moreover, the program offers a set of useful images and libraries of frequently used text and code.

Tip: When it comes to images, the Web is alive with choices. Numerous sites provide free graphics in the GIF and JPEG formats most common on the Web. Check any of the following:

Barry's Clip Art (http://www.barrysclipart.com/)
Clip Art Center (http://www.geocities.com/SoHo/4112/)
Clip Art Universe (http://www.nzwwa.com/mirror/clipart/)
Clipart.com (http://www.clipart.com/)

You can see the Claris Home Page main screen in Figure 10.20. Notice the familiar icon-based toolbar across the top of the screen, and the pull-down menus above it. We're in an environment that reminds us of a typical word processor, save that the tools here have been adjusted to meet the demands of HTML. In the figure, I have called up a text that I'd like to put in HTML format. It's a simple piece, based on a column I write every week for a local newspaper. To call it up, I simply opened it as I would a word processor document, pulling down the File menu to do so, although first I made sure the document was saved in text format; otherwise, I would have to deal with the format codes inserted by my word processor, and those aren't the ones I want to work with on the World Wide Web.

Why might I want to put a newspaper column of mine onto the Web? For one thing, as a freelance writer, I can always use the promotion; people looking through search engines may run across some of my material and recommend it to others. For another, I'm a great believer in creating archives. What I have on my hard disks, spread over about five different computers, is 12 years' worth of computer writing. Putting this material on-line makes it acces-

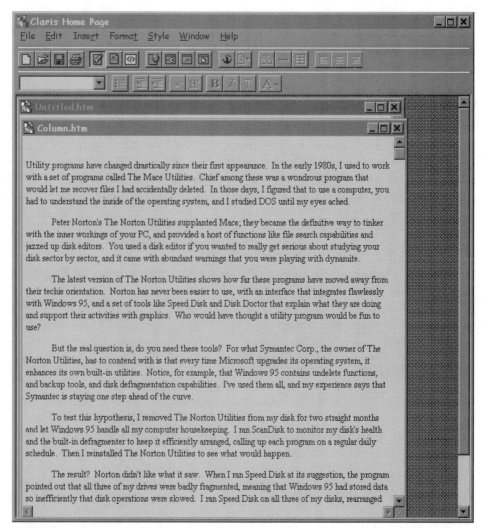

Figure 10.20   The primary screen for Claris Home Page, an HTML editor and Web publishing tool. Here I'm viewing an ASCII document.

sible; leaving it on the hard disk effectively shuts it off from the world. So it would be useful to create a library space where I can, ultimately, store all older columns, reviews, essays, short stories, and whatever materials on which I hold copyright. It would be my small corner of the virtual library, and I can build it with a tool like Home Page.

To do basic Home Page tasks, I need only select a part of the text by dragging my mouse across it while holding down the left mouse button. I can then apply formatting or style features by choosing the appropriate menu and clicking on a feature. My options are numerous. I can choose between six levels of headings, adjusting the size of the text. I can show the newly created header as plain text, or in bold, or in italics. I can underline it and adjust its color. I can manipulate its alignment or indentation.

It's important to realize what a difference this is from the previous way of inserting HTML codes by hand. In each case, HTML insisted that you insert a specific tag. Thus to experiment with a header, I would have to use a tag like this one:

```
<H2>Utility Program Update</H2>
```

Here, I've set up the statement as a level 2 header. You can see that it's preceded by the <H2> tag, but it must be concluded with a slash; thus </H2>. Needless to say, a mistake in the coding would cause the effect to fail. With the Home Page editor, I can create the effect by choosing an item from the pull-down menu. More significantly, I can highlight the item, change its header statement, and experiment with different header sizes all within seconds. Thus my ability to work with the page and to adjust its parameters is significantly heightened; I'm encouraged to keep editing until the effect I want has been achieved. In Figure 10.21, I've given this particular column, about utility programs and The Norton Utilities in particular, a title, and I've set that title up as a level 1 header.

Of course, straight text is a bit formidable on the computer screen. It's one thing when we're reading it in a newspaper, where it can be adjusted in columns, wrapped around photographs, or folded on the page for easy viewing. On a computer screen, text is harder to read than on paper, and can benefit from some graphical boosting. Adding an image to the text is managed by choosing a site for it on the page and clicking on the Insert Image button. I can then choose the image on my hard disk that I want to insert; I then click on it, move it into position, drag it into the proper size, and release the mouse button. In Figure 10.22, you can see an image I have inserted into the page from the library of images included in the Claris package; I could also easily link to any image on my hard disk.

I can also give this page some background color. I can click on the Document Options button and choose Colors and Backgrounds to play with a wide variety of possibilities. When I click on the Preview in Browser item in the File menu, I can see the result of these background changes; I can also view the page in my browser to verify that it's coming along as I want. The main criterion other than aesthetic ones is that the text must remain readable, no matter what background I use.

Has HTML editing the Home Page way saved me time? To answer the question, consider how simple creating this page has been. I spent little time on it; but if I had coded it by hand with HTML, here's what it would look like:

```
</HEAD>
<BODY
background="/E:/Program%20Files/Claris/Clipart/SuprSmpl/wood%26.jpg">
<H1>The Norton Utilities: Vital Diagnostics and Repair</H1>
```

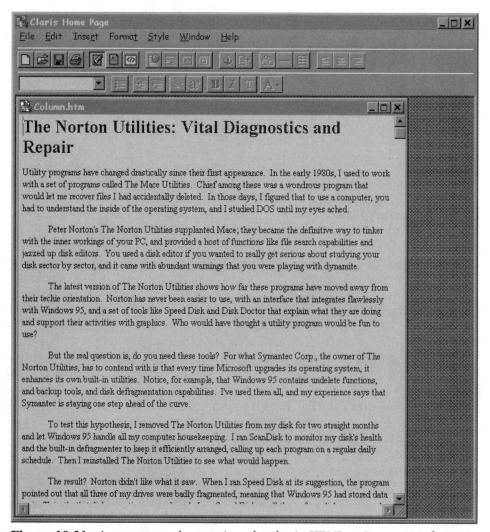

Figure 10.21 A computer column gains a header in HTML as I prepare it for entry onto the Web.

```
<P><IMG SRC="/E:/Program%20Files/Claris/Clipart/CClipart/pencil.gif"
ALT="pencil" WIDTH=67 HEIGHT=69 BORDER=6 ALIGN op></P>
<P>Utility programs have changed drastically since their first appearance.
In the early 1980s, I used to work with a set of
```

And this just represents the header section, the body, and the first two lines of text, completely trivial stuff as far as HTML is concerned; we haven't even considered frames, or tables. As you can see, Home Page, like a good word processor, has helped me manipulate display features without having to understand their complexity.

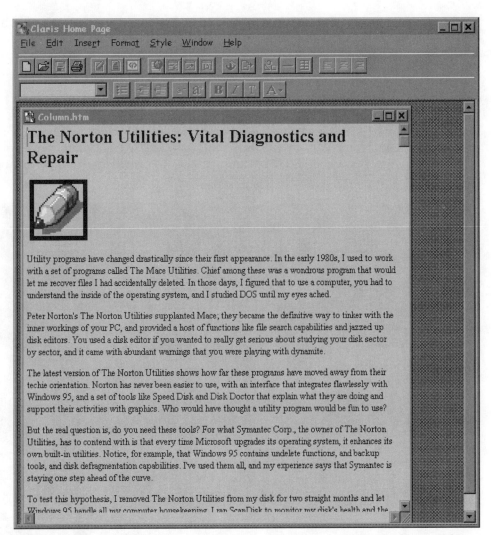

Figure 10.22   A simple image inserted into the text by using the Home Page library of clip art.

Of course, we've only begun to scratch the surface of what an HTML editor can do. I might, for example, want to add hyperlinks to my text. If I have background materials or other columns that supplement the information on this page, or links to external sites that represent companies I mention in the text, I can quickly establish links to them. Home Page's Link Editor lets me select text to use as my hyperlink, and to insert a URL to which that link will point. In Figure 10.23, you can see my text with a series of hyperlinks; in this case, two of these are internal links, meaning they point to files on my own hard disk, rather than to external Web sites. I've also changed the size of the text to make it more readable. Now I can begin thinking about what else I'd like to make available on this and other pages. A good HTML editor offers you a full range of options.

Critical Jobs for the HTML Editor

What I've done so far is to experiment with the most rudimentary features of Claris Home Page to illustrate that a good HTML editor can save you time and effort. But a good HTML editor also has to provide the complete range of Web

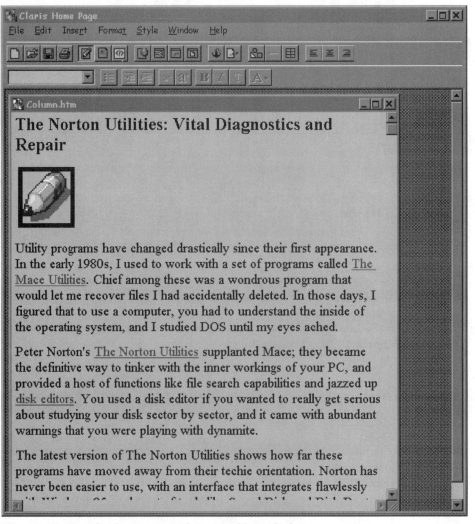

Figure 10.23 The document with inserted hyperlinks.

effects. With any editor, you should be looking at how the software does the following tasks:

Inserting hyperlinks: The key to any hypertext document is its ability to include links to external information, or to other documents on your hard disk. Home Page, for example, allows you to click a button to call up the Link Editor. You then type in the URL of the file you want to access. You can also link to a local file; in either case, the text changes to the familiar blue color that indicates the link.

Inserting anchors: Anchors are internal links that can take you to a specific spot on a page, rather than just calling up the page and positioning you at the top of it. Home Page's Insert Anchor button lets you give the anchor a name and choose its location. The anchor symbol then appears in your document.

Other types of links: Images, too, can be made into hyperlinks; click on them and go to the URL. Image maps are another possibility; they allow different parts of the same image to link to separate destinations. Or you could set up a link to an e-mail address. The latter is a significant link to make; it allows your readers to contact you easily, and thus keep you posted about news that might affect your site. The text of each link as it appears on the screen is easy to edit, and links are as easy to remove as they are to create.

Tables and data entry: Tables can be used for any data that needs to be formatted in rows and columns. An Insert icon handles the job for Home Page; once created, the table can be edited to insert or delete further rows and columns, and can be dragged and clicked to adjust position, height, and width. Images can also appear in tables, as can standard text, which could be used to emphasize particular points or set up as a table of contents. A good editor will use standard drag and drop procedures.

Frames for multiple field viewing: Frames let you divide the basic screen window into different sections, called panes. Browsing through pages on the Web, you'll find that the most obvious use for this technique is to set up a table of contents that can be clicked upon to cause changes in the second frame. A narrow table of contents running down the side of the screen will remain visible, making page navigation easy as you work your way through the site. In Home Page, this is done by creating separate home pages for each pane and then inserting each into the separate panes you've created with the Frame List Editor. You can then adjust the parameters of each pane, creating titles, links, and backgrounds.

Libraries for quick retrieval: Libraries of graphics and photographs are useful places to store those images you'll refer to frequently; text files can also be placed here for later use in other pages. In fact, you can insert anything from pictures to links, tables, buttons, and entire documents into Home Page's libraries; or use the files that come with the program. A good clip art library should include not only images for direct insertion into your pages, but also the supporting graphics like backgrounds, buttons, dividers, and other tools.

Creating forms: Forms allow you to create text areas for data entry, password fields to restrict users of your pages, or effects like radio buttons and checkboxes. A good HTML editor makes these easy to create and provides easy linkages to the CGI scripts that make the underlying forms work. If you're putting a business site on the Web, you may want to include forms for such things as user identification, so you can compile a list of the people who come to your site. For this purpose, however, it makes sense to hire a programmer, unless you're willing to go deep into the complexities of CGI, or, for that matter, other tools like JavaScript or VBScript. Most of today's tools still come up short when it comes to CGI, Java, ActiveX, and VRML techniques for page creation.

Tip: What do you do when you see a great effect on a Web page and want to re-create something like it at your site but don't know how? The answer is to study how the original page designer did the work and then modify his or her ideas in your own site. You can study any page's HTML coding by pulling down the View menu and clicking on Document Source. Consider this a learning experience—you're not out to plagiarize somebody else's work, but to understand what they did so you can re-create it on your pages. The simplicity with which you can study the work of good page designers is a great incentive to improving your own pages.

Inserting Java applets: While Home Page doesn't provide for creation applets in Java and JavaScript, it does make it possible to refer to them in your pages. JavaScript can be inserted in your home page as source code if you click on the Edit HTML Source button and paste the JavaScript data into your page. A click on the Preview in Browser button will then call up the page in Netscape with the Java script available.

HTML Reference Sites

No matter which editor you use, it's always a good idea to learn as much about how HTML itself works. The following are some Web sites that can help you understand its tags and quickly track down the answers to nagging questions.

The ABCs of HTML (http://www.ncsa.uiuc.edu/General/Training/HTMLIntro/Intro.html): A full-featured course that walks you through HTML basics and helps you create a sample document that includes titles, headers, page formatting, character formatting, images, and links to other sites.

HTML Reference Manual (http://www.sandia.gov/sci_compute/html_ref.html): Nicely presented backgrounder with helpful list of HTML elements.

D.J. Quad's Ultimate HTML Site (http://www.quadzilla.com/): Links to HTML tutorials, editors, standards, discussion groups, mailing lists, and publishing tips.

The Global HTML Directory (http://zion.gt.ed.net/html/index.htm): Tutorials, links to resources, useful information about books and journals devoted to HTML.

Introduction to HTML (http://www.cwru.edu/help/introHTML/toc.html): A tutorial to walk you through the basics, followed by an intermediate tutorial and a helpful quiz system.

HTML Quick Reference Guide (http://kuhttp.cc.ukans.edu/lynx_help/HTML_quick.html): The basic HTML tags defined.

Composing Good HTML (http://www.cs.cmu.edu/~tilt/cgh/): Stylistic issues raised by publishing in HTML, along with common mistakes and practices to avoid.

Comprehensive Guide to Publishing on the Web (http://www.webcom.com/html/): Helpfully arranged background information about all kinds of publishing issues and HTML references.

Beginner's Guide to HTML (www.ncsa.uiuc.edu/General/Internet/WWW/HTML-Primer.html): A good place to start, with background information on HTML laid out in plain English.

Tips on Page Design

How to build a home page is a topic that could occupy an entire book; in fact, it has, which is why I steer you to Horton, Taylor, Ignacio, and Hoff's *The Web Page Design Cookbook* (John Wiley & Sons, Inc., 1996), which includes templates for creating Web pages of all descriptions. But let me at least offer you some tips here, because the way a page is laid out will play a pivotal role in its success.

Create an outline before you open your editor: A basic outline of your site, or a flowchart that shows exactly how it will be built, is essential to help you avoid cumbersome rewriting of your links. Figure out what will be the major sections of your site and decide how they should be displayed on the home page. Do this *before* you start working with text so that the overall shape of your site is consistent and easy to navigate.

Think thrice about graphics: Graphics of all kinds, from photographs to logos to animated icons, can provide emphasis and visual depth to a page. But we've all been frustrated by home pages that take too long to load. Graphics files can be large, after all, and placing too many of them on a single page may make your readers impatient while they wait for the download to be completed. No matter how attractive the finished product, a torturous download experience will not win you friends. It's amazing how many Web designers don't seem to have grasped the fact that we don't all use T-3 connections. A good HTML editor can help you with this. Claris Home Page, for example, provides a Document Statistics window that includes minimum download times for the pages you create. Bear in mind that minimum times presuppose ideal network conditions, which are not often encountered in the average day. The Document Statistics window, however, does give you a good idea of what your readers will encounter; use it to eliminate overly ambitious imagery on your pages.

Use accurate and descriptive titles: Today's Web is both publishing archive and catalog. We all use search engines to find our way around. That means your page needs to be designed and labeled so that people can locate it by subject. Choose words your readers will use when conducting keyword searches. Remember that if someone bookmarks your site, its title will appear on that person's bookmark list. Ask yourself how easy it will be to recognize the subject of your page based on the title you've given it, and adjust the title as necessary.

Use META tags: META tags are used by Web search engines to classify your pages, making it easier for other people to find them by subject. They're easy to insert with a good HTML editor. It's always better to make your own call on how your pages are categorized by using META tags than to let someone else's search engine make the decision for you.

Create a site map or table of contents: Your visitors will need to know how to find their way around your site and what's available within it. Make sure you lay out the site's contents either through a table of contents or a site map that shows what's where.

Sprinkle navigation aids throughout your pages: Navigation aids should be sprinkled throughout your pages to help your readers find a way through the site, and the most important of these is a link on each page that takes the reader directly back to your home page.

Avoid mixing fonts and point sizes: Just because you have the ability to vary the display of text doesn't mean it's always a good idea. Ask yourself whether you need to congest your pages with a series of textual changes that do nothing but call attention to themselves. Do you really need italics, bolding, blinking lines, and other visual effects? If they can be spared, leave them out. Their effectiveness at adding emphasis is inversely proportional to how often you use them.

Make sure your text is readable: How many sites have you seen that were rendered unreadable due to the designer's fascination with strange screen backgrounds? Colors and special effects seem captivating when you first try them, but put yourself in the readers' shoes. If your text is not readable, your site has lost 90 percent of its value. A neutral background color—preferably solid—is the way to proceed. As you get a feel for what your audience likes, you can experiment with other effects later, but initially be sure to emphasize clarity.

Balance your hyperlinks: A good Web site should contain a mixture of links that point inward and outward. Inward-pointing links are those that take the reader to other pages at your site. Outward-pointing links connect to external Web sites with information that augments what you are providing. A balance between the two ensures that your site references its own information cache as well as indicating where to go for further study.

Choose external links cautiously: When you display a page in hypertext format, the links become part of the rhetoric of the page; they indicate what you find important, whether they be concepts that need explanation or other sites that people can use. Make links to external sites as representative as possible (and always clear them with the other site) so that your readers see you are providing them with a diverse set of viewpoints. You will be evaluated on how well you connect to the universe of information around you.

Link to your e-mail address: Home pages should be designed so that people can quickly contact their creators. One of the great beauties of the medium, after all, is that the same tool we use to read information is the one we use to send comments, and the comments can be sent almost immediately after reading the pages. Putting your e-mail address on your home page ensures that people will be able to contact you if they want to ask a question, confirm a notion, or simply discuss what you're doing.

Create a background page about yourself: One of the major issues raised by the Web is that it's so hard to verify content. Authors need to be sure that Web pages include information about themselves, so that readers can decide whether a particular author has the credentials to be making his or her argument. You can set up a page, linked off your home page, that lets you present your credentials and explain your philosophy; it might also include links to other material you've written that may be peripheral to the current site but nonetheless illuminating.

Maximize screen space: In this era of 17- and even 21-inch monitors, it's a natural temptation to use every high-tech tool built into the latest HTML editor. But bear in mind that many people are still working on smaller screens, or laptops, and what they read may be appearing in a far more confined space than you have in mind. While frames, for example, can be useful in setting up tables of contents, you must always ask yourself whether they take up more screen space than they should. Would you be better off without frames, thus providing maximum content area for the material at your site?

Keep your content fresh: A few trips to a Web site should convince you of the need to keep content updated. Your readers want—and expect—to find at least one new thing every time they come back to your pages. That doesn't mean you have to write reams of content every day, but the more often you can add something timely, the more likely people are to return. Nothing damages a site's reputation more than stale information. And keep your links up to date. When a user clicks on one of your hyperlinks and winds up with an error message, he or she will realize that you haven't been keeping up with your links. Readers want to know that they're involved in a Web site that is constantly monitored and improved. Check all your links to external sites on a regular basis.

Test your pages in multiple browsers: Given the fact that browsers have adopted different de facto standards as the Web has developed, it's always a good idea to make sure that the pages that look so good in Netscape will also look good in Internet Explorer, and so on. If you're going to become a Web publisher, download several of the major browsers and check your pages in each.

Keep your files in one directory: A Web page may include text as well as graphics, moving video, audio, and other formats. Put all your HTML materials in a single directory, using subdirectories for major categories like graphics. You may not think you need such organization while your site is small, but if your goal is to grow, you'll be glad you imposed a structure early.

Where to Publish Your Web Pages

Once your pages are complete, publishing them involves uploading them onto a computer that can be accessed over the Internet. This can be arranged in two ways: You can set up your own server and place your Web pages on it, or you can use a server designated for the purpose at your service provider's site. Individual dial-up users will definitely seek the latter option because of cost.

Consider what's involved with a dedicated server. First, you'll need a machine that can remain on-line 24 hours per day to offer access to your Web pages; even a relatively cheap Pentium will cost you in the range of $2,000. You'll also need server software, and this is where the big browser companies like Netscape up the ante; the Netscape Commerce Server, designed for business, and carrying encryption capabilities, costs around $5,000. But you're not finished yet, because to get onto the Net, you'll need a router, which runs an additional $3,000. And, of course, you need to factor in the cost of access; a T-1 connection to the Internet can run $1,000 per month and more. Be aware, too, that a dedicated server requires regular maintenance; nothing is more frustrating than a site that is down more than it is up. In other words, you need a trained staff.

But even if you have solid monetary backing and business aims, the choice still isn't clear-cut. Ask yourself these questions:

1. **Who is the target audience?** Many of us have ideas or enthusiasms we would like to share. If your interest in building Web pages is that of a hobbyist or scholar, you should probably consider renting space on someone else's server; the alternative is just too expensive. The same is certainly true for anyone attempting to build personal pages for anything other than business reasons. But if your audience is made up of customers for your services or products, the call is more difficult. Then the question becomes at what point will a dedicated Web server begin to justify its expense? Read on.

2. **If this is a business venture, how do you want it to grow?** Some businesses migrate to the Web by way of experiment. Their owners want to see whether markets can be found and developed on-line that would otherwise not be available. Other companies build their sites from day one on the Net; their whole marketing concept is to use the Internet to make money, and they may have no analog in the physical world. Amazon.com, for instance, is a bookstore without a physical storefront; it does all its business through the Web. Are you prepared for slow and steady growth, or do you anticipate making an all-or-nothing venture on-line? If you have a well-drawn marketing plan and major money, you'll need your own server and the support team to keep it running. Otherwise, rent space on someone else's machine.

3. **How much control do you need?** The only way to have complete control over your Web pages is to run your own server; this means you can change page content at will and perform whatever security checks you deem necessary to protect your site. Having your own server also allows you to decide how your pages connect to other services within your company; you may, for example, have a corporate database you'd like to link to, or a program that helps you analyze responses to your pages through fill-in forms. Security issues may make this an in-house project.

4. **Do you require maximum responsiveness?** Using a Web service means you are sharing bandwidth with other users of the same server. Depending on your service provider and his or her connection, this could mean a substantial setback in performance for your users. Before signing up with anyone, check out the site yourself to see how others who use the services provided are faring. Well-designed pages with reasonable performance are a powerful advertisement for a given provider. If it's maximum speed you require, a dedicated server is the only answer.

5. **Do you have the expertise and the staff?** Personal Web pages require only you and a service provider with hosting capabilities. A dedicated server requires a trained staff with the know-how to keep the site up and running around the clock. Both connection and personnel require a major outlay that

most end users and small businesses couldn't begin to consider. If you're involved in a business big enough to swallow such expenses (discussed shortly), then moving to a dedicated server makes sense.

You can see why using a third-party hosting service makes sense, at least until you're sure you can make your Web pages pay for themselves. And certainly for individuals who want to post information for personal or business purposes, a third-party service is the only way to go. My assumption is that end users will be working through service providers. Even if you're a small business owner and want to establish a Web presence, it's not wise to plunge immediately into running your own server until you've built up the necessary Net publishing experience. Make sure that your Web site investment pays off; if it does, then moving to your own server can be accomplished easily later, and with a better idea of what you need.

Posting Pages on a Commercial Information Service

It's not absolutely necessary that you use a dedicated Internet service provider to house your pages. Indeed, the simplest of all methods is to use a commercial on-line service like CompuServe or America Online; both of these include page publishing as part of their fees, allowing you to experiment with various formats and get a handle on basic issues. Moreover, the commercial services include their own templates that walk you through the creation of your pages, albeit without the flexibility you'll find with full-featured HTML editors and dedicated publishing tools.

The CompuServe OurWorld site includes links to over 100,000 home pages (http://ourworld.compuserve.com/). Simplifying the task of page creation are several authoring tools including a home page builder that comes with the associated software for uploading the pages you create. The service also makes available a set of publishing tools such as image collections, counters that show how many times your page has been accessed, background texture and color samplers, and HTML primer documents. One benefit of using a commercial service is, of course, that it is backed by support from the various forums of users; thus CompuServe can quickly link its members to audiences in its Publishing Forum, and similar venues for Webmasters, New Users, Java User Support, and Internet Resources. In Figure 10.24, you can see a Web page housed on CompuServe's member area. CompuServe also provides a search engine that lets you examine its pages by name, city, state, country, occupation or hobbies.

Both Prodigy and America Online likewise offer authoring software and a variety of tips and techniques on-line. AOL offers Personal Publisher and My Place, two areas where help is plentiful; the Web Diner feature offers tips and design techniques, while the InBusiness feature is designed to help you understand how to use the Web in marketing your business. Prodigy's authoring

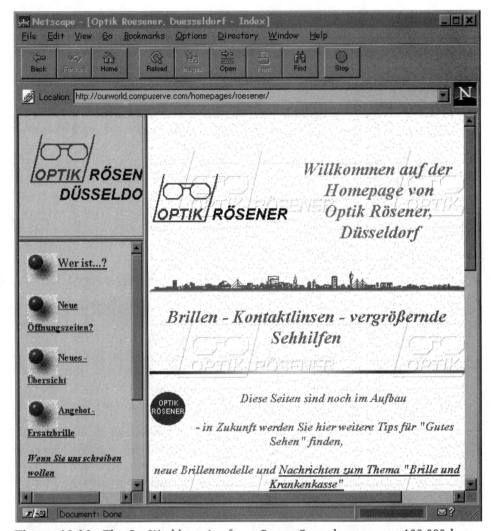

Figure 10.24 The OurWorld service from CompuServe houses over 100,000 home pages from members. Note the use of frames on this German page.

tools help you create pages based on your personal links and to customize your pages through personalized news and greetings. Its Web tools can help you create a customizable home base for your own use, with news, pointers, and built-in stock ticker, in a matter of minutes.

Commercial on-line services like these sound like a good idea until you begin to add up the incidentals. While a free Web site is the obvious place to begin your experiments, these services come up short by way of features, especially if you have business uses in mind; figuring out complex forms or creating documents with the latest display technology may well be beyond them (of the three, Prodigy is perhaps the most responsive to the business user). Further, both CompuServe and America Online have limits on the disk space available for your site; CompuServe limits you to 1MB of storage, America Online to 2MB. In a world of high-resolution graphics, moving video and sound, that's precious little room to maneuver.

Using an Internet Service Provider

Using a given information service's set of tools can be limiting, too, boxing you within certain design parameters; indeed, many of the pages on both CompuServe and America Online show a certain sameness that could benefit from exposure to some of the more creative Web publishing software. The alternative is to use an Internet service provider (ISP), but you'll get less help; indeed, the standard procedure is to create your site using whatever set of tools you choose and then to upload the finished product to the provider. Most providers will offer you a certain amount of disk space as part of the monthly fee you are paying anyway to access the Net; this fee can be increased in return for more disk space if you decide that expanding your site is worthwhile.

To be considered for Web hosting, an ISP obviously must maintain a 24-hour connection to the Internet, because you're hoping to reach an audience that could be logging on from almost any time zone. Because Web hosting has become a major revenue generator for the service providers, your choices should be wide. Most providers will offer a full set of instructions on how to post Web pages to their servers, but you should also find out about the quality of their technical support by asking pointed questions. Start out by getting directions on how to upload your pages to the server. Most pages are posted through FTP programs, as we'll see next, and your provider should be able to explain how and where to get the software.

How to learn about ISP possibilities? Through the Web itself. In Figure 10.25, you can see the Web hosting services offered at MindSpring, a national provider based in Atlanta. MindSpring offers virtual Web hosting, which means that you can use your own company name in your Web site's URL. Let's say you run a small company called Bookends, Inc. Without virtual hosting, your URL would have to use your provider's domain name, thus flagging the fact that you were not running your own server. With virtual hosting, you could set up a URL like http://www.bookends.com/, provided the same name wasn't already registered to some other company. But a variety of other Web hosting options are also provided, some of them cheaper because no registration with the InterNIC—the body that controls network domain names—is required (the InterNIC requires an annual maintenance fee).

Pricing varies depending upon which type of service you sign up for. MindSpring's standard pricing plan, for example, offers Web access as part of the basic package. For personal Web space 5MB of disk space is reserved, with a

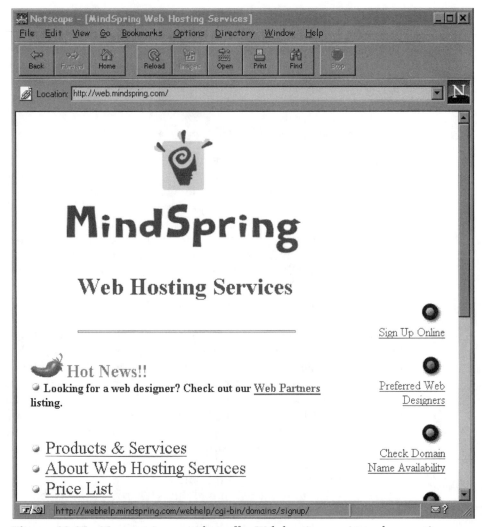

Figure 10.25 Most service providers offer Web hosting services whose options can be explored on the Web.

limit on bandwidth usage (determined by the amount of bandwidth used by other people reading your Web pages or accessing any FTP files you store on the server). If your needs go beyond 5MB, a wider variety of options is available. One offers up to 10MB of disk space for your Web pages for $50 per month, with a $75 start-up fee. Fees then rise depending on additional storage: 20MB of disk space costs $100 per month, 100MB of disk space is $250 per month, and so on. The bottom line: experimenting on the Web may well be built into your basic ISP fee anyway; as you gain in expertise, you may expand and need to pay more.

Tip: A major factor in choosing a provider for your own pages is access speeds. The surest deterrent for anyone trying to explore your work is a slow connection. Always check to see what kind of connection your ISP offers. The provider can't do much about general network slowdowns, but it helps if he or she offers a T-1 or, better still, a T-3 connection so your readers won't be left staring at a frozen screen while their browsers try to access your pages.

Uploading Your Pages to the Server

Once you have checked your Web pages in your browser to make sure they display correctly, you're ready to send them to your service provider (a common term for this is *mounting* your pages). The easiest way to do this is to use an FTP program, numerous examples of which are available for free or as shareware programs that you can try before you buy. You can track these down at any of the major software sites, like Windows94.com (http://www.windows 95.com/), The Ultimate Collection of Windows Software (http://www.tucows. com/), Stroud's Consummate Winsock Applications (http://www.stroud.com/), or Shareware.com (http://www.shareware.com/).

I've often used WS_FTP, an excellent file transfer program created by John Junod. WS_FTP provides an intuitive screen that shows directories at the remote site next to your own computer's files; you can then click on an icon to send a file from one machine to the other. The program is freeware, although a professional version is available for a fee. Another popular FTP program is CuteFTP from Alex Kunadze; this one is shareware and costs $30. A final recommendation is Microsoft's Web Publishing Wizard, which can be downloaded for free from the company's Web site: http://www.microsoft.com/ windows/software/webpost.default.htm.

No matter which program you use, the principle is the same: Find out from your provider where your files need to be sent, and make use of his or her technical support to help you through the first file transfer. The main thing to ensure is that you know the precise location on your provider's disk that is being reserved for your upload. If a provider can't explain clearly how to handle the upload, you need a different provider.

Publicizing Your Site

Once your pages are available on the Web, it's your job to publicize them. A variety of services have become available that help you register your page. The following are places where you can announce your site by using a single form:

Submit It! (http://www.submit-it.com/): A free service allowing you to register with 15 different search tools.

Postmaster (http://www.netcreations.com/postmaster/index.html): Posts to roughly two dozen sites for free; a commercial service allows you to post to a wider list.

Add It! (http://www.liquidimaging.com/submit/): Registers with over 100 directories. You can see the Add It! home page in Figure 10.26.

wURLd Presence (http://www.ogi.com/wurld/): Registration with major search engines and What's New pages.

Many search engines also provide forms that allow you to register your site on-line. In Figure 10.27, for example, you can see the registration form at Lycos. I found this form simply by following a hyperlink from the Lycos home page. Other engines and directories that provide such services include

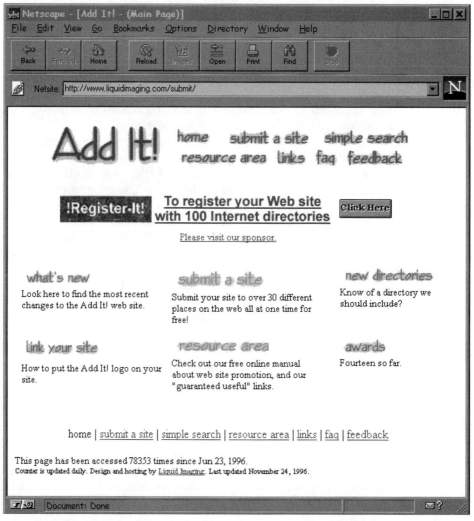

Figure 10.26   Add It! allows you to list your new pages with multiple directories.

WebCrawler, AltaVista, Yahoo!, OpenText, HotBot, Magellan, Excite and InfoSeek (although InfoSeek asks that you submit your URL by electronic mail to www-request@infoseek.com). A helpful master page of search engine submission pages can be found at http://www.tiac.net/users/seeker/searchengine-sub.html.

Be aware, too, that not all listing services are Web-based. The newsgroup comp.infosystems.www.announce, for example, is a moderated newsgroup dedicated to announcing new Web resources. You can also submit your URL to the Net-Happenings list at http://www.mid.net/NET/, which contains a sub-

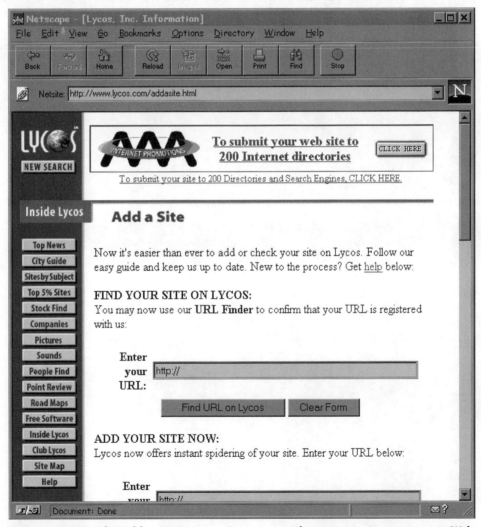

Figure 10.27 The Add a Site page at Lycos, a quick way to register your new Web pages.

mission form. Because many of the newer search engines are providing some form of registration service, it always pays to check for one when you examine their sites. The sooner you're listed by the search engines and any mailing lists and newsgroups that cover Net announcements, the faster your audience will appear.

Tip: Another good way to get word out about your site is to locate newsgroups that focus on the topics you discuss. Join such groups and include your Web site's URL in your signature file. Soon you'll be gaining readers from the population of newsgroup readers, who will, in turn, spread word of your activities. Like marketing of any kind, Web page promotion starts slow but can snowball if you have the content to merit a wider audience.

11

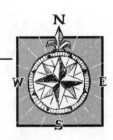

Commerce, Security, and Privacy

Business has changed the face of the Internet. From its beginnings in the research and scientific worlds, the Net has moved through successive incarnations as an educational connector (in the 1980s through the work of the National Science Foundation) and now as a consumer service. The latter, with all its implications for how we do business, buy products, research stocks, perform banking chores, and preserve our privacy, is the Internet we see trumpeted across our television screens and printed in our newspapers. It's the Internet that drives companies to put their Web address on their business cards, and convinces advertisers to allocate significant parts of their budget to cyberspace.

And it's an Internet that raises as many questions as it answers. When I can shop from my computer screen as easily as through a mail catalog or a trip to the mall, I've made my life easier. But is it safe to do so, considering that I'm consigning my credit card information to a service that was never designed to be secure? If I can look up a friend's address and telephone number by filling out a simple form on-screen, is my friend's privacy violated? And if I can hunt down an exciting new stock by using the World Wide Web, should I assume that the information I find there is sound? Just what shape will the Internet take as the growth into the commercial arena continues, and how successful will the new cyberspace entrepreneurs be?

The questions tug at all our notions of commerce within the larger social order. An unabashed free-marketer myself, a capitalist and buyer of stocks, I nonetheless sympathize with those who look upon the quicksilver growth of on-line business with concern. The Internet's great aesthetic has been the willingness to build, to give significant content to make it a better place, to help others connect so they can reap benefits, and not just profits. We'll have to consider in this chapter whether that notion of "giving to the Net" is imperiled by

417

on-line shopping malls and the unwelcome appearance of junk mail. Or are these things simply unavoidable as the Net learns to finance itself?

We know one thing without doubt. The people who study these phenomena say that on-line commerce is a gathering wave. New York-based Jupiter Communications, in a recent report, pointed out that some $3.5 billion went into some kind of network-assisted transaction in 1996; the firm projects that amount will rise to $14 billion by the year 2000. Much of today's Net dollar is going into advertising. Jupiter sees Web advertising passing the $5 billion mark by 2000, passing radio advertising revenue in the process. With huge growth possible in consumer spending, the total numbers for ad revenues are, however, still forecast to lag behind TV and newspapers: $36.3 billion were spent on television advertising in 1996; $11 billion went into print venues. An interesting picture should start to emerge shortly after the turn of the century as higher bandwidth data pipes help the Internet merge with broadcast television. In such a world, companies will have to target their ads in both directions.

The notion of security, at least, is one that's being actively addressed. Business needs airtight security—or, at least, security that can claim a reasonable chance of success—to survive in a world where hackers stalk the digital landscape and users wonder whether their information is secure. Advertisers rely on your ability to get to their products and buy them without concern; they'll ensure that companies like Microsoft, VISA, and Netscape succeed in setting powerful standards for encryption and secrecy. Banks will play a huge role in this. On-line banking from the home promises new revenue and additional savings for the banks, as long as people know their accounts are safe.

We'll need to ask as well whether the Net's current model of access can long survive in a world underserved by bandwidth. At $19.95 per month for a flat-rate account, the average user can leave his or her machine on all day long, creating huge strains in a telephone system designed for far shorter voice calls. Service-based billing may be on the horizon—you pay extra for guaranteed bandwidth, or for certain types of bandwidth-intensive services like videoconferencing. The long-distance carriers and Internet service providers have to find a way to make their books balance once the smoke of the coming ISP shakeout drifts off the battlefield.

Business Takes to the Net

The growth of business-driven sites on the Internet is visible from every economic angle. More and more companies have begun to feature their Web addresses prominently in their television advertising, a phenomenon that began with computer companies but now extends to everything from automobile manufacturers to pizza parlors. Some of these sites are designed to be come-ons for specific products; they feature information and order forms that can be filled out on-line. Others are support sites, offering an easy way to reach a company whose product you already own, or to query a database for further information about something you are thinking about buying. Some sites represent a corporate voice, making data about the company available to the press and the public at large, while others are one-person operations serving a cyberspace entrepreneur.

Grove Enterprises is an example of a company expanding to cyberspace as the logical outgrowth of an existing catalog operation. The company, located in Brasstown, North Carolina, sells shortwave equipment, including receivers, UHF scanners, antennae, and books; it's also a publisher, offering a magazine called *Monitoring Times* to radio enthusiasts. The Grove audience is a tightly defined one. As opposed to amateur radio operators, whose conversations are two-way, Grove targets monitors and listeners, those who like to eavesdrop on international communications and fine-tune everything from a radical antenna design to the parameters of a satellite dish.

You can see a page from the Grove site's on-line catalog in Figure 11.1. The site's URL is http://www.grove.net/. In the figure, I am looking at information about the Drake R8-A shortwave receiver, considered to be one of the finest of its type. Hyperlinks allow Grove to provide information about related products on the same page; thus I find entries for two types of antenna that can serve this receiver, along with a software program designed to enhance it through a computer interface and a sound enhancer to clean up murky shortwave signals. Ordering can be done through e-mail to the linked address, or by postal orders, phone orders or fax, and Grove notes that e-mail purchasers can call in their card number rather than placing it in the message itself if they are concerned about security.

The Grove site is an electronic version of an existing catalog; it mimics in digital form what the catalog offers in print, and provides roughly the same capabilities. Some sites enhance the model with interactive forms, accepting orders through direct entry into the company's computer system. Thus, Amazon.com, a bookstore based in Seattle. As opposed to Grove Enterprises, which began as a mail-order business and has moved recently into cyberspace, Amazon.com was conceived from the beginning as an on-line store. At its site (http://www.amazon.com/) you can search a database of over 1 million books by using a search engine. When you've found the titles you need, you can simply fill out the necessary information and they will be shipped to you.

Shopping for a book, I enter the keywords *terminal experiment* in the search field. I'm looking for Robert Sawyer's *The Terminal Experiment* (Harper Mass Market Paperbacks), a 1996 novel that won its author the prestigious Nebula Award. At Amazon.com, the entry for each book provides a synopsis of the title and assorted information that may include reader reviews or even authorial comments. The description also includes an on-screen button that lets me add the book to my digital shopping basket. When I click on this button and tell Amazon.com that I'm ready to pay, I see the screen shown in Figure 11.2.

Amazon.com is pointing out that an option exists that enhances the security of any information I send. The Netscape Secure Commerce Server has been specifically designed to encrypt—or scramble—any information it processes,

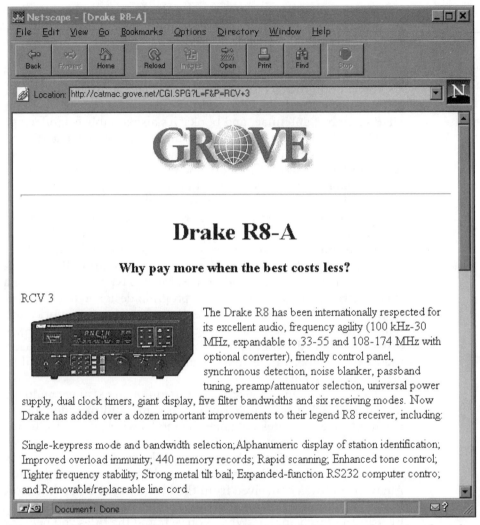

Figure 11.1   The Grove Enterprises site offers a digital version of its printed catalog on the Web.

thus keeping the data private. The Netscape browser supports these secure transactions in version 3.0 and later, but for those who use browsers that don't, Amazon.com makes it possible to choose another alternative.

A click on the secure server link pulls up the screen shown in Figure 11.3. You can see the familiar credit card logos at the top right. Using the secure server means that you are guaranteed greatly improved (though as we'll see shortly, not infallible) security for the transaction you are about to make. It takes only minutes to fill out the form, far less than that trip to the mall, and soon the book is on its way.

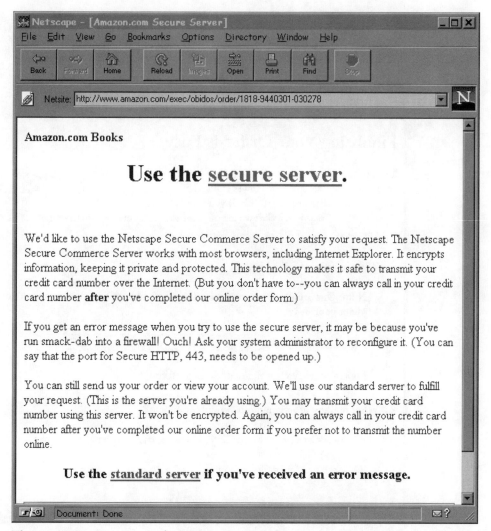

Figure 11.2 Amazon.com's security message alerts you to the fact that several channels exist for sending Internet data.

This model is explicitly retail; it focuses on individuals buying products through a new medium. But large companies are also exploring how their Web sites can provide consumers with the kind of information they need to make purchases on the local level. Take Ford Motor Company (http://www.ford.com/). Its site, The Ford WorldWide Connection, includes a dealer locator to help you track down the nearest place to buy a Ford, as well as a lease calculator to help you with financial considerations. It also provides a digital showroom that allows you to work through all options and specifications for any of the cars the company manufactures. You can see the specifications on a 1997 Mercury

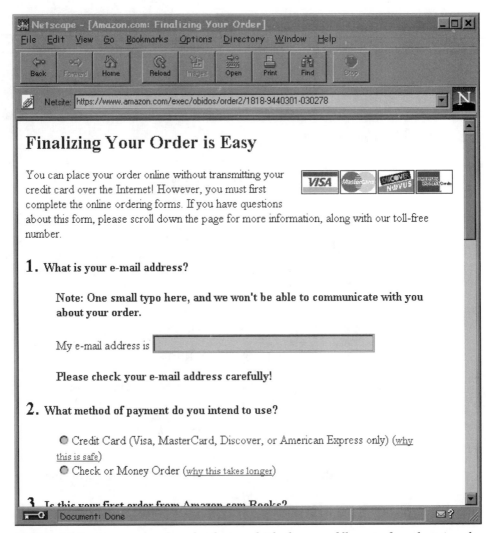

Figure 11.3 Amazon.com's order form, which the user fills out after choosing the items to be purchased. Note the key, a security icon, in the bottom left corner.

Mystique in Figure 11.4. Armed with these numbers and related data, you can approach your local dealer with confidence.

Of course, a corporation can also use its Web site for the benefit of its stockholders, as Ford does by linking to its annual reports, SEC EDGAR filings, and news briefs. A site that serves as an information stop for would-be customers and stockholders can boost a company's business in ways that may be hard to measure. But as commerce spreads on the Net, more people will check into such sites to determine whether a given product is in their price range or meets their needs before talking to a local supplier. The purchase

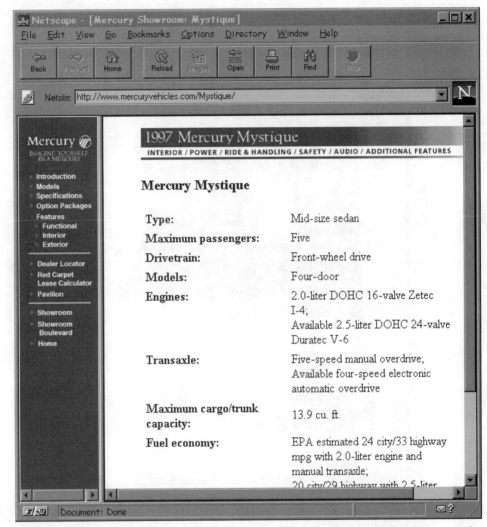

Figure 11.4 Ford Motor Company's Web site provides detailed information on the various models.

decision is deferred until on-line research is completed, making the development of information-rich product sites a useful tool for improving customer relations and boosting the bottom line.

And who knows how to measure the impact of a site like Disney's (http://www.disney.com/), which you can see in Figure 11.5. The company knows that the spread of the Web will bring people to its site in search of information and entertainment. Its latest movies can be supported with reviews and video clips, promoting the films and guaranteeing a wider audience for related products. Its television shows can be backed by channel guides and background

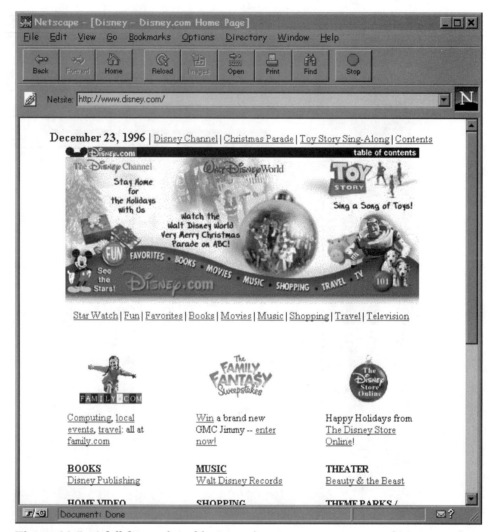

Figure 11.5 A full-featured site like Disney's can generate customers by enticing them with come-ons for movies and books.

stories. Its theme parks can be supported by tour guides and travel information, while the site at each level is enlivened by trivia games and videos of key events.

You as consumer benefit from the readily available information. A visit to the Windham Hill Records site allows me, for example, to sample the latest CD or read background information about the artist (http://www.windham.com/main.html). I can check George Winston's album Linus & Lucy/The Music of Vince Guaraldi and watch a video clip of Winston at work; and, of course, I can order a CD or cassette of the music on-line. In Figure 11.6, I'm examining information about Winston. Or I can search the Windham Hill catalog by key-

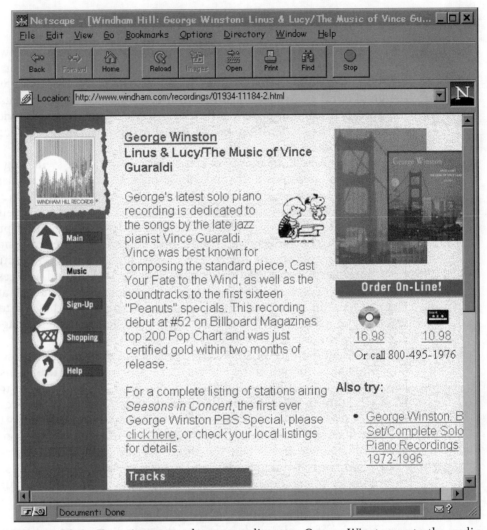

Figure 11.6 Targeting news about recording star George Winston; note the audio clips available for download.

words, working my way through the works of musicians like Philip Aaberg, John Gorka, the Modern Mandolin Quartet, and Shadowfax.

But the question that haunts all these proceedings is this: When I move beyond simply acquiring information and start talking about putting down money for a product, how safe is the transaction? On-line grocery shopping is upon us, as is the age of the cyberspace bank and the wired brokerage. If I routinely debit my account on-line, am I at risk of accessing it one day to find that it has been cleaned out? We turn now to security issues on the Internet and what can be done to solve them.

Business and Security

No one ever said the Internet was private, or that information on it was secure. In fact, the Net was never designed to be secure. As an experimental network verifying new communications technologies, the early ARPANET was hardly designed to be a carrier of business traffic, nor could its proponents have factored in the astounding growth in users, service providers, bandwidth needs, and content sites when they began transferring programs and manipulating remote computers in the 1970s.

Consider how data moves over the Internet. Packet switching puts data into separate envelopes and sends these packets over the Net, passing them from router to router until they arrive at their destination. There, they are reassembled and delivered to the person they're intended for. Their contents are in plain text form, straight ASCII, with address information provided in their headers. They cross numerous routers on multiple network sites as they make their way across the Internet. It doesn't take a computer genius to intercept those packets and read them; they can even be altered and resent if the purpose is to deceive. Send your credit card numbers over the Net and you do face the possibility that someone could access them. For that matter, a rogue employee at your service provider's site could get at your message directly, reading its contents and using it as he or she wishes.

Nor do all security breaches involve credit cards. Most of these explicitly target business, though some can be more personal in nature. Consider what happened to Josh Quittner and Michelle Slatalla, two writers who took on the hacker culture in an article in *Wired* magazine. After their service provider's computer was broken into, Quittner and Slatalla were ambushed by thousands of electronic mail messages, so many that their Internet connection was completely shut down. Even their telephone service was victimized; callers were routed to an out-of-state number and subjected to an obscene message.

A similar phenomenon, though using different methods, occurred when Panix, a Manhattan-based Internet service provider, was flooded with information requests in such numbers that the service was all but paralyzed. In this case, the use of invalid addresses was the culprit; Net servers are not able to process large numbers of such requests. The company, which acts as the hub for approximately 1,000 corporate sites, was apparently the victim of articles published in cracker magazines that exposed this weakness in the Net's infrastructure.

Tip: Always be careful when you hear the term *hacker* and ask yourself how it's being used. In the early days of computing, hacker was an honorable term, referring to those people who worked long hours to create elegant solutions to programming dilemmas. The term later took on a different meaning, coming to refer to those people who attack other people's computer systems for profit, revenge, or sheer malice. It is true that current usage is changing the meaning of the word hacker, but it seems a shame to lose a term so rich in history and honorable in intent. The better word to use for the work of computer vandals is *cracker*.

Password information is also vulnerable at many Net sites. It's your password that confirms you are who you say you are when you log in. A cracker can set up a network *tap*, usually called a *sniffer*, to dig out password information. A sniffer monitors the first 120 keystrokes of any newly opened session on the Net. Within those keystrokes occur such critical items as your password, account information, and information about the host computer. The UNIX operating system, which is in widespread use at Internet service provider sites, is particularly vulnerable to such tampering; crackers have found ready entry into such companies through Telnet, FTP, and mail applications, sometimes heisting valuable data.

Remember, it's not just at your own service provider's site that you may be vulnerable. Any computer on a local area network can see all the traffic that passes through that network. The message you send this morning on the Internet may pass through a large number of such networks at various ISP sites en route to its destination; it is therefore in danger of being compromised. Obviously, Internet service providers are popular targets for such attacks, as are corporations with extensive in-house networks. They carry a huge volume of traffic and thus yield passwords and other information in large quantities. Companies often use firewalls—computers specially designed to block unauthorized Net access—but these are of little use if a sniffer is used on a properly authorized computer.

The Assumptions of a Purchase

In a world of such dangers, how do we beef up Net security? By examining the assumptions we work with when we buy. The first of these is that no one else should know the details of your purchase, such as your credit card information or your billing address. You also need to know that you are dealing with a legitimate source for your merchandise. This isn't an issue in the physical world; standing in Sears Roebuck, you know you're dealing with a major company with a history. But on-line, the question becomes more nebulous. What do you know about the people you're dealing with? More to the point, can you be sure that the person(s) at the other end of the connection really are who they claim to be?

Questions of identity like these sound almost Orwellian, and in some ways they are, but we'll have to deal with them until sturdy Internet security is available so widely that we take it for granted. And consider this additional factor: When you buy something on-line, you need to be sure that your order is received and acted upon accurately. When you order something in the real world by filling out an order form, you know you can fall back upon your copy of the order to verify that you haven't been sent something you don't want. In the on-line world, it's too easy to alter information. What if a disreputable merchant changes your order so that you are billed for the wrong thing? For that matter, what if this merchant charges you for something and then fails to deliver it? Do you have accurate records that incontestably prove your case?

These are the issues that occupy on-line security experts, who have engineered a variety of solutions. They range from the use of encryption to secure vital information in transit to methods of verifying identity through digital signatures and certificates. The diverse nature of the Net requires security solutions that are widely accepted, but as we'll see, the work of the major credit card companies and computer software companies has conceived a workable standard. The first security bulwark is the browser itself.

Browser-Level Security

Web browsers like Netscape use their own security mechanisms to make sure your data arrives safely. Netscape's security method is called Secure Sockets Layer, or SSL. The Web is an open conduit, one that makes no attempt to encrypt the data flowing across it. For that reason, anyone who intercepts a Web data packet can gain access to everything in it, which could include credit card numbers, Social Security information, private telephone numbers, financial records, and more. To get around this problem, SSL encrypts HTTP data before it is sent and decrypts it on the receiving end. Without the special key needed to make sense of it, the data in transit is a meaningless jumble of binary arithmetic.

For all this to work, the browser must be equipped for security and must be in contact with a server that is likewise secure. In this scenario, Netscape offers security in three ways:

Server authentication	A means of confirming the identity of the party at the other end of the connection. This is essential for trusted business transactions to take place. Netscape delivers this using digital certificate technology (enhanced with digital signatures).
Encryption	To guarantee the privacy of content moving across the Net, the browser provides for encryption of data so that outsiders can't read the material even if they intercept it.
Data integrity	Encryption also allows users to be sure that the message they received has not been altered in transit.

The SSL protocol, operating independently of the other programs you're running at the time, is what delivers these safeguards. The fullest implementation of its security, however, only occurs when working with a secure SSL server.

SSL's encryption methods make unraveling the scrambled information out of the question for all but the most determined assaults. But putting computers to work on cracking such information is theoretically possible. In mid-1995, for example, a French doctoral student cracked a transcript of an SSL session by using 120 workstation computers and two supercomputers. The solution involved eight days of work during which the computers would guess at the numerical key that unlocked the encrypted information, see if it worked, and try again when it didn't. The cost of decrypting a single message in this way was high, but the point had been made that Net security remains crackable, even if the version of SSL that had been broken was the much weaker version Netscape was allowed to export overseas.

Tip: Netscape's encryption technology comes in two forms. The less powerful 40-bit method is what is used for overseas versions, while the U.S. domestic product comes with much more complicated 128-bit encryption. The use of encryption technologies for export remains controversial, as was demonstrated when Phil Zimmermann, creator of an encryption program called Pretty Good Privacy, ran afoul of the law. Zimmermann's program, which we'll install later in this chapter as a way of protecting electronic mail and other files, was introduced in 1991 and quickly became a standard on the Net.

Federal prosecutors pursued a case against Zimmermann under the Arms Export Control Act, which would classify such software as munitions and forbid its export. Their contention was that the introduction of the program onto the Internet was a form of export, since the Net crosses global boundaries with ease. Zimmermann, however, denied having placed the program on the Net in the first place. In early 1996, U.S. Attorney Michael J. Yamaguchi announced the government's decision not to prosecute Zimmermann, but the issues raised by the case regarding privacy, free speech, and the globalization of communications remain lively sources of contention.

Later that year, however, two graduate students at the University of California at Berkeley found a means of decoding both the overseas and domestic versions of SSL data. Worse yet, their technique required only a single workstation and a few hours of time. The students, Ian Goldberg and David Wagner, had uncovered a genuine security breach within the browser's security, one that involved the way Netscape generated its encryption key. Security problems were also uncovered in Sun Microsystems' Java and Microsoft's Internet Information Server. Version 3.0 of Netscape fixed the security bugs discovered so far, but the point has been made that Net security is a matter of keeping one step ahead of the crackers who would like to break into other people's computers, whether for gain or out of malice.

The Java environment, sure to be a major factor in Web programming in the future, contains its own security holes. Java lets a Web author execute a program on your PC, while the associated JavaScript, made available in version 2.0 of the Netscape browser, is a scripting language not dissimilar from HTML itself, its code embedded directly into hypertext files. Theoretically, the Java application arrives at the browser and is executed by a byte-code interpreter, which should limit what the program can do. But numerous breaches in Netscape's Java implementation have been uncovered, leading to changes and fixes in version 3.0.

ActiveX controls may pose even more of a problem; they contain none of Java's security restrictions because they process their code directly through the existing application rather than using links to associated programs. Aware of the problem, Microsoft advocates digital signatures for both Java and ActiveX applications; the incoming file would be checked against the public key used by the file's creator. Any modification to it would cause the signature test to fail. Until such digital signatures can be applied to the problem, both Java and ActiveX will bear watching.

But the tools for Net security, as seen through Netscape's evolving features, are developing fast. When working with a secure server, Netscape provides indicators about the security status of the document you're using:

- The URL will begin with https:// instead of http://.
- The security icon should appear in the browser window as a solid key on a blue background. You can click on the key icon to receive further security information about the site.
- The color line immediately above the content area on the Netscape screen should be blue when you're accessing a secure site; otherwise, it is gray.

You will also be shown various dialog boxes relating to the security of documents.

More security information about a given document can be found by pulling down the View menu and clicking on Document Info. In Figure 11.7, you can see information about a page on a secure server; here, I am accessing the bookstore at Amazon.com (http://www.amazon.com/) and have moved to its secure server to complete a transaction.

You can see that the security status field states the type of encryption used in the document. The 40-bit encryption used for export is called medium-grade encryption, while the 128-bit version (not shown here) is considered high-grade. Netscape also uses a variety of notification dialog boxes to inform you when you are entering or leaving a secure page.

The security problems uncovered in the Netscape browser have made it clear that securing data in transit is only part of the story. Even if we can be assured that our credit card numbers or financial data aren't going to be stolen while they make their way through the Net, how do we secure the transaction

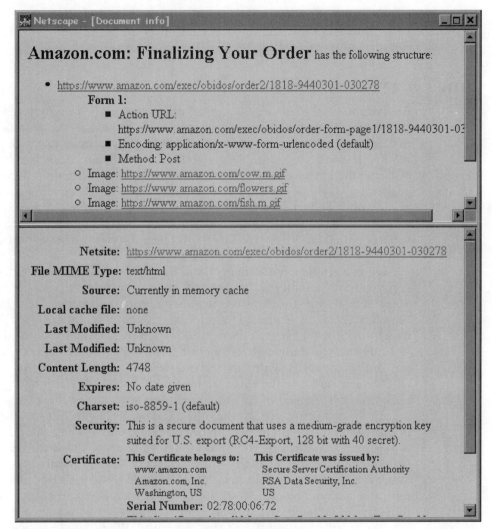

Figure 11.7 Security information about a document can be confirmed by taking the Document Info option on the View menu.

at the other end? We must find some way to use encryption to authenticate the business we are dealing with, so we can send information with confidence and be assured that it is not changed after we've sent it.

Notice the certificate information provided in Figure 11.7. A site certificate is what identifies the business we are dealing with, and each certificate is issued by a certificate authority, a firm recognized as a central point for certificate distribution and authentication. In this case, the authority was the Single Server Certification Authority at RSA Data Security, Inc. The certificate is signed with an encoded statement that verifies its authenticity. For its security features to work, a secure server must provide a digitally signed certificate. Let's now look a little more deeply into how authentication functions on the Net through the use of digital signatures and certificates.

How Encryption Works

Encryption performs a mathematical operation on data or, more precisely, on the binary coding that represents that data. At its heart is the presence of a key that can unlock the coded message. I might, for example, use various mathematical formulae to scramble the code of a particular message. I could then give you the key to this message so that only you and I could decode it. The problem with this technique is the presence of a single key. If I could put the key in your hands, I could feel secure in knowing no one else had seen it. But if we were working at opposite sides of the country, I would have to send it to you via e-mail, and then the key would be subject to the same security risks that the e-mail messages I was trying to protect were.

Using a single key to encrypt and decrypt a message is called secret-key cryptography; it assumes that both sender and recipient possess the same key. Many financial institutions use a secret-key method called Data Encryption Standard (DES) to send data to automated teller machines. Although the data may transit the telephone system, and is thereby insecure, it is considered sufficiently encrypted through its key technology to be safe. Single-key cryptography is also known as symmetric cryptography.

The alternative to the single-key method is public-key cryptography, which uses two keys instead of one for maximum security. Each of these keys can unlock the code generated by the other. The public key belongs to its owner but is known to everyone. The private key is known only to the owner. To send you a message, I would use your public key to encrypt the document, which I would then send to you. Only your private key—which requires a pass phrase known only to you—could decrypt it. Even if someone else intercepted the message, it would be useless without your private key. And at my end, I therefore know that you're the only one who will have seen the message.

Return information works the same way. When you send me a message that has been encrypted with my public key, you would know that it is secure because I am the only one who can decrypt it with my private key. We have thus opened up a secure channel of communication.

Public-key cryptography can also be used to verify identity. If you send me a message, for example, using your private key to encrypt it, I can decrypt it using your public key, thus verifying that it came from you, since no one else would have your private key. Or you could use a digital signature to sign the message, inserting a block of code that is created with your private key in a message that is otherwise unencrypted. The public key in my possession will verify that this is your signature, and thus confirm your identity.

Now if we combine the use of the two sets of keys, we can handle both authentication and security in one message. I can use my secret key to create a digital signature; I can then use your public key to encrypt the message. I am thus assured that only you will get my message and that you will be able to verify that it came from me. Only you can decrypt my message using your secret key, and you can verify my electronic signature by checking it against my public key.

Three cryptographers named Ronald Rivest, Adi Shamir, and Len Adleman devised public-key cryptography, and their cryptography algorithm bears their initials—RSA. An outstanding example of the RSA algorithm at work is in the previously mentioned program called Pretty Good Privacy (PGP), now being sold by ViaCrypt, but also available in a freeware version from MIT. PGP can be used to encrypt electronic mail or any other type of file. With adequate encryption, it hardly matters what anyone steals, because the material is rendered worthless to them. You can see the download site for PGP's freeware version (http://web.mit.edu/network/pgp.html) in Figure 11.8.

Tip: As Netscape's security glitches prove, encryption systems are not completely unbreakable. It's probably safe to say that no one has ever devised an infallibly secure system; indeed, it never fails to make the news when someone finds a security flaw in a Web browser or server. The real method behind cryptography is to design systems that would take so much time and expense to break into them that the effort wouldn't be worth the cost. Enough computer time applied to the task could pull up a result, but if you're a cracker trying to get, say, a credit card number, it won't do you much good to spend 10 times the credit limit of the card to extract the card number.

Digital Signatures and Authentication

The simplest form of authentication is the password and user identification system that most of us use when we log on to the Internet through a service provider. The user ID is one we can choose or that has been chosen by the service for us; the password is purely private and known only to ourselves. Thus, when I call the computer at Interpath, that machine assumes that I am who I purport to be because I have entered the correct password, and lets me into my account.

Of course, the problems with this system are manifold. For it to work, we have to assume that our password is secure. Yet we've just seen that so-called sniffer programs can trap passwords for someone else to use. Moreover, password security isn't tight on the individual level. Most people choose the name of a loved one or family pet, something obvious and definitely guessable, as their password. And how many times have you seen a business user's password written on a yellow Post-It note stuck on their computer monitor?

Figure 11.8 The download site for the Pretty Good Privacy program's freeware version.

This being the case, we need something tighter. Using encryption, we can create a so-called digital signature that proves conclusively that the person who signed the e-mail message you received truly is that person. In the real world, a person's signature provides that guarantee, but forgery remains a possibility. In the digital world, when properly implemented, a digital signature is unforgeable. Making electronic commerce viable over the Internet will require standardizing such signatures and the various ways of validating information that flow out of them. Aware of its significance, companies like IBM, Microsoft, Lotus, and Sun Microsystems have all incorporated encryption into their products. Sun, in fact, is adding digital signature capability directly into its Java programming language.

The encryption that creates a digital signature can also protect data so that you can be assured as you read it that it hasn't been changed since it was sent, whether by accident or deliberate forgery. And while its ability to identify the sender of the data is critical, the digital signature also proves the recipient of a given transaction, which keeps someone from denying he or she had received data or marked it with approval through his or her own digital signature. One day, digital signatures are likely to be as legally binding as written ones; in some states, like Utah, they already are.

The Digital Certificate: Verifying the Transaction

But we also need a way of verifying not just a single person's identity, but the identity of the organizations involved in a transaction. For this we turn to the digital certificate. Digital certificates are ways of verifying the identity of both consumer and merchant; they go beyond the digital signature to identify you to the merchant and protect you against fraud. It is the certificate that ensures that a particular public key is associated with a genuine organization or a specific person. Think of the digital signature as an individual identifier, whereas digital certificates make the entire transaction possible by confirming an identity through a trusted third party.

These certificates are issued by certificate authorities, companies in the business of guaranteeing the identity of their clients; they include not only the name of the certificate holder, but also the public key and a time limit on the use of the certificate. They also include a statement of the certificate class, which tells how fully the user holding the certificate has been investigated by the licensing company. The two primary issuers of digital certificates are VeriSign and CyberTrust.

Digital certificates come in two forms:

- A site certificate identifies a site or certification authority.
- A personal certificate establishes the identity of an individual.

When you send information to a secure server, the site certificate ensures that the information goes only to the owner of the certificate. This is done by encrypting your order through the site's public key; your message can thus be decrypted only with that site's private key. The server can also request your personal certificate to identify you.

Here's how the digital certificate is meant to work with a typical transaction today:

1. You enter the necessary information to buy a product at a secure Web site, finally clicking on the button to submit your order.
2. The server at the merchant's end sends you a digital certificate and a digital signature.
3. The certificate is checked against the certificate authority to ensure that it is valid.

4. If the certificate is valid, the browser uses the merchant's public key to encrypt your order and all data associated with it.

5. If the merchant wishes to encrypt any information he or she returns to you, you will need your own digital certificate to verify your identity.

While not widespread today, personal certificates will take on great significance as Secure Electronic Transaction (SET) technology, discussed in the next section, begins to take hold.

In the case of my transaction at Amazon.com, my browser already had the necessary site certificate, thus verifying that I was dealing with who I thought I was. When you visit a secure site and your browser does not already possess its site certificate, a dialog box will alert you and present you with security information. You can accept the certificate identification information and add the site's certificate to your list of certificates, or you can decline to go to the site; another option is to visit the site for one time only without adding the certificate to your list of certificates. The list of site certificates in Netscape is found by pulling down the Options menu, choosing the Security Preferences item, and clicking on Site Certificates, as shown in Figure 11.9.

VeriSign's digital certificate technology is used in Netscape version 3.0. The VeriSign technology works on both sides of the data transaction to verify the identity of users on the client side and the servers they access. Using electronic certificates allows companies to set up major data exchanges through the use of Electronic Data Interchange (EDI), a means of linking firms financially, over the Internet; EDI usually connects large corporations like auto manufacturers with their suppliers. Such transactions have in the past been considered so sensitive that they could be managed only over dedicated connections between the two companies involved. Microsoft plans to use VeriSign technology in its ActiveX controls, while Sun will incorporate digital certificates in its Java language.

CyberTrust, a division of GTE, produces its own digital certificate technology using public-key cryptography. You can see the CyberTrust home page in Figure 11.10. CyberTrust provides a suite of certification services and products for secure consumer shopping, as well as corporate protection in intranets. The company's CyberSign product provides public-key security for individuals and business.

Tip: Digital certificates shouldn't be all that difficult to get once the new Secure Electronic Transaction (SET) infrastructure is in place. Each credit card account will need to have its own certificate. Card issuers will mail out forms to their customers which, upon being returned, will allow the companies to encrypt the user's card information before sending it to the issuing bank. The bank will then authorize the card issuer to act as a certificate authority for that account. The signs thus point to a future in which people

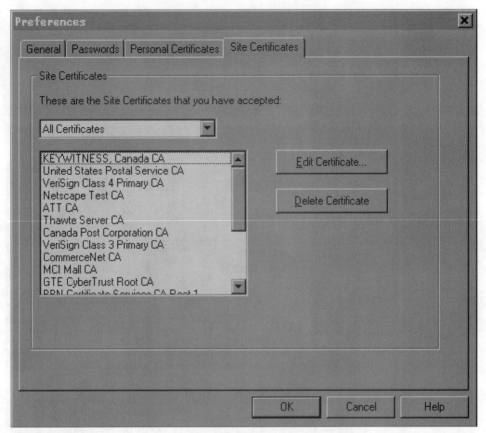

Figure 11.9 The site certificates currently available in Netscape are shown in this panel.

will sign up for digital commerce in the same way they fill out today's credit card applications. When the process is complete, we'll each get a public and private encryption key, and we'll be ready to shop.

SET: Toward a Secure Credit Card

If credit card transactions remain the biggest worry for customers of on-line commerce, they're among the largest issues for the banking industry as well. It was pressure from that industry that convinced MasterCard and VISA, which had been developing independent standards for such transactions, to work together to create a common standard. SET, for Secure Electronic Transactions, was the result. Moving to a set of unified principles means we can avoid a bruising standards fight that would have forced merchants and banks to have chosen between the two camps, one of which was embraced by Netscape,

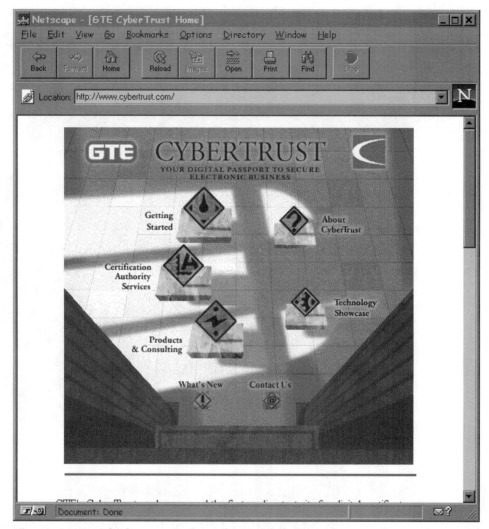

Figure 11.10 The home page for CyberTrust, a major player in the certificate and authentication business.

the other by Microsoft. VeriSign's authentication mechanisms would be used within SET along with technology from GTE to verify information.

The SET agreement draws together the major players in the secure transactions area to solve the thorniest problems of on-line business. Data is sent with digital signatures to ensure that orders and payments match. It provides for confidentiality through the use of message encryption. SET also creates a means of verifying that a particular credit cardholder is a legitimate user of that account, and that the account itself is viable. On the other side of the transaction, SET verifies the identity of the merchant and his or her relationship with a bank. Finally, SET is designed to work across all hardware and software systems.

Could SET security be broken? Presumably so, given the history of network security as a constant race to stay ahead of the crackers. But SET seems to offer a level of security that exceeds what we use in the physical world. The question of credit card security has a practical side. Many of us use credit cards on-line today even though the Net has yet to be secured through SET or other means. Why? Consider how we use our cards every day. Every year at Christmas, for example, I work my way through the hundreds of catalogs that arrive in our mailbox to find a present for my wife. Since I detest shopping malls, I invariably order by mail. And when I do, I call up someone I will never meet, whose name I don't even know, and read to that person my credit card information. I have yet to suffer as a consequence. For that matter, every time I eat out, I use my credit card, giving it to a waitress who disappears with it for several minutes. Are my credit card numbers compromised? Yes, but I've never been defrauded as a result.

The chance of your losing money because you use your credit card information on the Net today is in the same category. Yes, it could happen, but the chances of its happening are relatively slim. SET, which should be implemented widely in 1997, points to a mode of network security that will reduce that chance still further. It will move us beyond using credit cards for retail purchases and provide assurance that we can use the Net to maintain our checking accounts and manage our stock transactions. SET may well be what makes Internet business ubiquitous.

Payment Methods: Varieties of Digital Money

Encryption is one way of handling the electronic transaction, and the SET standard seems certain to play a major role in the way we deal with on-line shopping. But other mechanisms are already in use, each with its own take on security and authentication. Companies that don't want to wait for industry-wide standards to coalesce therefore have numerous, if proprietary, options.

First Virtual Holdings, for example, provides a self-contained system that uses no cryptography whatsoever. Reasoning that the biggest security risk is the illegal interception and decrypting of sensitive data, First Virtual chooses not to put that data on the Net in the first place. Consumers send a personal identification number (PIN), available for a small fee, to merchants, who then forward it to First Virtual. The company can confirm the transaction by sending electronic mail to the customer, who sends payment only when that confirmation has been received.

Many Web businesses offer products using a similar model. You browse a catalog and decide what you want; you then order on-line but place a call direct to the company to supply credit card information. First Virtual simply takes this reluctance to rely on cryptography to a further level, by offering a validation process through the exchange of e-mail that confirms the order. The user's own credit card information can be provided to First Virtual by telephone. You can see the First Virtual Web site (http://www.fv.com/) in Figure 11.11.

CyberCash, on the other hand, does use encryption. Merchants send electronic invoices to their customers for goods purchased. Customers attach their credit card numbers to the invoice and use the CyberCash software, called Wallet, to encrypt the document, which is then returned to the merchant and, in turn, forwarded to CyberCash, which will encrypt it in standard banking format and pass it along to the bank networks. CyberCash can also handle debit and cash transactions. The CyberCash home page appears in Figure 11.12.

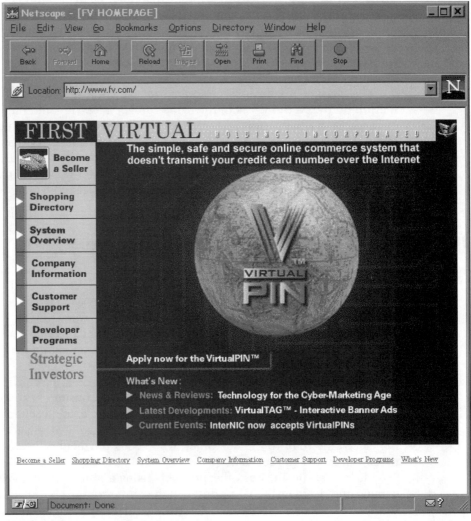

Figure 11.11 First Virtual Holdings solves the security problem by keeping sensitive data off the Internet altogether.

Figure 11.12 The home page for CyberCash, which uses encryption to pass data between the Internet and banking networks.

Note that under a model like this one, not every merchant will be able to offer a particular payment option; buyers must look for the Web pages of merchants who do participate, which should display a CyberCash icon. This, again, is the problem of working with diverse and proprietary systems. The CyberCash home page provides a list of participating merchants.

The CyberCash model is an interesting one because it draws the contrast between the relatively open Internet and the large private networks that operate daily around us. The banks have used secure networking for years, just as businesses have communicated with suppliers and arranged fund transfers over private networks whose security was never in doubt. The Internet's challenge is to become a vehicle for many of the same kinds of transaction, even if it was never designed with security in mind. CyberCash currently acts as a link between these two worlds using its own software to moderate the transaction.

CyberCash has worked with CheckFree, a company specializing in credit card transactions, to develop the digital "wallet" that contains the user's credit card number and the necessary encryption to return invoice and payment information to the merchant. The merchant never actually sees the credit card information; instead, he or she removes the order information and forwards the encrypted and digitally signed payment data to CyberCash. The order is reformatted and encrypted using the same technology banks use with automated teller machines. It is then forwarded to the merchant's bank over the dedicated banking network. The merchant's bank forwards the authorization request to the issuing bank or, in the case of American Express and Discover, directly to the credit card issuer, which returns an approval or denial code to CyberCash. This code is returned to the merchant and passed along to the customer in a process that takes about 20 seconds.

CheckFree's own background is in bill-payment transactions, including payments for commercial information providers like CompuServe and America Online. Its current software allows merchants to validate credit card information. Payment information travels to CheckFree via telephone or modem; the company then transfers funds from the subscriber's checking account to the merchant. This method of keeping the most sensitive data off the Internet itself offers obvious security advantages, enough that the company's bill-paying software has been included in such products as Intuit's popular Quicken program. You can visit the CheckFree Web site at http://www.checkfree.com/.

DigiCash is a different take on the idea of electronic payments. A Dutch company, DigiCash has developed a system of electronic cash based on cryptography and digital signatures. The user first sends money to a bank through a credit card or automated teller transaction. To retrieve electronic cash, the user's computer generates a random number, which is sent to the bank after being put through a mathematical operation (called *blinding*); the bank then digitally signs the note and returns the result to the user. The resulting cash tokens, each for a specific amount, are kept in the user's digital wallet until being used to pay for something. The merchant verifies the digital signature on the note and returns it to the bank, which checks the signature again and pays the merchant. You can see the DigiCash home page in Figure 11.13.

Created by cryptography expert David Chaum, DigiCash offers a model of electronic cash that is completely anonymous. The merchant does not know who is behind the electronic tokens, but he or she can verify that they are good. Public-key cryptography guarantees that no one can forge the bank's signature, but the merchant can verify that the payment is valid by using the bank's public key, while purchasers can prove they paid the cash because they can produce the blinding factor used on the original note.

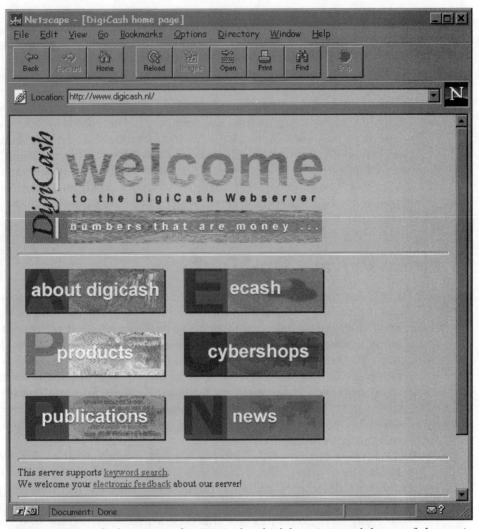

Figure 11.13 The home page for DigiCash, which has pioneered the use of electronic cash tokens.

Tip: The trick to using DigiCash and other technologies is going to be finding merchants that accept them. It's hard to track down many sites that use the DigiCash format, although the ones that do have a certain fascination. You can visit various image galleries, for example, make donations to the Samaritans of Cheltenham and District, or download snatches of song from a shop called Homunculus Productions. Obviously, digital money will have to move into the realm of mainstream business before it becomes a

> serious factor in commerce. The idea that merchants will offer numerous competing standards to settle payments is far-fetched. Of the technologies we've viewed, First Virtual seems to have the widest range of stores.

Finally, VeriFone is a leader in point-of-sale credit card systems that has adapted its expertise to Internet commerce. The company offers an Internet gateway that uses standard bank protocols for data, and is also behind a product called vWallet that lets consumers make Net purchases through their Web browsers rather than proprietary software. VeriFone technology is going into Microsoft's commerce server based on Windows NT, and both Netscape and Oracle are also planning to integrate VeriFone's transaction-management system with their own servers.

Is There Privacy On-Line?

The other night a caller rang my phone and hung up when I answered. Curious, I punched in the telephone code that traces the call and found the number. I then ran the number through an Internet site that returned the person's name and address. This kind of access to personal data makes most people edgy. The other day on a radio show, I looked up the host's address and phone number while we were talking. Like many, she was appalled that information she considered private was now available by keyword search on the Internet. I took the issue one step further by generating a map that showed me exactly where her house was by using the Yahoo Maps site. The days of safe anonymity seem to be ending.

Privacy is one of the Internet's most controversial topics. When Lexis-Nexis Corp. briefly made available a database that offered Social Security numbers along with credit and medical histories, the reaction was immediate; the company was deluged with electronic mail, phone calls, faxes, and letters, decrying its decision to make this data available. The data, in a system called P-TRAK, was designed to be used by the legal community, and once the Social Security numbers were removed (which occurred almost immediately after the system was brought on-line), it contained only publicly available information. But perhaps that is the point: The average person doesn't realize how much computerized information is already available about our lives.

Tracking Your Mail and Newsgroup Habits

A few turns around the Internet may clarify the issue, for individual users are often the source of unexpected information. Your electronic mail address, for example, can be determined in several ways. When you log on at an FTP site to download a file, your address is sent to the host computer by your browser.

Web sites can easily get your e-mail address as well by offering file downloads or setting up forms for user information—if you don't fill out the form, you don't get access to the site. The growing problem of Internet junk mail can be traced back to such activities.

E-mail addresses themselves tell people much about you. They're designed to trace a specific route to your computer. Thus sam_jones@mercator.maps.com is obviously a user at a commercial site with the word maps in its name. Users at universities sport e-mail addresses with the .edu domain, which can then be used to trace more information through campus directories. Information that users put on-line intending it to be for local consumption only thus becomes available widely, and usually without the person's knowledge. A UNIX program called finger can read personal information posted on Net machines, revealing to people when you last logged on and whether you have any e-mail.

And while e-mail seems like a safely stored item on your own hard disk, both students and employees should realize that their correspondence does not belong to them. It is actually company or university property, making it possible for system administrators or managers to read it for whatever reason they deem necessary. The general rule is, don't write anything in electronic mail that you wouldn't mind seeing being written across the sky, and it's the only rule to follow if safety of your data is a concern.

For that matter, your habits in other parts of the Internet can also be monitored. Consider the newsgroups. If you go to the DejaNews site (http://www.dejanews.com/), you'll find a searchable database of newsgroup postings that can reveal extensive information about posters. In Figure 11.14, you can see the DejaNews Query Filter option. By submitting a keyword to DejaNews and calling up a series of articles about that subject, I can then click on any poster's name to see how many articles this person has posted to which newsgroups. Or I can enter a particular author's address and use it as a filter against which to run my search. It is thus fairly easy to build up a picture of what a particular person is interested in, or to read postings that person has made to any of the newsgroups. In other words, a message you entered into a newsgroup years ago, expecting that it would be viewed in the context of an ongoing discussion by people interested in the issue, is still available simply by entering the user's name. The growth of such archives means that your messages may be as readily available today as they were 10 years ago.

Monitoring Web Use

If employers have the option of reading the mail of their employees, it's also true that they can monitor ongoing use of the Web at workstations under their control. It's an understandable impulse; after all, workers who spend their time at Internet game sites or in pornographic newsgroups are not contributing to the company's productivity. And developers like Webster Network Strategies and Tinwald Network Technologies have developed extensive options for tracking employee Web use.

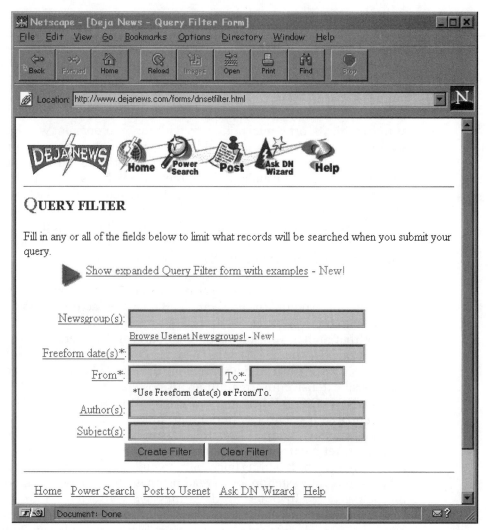

Figure 11.4   DejaNews offers a Query Filter option that lets you track a newsgroup poster's activities over time.

Webster's WebTrack, for example, can monitor Web browsing, file transfer, and newsgroup activity while running behind a corporate firewall. The program blocks access to sites in a variety of categories, from hate-speech to sports and nonessential sites that don't fit the worker's job description. Tinwald's Internet Snapshot offers Net activity summaries that identify what users are doing. ANS, the network infrastructure player now owned by America Online, also has entered this arena with a product called Interlock, which provides reports on Internet use by the hour, and includes sites that have been visited the most.

This is a snapshot of your on-line activities that you probably hadn't realized was being taken. Compaq Computer and Lockheed Martin Space & Missiles Co. are but two of the firms who have actually fired employees after examining their on-line activities and deeming them inappropriate. Clearly, workers in large corporations can't assume that their Web use goes unnoticed. But neither can the individual Web surfer. IBM provides a product called Surf-Aid, for example, that analyzes the behavior and usage patterns of visitors at a particular site. If a user is willing to identify him- or herself, the software can set up an individual tracking service that will follow customer preferences and simplify future access at the site. Other companies are following IBM on this; Bellcore provides Adapt/X, a program that creates user profiles for customized Web pages, thus tracking usage and generating reports. Programs like these can provide many user benefits, such as simplifying sign-on procedures at password-only sites, but be aware that more and more databases of consumer information are being generated as the Web grows. A particular Web site have a record of the pictures and files you examined while at the site, which material you read and which you didn't, and which site you last visited.

Tip: Although they're not significant to home users, firewalls are a corporate solution to various data security problems. A firewall is a set of tools, usually a host computer and a router, with appropriate software that is configured to protect internal company networks. The firewall is usually installed where the network connects to the Internet, and monitors ongoing traffic to and from the company to make sure that intruders can't violate security.

Recording Your Personal Information on Disk

Your own hard disk holds a personal usage pattern that could pose a security risk. Netscape leaves a trail of cache files, history files, bookmarks, and various other options for tracing where you have been, including particularized information that tells the Web server what you did when you were last logged on at the site. It's obvious why marketers love this aspect of the Net. They can learn about their customers' preferences while looking at the company's site.

Many commercial sites include forms that allow users to register before moving past the home page. Fill out the form and you are granted full access to the site; leave it blank and you may not be allowed in at all, or may be given only a partial view of the entire contents. Registration forms are voluntary, but can include personal information like addresses, telephone numbers, personal preferences, and so on. Mixing this information with what can be gained simply by analyzing user actions at the site yields an ever-evolving image of who you are and what you do.

Such materials could be reachable not only by remote marketers and crackers, but also by anyone who takes a look at your machine while you are away from your desk. Consider Netscape's disk cache. The cache is a temporary storage space on your hard disk; if you request to see a page you've already examined, the browser checks to see if the page is already in the cache. If it is, the cache can display the page much faster than it can be accessed and displayed over the Net. Netscape also uses a memory cache, but the latter is emptied when you exit a session, whereas the disk cache is not. Many people don't realize that this trail of their on-line activities remains on their disk after they quit for the day. It's true that no pages are permanently stored in the cache; as it fills, newer materials are added. But if you maintain a cache of, say, 5MB, which is the default, you're holding on to quite a bit of data in that niche.

 Tip: Documents from a secure transaction via SSL are not automatically cached to disk, which provides some security assurances. But SSL is not widely implemented, and most Web pages you access aren't found on secure servers. In fact, a recent study by O'Reilly & Associates and Netcraft, Ltd. found that fewer than 1 percent of the public sites on the Web are able to host fully secure transactions. For that reason, be aware that Web pages you visit are in most cases left on your disk when you exit the browser for the day.

Materials stored in your disk and memory caches can be cleared when you end your Web sessions for the day. The memory cache will be emptied automatically when you leave the browser, but you can also clear it on demand. The disk cache can be cleared at any time. Here's how:

1. Pull down the Options menu.
2. Click on Network Preferences.
3. In the Cache panel, click on either or both of the Clear Memory Cache Now and Clear Disk Cache Now buttons.

It would be nice if this cache clearance were automated, so that the browser emptied the cache at the end of each session without user intervention. As is, most users aren't aware of the option and fail to exercise it.

Why not just set a disk cache size of zero so that no pages are cached? The problem with that is performance; loading Web pages will be drastically slowed if the browser can't pull recently viewed material out of the cache.

If you're worried about the trail your browser leaves on your hard disk, check out a product called NSClean (and its companion called IEClean for Internet Explorer). This program, created by Kevin McAleavey, erases the identity trail left behind by the browser. NSClean can empty the history database that lists URLs and names of Web sites visited as well as documents saved; it can also clear your disk cache, Cookie list, newsgroup directory, URL list of sites most recently visited, and bookmark settings. The product is available at http://www.axxis.com/.

Storing Information in Cookies

But disk caches aren't Netscape's only information trail. The browser also includes a feature known as Cookies (Microsoft's Internet Explorer and various other browsers also support the use of Cookies). A Cookie can tell a merchant what you've been doing at the site; it can be used to gather information such as user name, password, payment information, and various demographic data. In the Cookie model, the server sends information to the browser, which the browser will return every time it accesses that server.

Used properly, a Cookie simply smoothes a commercial transaction. You might, for example, frequently go to a site that offers password-only access (many newspapers do this). Rather than having to enter your password each time you check in at the site, you could count on the help of the associated Cookie to submit your password automatically. Cookies can also be used to create digital shopping carts, storing information about purchases until the user decides to total up the order, or to remember your preferences so that you can create customized Web pages at a site.

Tip: Curious to find out more about Cookie information on your hard disk? There's a quick way to see what's there. Cookies are stored in a file called cookie.txt. It's in plain ASCII, meaning you can open it in any text editor; you will then see which sites have stored information on your system. But be advised that much of the information placed in it is encoded, so you may be able to tell little other than the address of the site that created the Cookie.

Used improperly, however, a Cookie could be used to track user actions on particular servers to generate statistics on your habits and interests. Fed into a database of such information, this becomes a valuable marketing tool, but it's one that was collected without knowledge or permission of the people from whom it came.

To find out what can be done with simple Cookies, check the Center for Democracy and Technology page at http://www.cdt.org/. There you'll find a privacy demonstration that reveals what marketers can learn about you. When I logged on recently, the site told me who my service provider was, where I lived, what operating system I was using, which Internet browser I was viewing the site with, which host computer I was connected to, and the Web site I had visited previously.

How did CDT pull up all this information? In a variety of ways. The site runs WHOIS and finger searches to pull up any information stored on network servers. It can use a so-called browser loophole to find e-mail addresses for some people, although not all browsers make this loophole available. In addition, when some Web browsers perform anonymous FTP downloads, they automatically supply the user's e-mail address, which can then be taken from the browser's transaction log. This option has changed now that the latest browsers have gone to a standard password for such transactions rather than using your actual e-mail address. Clearly, there are a variety of ways besides Cookies themselves that enable people to learn about you.

Cookies can be set up to handle site customization, so that Webmasters can offer users options for what they see whenever they log on. They can also provide counts on how many people have been to what page on your site. For that matter, they can track habits down to the level of the individual ordering products, allowing the site manager to build up a personal customer profile. We call this phenomenon *client-side persistent information;* it's material that stays on your hard disk and is read by the remote site when you visit it. Most users are unaware that it exists.

Cookies are clearly an issue for the privacy-minded. Marketers point out that much of the information they gain from Cookies could be learned through user forms and voluntarily supplied information; and in any case, many Cookies are set up to expire quickly at the sites that send them. But if you're worried about what might be in your own Cookies, Netscape offers a way out. If you want to turn off the Cookies feature, do the following:

1. Pull down the Options menu.
2. Select the Network Preferences item.
3. Select the Protocols pane.
4. Find the section marked Show an Alert Before.
5. Check the box marked Accepting a Cookie.

You can see the Protocols pane in Figure 11.15.

From this point on, when you log on to a site that wants to send your browser a Cookie, Netscape will pop up a warning box telling you of the attempt, where it will be sent, and how long it will persist on the remote server. You can then click on OK to send the Cookie or Cancel to refuse it. You'll be amazed how often you're asked to supply a Cookie.

Making Yourself Anonymous

Another way to secure your privacy on the Web is to use The Anonymizer. Created by the Community Connexion, The Anonymizer is a site that helps you shield your personal information from eavesdroppers. When you visit its Web site (http://www.anonymizer.com/), you are assigned an anonymous identity that is revealed when you move around the Internet. Any attempt to track your true identity is thus foiled. You can see The Anonymizer's home page in Figure 11.16.

The Anonymizer server retrieves any information you request and then passes the document along to you. It then purges your host name so that your

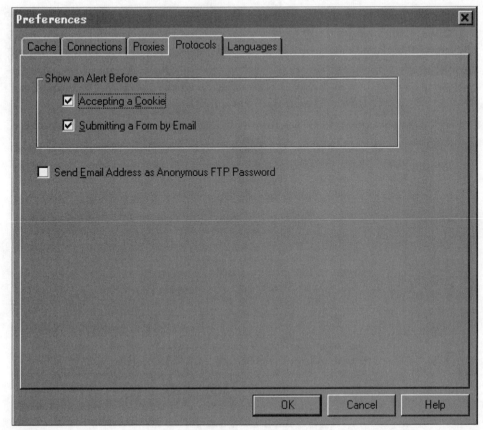

Figure 11.15 The Protocols pane allows you to be warned whenever Netscape is being asked to accept a Cookie.

identity doesn't appear in any logs. All references to personal information are stripped out before the Web pages are passed along to you.

And if secure e-mail is your goal, you may want to consider an anonymous remailer site. By logging on through one of these, you are acquiring an e-mail pseudonym; any mail you send goes out under the pseudonym, providing you with a new identity. But here, too, there are two obvious issues. A database at the remailer site matches your true identity with your pseudonym, so you're still known to somebody. And like any Web site, a remailer's site can be attacked by crackers, potentially exposing your identity.

One good site for learning about remailers is http://www.stack.nl/~galactus/remailers/. You can see this page, dedicated to anonymity on the Web, in Figure 11.17. Another remailer list can be found at http://kiwi.cs.berkeley.edu/~raph/remailer-list.html. The most famous remailer site of all, anon.penet.fi, was forced to close recently, but numerous other options are found on the pre-

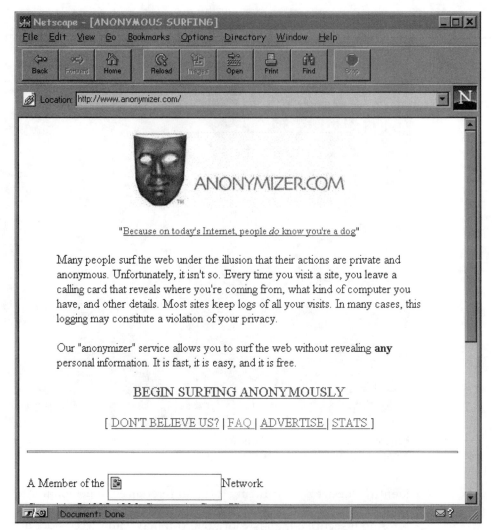

Figure 11.16   The home page for The Anonymizer, a site that lets you purge your real identity and travel the Net anonymously.

ceding page. Remailers can even be chained together to maximize your chances for complete anonymity.

Pretty Good Privacy for Secure E-Mail

If you're interested in trying out Phil Zimmerman's Pretty Good Privacy program, you can find it at http://bs.mit.edu:8001/pgp-form.html. The program is DOS-based, making it ideal for those who enjoy command-line complexity. But if you'd prefer a Windows interface, numerous front ends are available.

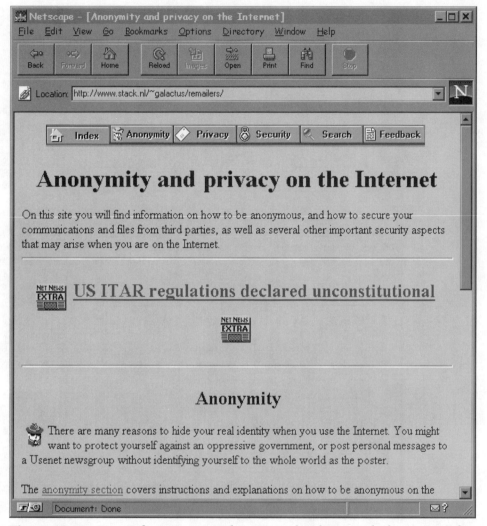

Figure 11.17 Issues of anonymity can be examined at this site, which contains information about using remailers for privacy.

Figure 11.18, for example, shows Scott A. Hauert's collection of front ends (http://www.primenet.com/~shauert/pgpwins.htm). Some are relatively specialized, attaching to specific mail programs, while others work with multiple applications.

  For my use, Walter Heindl's Lock & Key works as well as any, and includes an excellent Windows interface. You can find the program, now in version 3.0, at Heindl's home page (http://www.voicenet.com/~wheindl/). Lock & Key is tightly integrated with the Windows Explorer. To decrypt files, you simply double-click them; a right-click encrypts them. Text can be encrypted in the

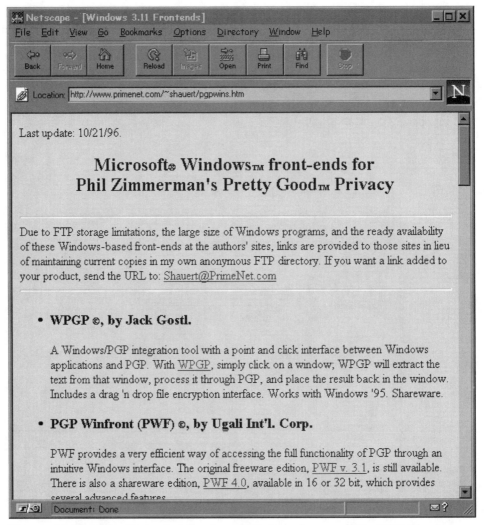

Figure 11.18 Scott Hauert's collection of Windows front ends for PGP, allowing you to use encryption in the Windows environment.

clipboard and then pasted into your mail program. You can easily view the digital signature of any encrypted message you have received. The program is shareware and carries a $15 registration fee.

With both PGP and Lock & Key on hand, we're ready to install the software. The PGP installation involves unzipping the downloaded archive file to a directory of your choice. You then add a reference to this directory in your autoexec.bat file by adding the following line:

```
set pgpath=c:\pgp
```

In my case, the file reads set pgpath=e:\pgp, because I keep many of my executable programs on the E: drive, but you can adapt the line to your own storage requirements.

You also need to set another line into your autoexec.bat file. This is the MS-DOS tz variable, which tells the operating system which time zone you are in. PGP will use this to create time stamps for its keys and signatures. Since I am on the East Coast, I insert this line into autoexec.bat:

    set tz=est5edt

Someone on the West Coast would insert this:

    set tz=pst8pdt

And so on. The numerical value is based on the differential between the site and Greenwich Mean Time. Thus my East Coast setting tells the software that in standard time I am five hours behind Greenwich Mean Time. London, then, would have a tz value of tz=gmt0bst, the 0 reflecting the fact that London is in the same time zone as Greenwich. A full explanation of the tz variable is found in the PGP documentation, which comes with the program download.

The easiest way to edit your autoexec.bat file is to use the Windows Notepad, which is a basic text editor (you could also do it by giving the **edit autoexec.bat** command at the DOS command prompt). In Figure 11.19, you can see my autoexec.bat file being edited in Notepad. Once you've added this line to your file, your computer will be ready to deal with PGP each time it is booted up.

The next step is to create the public and private keys that will be the basis of your security system. This requires you to go to a DOS prompt in the directory where you put the PGP files.

    1. From the DOS prompt, enter **pgp -kg**.

PGP will then take you through a set of prompts that allow you to create the public and private key pair. You will have a choice of three levels of security:

512 bits	Low commercial grade; fast but less secure
768 bits	High commercial grade; medium speed, good security
1024 bits	Military grade; slow, highest security

I recommend you begin with 768 bits; you can always change this value later.

You will next be asked to create a user ID for your public key. This is usually done by adding your mailing address in brackets to your name. Thus a typical user ID might be George Wilson <gwilson@unc.edu>. Type in the user ID of your choice, spaces and all, as shown in the example.

Finally, you will be asked to choose a pass phrase that will protect your secret key. The pass phrase can be any sentence or phrase and can include words, spaces, punctuation, or any other printable characters. You will be asked to type this information twice, after which PGP will create your keys.

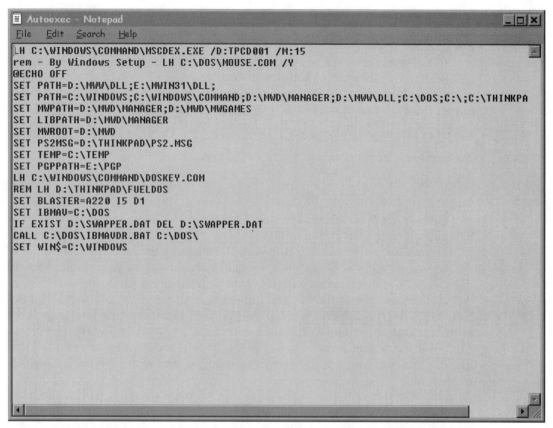

```
Autoexec - Notepad                                                    _ □ X
File   Edit   Search   Help
LH C:\WINDOWS\COMMAND\MSCDEX.EXE /D:TPCD001 /M:15
rem - By Windows Setup - LH C:\DOS\MOUSE.COM /Y
@ECHO OFF
SET PATH=D:\MWW\DLL;E:\MWIN31\DLL;
SET PATH=C:\WINDOWS;C:\WINDOWS\COMMAND;D:\MWD\MANAGER;D:\MWW\DLL;C:\DOS;C:\;C:\THINKPA
SET MWPATH=D:\MWD\MANAGER;D:\MWD\MWGAMES
SET LIBPATH=D:\MWD\MANAGER
SET MWROOT=D:\MWD
SET PS2MSG=D:\THINKPAD\PS2.MSG
SET TEMP=C:\TEMP
SET PGPPATH=E:\PGP
LH C:\WINDOWS\COMMAND\DOSKEY.COM
REM LH D:\THINKPAD\FUELDOS
SET BLASTER=A220 I5 D1
SET IBMAV=C:\DOS
IF EXIST D:\SWAPPER.DAT DEL D:\SWAPPER.DAT
CALL C:\DOS\IBMAVDR.BAT C:\DOS\
SET WIN$=C:\WINDOWS
```

Figure 11.19 The Windows Notepad is the best place to edit your autoexec.bat file.

When key generation is complete, you can extract your public key to a separate file so it can be sent to other people. Here's how:

2. At the DOS prompt, type **pgp -kx** *name*, where *name* is all or part of the name you entered when you generated your key.

PGP will prompt you for an output filename, which must have the extension .pgp. Give it any name you choose. You can then send this file to anyone who wants to send you an encrypted message; it's your public key.

PGP is now installed and you can proceed with the installation of Lock & Key to provide a graphical interface to it. Before proceeding, reboot your computer to make sure that the changes you have made to the autoexec.bat file take effect. Lock & Key is downloaded as an archived zip file; once unpacked, you can simply click on the install program to activate it. Note: The program is written in Microsoft Visual Basic and requires that a file called vb40032.dll be available in your c:\windows\system\ directory. The installation program will prompt you if you don't already have this file on your system. If you don't, it is available for download from Walter Heindl's home page.

Let's assume that I want to send an encrypted file to an associate. The method is simple:

1. Right-click on the file in Explorer.
2. Select Send To.
3. Click on Lock & Key. The Lock & Key panel should appear, as shown in Figure 11.20.
4. Enter the name (or part of the name) of the public key of the intended recipient.
5. Click the Windows Clipboard button under Output.

After being encrypted, the file will be sent to the Windows Clipboard. In my mail program, I can simply choose the Paste function to put the file into my open message to that party. If I had chosen a different output option, the file would have been encrypted and renamed with a .pgp extension in the same directory where the output file was located. The original file is not affected by this operation. Notice that if I had chosen to provide a digital signature, I could have done so by clicking on the Signature box, at which time I would have been prompted to insert my pass phrase.

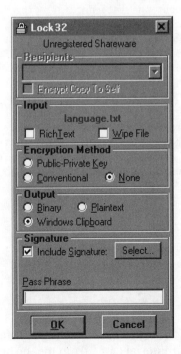

Figure 11.20 The Lock & Key panel provides quick conversion options for documents through Windows Explorer.

Tip: Lock & Key provides two other output options. Binary should be used if your electronic mail format allows you to deliver mail in binary form, or if you plan to deliver the file on diskette. Encrypted binary files are given the .pgp extension. Armored is for mail programs that cannot manage binary files; it provides files with an .asc extension.

As you can see, using **PGP** with Lock & Key is relatively simple; you can encrypt a message to anyone as long as you have his or her public key, and Lock & Key provides a keyring feature that stores these keys. Double-clicking a file allows you to decrypt it using your private key. Notice that it's possible to send a file in unencrypted form but with a digital signature attached to verify who sent it. If the recipient can unlock the message with your public key, then he or she knows it is actually from you.

Here is what a message with a digital signature looks like. In this message, I am sending a standard bio to the publicist for an organization I will be addressing in a few days:

```
-----BEGIN PGP SIGNED MESSAGE-----
Paul Gilster -- biographical information


Paul Gilster is a freelance writer specializing in computers and technol-
ogy. He is the author of six books about the Internet, all from John Wiley
& Sons: Digital Literacy (1997), The New Internet Navigator (3rd Ed.,
1995), Finding It on the Internet (2nd Ed., 1995), The Mosaic Navigator
(1995), The SLIP/PPP Connection (1995), and The Web Navigator (1997).
Gilster is a regular columnist for Carolina Computer News and a frequent
contributor to CompuServe Magazine; he has written essays, feature stories,
reviews and fiction for a wide range of publications both in and out of the
computing field. For the past nine years, he has written the weekly  Com-
puter Focus  column, which now appears in The News & Observer (Raleigh,
NC). Before launching his writing career in 1985, he was, at various times,
a specialist in medieval literature, a commercial pilot, and the owner of a
wine shop. Even his wife got confused.

-----BEGIN PGP SIGNATURE-----
Version: 2.6.2


iQB1AwUBMrGiJTuubARFzx8RAQE1OwMAvFUDgi8tvOy9MbH/fIeIRJTQiG/Lv131
7x1dmwkYZG7rW6zfdJDgI6q819rGh6Q7XfYaWdgOG1UjKOjCxaWU/OSyYbJnHhT+
AHoqizol6mSZjfVkQG1uSdg49cBcxP2C
=o6zV
-----END PGP SIGNATURE-----
```

You can see that **PGP** has inserted the signature following my statement. If my recipient wanted to verify that this material came from me, he or she could use my public key to decrypt the signature. Only my private key could have created it.

PGP creator Phil Zimmermann, incidentally, has introduced a new security product called PGPcookie.cutter, a plug-in for Netscape that will let users block Cookie files selectively. The program tracks Cookie requests and who made them. You can read more about this new plug-in at http://www.pgp.com/.

The Rise of the Junk Mailers

Extracting information about users can only profit junk mailers, those people and companies who obtain your electronic mail address and send messages through the system to promote their services or products. Whether this is truly an invasion of privacy depends on your definitions, since we're all subjected to junk mail through the postal service and tend to accept it with resignation, if not enthusiasm. But junk mail on the Net does tell us that people are extracting information from us without our knowledge and using that information to try to sell us things, very much like the situation when a magazine sells its subscription list to marketers.

Users are clearly unhappy with the amount of junk mail now being generated. America Online, reacting to user complaints, began to block unsolicited e-mail from some of the larger bulk mail senders in 1996, prompting a court fight that AOL won when a federal judge determined that no First Amendment right exists to send unsolicited mail. Mass mailings like this, based on databases created from various sources, are known as spam, and despite the efforts of AOL and other providers, the phenomenon is likely to continue. One response is to tune up your e-mail program. A program like Eudora, for example, allows you to set up filters that automatically send certain types of content, based on keywords you provide, to your trash bin.

For Web discussions about the junk mail phenomenon, and suggestions on how to trace spam attacks and work with ISPs on the subject, consult some of the following pages:

> http://kryten.eng.monash.edu.au/gspam.html: Helpful tips for identifying the origins of junk mail.
> http://www.ee.umd.edu/medlab/filter: The Information Filtering Resources page maintained by the University of Maryland. Filtering systems can sift junk mail out of your system.
> http://www.mcs.com/~jcr/junkemail.html: The Stop Junk E-Mail page, replete with case histories and news from the battle to stop junk mail. Here you'll find the most complete set of tips I've seen for lodging complaints against junk mailers.

The Clipper Chip: Federal Law and Privacy

What would you think about a chip embedded in your telephone that provides you with unbreakable encryption of your calls for maximum privacy?

How about using the same technology for your electronic mail? Sounds like a good idea.

But what if you then combined that chip with a secret code methodology known only to the National Security Agency? And what if the law required you to give your encryption keys, which could unlock any or all of your communications, to the federal government? The idea, floated under the name Clipper, was controversial from the moment it was voiced by the Clinton administration in 1993. And while public reaction to the chip and its own flawed design sank it, the administration has unveiled a new variation on the theme.

Today, under the name Clipper III, the chip has given way to a software-based encryption tool using methods that are standard within the computer industry. In all three versions, Clipper has shared the idea that you should yield your encryption key to a third party. In this way, the government maintained the option of listening in on conversations that could presumably involve terrorism, or drug dealing, or other activities well outside the law. Programs like PGP, on the other hand, use key technology the way it was designed to be used; only you have access to your secret key, and the use of the technology is to validate that a particular message comes from a particular person. The private key remains your possession.

You can check the latest Clipper proposal at the site of an organization that continues to scrutinize and criticize government policy in this area, the Electronic Frontier Foundation. The address is http://www.eff.org/pub/Privacy/Key _escrow/. You can see this page, which includes links to numerous archives, in Figure 11.21.

The first Clipper proposal revolved around an encryption standard that would have been designed in Washington. Its new incarnation looks to nongovernmental agencies to hold the vital keys to decrypting messages. The policy is aimed at the export market, in hopes of keeping encryption software of the most powerful kinds out of the hands of criminals.

The U.S. government presently limits the export of heavy-duty encryption technology, under the assumption that having it fall into the wrong hands is tantamount to arming its enemies. The Clipper proposal would continue to make encryption available within the United States while supposedly keeping it out of the hands of foreign governments and individuals because of its tight control by the government. What the proposal seems to ignore is that encryption software of various kinds is already widespread. The Internet is one vehicle by which such software readily crosses international boundaries, and it has been doing so for some time.

The ongoing battle over export controls for encryption will be one to watch. As this book went to press, a report by the National Research Council endorsed relaxing although not eliminating export controls on the technology. The debate over individual privacy versus government's need to know remains one of the Net's most controversial.

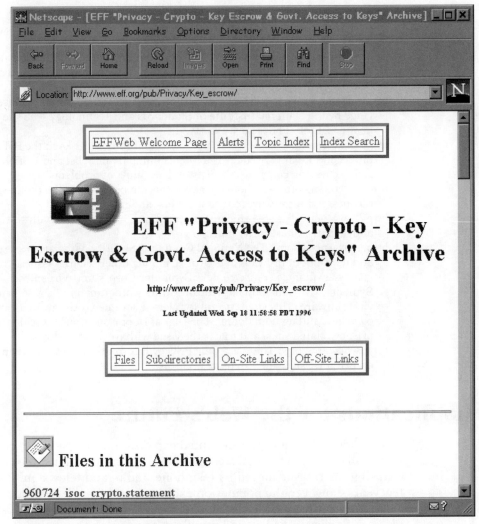

Figure 11.21 The Electronic Frontier Foundation maintains extensive archives on the issue of exporting encryption software.

Privacy and Security-Related Sites

Numerous sites are tracking developments in Internet security and the related question of privacy. You may want to examine some of the following to keep up with the news:

> http://www.gocsi.com/: The Computer Security Institute in San Francisco offers a variety of informational material on computer security. Includes numerous links for professionals in the field.

http://ciac.llnl.gov/: The Computer Incident Advisory Capability site for the
 U.S. Department of Energy provides updates on recently uncovered security
 problems.

http://www.genome.wi.mit.edu/WWW/faqs/: Among other Frequently Asked
 Questions documents available here, MIT offers a useful breakdown of Web-
 based security problems.

http://csrc.ncsl.nist.gov/: The Computer Security Resource Clearinghouse is provided by the National Institute of Standards and Technology. The site offers publications, tools, and security alerts.

http://catless.ncl.ac.uk/Risks/VL.IS.html: The Forum on Risks to the Public in Computers and Related Systems is a long-running mailing list and USENET newsgroup covering computer security and accounts of problems.

http://www.rsa.com/: The home page for this major player in the on-line security
 business, with software, position papers, and news.

http://www.netwalk.com/~silicon/episteme.html: Infinity Void, with software tools
 and hacking and security links.

http://www.ncsa.com/: The National Computer Security Association site offers tips
 and news about firewalls and viruses, among other security issues.

http://www.symantec.com/avcenter/: Symantec Corp.'s Anti-Virus Research Center.
 Symantec owns the popular Norton Utilities program and its associated anti-
 viral software. This site is useful for alerts about newly discovered viruses.

http://www.CataLaw.com/doom/: The Digital Doomsday Clock provides links to
 privacy-related sites, and tracks the issue with frequent updates.

http://www.epic.org/: The Electronic Privacy Information Center contains updates
 on privacy issues and extensive archives.

Implications for the Web's Future

Business is fueling an unprecedented expansion in the Net; in fact, this technology has become the fastest-growing communications tool in history,
eclipsing the rates achieved by telephone, radio, and television. For the next
few years, however, the population explosion on-line will continue to sap network bandwidth, causing slowdowns that frustrate all but the most committed user. Service providers will soon have to adapt to the changing scale of the
market. Flat-rate pricing, now becoming a norm not only in this country but
in some parts of Europe, is in the long run a nonstarter; it will soon be
replaced by usage-based pricing, in which customers pay for the bandwidth
they consume. We can envision, for example, a flat-rate e-mail and newsgroup
service, with value-added pricing for such high-bandwidth accessories as
video teleconferencing.

Changing the pricing model will relieve pressure on the infrastructure and
allow time for building new capacity. Two years from now, the growth in cable
television modems and satellite Internet delivery, and the emerging deployment of fast modems equipped with Asynchronous Digital Subscriber Loop
(ADSL) technology, will begin to ease that pressure even more. Data downloads that would freeze the clock today will become commonplace. Live audio

and video on the Web will be standard fare, leading to numerous experiments from broadcasters of all stripes, while the tools of video production will rapidly be deployed among end users. Web-based video software will become the desktop publishing tool of the new millennium, allowing anyone with a minimal investment to go live on-line with home or office-produced content. This content will doubtless be highly variable, but as with television today, a few gems will shine through.

The Internet security crisis will never be fully resolved, for it is in the nature of human business that every time you put a new lock on the door, thieves figure out a new way to pick it. But we are at the edge of an era in which Net commerce is as resistant to tampering as other forms of transaction, and that should force rapid developments in the areas of on-line banking and brokerage services. Retail purchases will shake out according to product; we don't know yet what goods are most compatible to on-line selling, although it's clear that books are a winner; and the ability to search databases makes using on-line catalogs significantly faster than their paper-based alternatives. Supplementing shopping with access to other purchasers for comments and questions is a natural outcome.

Bringing Web technology into the living room has already begun to happen, as witness the arrival of so-called WebTVs, which allow you to surf the Net from the comfort of your couch. The products are unlikely to succeed, however. The Web remains both a graphic and textual medium, while reading text on a television screen is demanding and unproductive. Nor does the WebTV provide the flexibility offered by even the simplest computer, with its ability to download and try out new software, move quickly between Net sessions and local chores like word processing or family finances, and adapt to the preferences of the individual user. This same drawback will limit the spread of NetPCs, machines stripped down for targeted Net use, to business. Their ability to be standardized and managed from a central server suits large corporate environments, but is unattractive to the average user, who counts on the power of the local processor and its liberating range of choice.

Browser technology will continue to evolve, though perhaps at a slower pace as the market begins to settle. Despite predictions to the contrary, I do not believe that Microsoft will destroy Netscape, whose browser is already widely deployed and appreciated for its elegance of design. One factor holding back conversion to other browsers is the wide range of helper applications and plug-in programs we use to view various types of content. Changing browsers can mean upgrading that software, not always a task for the faint of heart, and one that home users may choose to avoid. Netscape, meanwhile, will press its advantage in the corporate intranet market, connecting business to business through private networks that resist standardization around a single standard dictated by Microsoft.

Expect developments in virtual reality to come fast and furious as the Web grows. VR offers advantages in terms of modeling complex environments that other forms of training cannot match. Crafting virtual worlds and manipulating them over tomorrow's broad bandwidth network will allow us to develop education and corporate training packages that simulate everything from nuclear reactors to weather patterns. The early impetus for VR has been in the realm of chat and community building, but its potential as an educational tool is breathtaking. While the standard interface will continue to be the browser, with its pull-down menus and mouse-driven commands, virtual reality displayed through that browser will become a factor at more and more sites, making Web content manipulable and didactic.

A commerce-driven Internet is a great departure from the research-based network that emerged in the 1970s and gradually changed the way we communicate. Adapting to the commercial model is inevitable if the Net is to continue its growth into the mainstream of our culture. But commerce and social responsibility must coexist, and the great rush into cyberspace must not occur without consideration of its implications for education, art, and the public welfare. The questions this chapter has raised about privacy and security point to the broader questions we must ask about technology. Specifically, how does it help us? How does it help the broader culture? We know that the Net can be used to make money. But we must also ask whether it can be used as a driver for the moral and ethical enhancement of society.

These issues are not peculiar to the Net. They tug at the nature of libertarian democracy, calling us to defend the right of deregulated commerce at the same time that we point to an obligation of public service. The World Wide Web simply makes this fault line stand out more distinctly on the intellectual map. Its terrain is seemingly limitless; its future is at our discharge. We need to put libraries into that landscape as well as storefronts. We need to enhance the people's access to government, as well as offering them more things to buy. We need to defend privacy. Such commitments will keep the tension between unbridled capitalism and the social welfare vibrant, a dynamism that can foster cultural change and economic growth.

A Web without adequate attention to education, learning, and the possibility of universal access is a disturbing compartmentalization of a great technology. If today's Web is largely a phenomenon of the developed world, we must press for its growth in Africa, southern Asia, and Latin America, making it worldwide in more than name. A major task as we end the decade must be the digitization of our books, magazines, and newspapers (especially older, archival materials), and a resolution of the nagging problems of intellectual property that restrict their spread. All these issues demand rigorous inquiry and honest labor, but I have learned to be an optimist. If we can build a World Wide Web out of nothing but silicon and wire, we can surely defend the high ground of its principled deployment.

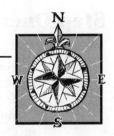

Appendix: Configuring Windows 95 for the Internet

Many Windows 95 users work with third-party software to run their TCP/IP connection to the Internet, often because that's what they were given when they first opened their account. The problem with this is that many of these TCP/IP 'stacks' are 16-bit software, whereas the stack built into Windows 95 allows you to run 32-bit versions of the major Net programs, offering performance increases that are worth acquiring. And in my own experience, the Windows 95 stack is also more stable. We're moving into a 32-bit world, and it makes sense to put Windows 95 to work for your connection.

The problem, however, is that the setup isn't easy to fathom. So here is a methodology which should get you up and running with Windows 95. Using these methods, you'll be able to dial into your PPP account and launch client programs with the Windows 95 stack. You'll need to have by your side the documentation your provider gave you when you signed up for an account. This should contain all the necessary information to fill in the necessary fields in TCP/IP, including: your user name and password; your host name; the domain name of your service provider; the provider's gateway address; the provider's DNS address; the provider's IP subnet mask; and the telephone number you'll need to call. Don't hesitate to call your provider if you don't know which value to plug into a particular field.

Step One: Dynamic or Static Addressing?

A crucial piece of information for your installation is to determine the type of addressing that your provider offers. Chances are your account uses a dynamic IP address, which means that the address can vary each time you sign on. But some providers work with static IP addresses that stay the same each time you log onto the Net. Check the materials your provider gave you when you signed up for an account; if you still can't tell which kind of addressing is being used, call your provider. We'll use this information below as we configure the Windows 95 TCP/IP options.

Step Two: Install Dial-Up Networking

We now need to see whether the Windows 95 Dial-Up Networking component has been installed. To do this, click on the My Computer icon. You should see various icons in the resulting window, including one marked Dial-Up Networking, provided it has already been installed on your system. If it has, you can skip to the Installing TCP/IP section below. If it hasn't, you'll need to follow these procedures. Be sure to have your installation disks or CD-ROM at hand.

1. Click Start.
2. Select Settings.
3. Click Control Panel.
4. Double-click Add/Remove Programs.
5. Click the Windows Setup tab.
6. Double-click on Communications. The Communications box will appear, as shown in Figure A.1.

A check mark should appear next to the Dial-Up Networking option. If it doesn't, click on the box to insert it.

7. Click OK.
8. Click Apply in the Add/Remove Programs box.

The Dial-Up Networking component is now installed and you can proceed with the rest of the TCP/IP installation.

Step Three: Installing TCP/IP

It is now time to install the TCP/IP protocol and the Dial Up Adapter software that allows you to connect via your modem. First, it's necessary to check to see if TCP/IP is already present.

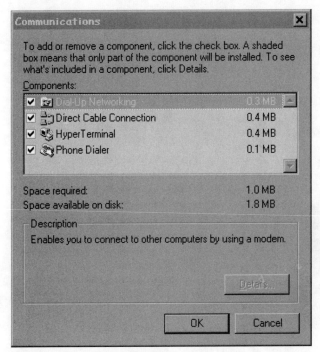

Figure A.1 The Communications box, where you should check to see that Dial-Up Networking is installed.

1. Click on Start.
2. Choose Settings.
3. Click on Control Panel.
4. Double-click on the Network icon.
5. Click on the Configuration tab.

Both Dial-Up Adapter and TCP/IP should appear in the window.
   If TCP/IP is not present there, do the following:

1. Click on Add. The Select Network Protocol box will appear, as shown in Figure A.2.
2. Double-click Protocol.
3. Select Microsoft.
4. Select TCP/IP.
5. Click on OK.
6. In the Select Devices box, select Microsoft.
7. Select Dial-Up Adapter.

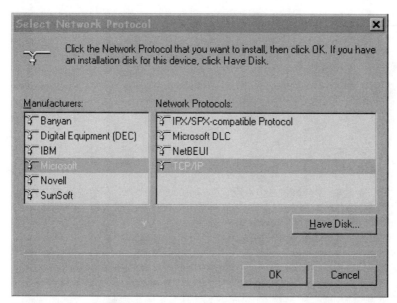

Figure A.2 The Select Network Protocol box, where I have selected Microsoft and TCP/IP.

8. Click OK.
9. In the Network dialog box, click OK.

If the Dial-Up Adapter alone is not present, do the following:

1. Click on Add.
2. Double-click on Adapter.
3. Select Microsoft.
4. Select Dial-Up Adapter.
5. Click OK.
6. In the Network dialog box, click OK.

Both TCP/IP and Dial-Up Adapter should now be visible in the Network dialog box.

Windows 95 will have probably installed other protocols that you don't need. You can remove any of these except Microsoft Client, Dial-Up Adapter, and TCP/IP. For example, if you find the IPX/SPX-compatible Protocol installed, highlight it and click the Remove button.

1. Now double-click on Dial-Up Adapter in the Network dialog box.
2. Click on Bindings.
3. Verify that the TCP/IP box is checked.

4. Click on OK.

5. In the Network dialog box, click on OK.

Step Four: TCP/IP Configuration

To configure TCP/IP, take the following steps:

1. Go back to the Control Panel.

2. Double-click the Network icon.

3. Select TCP/IP in the Network box.

4. Click the Properties button.

5. Select the DNS Configuration tab. This tab is shown in Figure A.3.

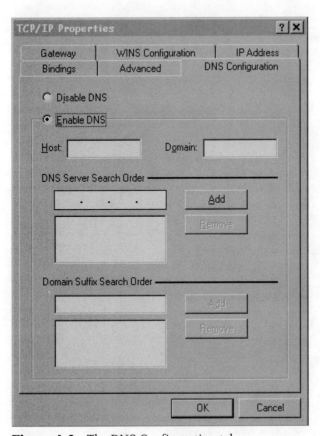

Figure A.3 The DNS Configuration tab.

In The DNS Configuration Tab

1. Click on Enable DNS.

2. Enter your username in the Host field.

3. Enter the domain name of your service provider in the Domain: field.

4. Enter the IP address of your service provider's name server in the DNS Server Search Order section. This number should have been provided by your service provider. If you have any questions about what these numbers should be or what order they should be entered in, call your provider or double-check the documentation that came when you opened your account.

5. In the Domain Suffix Search Order box, enter the domain suffix for your provider; this is usually the same as the domain name.

6. Click the Add button.

7. Select the Gateway tab. This tab is shown in Figure A.4.

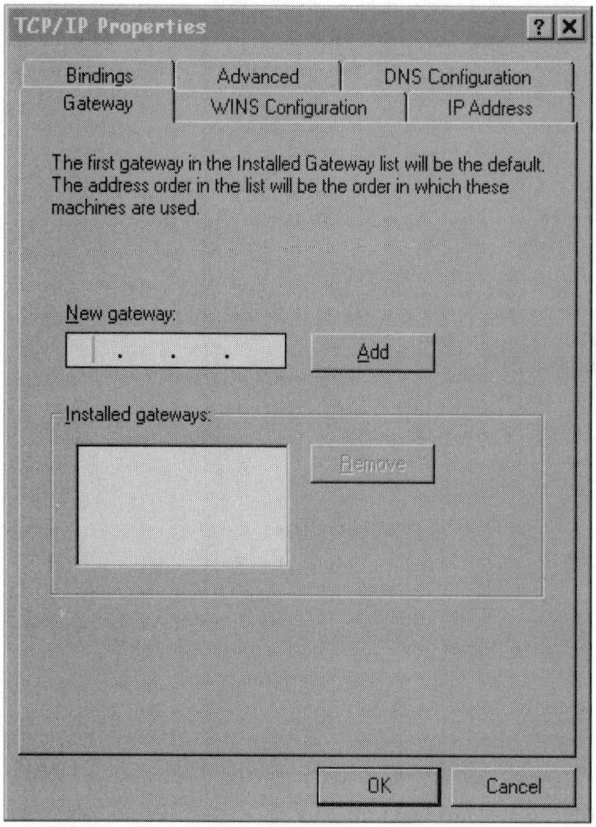

Figure A.4   The Gateway tab.

In the Gateway Tab

1. Enter a value for Installed Gateways that corresponds to the value given by your service provider. A value of 0.0.0.0 can be tried if you don't know the correct number; if this doesn't work, check with your provider.
2. Click Add.
3. Select the IP address tab. You can see this tab in Figure A.5.

In the IP Address Tab

If your service provider offers a static IP address (i.e., the address doesn't change every time you log on), do the following:

1. Select Specify an IP Address.
2. Enter the IP address that came with your documentation.

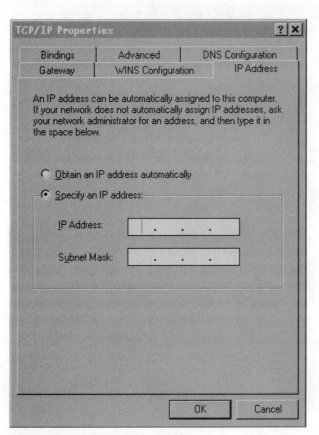

Figure A.5   The IP Address tab.

However, if your service provider offers a dynamic IP address (changing it every time you log on), select Obtain an IP address automatically.

If you're using static addressing, enter the Subnet Mask: value given by your service provider.

Click on WINS Configuration. The WINS Configuration tab will appear. You can see this tab in Figure A.6.

In the WINS Configuration Tab

Confirm that Disable WINS Resolution is checked.

TCP/IP has now been configured. To implement these changes:

1. Click on OK in the TCP/IP Properties box.
2. Click on OK in the Network box.

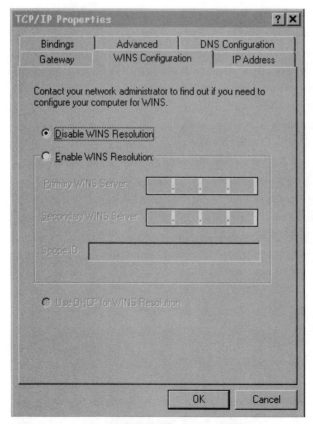

Figure A.6 The WINS Configuration tab.

3. You will be prompted to re-start your computer so the new settings can take place. Click Yes to choose this option and re-start your machine.

Configuring Dial-Up Networking

We must now configure the connection you are using to your service provider. Here's how:

1. Click on the My Computer icon.
2. Double-click the Dial-Up Networking icon.
3. Double-click Make New Connection.
4. The Microsoft Make New Connection Wizard will appear, as shown in Figure A.7.
5. Choose a name for the connection, based on the name of your service provider.
6. Click the Configure button.
7. Click the General tab.
8. Set your modem speed. Due to data compression, you can set a 14.4 Kbps modem to 57600, while a 28.8 modem should be set to 115200. Do not click the Only connect at this speed box; doing so may prevent your modem from connecting at different speeds.

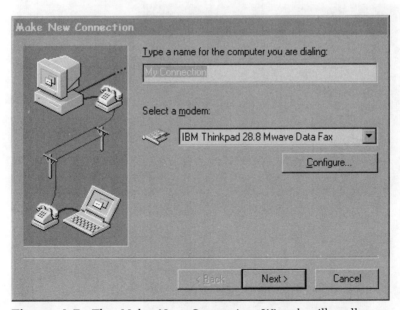

Figure A.7 The Make New Connection Wizard will walk you through the process of configuring your connection.

9. Click the Options tab.

10. Leave the Bring up terminal window after dialing option unchecked.

11. Click OK.

12. Click Next.

13. Enter the phone number to dial, as provided by your service provider.

14. Click Next.

15. Click Finish.

The Dial-up Networking folder should now have an icon for your new connection.

Step Five: Configuring the Connection

In the Dial-Up Networking window, select the connection you just created.

1. Click the right mouse button to call up a menu.

2. Click on Properties.

3. Click the Server Type button. You can see the Server Types dialog box in Figure A.8.

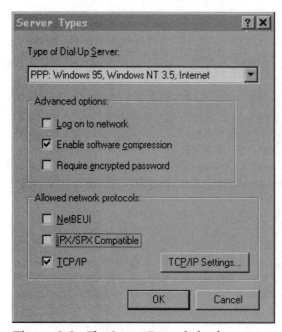

Figure A.8   The Server Types dialog box.

4. Check that the Type of Server reads PPP:Windows 95, Windows NT 3.5, Internet.

5. In the Advanced Options box, verify that Enable Software Compression is selected and nothing else.

6. In the Allowed Network Protocols selection, verify that only TCP/IP is selected.

7. Click on OK.

8. Click on OK in the Properties box.

Step Six: Making the Call

To dial your provider, double-click on the provider's icon in the Dial-Up Networking box. In the Connect To dialog box, enter your user name and password.

Click on Connect.

Your modem should now dial your provider's number. You can now run your client programs as needed as soon as Windows 95 logs you into your provider's computer.

In Case of Trouble

If the connection fails to work, try the following:

1. Double-click on My Computer.
2. Double-click on the Dial-Up Networking icon.
3. Select the icon for your connection.
4. Click the right mouse button.
5. Click on Properties.
6. Click on Configure.
7. Click on the Options tab.
8. Click on Bring up terminal window after dialing.
9. Click on OK.
10. Click on OK in the Properties box.

Changing this setting will result in the connection being handled somewhat differently. When you place your call, the terminal window will appear after you connect. You can then enter your user name and password. When it appears:

1. Enter your user name.
2. Press RETURN.

3. Enter your password.

4. Press RETURN.

5. Click on Continue.

The connection should now proceed. You will receive a dialog box that shows you are connected.

If the connection still fails, try disabling software compression in the Server Type dialog box.

And be aware that further connection help is available on-line. The Windows 95 TCP/IP Setup How-To FAQ is available at this URL:

http://www.aa.net/pcd/slp95faq.html

Index

A

Access to the Internet, 99
  evolution of, 64–67
  local, 98. *See also* Service providers
  telephone, *see* Telephone service
  types, 72–80
Access Net Directory, 97. *See also* Prodigy
Acrobat Reader, 177–179
ACTA, *see* American Carriers Telecommu-
    nication Association
ActiveX, 275–276, 277–278, 285–287
  security and, 430
  Web pages featuring, 287, 288
Adapt/X, 447
Add-ons, 146, 147. *See also* Helper appli-
    cations; Plug-ins
Addresses:
  E-mail, 40, 55
  Internet, 39–41. *See also* URL
  IP, 39–41
Adobe, 178
Adobe Acrobat, 176–179
ADSL, 76–77
  vs. ISDN, 76–77, 79–80
Advanced Research Projects Agency, 29

@dver@active, 158
Advertising, Net-based, 60. *See also*
    Commerce, on-line
Agents, 307–318, 358–363
  defined, 307, 308–309
  limitations of, 318
  possibilities of, 308, 310–311
  search engines and, 307
  standards, 311
  up-and-coming, 316–317
Agents Inc., 308
Aliasing domain names, *see* Domain
    names
AlphaConnect, 311
Alpha Microsystems, 311
AlphaWorld, 298
Alta Vista, 20, 21
  vs. HotBot, 329–331
  how it works, 324
  using, 320–324, 326–329
amazon.com, 60, 419–421, 422
American National Standards Institute,
    see ANSI
America Online, 67, 80, 92–94, 446
  front-end interface superior to Compu-
    Serve's, 95

posting personal Web pages on,
    409–411
ubiquity of, 106
America's Carriers Telecommunications
    Association, 294
Analog information, 69, 74
    vs. ISDN, 74–76
Andreessen, Marc, 56, 58
Animation, 158
Anonymity, on-line, *see* Privacy
Anonymous FTP, *see* FTP
ANS, 446
ANSI, 260, 261
AOL, *see* America Online
API, 148
Applets, 278, 279, 282, 285
    vs. applications, 281–282
    hostile, 280
Application Program Interface, *see* API
Applications, Java, *see* Applets
archie, 43, 44, 319
ARPANET, 31, 33, 36, 206, 233, 426. *See
    also* MILNET
ASCII files, 176, 249
Asymetrix, 148
Asymmetric Digital Subscriber Line, *see*
    ADSC
AT&T, 64, 80–83, 86
AT&T WorldNet, 80–83, 86, 96
Audio, *see* Sound
Authentication, methods of, 433–435
Autonomy, 358–360
Avatars, 42, 298. *See also* Virtual reality
AVI, 167–168
Aware, 77

B

Backstage Designer Plus, 396
Bandwidth:
    expansion of, 37, 66, 78, 175
    flagrant waste of, 205
    maximizing available, 74
    problems involving, 74–75, 169,
        306–307
    wholesalers of, 89
Baran, Paul, 30
BBS, *see* Bulletin boards

Bell Telephone, 67, 77
    RBOCs, 81, 85
Bellcore, 447
Bennahum, David, 389–390
Berners-Lee, Tim, 45, 297
Bina, Eric, 56
Binary information, 69
BITNET, 206, 207, 210
BIX, 65
Blinding, 442
Bolt, Beranek, and Newman, 31
Bookmarks, 121–130
    changing, 125
    creating multiple bookmark lists, 126
    creating new folders, 123–124
    inserting, 129–130
    limiting display of menued, 130
    search result pages and, 351
    smart, 315–316, 317
    sorting, 124
    updating, 127–128
    using separators, 127
Boolean operators, *see* Searching
Browsers, 3, 25, 56–58, 73
    basic operation of, 107–112
    best available, 105–106
    bookmarks, *see* Bookmarks
    choosing, 94
    e-mail and, *see* E-mail
    interface of, 106–107
    features of, 20, 25, 40, 112–131
    newsgroups and, *see* Newsgroups
    proprietary, 93–94
    ubiquity of, 106
    using more than one at the same time,
        119–120
Bulletin boards, 35, 65, 262, 263
Bush, Vannevar, 27–29, 62
Business, on-line, 418–419. *See also*
        Commerce, on-line

C

C++, 281
Cable modems, *see* Modems
Cable television, 74
    Internet connection via, 38, 77–78
    wireless, 79

Caches, 59, 111, 143
    privacy issues and, 447–449
Cailliau, Robert, 45
Carter, Jimmy, 166
CD-ROM, 168
Cellular modems, *see* Modems
Cellular telephone, Internet connection
    via, 38
Cerf, Vinton, 31, 83
CERN, 45, 49, 53
Certificates, digital, *see* Digital certifi-
    cates
Chatting, *see* Virtual communities
CheckFree, 442
City University of New York, 207
CJLI, *see* Mailing lists
Claris Home Page, 397–402
Client programs, 42–43
Client/server computing, 42–43
    thin clients, 285
Clipper chips, *see* Privacy
Clock speed, 168
C/Net, 12
CNN Interactive, 11–13, 167
Coaxial cable, 77
Codecs, 161, 289
Comic book companies, 158
Command Job Language Interpreter, *see*
    Mailing lists
Commerce, on-line, 14, 15, 417–427
    purchase assumptions, 427
    strategies, 421–425
Commercial information services, *see*
    Information services
Common Gateway Interface, 59–61,
    279–280
Common Ground, 177
Communities, on-line, *see* Virtual com-
    munities
Compression, 166–167, 168, 169,
    251
    described, 161–162
Compaq Computer, 447
CompassWare Development, 364
CompuServe, 35, 65, 67, 75, 80, 94–96.
    See also Sprynet
    posting personal Web pages on,
    409–411
Computer Database Plus, 94

Computer languages, 61, 281
    interpreted, 283
    multithreading, 283
    object-oriented, 283
    old-style, 30
Computer programs, encoding and
    decoding, 250–251
Computers:
    vs. humans, 30
    laptops, 78
    mainframes, 30, 260
    NetPCs, 463
    network (NCs), 284–285
    networked, 64. *See also* Networking
    supercomputers, *see* Supercomputers
Cookies, 449–450, 451
CoolTalk, 147, 175, 292–294
    chat tool, 294
    whiteboard, 293
Copper wire, 74, 76–77
Cornell University, 174
Corporation for Research and Educa-
    tional Networking, 207, 221
Counters, 60
Country codes, 41
Crackers, 426–427, 429, 433
    vs. hackers, 427
CREN, *see* Corporation for Research and
    Educational Networking
CRT, 256
CUNY, *see* City University of New York
CU-seeMe, 151–152, 174–175
    configuring for your browser, 174
Customizing, 131–143
    importance of, 24
CyberCash, 440–442
Cybercasting, 166. *See also* Video
CyberTrust, 435, 438

D

da Silva, Stephanie, 221
Data packets, *see* Packets
DCA, *see* Defense Communications
    Agency
DC Comics, 157, 158
Defense Communications Agency,
    33

DejaNews, 347–349
DELPHI, 35, 65
Department of Energy, 35
Deutsch, Peter, 43
DigiCash, 442–444
Digital certificates, 435–437
Digital Equipment Corp., 260
Digital modems, 74. *See also* ISDN
Digital money, 439–444
Digital paper, 177
Digital signatures, 433–435
DirecPC, 78
Directories, Internet, 355–357
    vs. search engines, 351
DirecTV, 78
Discussion groups, on-line, *see* Mailing
        lists; Newsgroups
Disney, 423–424
Domain names, 39–40
    aliasing, 101–102
    FQDNs, 40
Domain Name System (DNS), 39
DOOM, 8
Downloaders, 276
Downloading, 113–117, 137–138
    plug-ins, 153–157, 162, 170
    a Telnet client, 256
    video, 167–168
Drop-down menus, 14
Duke's Diner, 300–303
Duke University, 232

E

Edify, 311
Education, use of the Web for, 14–17
Educom, 229
Edupage, 229
Electronic Frontier Foundation, 460,
        461
Electronic mail, *see* E-mail
Electronic Workforce, 311
Emtage, Alan, 43
E-mail, 19, 26, 35, 40, 72–73, 166
    addresses, *see* Addresses
    as asynchronous, 181–182
    browsers and, 20, 181–187

checking frequency, 185
    embedded hyperlinks and, *see* Hyper-
        links
    encrypting, 433
    etiquette, *see* Etiquette, on-line
    forwarding, 102
    how it works, 183–184
    identity tab, 185–186
    junk e-mail, 197, 444–445, 459
    leaving on the server after reading,
        185
    mail directory, 184–185
    maximum message size, 183
    multimedia and, 20, 166
    multiple mailboxes, 102
    Netscape Navigator and, 184–199
        address book, 199, 200
        alternatives to, 199–202
        creating a new message, 196–197
        deleting, 195–196
        folders, 198
        organizing, 187, 197–199
        quoting from previous messages,
            204–205
        reading, 188–192
        saving, 199
        sending replies, 192–195
    privacy and, *see* Privacy
    wide use of, 181
Emoticons, 203
    tediousness of, 204
Encryption, 428–435
    of e-mail, 453–454, 459–460
    grades of, 430
    how it works, 432–433
Encyclopaedia Britannica, 6, 22
Engelbart, Doug, 29
Envoy, 177
Ericson, 74
Etiquette, on-line, 202–205, 246–248,
        252–254, 258
Euclidean geometry, 249
Eudora, 199–202
Eudora Pro, 201, 202
European Laboratory for Particle
        Physics, *see* CERN
Excel, 287
Excite, 340–343

F

FAQs, 252, 253
FedWorld, 257–258, 259, 260
Fiber-optic cable, 38, 41, 69, 77, 83
File transfer, 43. *See also* FTP; TCP/IP
File Transfer Protocol, *see* FTP
Firefly, 308–311
Firefly Network, 308
Firewalls, 427, 446, 447
First Floor Software, 315
First Virtual Holdings, 439–440, 444
Flaming, 254
Fonts, 135–136, 137
Ford Motor Company, 421–423
Form, bad, *see* Etiquette, on-line
Forms, 60, 154
Forte Agent, 255–256
Four11, 355, 356
Fractal geometry, 249, 250
Frames, *see* Netscape Navigator
Free Agent, 256
Freenets, 263
Freeware, 7
Frequently Asked Questions, *see* FAQs
Friends, on-line, *see* Virtual communities
Freeloader, 365
Freeman, Greydon, 207
FrontPage, 396
FTP, 25, 26, 33, 41, 43, 48, 55, 183, 320
   anonymous FTP, 43
   downloading, 114–115
   programs, 413
Fuchs, Ira H., 207
Future of Hope, 166

G

Gates, Bill, 78, 275
General Magic, 316
GEnie, 65
Gilder, George, 392–394
Gleick, James, 391–392
Go-Get-It, 363
Goldberg, Ian, 429
Gold Disk Astound, 148

Gopher, 25, 26, 43–44, 48, 54, 55, 268–274, 320
   sources of information about, 272
   using, 269
Gopher Jewels, 272, 273
Graphical interfaces, 29, 56, 63, 92, 106, 145. *See also* User interfaces
Graphics, 11, 59, 73, 166, 176
   decoding newsgroup, *see* Newsgroup
   downloading options, 137–138, 139
Grateful Dead, 166
Grave Enterprises, 419, 420
GTE, 77

H

Hackers, 426–427
   vs. crackers, 427
Harris organization, 267–268
Hart, Michael, 386–388
Hauert, Scott A., 453
Heindl, Walter, 453
Heinlein, Robert, 29
Helper applications, 147, 150–153. *See also* Add-ons; Plug-ins
   vs. plug-ins, 150–151
High-speed networks, 36, 64
Home pages, selecting, 132, 134
Horton, Mark, 254
Hostile applets, *see* Applets
HotBot, 329–336
   vs. Alta Vista, 329–331
   using, 329–333
HoTMetaL, 396
HotWired, 329
HTML, *see* HyperText Markup Language
HTTP, *see* HyperText Transfer Protocol
Hyperlinks, 5, 9, 11–13, 14, 17, 20, 28, 42, 45, 48–49, 62, 106, 107–108, 112, 263
   colors of, 57, 106, 107–108
   defined, 5
   embedded in e-mail, 182, 196–197, 201, 226
   expiration of, 135
   in on-line publications, 371, 401–402
Hypermedia, 45

HyperTerminal, 256
hypertext, 3, 20, 45, 61
HyperText Markup Language, 47, 49–53,
    54, 56, 59
    editing tools, 395–397
    reference sites, 404–405
    writing with, 394–397
HyperText Markup Language editors,
    402–404
    features of good, 402–404
HyperText Transfer Protocol, 25, 47–49,
    54, 56
    definition of, 47
HYTELNET, 263–267

I

IBM, 83, 97, 207, 447
    terminal connections, 267–268
IBM ThinkPad, see ThinkPad
Icons, 258
IEClean, 448
Images:
    printed vs. on-line, 4–6
    real time, see Real time images
Individual Inc., 309
Information services, 35. See also individual entries
Infoseek, 344, 345
InSoft, 291
Integrated Services Digital Network, see
    ISDN
Inline images, 142
Interactive games, 80
Intel Corp., 175
"Intergalactic Computer Network," 29
Interlock, 446
International Telecommunications
    Union, 176
Internet, 233. See also Networking
    access to, see Access to the Internet
    birth of, 33–35
    vs. broadcast media, 312
    coining of the term, 34–35
    as a government-funded operation, 35
    growth of, 24
    vs. intranet, 37–38
    lack of a single backbone, 37

price of, 35, 37
service providers, see Service providers
standards, 31, 32
as an unsubsidized, commercial-free
    enterprise, 37
vs. World Wide Web, see World Wide
    Web
"Internet Catch," 23–24
Internet Explorer, 3, 17, 20, 58, 63, 83,
    92, 95, 162, 175, 177, 312
    ActiveX and, 285–286
    Java and, 285–286
    vs. Netscape Navigator, 105–106, 276
internetMCI, 83–85
Internet Relay Chat servers, see IRCs
Internet shortcuts, 108–109
Internet Snapshots, 446
Internet Society, 31, 32
Internet suites, 73
Internet telephony, see Telephone service
Internetwork (internet), 37
InterNIC, 102
InterRamp, 89
InterSoft International, 256
InterText Magazine, 177, 178, 179
InterVU, 168, 169
Intranet, 37, 38. See also Internet, LANs,
    WANs
IP addresses, see Addresses
IRCs, 290
ISDN, 74–76, 89
    vs. ADSL, 76–77, 79–80
ISPs, see Service providers
ITU, see International Telecommunications Union

J

Java, 61, 147, 275–276, 277–285
    vs. CGI, 279–280
    modularity of, 281
    network computer and, 284–285
    platform-neutrality of, 278–279
    vs. plug-ins, 278
    security and, 280, 430
    upgrading and, 282
    uses of, 281–282
JavaScript, 147

JavaStation, 285
Java Virtual Machine, 278
Jobs, Steven, 29
JPEG format, 152
Junk e-mail, *see* E-mail

K

Kahn, Robert, 31
Keyword search, *see* Searching
Keyword shortcuts, 4, 141–142

L

Language preferences, *see* Browsers
Languages, computer, *see* Computer
    languages
LANs, 33, 37, 38. *See also* Intranet, WANs
Latency, 290
Libraries, on-line, 263–264
Licklider, J.C.R., 29, 62
Line-of-sight laser communication, 38
Linked computers, *see* Networking
Links, *see* Hyperlinks; Hypertext
ListProcessor, 221
LISTSERVs, *see* Mailing lists
Liszt, 221
LiveAudio, 160–161
Live3D, *see* Netscape Navigator
Live video, *see* Video
Local area networks, *see* LANs
Lock & Key, 453–459
Lockheed Martin Space & Missiles Co.,
    447
Logging on, 63–64
look@me, 176
L-Soft, 208
Lucent Technologies, 74
Lycos, 339–340

M

Macintosh, 9, 37, 83, 85, 89, 250
    designing of, 29
Macromedia, 396
Macromedia Director, 148

Macromedia Shockwave, *see* Shockwave
Magazine Database Plus, 94
Magazines, on-line, *see* Publications,
    on-line
Magellan, 352
Mail, *see* E-mail
Mailbase, 221
Mailing lists, 19–20, 35, 205–229
    finding non-LISTSERVs, 221
    finding the right, 221
    LISTSERVs, 206–221, 226
        alternatives to, 221
        canceling, 212
        Command Job Language Interpreter
            (CJLI), 219
        database function, 217–220
        distributing messages to fellow mem-
            bers, 213
        finding the right, 208–209
        managing, 213–214
        searching, 214–220
        sending messages to the list adminis-
            trator, 213
        subscribing to, 211–213
    vs. newsgroups, 19
    sources of information about, 227–
        228
Mailserv, 221
Mainframes, *see* Computers
Majordomo, 221
Mandela, Nelson, 166
Mandelbrot, Benoit, 249
Manners, on-line, *see* Etiquette, on-line
Marks, Richard, 262
Marvel Comics, 158
MBONE, 166
McAleavey, Kevin, 448
McCahill, Mark, 43, 268
McCaw Cellular, 78
McCaw, Craig, 78
MCI, 64, 80, 175
Memex, 28–29
Menus, in Gopher, 268–269
Merit, Inc., 38
Meta-engines, *see* Metasearching
Metasearching, 357–358
MFS Communications, 85, 86
Microelectronics Center of North
    America (MCNC), 65

Microphone, 289
Microsoft, 53, 106, 175, 275, 280, 285–286, 299
Microsoft Explorer, *see* Internet Explorer
Microsoft Network, 75, 96–97, 275, 314
Microsoft Office, 287
Microsoft Visual Basic, 456
Microwave transmission, 38, 41
MIDI, 161, 165, 166
Milles, James, 226
MILNET, 35. *See also* ARPANET
MIME, 150–153
Mindspring, 89–91
MIT Media Lab, 308
Miya, Eugene, 33
Modems, 38, 43, 64–67, 72, 76
    analog vs. ISDN, 74–76
    cable, 77–78
    cellular, 78. *See also* Cellular telephone
    digital, *see* Digital modems
    how they work, 68–70
    obsolescence of, 69
    speed of, 100, 161, 174, 289
        vs. network speed, 74–75
Money, digital, *see* Digital money
MoreLikeThis, 363
Mosaic, 3, 20, 56–58, 145
Mouse, invention of, 29
Movies, 80. *See also* Video
MPEG, 168
MPEG player, 168
MrTerm, 256
Multimedia, 11, 36, 147, 148, 153–154, 157–158, 166. *See also* Shockware
    e-mail and, 20
Multimedia Backbone, *see* MBONE
Multiple communications programs, problems with, 71–72
Multiple Internet service providers, *see* Service providers
Multipurpose Internet Mail Extensions, *see* MIME
Multitasking, 157
Museums, virtual, *see* Virtual museums
Music, 11, 58

N

NASA, 35
National Center for Supercomputing Applications (NCSA), 56
National Institutes of Health, 35
National Science Foundation, 35
NCs (network computers), *see* Computers
NetAttache, 364
NETCOM, 66, 67, 86, 87, 88–89, 90
NetCruiser, 88
NetFerret Utilities, 363
Netfind, 265, 319
Netiquette, *see* Etiquette, on-line
NetMeeting, 175
NetPCs, *see* Computers
Netriever, 365
Netscape, 53, 175, 280, 299
Netscape Navigator, 3, 4, 17, 42, 58, 63, 88, 92, 95, 105–143, 162, 175–176, 177, 250, 312
    as best browser available, 105–106
    bookmarks, *see* Bookmarks
    copying and pasting, 120
    customizing for personal use, 131–143
    custom version for AT&T WorldNet, 82–83
    custom version for internetMCI, 83
    directory buttons, 111–112
    display of, 4, 140–141, 142
        parts defined, 108, 109–112
    e-mail, *see* E-mail
    finding text, 119
    frames and tables, 112, 113
    fonts, 135–136, 137
    history list, 130–131
    inline images, 142
    vs. Internet Explorer, 105–106, 276
    keyboard shortcuts, 141–142
    language preferences, 139–140
    Live3D and, 300–305
    newsgroups and, *see* Newsgroups
    plug-ins, 147, 149–150
        system crashes caused by, 148
    screen colors, 137
    security and, 429
    for Sprint Internet Passport, 85

Telnet and:
  configuring, 257
  fiding a client, 256
toolbar, 108, 110–111, 131–132, 133, 134
NetTerm, 256, 261
Network computers, *see* Computers
Networking, 2–3, 6, 14, 17, 38, 64
  advantages of, 34
  early experiments in, 17, 27–33
  international, 38
  military, 33. *See also* Defense Communications Agency; Internet
  nature of, 37
  routing and, *see* Routing
  software, 37
  transcontinental, 31, 38
  UNIX computers, 232, 233
  visionaries, 27–30
  wireless, *see* Wireless networking; individual entries
Network News Traffic Protocol, 41, 233
Networks, *see* Networking
Networks, high-speed, *see* High-speed networks
Newsgroups, 17–19, 26, 41, 55, 73, 98–99, 166
  best for a new user, 245–246
  decoding graphics without Netscape Navigator, 249
  etiquette, *see* Etiquette, on-line
  examples of excellent, 18
  Forte Agent and, *see* Forte Agent
  how they work, 233
  language-defined, 238
  local, 238
  vs. mailing lists, 19, 20
  major categories of, 234–238
  Netscape Navigator and:
    configuring, 239–240
    graphics use with, 249–251
    marking as read, 244
    posting a new message, 249
    reading, 240–244
    responding to articles, 247–249
    saving a posting, 249
    searching for message, 247
    subscribing, 244–246

organization into hierarchies, 233–238
privacy, 445, 446
regional or statewide, 238
selecting carefully, 253
USENET, 17, 29, 33, 231–233
use of quoted material in postings, 247–248
using to promote your Web site, 416
NewsPage, 309–311, 313
News services, on-line, 11–13
Newspapers, on-line, *see* Publications, on-line
NeXT, 45
NNTP, *see* Network News Transfer Protocol
Nodes, 29, 31, 33, 34
Northern Telecom, 74
NSClean, 448
NSFNET, 35, 36, 83

O

Object Linking and Embedding (OLE), 286–287
Off-line browsers, 276, 364–365
  vs. intelligent search engines, 364
On-line shopping, *see* Commerce, on-line
Open Text, 344–347
OS/2, 250

P

Packet radio, 38, 79
Packets, 38, 41
Packet switching, 30–31
  beauty of, 34
  definition of, 30
Palo Alto Research Center (PARC), 29, 166
Panix, 64
PARADISE, 265
PARC, *see* Palo Alto Research Center
Passwords, 433
PCs, 83, 84, 87, 89, 176

PCT, *see* Private Communications
    Technology
PC-WRITE, 7
PDF, 176–180
    vs. HTML, 176
Pentium, 168
Peres, Shiman, 166
Performance Systems International, 67, 80
Personal communicators, 316
Personal Web pages, 389–394
    for self-promotion, 391–394
Pesce, Mark, 390–391
Philosophy, 221
Pipeline, 89
Plug-ins, 12, 16, 147–150, 151, 152. *See
    also* Add-ons; Helper applications
    downloading, *see* Downloading
    vs. helper applications, 150–151
    miscellaneous, 180
    potential problems with, 148–149, 154
    qualities of a good, 158
    VRML, 300
    Web interactivity and, 277–278
Pobox, 102
PointCost, 311–314
Points of presence (POPs):
    of AT&T WorldNet, 80, 82
    defined, 69
    of internetMCI, 83
    local vs. national, 98
    of NETCOM, 89
    for Sprint Internet Passport, 85
Point-to-Point Protocol (PPP), 42, 71, 72,
    73, 84, 96
POP (Post Office Protocol), 184
POPs, *see* Points of presence
POP3, *see* POP
Pop-up menus, 4
Portable Document Format, *see* PDF
Post Office Protocol, *see* POP
PostScript, 176
PowerPoint, 148
PressAgent, 359
Pretty Good Privacy, 454–459
Privacy, 205, 444–462
    anonymity and, 450–452
    clipper chips and, 459–460
    e-mail and, 205, 433, 451, 452–459
    programs for, 452–459

Private Communications Technology, 280
PRO-COMM, 7–8
Prodigy, 65, 67, 80, 92, 94, 97. *See also*
    Access Net Direct
    posting personal Web pages on,
    409–411
Programming, *see* Computer program-
    ming
Progressive Networks, 159
Progressive rendering, 108
Project Gutenberg, 386–388
Proprietary interfaces, 88–89, 299–300
ProShare, 175
Protocols, 183. *See also* individual entries
Providers, Internet service, *see* Service
    providers
PSI, 37
PSINet, 64, 86, 87, 89
Publications, electronic vs. printed, 177
Publications, on-line, 368–388
    advantages of, 369–374
    books, 382–388
    magazines, 368–378
        independents, 374–378
    newspapers, 378–382
Publicly Accessible Mailing Lists, 221,
    222
Publishing software, 367–368
Pull-down menus, 4, 58, 106, 112, 258
    invention of, 29

Q

Quarterdeck, 360, 361
QuickTime, 12, 145, 167
QuickTimeVR, 305
QVT/Term, 256
QWS3270, 267–268

R

Raggett, David, 297
Rand Corporation, 30
RBOCs, see Bell Telephone
RealAudio, 11, 117, 151, 159–167, 295,
    302
Real time images, 9–10, 147

Real-time Transport Protocol, 176
Reflectors, 174. *See also* CU-seeMe
Remailers, 451–452
Rerouting, *see* Routing
Resource Preservation Protocol, *see*
    RSVP
Roberts, Larry, 31
Robots, *see* Software robots
Rolling Stones, 166
Rospach, Chuq Van, 254
Routers, 37, 38–39, 41
Routing, 30–31, 34, 41, 70. *See also*
    Packet switching
  complexities of, 41
RSA, 280
RSVP, 176
RTP, 176

S

Sanford Research Institute, 29
Satellite transmission, 33, 38, 41, 78
SATF, *see* Sample Agent Transfer Protocol
Sausage Software, 396
SavvySearch, 357
Search engines, 20–22, 23, 24, 43, 48, 59,
    320–358
  agents and, 307
  vs. directories, 349–351
  future of, 353–355
  how they work, 324–325
  major, 338–349
  meta-engines, *see* Metasearching
  ongoing development of, 61–62
Searching:
  Boolean operations, 332, 344
  by concept, 340–343
  fine-tuning, 326–329
  metasearching, *see* Metasearching
  miscellaneous tools, 363–364
  natural language, 344, 347
  for people, 355
  relevancy ranking, 325–326, 329
  targeting, 338
  typical issues associated with, 336–338
  using capitalization in, 336
  with wildcards, 337
Sears, 97

Secure Electronic Transaction technol-
    ogy, *see* SET technology
Secure servers, *see* Servers
Secure Sockets Layer, 280, 428–429,
    448
Security, 56, 101, 154, 280, 426–439. *See*
    also Privacy
  ActiveX and, *see* ActiveX
  browser-level, 428–432
  e-mail and, *see* Privacy
  encryption and, *see* Encryption
  Java and, *see* Java
  Netscape Navigator and, *see* Netscape
    Navigator
Serial Line Internet Protocol (SLIP), 42,
    71, 72, 89
Servers:
  definition of, 42
  secure, 14, 419–420, 428, 435
Service providers, 63, 64, 67
  choosing the right one, 99–103
  instability of, 85–86, 89, 97
  ISDN and, 75, 89
  local, 64, 76, 97–99
  multiple, 88
  national, 64, 67, 80–97
  posting a Web page on, 411–413
  that also provide telephone service, *see*
    Telephone service
Sessions, *see* Web sessions
SET technology, 436–439
Shareware, 6–9, 22
  origins of, 6–7
Shell account, 72
Shockwave, 153–159
  downloading, 154–157
  installation, 157
Shopping, on-line, *see* Commerce, on-line
Signatures, digital, *see* Digital signatures
Silicon Graphics, 297
Simple Agent Transfer Protocol, 311
Simple Mail Transfer Protocol, *see*
    SMTP
Slash, *see* URL
SLIP, *see* Serial Lie Internet Protocol
Slurp, 332
SMTP, 183–184
Sniffers, 427, 433
SoftQuad, 396

Software:
 networking, 37
 supplied by Internet service provider,
  101
Software robots, 324, 351
Sony Magic Link Personal Communica-
  tor, 316
Sound, 11, 145, 147, 158. *See also*
  Streaming audio and video virtual
  reality and, *see* Virtual reality
Sound card, 289
Sound file formats, 161
Source, 35, 65
Sovereign 7, 158
Spoofing, 334
Sprint Internet Passport, 85, 86
Spry Mosaic, 96
SpryNet, 94, 96. *See also* CompuServe
Spyglass, 58
SRI, *see* Sanford Research Institute
SSL, *see* Secure Sockets Layer, 280
Streaming audio and video, 11, 61,
  147, 159–162, 164–165, 166–176,
  172–173. *See also* Sound;
  Video
Streamworks, 11, 169–171
Sun Microsystems, 147
Supercomputers, 35, 37, 83
Superheroes, 158
SurfAid, 447
Switchboard, 355
Synapse–The Movie, 159

T

Tables, *see* Netscape Navigator
Tabriz, 316–317
Taps, 427
TCP/IP, 31, 34, 38–42, 48, 63, 70, 71, 94,
  97, 98, 171
 e-mail and, 193
 vs. UDP, 171
TCP/IP stacks, 70–71
Technology, nature of, 27, 29
Teledesic, 78
Telephone service, 73–77
 cellular, *see* Cellular telephone
 800 numbers, 103

Internet access from same provider
  and, 80–83, 86
 using the Internet to place regular
  phone calls, 24, 147, 275, 288–295
 legality of, 294
 problems with, 289–291, 295
Teleport Pro, 365
Telescript, 316
Telnet, 25–26, 183, 256–268
 clients, 256
 commands, 258
 logout, 258
 reasons for its decline, 261–262
 terminal emulation, *see* Terminal emu-
  lation
 why you shouldn't dawdle at a site,
  262–263
Terminal adapter, 74
Terminal emulation, 251–263, 267–268
Terminals, 64, 66, 72, 260
ThinkPad, 37
Thomas, Eric, 206, 208
Time-sharing, 29
 definition of, 29
Tinwald, 446
tn3270, 267–268
Toolbars, 4
traceroute, 41
Transferring files, *see* File transfer
Trash folders, 198
Transmission Control Protocol/Internet
  Protocol, *see* TCP/IP
Transoceanic cable, 41
Trumpet Winsock, 71

U

UDP, 171
 vs. TCP/IP, 171
University of Minnesota, 268
UNIX, 9, 41, 43, 221, 232, 233, 258
UNIX-to-UNIX Copy Protocol, 233
URL (Uniform Resource Locator), 24–26,
  48, 54–56
 for Access Net Direct, 97
 for Acrobat Reader, 177
 for ActiveX sites, 287
 confusion with, 54

definition of, 24, 54
slash in, 55
USENET, *see* Newsgroups
User Datagram Protocol, *see* UDP
User interfaces, *See also* Graphical inter-
        faces:
    earliest, 30
    intimidation and, 30
    problems with, 30
UUCP, *see* UNIX-to-UNIX copy protocol
uudecode, 249
uuencode, 249
UUnet, 37, 38, 67, 80, 85–88
UUnet Alter Dial, 85–88

V

VAG, 298
VDOLive, 169–170, 171, 173
VDONet, 169, 171
Verity, 317
VeriSign, 435
Veronica, 44, 274, 319
Video, 11, 15, 145. *See also* Streaming
        audio and video
    downloading, *see* Downloading
    live, 11, 12, 42, 147, 166, 173
Videoconferencing, 11, 24, 151, 173–176,
        294
Video file formats, 167–168
    incompatability of, 171–172
Video for Windows, 167–168
Virtual communities, 17–20, 35, 166
    mailing lists and, 228–229
    newsgroups and, 252–254
Virtual museums, 14–17
Virtual reality, 17, 24, 42, 276, 295–307,
        463
    as a challenge to programmers and
        designers, 298–300, 306–307
    configuring browsers for, 305–307
    how it works, 296–297
    limitations, 303
    sound and, 298
    uses of, 296–297
Virtual Reality Modeling Language, 276,
        297–300
VISA, 280

VRML, *see* Virtual Reality Modeling Lan-
        guage
VRML Architecture Group, *see* VAG
VRML Forum, 298
VRML Repository, 298, 299, 300
VSDL, 76

W

WAIS, 319–320
Wagner, David, 429
WANs, 37
Web Compass, 360–363
Web Compass Professional, 361–363
WebCrawler, 94, 347, 348
WebEx, 365
Webmaster, 53–54
Web pages:
    creating, 394–407
    personal, *see* Personal Web pages
    posting on an Internet service provider,
        411
    posting on an on-line service, 409–411
    printing, 118–119
    publicizing, 413–416
    saving, 118
    tips on designing, 405–407
    uploading, 413
    where to publish, 407–413
Web Player, 148
Web Retriever, 365
Web sessions, 277–278
Web sites, rating, 352, 354
Web spiders, *see* Software robots
Websters, 446
WebTamer, 363
WebTrack, 446
WebTVs, 463
Web use, monitoring, 445–447
WebWhacker, 364
WELL, 64, 65
Westell, 77
Wheelan, William, 43
White Pine Software, 11, 174
WHOIS, 319
Wide Area Information Servers (WAIS),
        45
Widea area networks, *see* WANs

Wildcards, *see* Searching
Windham Hill Records, 424–425
Windows Explorer, 453
Windows 3.1, 70, 71, 83, 84
Windows 95, 9, 70, 108, 256
    AOL and CompuServe integrated with,
        94
    configuring for the Internet, 465–476
Winsock, 71–72, 92
WinZip, 251
Wired, 426
Wireless cable, *see* Cable television
Wireless transmission, 38, 69, 78–80
Word for Windows, 287
Word processors, 147
World in Massachusetts, 64
Worlds Inc., 298
World Wide Web:
    future of, 462–464
    interactivity of, 276–284, 316
    vs. the Internet, 22–23
    origins of, 43–46, 53
    as platform-neutral, 279
    as a publishing tool, 28, 57, 62,
        176–180, 367
    responsibilities of, 464
    searching, *see* Searching the Web
    ubiquity of, 17
    unprecedented growth of, 275

World Wide Web Consortium, 45, 46–47,
    49, 50
World Wide Web Journal, 45, 46, 47
W3 Servers Web page, 49

X

Xerox, 29, 166
X.500, 265
Xing Technologies, 11, 169, 170,
    171
X-Men, 158

Y

Yahoo!, 21, 22, 64, 352
Yahoo! Maps, 22
Yale, 207

Z

Zen Buddhism, 221
Ziff-Davis site, 314
Zimmerman, Phil, 452
.zip format, 251